D1072761

This book situates Romans 14.1–15.13 in the context of first-century Roman thought, using the lenses of asceticism (especially vegetarianism), superstition, and obligation. It also seeks to situate this section of Romans within the letter as a whole, and concludes by arguing that the section illustrates the theme, or primary topos, of the letter: that Paul, his gospel, and those who follow it are not shameful. New contributions to Romans research surface where this book examines the terms "strong" and "weak" in light of their use within Roman social discourse; identifies the Roman social value of obligation throughout the letter as a key element both within Paul's self-understanding and in his ethical teaching; raises previously unrecognized implications of the letter's occasional nature for how we read and use Romans; and traces the topos of not being ashamed through the letter and back to its roots in the LXX.

SOCIETY FOR NEW TESTAMENT STUDIES

MONOGRAPH SERIES

General editor: Richard Bauckham

103

THE STRONG AND THE WEAK

The Strong and the Weak

Romans 14.1–15.13 in Context

Mark Reasoner

Bethel College, St. Paul

CAMBRIDGE
UNIVERSITY PRESS

PUBLISHED BY THE PRESS SYNDICATE OF THE UNIVERSITY OF CAMBRIDGE
The Pitt Building, Trumpington Street, Cambridge CB2 1RP

CAMBRIDGE UNIVERSITY PRESS
The Edinburgh Building, Cambridge CB2 2RU, United Kingdom
40 West 20th Street, New York, NY 10011–4211, USA
10 Stamford Road, Oakleigh, Melbourne 3166, Australia

© Mark Reasoner 1999

First published 1999

Printed in the United Kingdom at the University Press, Cambridge

Typeset in Times 10/12pt [CE]

A catalogue record for this book is available from the British Library

Library of Congress cataloguing in publication data

Reasoner, Mark.
The strong and the weak: Romans 14.1–15:13 in context / Mark Reasoner.
    p.   cm. – (Society for New Testament studies monograph series; 103)
Includes bibliographical references and index.
ISBN 0 521 63334 6 hardback
1. Bible. N.T. Romans XIV, 1–XV, 13 – Socio-rhetorical criticism.
I. Title.   II. Series: Monograph series (Society for New Testament Studies); 103.
BS2665.2.R33   1998   98–20168   CIP
227′.106–dc21

ISBN 0 521 63334 6

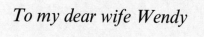

To my dear wife Wendy

CONTENTS

Contents

PREFACE

The opportunity to write a book on Romans has reminded me of my first Christmas visit to my in-laws' home. Everyone was talking in a crowded room, and it wasn't clear who was listening to whom. Just as it was difficult to listen and converse with everyone that first visit, so it is a challenge to interact well with everyone writing on Romans. Sometimes a nod or a glance is given, when an in-depth conversation is preferable. In any case, I have done my best in this book to recognize and converse with many who are writing on Romans.

This book began as my dissertation, "The 'Strong' and the 'Weak' in Rome and in Paul's Theology," accepted at the University of Chicago in the summer of 1990. I express thanks to the director of my dissertation, H. D. Betz, for mentioning this passage of Romans as a text that needed work. His suggestion of looking at the text through the lenses of asceticism, superstition, and obligation has been formative and helpful in the project. I also thank Arthur J. Droge and Richard P. Saller, the other members of my committee.

Since 1990 I have undertaken a thorough revision of the project, omitting an exegetical chapter, conversing with authors who have published on Romans since 1990, and integrating my findings on this section of Romans with the whole letter.

An earlier version of chapter 3 was presented by invitation in November of 1992 at an SBL session on the social history of Judaism and Christianity. An earlier version of chapter 12 was presented in February of 1997 to the Twin Cities NT Trial Balloon Society. I thank those present at those occasions for their comments on the papers. In addition, I wish to thank Steven E. Enderlein, Robert Hodgson, Jr., Robert Jewett, and Mark D. Nanos for their conversation and encouragement along the way. Of course, I alone carry the responsibility for all the weaknesses of this book. I hope that my readers may share some of the pleasure and excitement that I experience in studying Romans.

I have done my best to indicate where I have used existing translations. If no such indication is found with regard to a given quotation, the translation is my own.

ABBREVIATIONS

AAA	American Anthropological Association
ABD	*Anchor Bible Dictionary*
AGJU	Arbeiten zur Geschichte des antiken Judentums und des Urchristentums
AHR	*American Historical Review*
AJPh	*American Journal of Philology*
AnBib	Analecta Biblica
ANRW	*Aufstieg und Niedergang der römischen Welt*
Aristotle:	
EN	*Ethica Nicomachea*
Rh.	*Rhetorica*
AS	*Ancient Society*
Athenaeus:	
Deip.	Δειπνοσοφισταί
AUS	American University Studies
AUSS	*Andrews University Seminary Studies*
Bauer–Aland	Bauer, Walter. *Griechisch-deutsches Wörterbuch zu den Schriften des Neuen Testaments und der frühchristlichen Literatur.* 6th ed., eds. Kurt and Barbara Aland. Berlin/New York: Walter de Gruyter, 1988
BBB	Bonner biblische Beiträge
BDB	Brown, Francis; Driver, S. R.; and Briggs, Charles A. *A Hebrew and English Lexicon of the Old Testament.* Oxford: Clarendon, 1951
BDF	Blass, F.; Debrunner, A.; Funk, Robert W. *A Greek Grammar of the New Testament and Other Early Christian Literature.* Chicago: University of Chicago Press, 1961
BFCT	Beiträge zur Förderung christlicher Theologie
BHT	Beiträge zur historischen Theologie

BibS (F)	Biblische Studien (Freiburg, 1895–)
BJS	Brown Judaic Studies
BLib	The Bible and Liberation Series, Maryknoll, New York: Orbis
BMS	Benedictine Monographic Series
BR	*Biblical Research*
BWANT	Beiträge zur Wissenschaft vom Alten und Neuen Testament
BZNW	Beihefte zur *ZNW*
CAH	*Cambridge Ancient History*
Can. Ap.	*Canones Apostolorum*
CBA	Catholic Biblical Association
CBQ	*Catholic Biblical Quarterly*
CBQMS	Catholic Biblical Quarterly Monograph Series
Cicero:	
Att.	*Epistulae ad Atticum*
de Orat.	*de Oratore*
Div.	*De divinatione*
Fam.	*Epistulae ad familiares*
Flac.	*Pro Flacco*
Mur.	*Pro Murena*
ND	*De natura deorum*
Off.	*De officiis*
Phil.	*Philippicae*
Q. fr.	*Epistulae ad Quintum fratrem*
Tusc.	*Tusculanae disputationes*
1 Clem.	*1 Clement*
Const. Ap	*Constitutiones Apostolorum*
CQ	*Classical Quarterly*
Did.	*Didache*
Dig.	*Digesta Iustiniani*
Diog. L.	Diogenes Laertius
EA	Das Erbe der Alten
Ebib	Etudes bibliques
EDR	*Enciclopedia delle religioni*
EKKNT	Evangelisch-katholischer Kommentar zum Neuen Testament
ER	*Encyclopedia of Religion*
ET	English translation
Eusebius:	
HE	*Historia ecclesiastica*

FAS	Frankfurter althistorische Studien
FRLANT	Forschungen zur Religion und Literatur des Alten und Neuen Testaments
Gel.	Aulus Gellius, *Noctes Atticae*
Herm.	*Hermas:*
Man.	*Mandate(s)*
Sim.	*Similitude(s)*
Vis.	*Vision(s)*
Hesiod:	
Theog.	*Theogonia*
HKAW	Handbuch der klassischen Altertumswissenschaft
HNT	Handbuch zum Neuen Testament
HNTC	Harper's NT Commentary
Horace:	
Carm.	*Carmina*
Sat.	*Satirae*
HTKNT	Herders theologischer Kommentar zum Neuen Testament
HTR	*Harvard Theological Review*
HUT	Hermeneutische Untersuchungen zur Theologie
ICC	International Critical Commentary
IESS	*International Encyclopedia of the Social Sciences*
Ign.	Ignatius:
Eph.	*Ephesians*
Rom.	*Romans*
Trall.	*Trallians*
Interp.	*Interpretation*
JBL	*Journal of Biblical Literature*
JJS	*Journal of Jewish Studies*
Josephus:	
AJ	*Antiquitates Judaicae*
BJ	*Bellum Judaicum*
C. Apion.	*Contra Apionem*
JR	*Journal of Religion*
JRS	*Journal of Roman Studies*
JSNT	*Journal for the Study of the New Testament*
JSNT Sup	*JSNT* Supplement Series
JSS	*Jewish Social Studies*
JTS	*Journal of Theological Studies*
Justin	Justin Martyr
1 Apol.	*First Apology*

KEK	Kritisch-exegetischer Kommentar über das Neue Testament (Meyer)
LCL	Loeb Classical Library
LEC	Library of Early Christianity
LSJ	Liddell, H. G.; Scott, R.; Jones, H. S. *A Greek–English Lexicon*. 9th ed. Oxford: Clarendon, 1940

Lucian:

Demon.	*Demonax*
Peregr.	*Peregrinus*
LXX	Septuagint
MAPS	Memoirs of the American Philosophical Society

Martial:

Epig.	*Epigrammata*
MH	*Museum Helveticum*
MNTC	Moffat NT Commentary
MT	Masoretic Text
NovT Sup	Novum Testamentum, Supplements
n.s.	new series
NTAbh	Neutestamentliche Abhandlungen
NTD	Das Neue Testament Deutsch
NTS	*New Testament Studies*
NTTS	New Testament Tools and Studies
OCD	*Oxford Classical Dictionary*. Eds. N. G. L. Hammond and H. H. Scullard. 2nd ed. Oxford: Clarendon, 1970
OF	*Orphicorum Fragmenta*. Ed. by Otto Kern. 2nd ed. Berlin: Weidmann, 1963
PG	*Patrologia Graece* (Migne)

Philo:

Anim.	*De animalibus*
Cont.	*De vita contemplativa*
Legat.	*Legatio ad Gaium*
Mut.	*De mutatione nominum*
Plant.	*De plantatione*
Praem. poen.	*De praemiis et poenis*
Spec.	*De specialibus legibus*

Plato:

Laws	*Leges*
Phileb.	*Philebus*

Pliny:

HN	*Historia naturalis*

Plutarch:
Esu carn.	*De esu carnium orationes* (*Moralia* 993A–999B)
Quaest. conv.	*Quaestiones convivalium*
Superst.	*De superstitione* (*Moralia* 164E–171F)
PTWECL	*Plutarch's Theological Writings and Early Christian Literature.* Ed. by H. D. Betz. Leiden: Brill, 1975
PW	Paulys Real-Enzyclopädie der klassischen Altertumswissenschaft (Pauly–Wissowa)
PW Sup	Supplement to PW
RAC	*Reallexikon für Antike und Christentum*
RevQ	*Revue de Qumran*
RGG	*Die Religion in Geschichte und Gegenwart: Handwörterbuch für Theologie und Religionswissenschaft*, 3rd ed. Tübingen: J. C. B. Mohr (Paul Siebeck), 1958
RHLR	*Revue d'histoire et de littérature religieuses*
RVV	Religionsgeschichtliche Versuche und Vorarbeiten

Sallust:
Cat.	*Catilina*
Jug.	*Jugurtha*
SANT	Studien zum Alten und Neuen Testament
Sat.	*Satirae*
SBAW	Schweizerische Beiträge zur Altertumswissenschaft
SBLDS	Society of Biblical Literature Dissertation Series
SBLTT	Society of Biblical Literature Texts and Translations
SBS	Stuttgarter Bibelstudien
SBT	Studies in Biblical Theology
SCHNT	Studia ad Corpus Hellenisticum Novi Testamenti
SCL	Sather Classical Lectures
SD	Studies and Documents
SEÅ	*Svensk exegetisk årsbok*
SEHRE	M. Rostovtzeff, *The Social and Economic History of the Roman Empire.* 2nd ed. Oxford: Oxford University Press, 1957

Seneca:
Ben.	*De beneficiis*
Ep.	*Epistulae*
SHA	*Scriptores Historiae Augustae*
SHJ	Studies in Hellenistic Judaism

SIHC	Studies in the Intercultural History of Christianity
SJT	*Scottish Journal of Theology*
SNT	Studien zum Neuen Testament
SNTW	Studies of the New Testament and its World
Sophocles:	
Aj.	*Ajax*
OT	*Oedipus tyrannus*
SPIB	Scripta Pontificii Instituti Biblici
SSRH	Sociological Studies in Roman History
Suetonius:	
Aug.	*Augustus*
SUNT	Studien zur Umwelt des Neuen Testaments
SVF	*Stoicorum Veterum Fragmenta*
Tacitus:	
Agr.	*Agricola*
Ann.	*Annales*
Dial.	*Dialogus de oratoribus*
TDNT	*Theological Dictionary of the New Testament*
Theophrastus:	
Char.	*Characteres*
THKNT	Theologischer Handkommentar zum Neuen Testament
TLL	*Thesaurus Linguae Latinae*
TPINTC	Trinity Press International New Testament Commentary
TRE	*Theologische Realenzyklopädie.* Eds. Gerhard Krause and Gerhard Müller. Berlin/New York: Walter de Gruyter, 1977–
TSK	*Theologische Studien und Kritiken*
TSR	Texts and Studies in Religion
TU	Texte und Untersuchungen zur Geschichte der altchristlichen Literatur
TynBul	*Tyndale Bulletin*
TZ	*Theologische Zeitschrift*
Varro:	
L.	*De lingua Latina*
Vg	Vulgate
VKHSM	Veröffentlichungen aus dem kirchenhistorischen Seminar München
VLGLB	Vetus Latina: Aus der Geschichte der Lateinischen Bibel

WMANT	Wissenschaftliche Monographien zum Alten und Neuen Testament
WTJ	*Westminster Theological Journal*
WUNT	Wissenschaftliche Untersuchungen zum Neuen Testament
ZNW	*Zeitschrift für die neutestamentliche Wissenschaft*
ZTK	*Zeitschrift für Theologie und Kirche*

1

"STRONG" AND "WEAK" IN ROMANS:
PAST PORTRAITS AND SIGNIFICANCE

Le chap. XIV soulève une question très difficile: *Quels sont les faibles que les forts doivent ménager?* M.-J. Lagrange[1]

Romans challenges its readers with a problem. As a letter written to a church Paul had never visited (Rom. 1.13; 15.22–24) it causes those who read it today to wonder if the letter is a general summary of doctrine, or a memorandum addressing specific needs in the Roman church.[2] In its selection and treatment of topics, is Romans a general treatise constructed from Paul's past interactions with churches, or is it focused on the situation within the Christian community of Rome? Donfried has effectively presented this difference in terms of the history of scholarship,[3] but perhaps some interpretive examples will help to sharpen the question. For this question of the nature of Romans, general versus specific, abstract versus occasional,[4] affects how the letter is understood.

For example, Paul presents his gospel as containing the message of God's righteousness that is grasped by faith (1.17). Is this actually the theme of Paul's letter (and even the center of his theology), or simply the frame in which Paul places his message when writing to Roman people, who valued *iustitia* and *fides*?

Another example can be found in a consideration of Rom.

---

[1] M.-J. Lagrange, *Saint Paul: Epître aux Romains* (4th ed.; Ebib; Paris: Gabalda, 1931), 335.

[2] For the former option, Philipp Melanchthon's description of Romans as a *doctrinae christianae compendium* is representative, *Loci communes, 1521* (ed. R. Stupperich; Werke in Auswahl 2.1; Gütersloh: Bertelsmann, 1952), 7. For the latter option, see K. Haacker, "Der Römerbrief als Friedensmemorandum," *NTS* 36 (1990) 25–41.

[3] K. P. Donfried, "False Presuppositions in the Study of Romans," *The Romans Debate* (ed. K. P. Donfried; rev. ed.; Peabody, Mass.: Hendrickson, 1991), 102–103.

[4] To be sure, we can also speak of an occasion in Paul's own experience that prompted the letter (R. J. Karris, "The Occasion of Romans: A Response to Professor Donfried," in Donfried, *The Romans Debate*, 127). I shall consider that in chapter 11 below.

13.1–7. Did Paul intend his directives on obeying the government to be the definitive statement on the Christian's relationship to civil authority?[5] Or are Paul's words meant to prescribe Christian behavior in relation to a specific government at a specific time in history?[6]

This question of the focus of the letter is particularly pressing in Paul's section on the "strong" and the "weak," identified in the next chapter as extending from Rom. 14.1 through 15.13. In this part of Romans, it seems that Paul knows of two groups within the Roman church at odds with one another. At the same time, he has not been to Rome (Rom. 1.13) and we notice that the text bears real similarities to 1 Cor. 8–10,[7] which describes a food-related controversy in another Christian community. Is Paul's section on "strong" and "weak" addressed to two groups actually scorning and judging each other in Rome? Or is this section modeled after 1 Cor. 8–10, and simply an hypothetical case study in Paul's letter?[8] What makes this section of Romans especially exciting is that the question regarding the occasional nature of the letter intersects in this passage with another pressing question: Just how Jewish- and Torah-friendly is Paul in this letter?

Answers to our questions about this part of Romans will help to clarify what part this section of Romans plays in the context of the whole letter. These answers may also help us understand more clearly how this section of Romans fits into the context of first-century Rome and its believing communities. Both contexts are of compelling interest, since the letter to the Romans has been accorded first place in the Pauline canon,[9] and since it was Roman Christianity that became normative for the Western church.

This monograph goes beyond the limited number of pages that Romans commentators can spend on this part of the letter. The last book written on this topic was written over a generation ago,[10] and while some recent monographs and articles include material on the

---

[5] See H. Ridderbos, *Paul: An Outline of his Theology* (trans. J. R. de Witt; Grand Rapids: Eerdmans, 1975), 320–23.

[6] See N. Elliott, *Liberating Paul: The Justice of God and the Politics of the Apostle*, BLib (Maryknoll, N.Y.: Orbis, 1994), 217–26.

[7] I use 1 Cor. 8–10 to designate the discussion in 1 Corinthians on meat offered to idols. Its precise parameters are 1 Cor. 8.1–13; 10.14–11.1.

[8] See R. J. Karris, "Romans 14:1–15:13 and the Occasion of Romans," in Donfried, *The Romans Debate*, 65–84.

[9] Jerome, "Prologus in epistulis Pauli apostoli," lines 27–35.

[10] M. Rauer, *Die "Schwachen" in Korinth und Rom nach den Paulusbriefen* (BibS [F] 21.2–3; Freiburg im Breisgau: Herder, 1923).

"strong" and the "weak" in Rome,[11] no monograph has been published in English on this topic in this century.

This book does not simply rehash what commentators have said, sifting through various proposals to find probable answers. While the work is done in conversation with those who have written and are writing on Romans, I examine the text with concepts and comparative texts that hitherto have not been applied to the study of "strong" and "weak" in Romans.

But it is not as though no valuable work had been done before. Indeed, it may be helpful to place this study within the flow of those who have studied and written on "strong" and "weak" in Romans. What follows is a brief survey of past work on this topic, to trace the contours of past discussion on the "strong" and "weak" in Romans, before I identify what is new in this study. Figure 1 outlines the survey to follow.

Since the time of Origen, the interpretation of "strong" and "weak" in Romans has been a controversy in its own right. While it is not necessary here to repeat the surveys of research done by Rauer,[12] Nababan,[13] and Schneider,[14] I set out the landmarks of the various positions in order to establish the background for an investigation of the problems. Relevant works on Romans that have appeared since 1988 are included under headings of their authors' names and presented within the appropriate category on "strong" and "weak."

The investigations may first be categorized on the basis of one's

[11] Karris, "Occasion"; P. S. Minear, *The Obedience of Faith: The Purposes of Paul in the Epistle to the Romans* (SBT 2.19; Naperville, Ill.: Allenson, 1971); A. E. S. Nababan, "Bekenntnis und Mission in Römer 14 und 15: Eine exegetische Untersuchung" (D.Theol. dissertation, University of Heidelberg, 1962); M. D. Nanos, *The Mystery of Romans: The Jewish Context of Paul's Letter* (Minneapolis: Fortress, 1996), 85–165; N. Schneider, "Die 'Schwachen' in der christlichen Gemeinde Roms: Eine historisch-exegetische Untersuchung zu Röm 14, 1–15, 13" (D.Theol. dissertation, Kirchliche Hochschule Wuppertal, 1989); F. Watson, "The Two Roman Congregations: Romans 14:1–15:13," in Donfried, *The Romans Debate*, 203–15; F. Watson, *Paul, Judaism and the Gentiles* (SNTSMS 56; Cambridge: Cambridge University Press, 1986), 88–98.

[12] In his chapter "Die Frage in der älteren Exegese," Rauer surveys interpretations of the problem from Augustine through J. A. Bengel (*Die "Schwachen,"* 108–20). He catalogs in detail scholars' views on the problem from the nineteenth century through his own time in his next chapter, "Die zugrunde liegenden Anschauungen," 121–69.

[13] A. E. S. Nababan describes the history of research from F. C. Bauer to his own time in his dissertation "Bekenntnis und Mission," 9–25.

[14] The preceding sixty years of research are surveyed and categorized in Schneider, "Die 'Schwachen,'" 8–49.

Literary construct based on situation in Corinth
(*Sanday–Headlam, Karris*)

INTERPRETIVE STRATEGY: Use 1 Cor. 8–10 as a lens through which to read Rom. 14–15.

IMPLICATIONS: Romans is more like a general, theological essay than an occasional letter.

Situation actually occurring in Rome

INTERPRETIVE STRATEGY: Use what we know of Roman society and Judaism in the diaspora to help interpret the letter.

"Weak" cannot be identified
(*Lietzmann, Dodd, Sampley*)

IMPLICATIONS: Romans is more like a general, theological essay than an occasional letter.

"Weak" are non-Christian
(*Nanos*)

IMPLICATIONS: Romans is thooroughly Jewish- and Torah-friendly, an ecumenical letter.

"Weak" are Christian

Jewish Christians
(*Origen, Cranfield, Schneider, Fitzmyer, Moo, Dunn, Schmithals, Stuhlmacher, Lampe, Tomson, Barclay, most commentators*)

IMPLICATIONS: Jewish/Christian tension drives the whole letter.

Both Jewish and Gentile Christians
(*Lagrange, Wedderburn, Ziesler, Reasoner*)

IMPLICATIONS: Roman churches are a melting pot of Jewish and Gentile concerns.

Gentile Christians
(*Rauer, Kümmel, Stowers*)

IMPLICATIONS: Jews are interesting to Paul as a matter of theological speculation, but they were not as significant in the church as others think.

Figure 1 Romans 14.1–15.13: interpretive options

understanding of the text's relationship to the historical situation in Rome. While the majority of scholars do see an actual situation reflected in Rom. 14.1–15.13, some think that the similarities with 1 Cor. 8–10 indicate that Paul has written to Rome with no historical referent in mind except the situation of the Corinthian church.

"Weak" are a literary construct based on situation in Corinth

Those who see the situation in the text as related only to the situation described in 1 Cor. 8–10 may be represented by Sanday and Headlam's commentary. They write, "When St. Paul says in ver. 2 'the weak man eateth vegetables,' he does not mean that there is a special sect of vegetarians in Rome; but he takes a typical instance of excessive scrupulousness."[15] Their basic position is that the argument lacks specific reference and can only have been written on the basis of Paul's past experience, rather than from his knowledge of conditions in the Roman church. Leenhardt essentially approaches 14.1–15.13 in this way as well.[16]

A more recent expression of this position may be found in Robert J. Karris's essay, "Romans 14.1–15.13 and the Occasion of Romans."[17] Karris argues that since the history-of-religions view is bankrupt and parallels can be identified between Rom. 14.1–15.13 and 1 Cor. 8–10, the text in Romans must have been constructed on the analogy of the situation in Corinth, with no reference to specific groups in the Roman church. This position of course has significant implications for how one reads the letter as a whole, since Rom. 14.1–15.13 is usually taken as evidence of the letter's occasional nature.[18]

In the former category, investigations usually result in an identification of the "weak" practices and attitudes either with Jewish or pagan[19] forms of abstinence and observance of days that were

---

[15] *A Critical and Exegetical Commentary on the Epistle to the Romans* (13th ed.; ICC 45; Edinburgh: T. & T. Clark, 1911), 401–402.

[16] F. J. Leenhardt, *The Epistle to the Romans: A Commentary* (trans. H. Knight; London: Lutterworth, 1961), 346.

[17] Donfried, *The Romans Debate*, 65–84.

[18] Cf. the range of occasions or motives suggested for Romans that are listed in Haacker, "Der Römerbrief als Friedensmemorandum," 25–29.

[19] The dichotomy "pagan or Jewish" is not without problems, given the syncretistic nature of Hellenistic Judaism in the diaspora. See J. Z. Smith, "Wisdom and Apocalyptic," in *Map Is Not Territory* (Leiden: Brill, 1979), 87. "Pagan or Jewish" is

purportedly occurring in Rome. Most numerous in the history of exegesis are those interpretations which see the "weak" as motivated by concerns related to Jewish-Christian observance of Mosaic law.

"Weak" are Jewish believers

Origen considered the "weak" to be Jewish Christians in Rome who distinguished themselves by their concern for Torah.

> Quod potest quidem videri dictum ad eos qui ex gentibus crediderunt, extollentes se in libertatem fidei, quia nihil commune aut immundum esse crederent adversum eos qui ex circumcisione crediderunt, observantes adhuc secundum traditionem legis ciborum differentiam: ut eos reprimere videatur et monere ne insultent eis quibus longa consuetudo in observandis cibis discretionem adhuc aliquam et cunctationem movebat.

> Thus one can see that this is addressed to those who believed from the Gentiles, elevating themselves in the freedom of faith, since they believed nothing to be common or unclean, as opposed to those who believed from the circumcision, who still observed a differentiation among foods according to the tradition of the law. So he seems to restrain them and warn them not to insult those who through long habit in observing discrimination up to now in foods were motivated by some reservation.[20]

At a later point in his commentary, on 14.16–17, Origen does suggest Jewish or Encratite practice as forming the background of the "weak," thus raising the possibility that Nanos has now developed, that the "weak" are Jews who do not believe in Jesus.[21]

Following Origen in the basic identification of Jewish concerns behind the "weak" abstinence of believers within the Roman churches is Chrysostom.[22] Greek fathers known for following

---

used here to designate the general orientation behind the practices and attitudes in question.

[20] Origen, *Commentaria in epistolam beati Pauli ad Romanos* 9.35 (*PG* 14:1234–35).

[21] Ibid., 10.1 (*PG* 14:1249). See discussion on Nanos later in this chapter.

[22] John Chrysostom, *Homiliae XXXII in epistolam ad Romanos* 25.1 (*PG* 60:627).

Chrysostom do so here as well, for example, Theodoret.[23] John Damascene, who is in the same interpretive tradition, may be cited as representative.

Πολλοὶ τῶν ἐξ Ἰουδαίων πεπιστευκότων. ἔτι τῇ τοῦ νόμου κατεχόμενοι συνειδήσει μετὰ τὴν πίστιν, τῶν βρωμάτων ἐφύλαττον τὴν παρατήρησιν, οὔπω θαρροῦντες τέλειον ἀποστῆναι τοῦ νόμου, εἶτα ὥστε μὴ γενέσθαι εὐφώρατοι τῶν χοιρίων ἀπεχόμενοι μόνον, πάντων ἐξῆς ἀπείχοντο κρεῶν, καὶ ἤσθιον λάχανα, ἵνα νηστεία μᾶλλον εἶναι δοκῇ, ἀλλὰ μὴ νόμου παρατήρησις.

Many from among the Jews had believed. But they still held in conscience to the law after faith; they kept the observance of foods, not yet having complete confidence to stand away from the law, for since it would not be easy to detect those who abstained only from pork, they therefore abstained from all meats, and ate vegetables, that it would rather appear to be a fast, though this was not the observance of the law.[24]

In more recent times this view has been held by Melanchthon,[25] J. J. Wettstein,[26] Godet,[27] Riggenbach,[28] Kühl,[29] Michel,[30] Jewett,[31]

---

[23] *Interpretatio epistolae ad Romanos* 140 (*PG* 82:200).

[24] Ἐκ τῆς καθόλου ἑρμηνείας Ἰωάννου τοῦ Χρυσοστόμου ἐκλογαὶ ἐκλεγεῖσαι, 51 (*PG* 95:549).

[25] P. Melanchthon, *Annotationes in epistulam Pauli ad Romanos et ad Corinthios*, in *Opera quae supersunt omnia* (Vol. XV; ed. C. G. Bretschneider; Halis Saxonum: C. A. Schwetschke and Son, 1848; reprint ed., New York: Johnson Reprint Corp., 1963), cols. 1024–28.

[26] J. J. Wettstein, Ἡ Καινὴ Διαθήκη *Novum Testamentum graecum*, Vol. II: *Continens epistolas Pauli* (Amsterdam: Ex officina Dommeriana, 1752; reprint ed., Graz: Akademische Druck- und Verlagsanstalt, 1962), 91 (on Rom. 14.22).

[27] F. Godet, *St. Paul's Epistle to the Romans* (trans. A. Cusin and T. W. Chambers; New York: Funk & Wagnalls, 1883), 467.

[28] E. Riggenbach, "Die Starken und Schwachen in der römischen Gemeinde," *TSK* 66 (1893) 675–76.

[29] E. Kühl, *Der Brief des Paulus an die Römer* (Leipzig: Quelle & Meyer, 1913), 444–46.

[30] O. Michel, *Der Brief an die Römer* (4th ed.; KEK 4; Göttingen: Vandenhoeck & Ruprecht, 1966), 334.

[31] R. Jewett, *Paul's Anthropological Terms: A Study of their Use in Conflict Settings* (AGJU 10; Leiden: Brill, 1971), 42–46; R. Jewett, "The Law and the Coexistence of Jews and Gentiles in Romans," *Interp.* 39 (1985) 354.

Käsemann,[32] Cranfield,[33] Wilckens,[34] and Watson.[35] The basic arguments for a Jewish background to "weak" abstinence are parallels for Jewish abstinence,[36] Paul's use of κοινος in 14.14,[37] and the general Jew versus Gentile tension that energizes much of the letter.[38] I can illustrate this position, that Jewish Christians represent the "weak" and Gentile Christians represent the "strong," from more recent publications on Romans,[39] presented in the order in which they have appeared.

J. D. G. Dunn[40]

Dunn notes the absence of the terms εἰδωλόθυτα, συνείδησις, and γνῶσις in this section of Romans, along with its description of a clean/unclean distinction (not found in 1 Corinthians), as evidence of a difference in reference from the situation depicted in 1 Cor. 8–10.[41] After acknowledging neo-Pythagorean parallels to the meat and wine abstinence found in Rom. 14.1–15.13, he states that "here Paul must have at least the dietary rules of Jews and Jewish Christians in view, whatever other practices can be included in its sweep."[42] Dunn supports this conclusion with three observations.[43] First, the orientation of the letter around the Jew versus Gentile

---

[32] E. Käsemann, *Commentary on Romans* (trans. and ed. G. W. Bromiley; Grand Rapids: Eerdmans, 1980), 368–69.

[33] C. E. B. Cranfield, *A Critical and Exegetical Commentary on the Epistle to the Romans*, ICC; Edinburgh: T. & T. Clark, 1979), 690–97.

[34] U. Wilckens, *Der Brief an die Römer* (EKKNT 6; 3 vols.; Neukirchen-Vluyn: Neukirchener, 1982), III.109–15.

[35] Watson, *Paul, Judaism and the Gentiles*, 94–98.

[36] These include Dan. 1.8, 10–16; Josephus, *Vita* 13–14; and Hegesippus' testimony (according to Eusebius, *H.E.* 2.23.5) about the abstinence of James.

[37] Examples of the word's occurrence in discussions of purity issues outside of a Jewish context have not been found.

[38] See Rom. 1.16; 3.9–31; 9–11; 15.9–12.

[39] Christoph Heil, *Die Ablehnung der Speisegebote durch Paulus* (BBB 96; Weinheim/Berlin: Beltz Athenäum, 1994), 260–65, identifies the "weak" as Jewish Christians. He is not featured in the survey here, since the focus of his monograph prevents him from contributing significantly to the arguments regarding the identity of the "weak."

[40] J. D. G. Dunn, *Romans 9–16* (WBC 38B; Dallas: Word, 1988).

[41] Ibid., 795. The absence of these terms and concepts related to them is significant, for they play a crucial role in the 1 Cor. 8–10 passage. On εἰδωλόθυτα, see 1 Cor. 8.1, 4, 7, 10; 10.19. On συνείδησις, see 1 Cor. 8.7, 10, 12; 10.25, 27–29. On γνῶσις, see 1 Cor. 8.1, 7, 10–11.

[42] Dunn, *Romans*, 799–800.

[43] Ibid., 800 for the following arguments.

theme in chapters 1–11 and the return to this theme in 15.7–13 make a similar background probable here. Second, the use of καθαρός and κοινός in 14.14, 20 fits with Jewish concerns on purity issues. Third, he adduces evidence from Hellenistic authors[44] to show that dietary concerns continued to be a central mark of identification for diaspora Jews.

He relates the controversy, as others have done,[45] to the return of Jews to Rome after Claudius' ban of 49 CE was lifted. Perhaps fewer facilities were available for providing kosher meat or Jewish Christians did not want to call attention to their Jewish orientation by asking for correctly slaughtered meat.[46] He concludes his identification of the "weak" by recognizing that not everyone in the Roman church may have been included in either the designation "strong" or "weak"; we simply do not know the proportions of the controversy.[47]

Walter Schmithals[48]

Schmithals eliminates explanations of pagan asceticism or sectarian (and vegetarian) Judaism as the background for the abstinence mentioned in Rom. 14.1–15.13.[49] Instead he chooses to see the abstinence as based on concern for contamination from εἰδωλόθυτα, and sees 1 Cor. 8.1–13; 10.14–11.1 and Col. 2.16–23 as close parallels to Paul's description of an actual situation in Rome.[50] He explains the obvious difference between the Romans and Corinthians texts first with the generalization that Paul speaks to the Corinthians about a special case of unclean meat, food offered to idols, since they

---

[44] Among them are Philo, *Legat.* 361; Plutarch, *Quaest. conv.* 4.5; Tacitus, *Hist.* 4.2; Juvenal, *Sat.* 14.98.

[45] See Wilckens, *Römer* III.95, 113 n. 547 and P. Lampe, *Die stadtrömischen Christen in den ersten beiden Jahrhunderten: Untersuchungen zur Sozialgeschichte* (2nd ed.; WUNT 2.18; Tübingen: J. C. B. Mohr [Paul Siebeck], 1989), 57 n. 149.

[46] Dunn, *Romans*, 801.   [47] Ibid., 802.

[48] W. Schmithals, *Der Römerbrief: Ein Kommentar* (Gütersloh: Gerd Mohn, 1988).

[49] Ibid., 490–91. For him, pagan asceticism is not in view because Pythagoreanism (the only specific form of this asceticism he considers) cannot explain the day observance (14.5); it is not concerned with cultic purity as the Roman "weak" apparently were (14.14); and the "weak" would not be likely to judge "strong" on the basis of pagan ideas. An asceticism from Jewish orthodoxy is denied primarily because meat and wine in themselves were not considered unclean within Judaism.

[50] Ibid., 491–94. He does not consider the differences between the Corinthians and Colossians texts. Colossians, which he thinks is Pauline (494), does not mention meat, and unlike Corinthians it does mention day observance.

had asked Paul about that. To the Romans Paul writes more comprehensively about unclean meat.[51] With this explanation it is difficult to understand how exactly the situation in Rome can be said to parallel that of Corinth, for if Paul is writing of unclean meat in general, there are more concerns than simply whether or not it was offered to idols, which is all that is in view in 1 Cor. 8–10.

He then suggests that Paul omits reference to wine abstinence or the observance of days in 1 Cor. 8–10 because they had not asked him about them. The problem in Rome is in principle the same as that in Corinth.[52] The issue is to be seen in light of Jewish legal prescriptions on diet and day observance, so that the observance of days relates to the Jewish calendar.[53]

Peter Stuhlmacher[54]

Stuhlmacher also sees the conflict narrated in Rom. 14.1–15.13 as an actual situation resulting from the influx of Jews and Jewish Christians who returned to Rome some time after 49 CE. He considers the "strong" to be Christians of a Pauline sort who emphasized freedom from Torah. He describes the "weak" as Jewish Christians who had a legalistic and ascetic viewpoint. The division between the groups was basically one of ethnic orientation (Jew versus Gentile), although this characterization cannot be absolute.

He relates the controversy back to the apostolic council and decree (Acts 15; Gal. 2.1–11). The controversy in Rome is therefore presented as an unresolved situation arising from the same Jewish versus Gentile tensions within early Christianity. While Stuhlmacher sees the situation in Rome as distinct from that described in 1 Cor. 8–10, he states that Paul argues in the same way in Romans as he did when he addressed the Corinthian problem.

Peter Lampe[55]

Lampe discusses the problem of the "strong" and "weak" in the context of his investigation of the relative numbers of Jews and

[51] Ibid., 493–94.   [52] Ibid., 494.   [53] Ibid., 499.

[54] P. Stuhlmacher, *Der Brief an die Römer* (NTD 6; Göttingen: Vandenhoeck & Ruprecht, 1989). The summary that follows comes from pp. 195–97 of the commentary.

[55] Peter Lampe, *Die stadtrömischen Christen in den ersten beiden Jahrhunderten* (2nd ed.; WUNT 2.18; Tübingen: J. C. B. Mohr [Paul Siebeck], 1989).

Gentiles in the church. He portrays Paul as writing Romans on the assumption that most of the audience had come to Christianity as σεβόμενοι (God-fearers). This is based on his reading of the letter as addressed mostly to Gentiles[56] who were familiar with their Bible.[57] Aquila and Priscilla therefore become representative of Roman believers who possibly had already come to participate in Gentile Christianity before they came to Corinth.[58]

Direct address to "strong" and "weak" in Rom. 14.1–15.13 and the differences between this text and 1 Cor. 8–10 combine to prove for Lampe that it is a real situation in Rome, distinct from the problem of Corinth.[59] He then presents the conflict of Rom. 14.1–15.13 as centering on observance of Mosaic law. The two factors that place this conflict in the context of Jewish law are the use of κοινός in 14.14 and the juxtaposition of Paul's consideration of this controversy with the salvation-historical problem of Israel's relation to the nations.[60] He marshals literary evidence to show that both food laws and observance of days were known to have been followed in first-century Rome by non-Jews who were attracted to Judaism (σεβόμενοι).[61] The concerns related to meat were that properly slaughtered meat might not have been available in Rome, as Josephus' account of the Jewish priests abstaining from meat in Rome shows (*Vita* 13–14). Wine abstinence was probably due to the uncertainty of knowing whether one's wine had been used in pagan libations.[62]

Nélio Schneider[63]

After a thorough comparison with 1 Cor. 8–10, Schneider concludes that Paul is addressing a real situation in Rome. Paul

---

[56] Ibid., 54 n. 131. He lists 1.5–6, 13–15; 6.17–21 in view of 1.18–32; 11.13, 17–18, 24, 28, 30–31; 15.9–12, 15–16, 18.

[57] The commonly recognized scripture citations and proofs are adduced: 1.17; 4.6–8, 17; 9–11; and direct address to the Jew in 2.17 (ibid., 54). Paul's agenda in Romans of showing that Israel and the law have no privileged place before Gentiles would be a pleasing reversal for God-fearers accustomed to synagogue teachings of Jewish superiority (ibid., 55).

[58] Lampe, *Die stadtrömischen Christen*, 53.

[59] Ibid., 56–57.   [60] Ibid., 57.

[61] Juvenal, *Sat.* 14.96–106; Horace, *Sat.* 1.9.68–72.

[62] Lampe, *Die stadtrömischen Christen*, 57. Lampe in n. 149 of this same page offers Wilckens's suggestion (*Römer*, III.95) that after the controversy among the Jews related to the Claudius edict of 49 CE, Jewish butchers in Rome may have refused to sell meat to Jewish Christians who had settled back in the city.

[63] Schneider, "Die 'Schwachen.'"

recognizes three characteristics of the Roman situation: the "weak" are abstaining from meat; the cause of this abstinence is a concern over impurity of food; and certain days are being observed.[64]

The body of Schneider's dissertation then considers three backgrounds for the abstinence of the "weak": a Hellenistic asceticism, exemplified by Apollonius of Tyana; a gnostic asceticism; and an abstinence originating from Judaism. He eliminates Hellenistic asceticism on the basis of four considerations. First, it does not account for the observance of days mentioned in Romans. Second, while the abstinence of the "weak" in Romans was religious in character, typical Greek abstinence of someone like Apollonius[65] was motivated more by a desire not to participate in mortality. Third, the Pythagorean asceticism of the Hellenistic world was for elite individuals and was not promulgated as something for the common people. This seems to differ from the abstinence of the "weak" as depicted in Paul's letter. Fourth, the use of the term κοινός as impurity in 14.14 cannot be understood in a Hellenistic milieu.[66]

He then moves to an examination of gnostic asceticism,[67] using Epiphanius, the apocryphal acts of various apostles, and the Nag Hammadi writings as evidence for various types of asceticism. He finds both chronological and geographical difficulties in finding gnostic influence in the situation described in Romans. The gnostic evidence usually comes from the eastern Mediterranean and is late; he thinks it unlikely that it could have been operative in mid-first-century Rome. Aside from these discontinuities, he notes the qualitative difference that the gnostic asceticism described in his sources was more concerned with sexual than dietary control.

Finally, he notes that the phrase κοινὸν δι' ἑαυτοῦ of 14.14, which seems to represent the difficulty the "weak" had with meat, is neither verbally nor conceptually present as a motive in gnostic asceticism.[68] The twenty pages in which he examines the gnostic evidence are decisive in the history of investigation, for they

---

[64] Ibid., 50–61.

[65] It is Schneider's decision to use Apollonius as a typical example of Hellenistic asceticism (ibid., 65–66).

[66] Ibid., 69–70, for these arguments.

[67] Ibid., 80–91. This comparison is preceded by a brief look at NT texts that might show gnostic influence: 1 Cor. 8–10; Gal. 4.1–11; Col. 2.6–3.4; 1 Tim. 4.3; Titus 1.15; Heb. 13.9 (ibid., 73–80).

[68] Ibid., 92.

represent the first reevaluation of the gnostic evidence since Rauer and arrive at an opposite conclusion.

In the final comparison of the dissertation, he examines evidence for dietary abstinence in Judaism. Examples of Jewish concern for purity when living among Gentiles are presented, and then more specific examples of Jews who abstained from meat in order to fulfill *kashrut* laws follow.[69] After examinations of the use of κοινός as a term for cultic impurity in Judaism,[70] and the question of table fellowship and dietary law in early Christianity,[71] Schneider reaches his conclusion. He portrays the controversy in Rome as one relating to table fellowship between Jewish and non-Jewish Christians. The "weak" are a minority of Jewish Christians whose law-observant tendencies related to diet are disregarded.[72]

Peter J. Tomson[73]

Tomson's work, which seeks to present Paul's positive stance to *halakha* in his letters, leaves two options open for an identification of the "weak" concern reflected in Romans. Tomson thinks that perhaps Paul is asking the Gentile believers in Rome to be sensitive to "basic Jewish food laws." His other option is that there may have been an extra sensitivity among some of the Jewish believers, manifesting itself in their refusal to eat with Gentiles unless the Gentiles abstained from meat and wine, because of a concern that such foods may have been offered to idols.[74] Tomson's reading of the text distills two principles from it: "nowhere does Paul argue abandonment of the commandments by Jews, and he always pleads for Jewish–gentile coexistence."[75]

A distinctive value of Tomson's volume is his use of rabbinic texts that deal with Jewish–Gentile commensality. He is the only author who deals with Rom. 14.1–15.13 who has pointed out how ἀσθενής appears as a loan word in the Mishnah.[76] Its occurrence

---

[69] Ibid., 100–104. Among the latter group of examples are Dan. 1.16 and the other accounts of Daniel (Josephus, *AJ* 10.190; *Vitae proph.* 16); Tobit 1.10–12; Judith 10.5; 12.1–2, 19; Letter of Aristeas 181–83, 186; 2 Macc. 5.27; Josephus, *Vita* 14. An excursus on the Therapeutae of Philo's *De vita contemplativa* follows (Schneider, "Die 'Schwachen,'" 104–107).

[70] Schneider, "Die 'Schwachen,'" 108–15.

[71] Ibid., 115–21.   [72] Ibid., 122–23.

[73] Peter J. Tomson, *Paul and the Jewish Law: Halakha in the Letters of the Apostle to the Gentiles* (CRINT 3.1; Assen/Maastricht: Van Gorcum, 1990).

[74] Ibid., 244.   [75] Ibid., 245.

[76] Ibid., 195, citing *m. Yoma* 3.5.

there leads him to identify Paul's connotation of ἀσθενής, both in 1
Cor. 8–10 and in Rom. 14–15, as " 'infirm, delicate,' stressing a
restrictive diet rather than a defective faith."[77] Tomson represents
the recent start of Jewish-sensitive readings of this text in Romans,
which has been extended further by Mark Nanos. Nanos follows
him in viewing "weak" as a respectful term, though Nanos does
focus it on some Jews' faith, rather than on their diet.[78]

Joseph A. Fitzmyer[79]

Fitzmyer presents the "weak" as "probably Jewish Christian
members of the Roman community."[80] He is cautious about Marxsen's idea that the "strong" are Gentile believers and the "weak"
are Jewish believers who returned when Claudius' ban on Jews was
lifted, because of Paul's vague references to the problems dividing
the community. But this is the only explanation that he uses when
he summarizes the situation, so he does seem to give it a qualified
endorsement.[81] At one point Fitzmyer notes that converts from
Orphism, the Dionysiac mysteries, and Pythagoreanism might have
thought it best to continue meat abstinence even after joining the
Christian community,[82] though this possibility does not figure in
his exegesis of the passage.

John M. G. Barclay[83]

Barclay's article presents succinctly the evidence for viewing the
"weak" position as motivated by respect for Mosaic law. The uses of
κοινόν and καθαρός in 14.14, 20, the literary context of this passage,
the likelihood that such concerns arose among early Christians, and
the difficulties with viewing pagan influence as part of the "weak"
behavior all combine for Barclay to support this view.[84] He also

---

77 Ibid., 195.
78 Nanos, *Mystery*, 157.
79 J. A. Fitzmyer, *Romans* (AB 33; New York: Doubleday, 1993).
80 Ibid., 687.
81 Ibid., 77–79; 687–88. Marxsen's ideas on the origin and characteristics of
Roman Christianity with which Fitzmyer interacts may be found in W. Marxsen,
Introduction to the New Testament (Philadelphia: Fortress/Oxford: Blackwell, 1968),
92–109.
82 Fitzmyer, *Romans*, 687.
83 John M. G. Barclay, " 'Do We Undermine the Law?' A Study of Romans
14.1–15.6," in *Paul and the Mosaic Law* (ed. J. D. G. Dunn, Tübingen: J. C. B.
Mohr [Paul Siebeck], 1996), 287–308.
84 Ibid., 289–93.

helpfully portrays the Jewish diet as distinctive and well known in first-century Rome. He presents Sabbath observance as popular among some Romans, though not because of an inherent attraction to Judaism.[85] With the social context before the reader, Barclay summarizes Paul's instructions and concludes his article with his most controversial points under the heading "The Social Effects of Paul's Advice." These points are: "Paul protects Law observance and Jewish Christianity"; "Paul allows Law-neglect and a Gentilized Christianity"; "Paul effectively undermines the social and cultural integrity of the Law-observant Christians in Rome."[86]

Significant in Barclay's presentation is his use of this section of practical teaching within Romans to inform our understanding of Paul's view of Torah. Rom. 14.1–15.13 does not explicitly mention Torah, so reading it with an eye to Torah observance is a step not everyone will follow. But the article is very valuable for the way in which it attempts to read the passage on "strong" and "weak" together with Rom. 3.31; 7.12, 14. And when this article is read alongside the works of Tomson and Nanos, distinguishing features in the rival portraits of Paul become clear. Barclay's article is stimulating to me in the way in which it uses the "strong" and "weak" section as a window onto the whole letter of Romans.

Douglas J. Moo[87]

Moo considers the "weak" to be "mainly Jewish Christians who refrained from certain kinds of food and observed certain days out of continuing loyalty to the Mosaic law."[88] He sees the conflict as a Jewish versus Gentile issue because of this theme's presence in the letter from the first chapter on, as well as in Paul's conclusion to this part of the letter in 15.8–13. Paul's use of κοινός in 14.14 also argues for a Jewish concern regarding consumption. Paul's general acceptance of the "weak" implies for Moo that their position was not opposed to Paul's gospel, thus eliminating Jewish sectarians from his list of candidates for the "weak." The omission of εἰδωλόθυτα widens the issue beyond food sacrificed to idols, as in 1 Cor. 8–10. Moo cites other cases of Jewish abstention from meat and wine as examples of diaspora Jews who abstained in order to

---

[85] Ibid., 294–98.   [86] Ibid., 303–308.
[87] Douglas J. Moo, *The Epistle to the Romans* (NICNT; Grand Rapids: Eerdmans, 1996).
[88] Ibid., 829.

be sure that their dietary laws were not violated, which is what he thinks is happening among Paul's audience.[89] The significance of Moo's commentary for this study is the link he makes between this section and the theme of Romans: "We find even in this hortatory section, therefore, further confirmation of our thesis that Romans is a general exposition of the gospel occasioned by the specific needs in the Roman community."[90] This statement is moving in the same direction that I am in this study; I also want to use an examination of Rom. 14.1–15.13 as a window onto the whole letter.

"Weak" are Gentile believers

Among those who view the text as referring to actual abstinence in Rome primarily motivated by pagan concerns, Rauer[91] is the main exponent. He argues that vegetarianism was not a part of Judaism, thinks that κοινός in the sense of unclean does not conclusively designate Jewish purity concerns, and takes gnosticism as the preferable background for "weak" concerns. Kümmel would have to be placed in this category, for he can recognize no evidence for a Jewish background to the "weak."[92] A moderate form of this position is held by C. K. Barrett. Though he thinks that orthodox Judaism is precluded, he thinks a Jewish–gnostic matrix probable.[93] The only representative of this position in recent publications is Stowers.

Stanley K. Stowers[94]

Stowers considers the parallels he finds with Greco-Roman philosophical literature on adaptability and the terminology of weakness to be the "compelling" reason why the "weak" cannot be understood as a group marked by distinctly Jewish concerns. He also

[89] Ibid., 829–31. The references he gives (831 n. 19) for Jewish abstinence are: Dan. 1.8; 10.3; Tobit 1.10–12; Judith 12.2, 19; Add. Esther 14.17; *Joseph and Asenath* 7.1; 8.5; Josephus, *Vita* 14; *m. 'Abot* 3.3.

[90] Moo, *Romans*, 832.

[91] Rauer, *Die "Schwachen."*

[92] W. G. Kümmel, *Introduction to the New Testament* (17th ed.; trans. H. C. Kee; Nashville: Abingdon, 1973), 310–11.

[93] C. K. Barrett, *A Commentary on the Epistle to the Romans* (HNTC; New York: Harper & Brothers, 1957), 257.

[94] S. K. Stowers, *A Rereading of Romans: Justice, Jews, and Gentiles* (New Haven/London: Yale University Press, 1994).

states that it is difficult to identify the "weak" with Jews because there is no evidence that there were Jews then following the "weak" practices mentioned in this section of Romans.[95] Another unique feature of Stowers's explanation is that he refuses to think of "strong" and "weak" as groups of people or theological positions. He borrows from his philosophical parallels and chooses rather to call them "dispositions."[96] While he does not go into detail on what sort of teaching or advising that he thinks Paul wants to occur between "strong" and "weak," Stowers does think that Paul expects some "psychagogic activities" to occur between "strong" and "weak." Stowers concludes his discussion on this mutual teaching Paul envisages by stating that Paul's point is that the "weak" and "strong" (in that order) must adapt to each other as Christ has adapted to them by accepting the ungodly.[97]

In regard to the letter of Romans as a whole, Stowers claims that once one sees that the letter is about Christ's example of adaptability to others, then the ethical section beginning at 12.1 naturally flows out of this. Since Paul's theology centers around the adaptability of Christ, according to Stowers, his social ethics follow suit.[98]

Though Rauer and Stowers must be placed in the same category, since they view the "strong" and "weak" tension as an intra-Gentile issue, their approaches are very different. Rauer thinks that the "weak" behavior is a type of gnostic asceticism, while Stowers identifies the same behavior as some form of immaturity, based on the use of the word ἀσθενέω in Rom. 14.1, since this word and cognates carry this significance in the moral philosophers. Stowers does not define exactly what he means by "immature" in this context.[99]

"Weak" are Jewish and Gentile believers

This position is a compromise between the preceding two positions. Its attraction is that it allows one to take the purity language of 14.14, 20 in its most likely sense, as referring to Jewish concerns, while at the same time noting that there were other reasons why people abstained from meat and wine in first-century Rome. Those who have held this position include La-

[95] Ibid., 317.   [96] Ibid., 321.   [97] Ibid., 322–23.
[98] Ibid., 323, 326.   [99] Ibid., 321.
[100] Lagrange, *Romains*, 338–39.

grange,[100] Huby,[101] and Lyonnet.[102] The foremost exponents of this position, in recent research, are Wedderburn and Ziesler.

A. J. M. Wedderburn[103]

Wedderburn makes the telling point that the number of views on the identities of "strong" and "weak" does not mean that Paul did not know who they were. Indeed, the way in which Paul's directions in Rom. 13.1–7 fit with Tacitus' testimony about popular sentiment over Roman taxation in 58 CE seems to indicate that Paul had a detailed knowledge about life in Rome while writing to the churches there.[104] Wedderburn identifies the abstinence of the "weak" with concerns of Jews in the diaspora who did not want to defile themselves with improperly slaughtered meat and so practiced vegetarianism. Wine abstinence among diaspora Jews is also attested, so Wedderburn places all the behavior of the "weak" – vegetarianism, wine abstinence, and observance of days – as Jewish practices that some church members in Rome felt that they should maintain.[105]

Yet he does not go so far as to state that the division between "weak" and "strong" was drawn exclusively along Jew/Gentile lines. He states that some Jews may have considered themselves liberated from Mosaic law and the traditions built up around it, while some of the ethnic Romans may have been attracted to Jewish practices, or come into the Roman house churches via the synagogues.[106] I agree with Wedderburn that the "weak" must have included both Jewish and Gentile believers. We differ in that I think it plausible that some of the "weak" were abstaining for extra-Jewish reasons. My work attempts to fill out his picture of the Roman churches and Paul's directions to them over "strong" and "weak."

---

[101] J. Huby, *Saint Paul: Epître aux Romains: traduction et commentaire* (rev. S. Lyonnet; Paris: Beauchesne, 1957), 453.

[102] S. Lyonnet, *Les Epîtres de Saint Paul aux Galates, aux Romains* (2nd ed.; Paris: Cerf, 1959), 126.

[103] A. J. M. Wedderburn, *The Reasons for Romans* (SNTW; Edinburgh: T. & T. Clark, 1988).

[104] Ibid., 62–63; Tacitus, *Ann.* 13.50–51.

[105] Wedderburn, *Reasons*, 30–35.

[106] Ibid., 60.

John Ziesler[107]

Ziesler considers the problem in Rome to have been "very similar to that in Corinth."[108] By that he means that it concerned εἰδωλόθυτα. Just as this problem occurred in the Gentile church of Corinth, so Ziesler thinks that Gentiles as well as Jews constituted the "weak," and that the "strong" and "weak" groups can therefore not be identified along Gentile- versus Jewish-Christian lines.[109] Since meat was controversial for more reasons than simply its possible status as εἰδωλόθυτα, I shall argue that the characteristic "weak" behavior was motivated by more concerns than this.

Among those who see Rom. 14.1–15.13 as a concrete situation in Rome that Paul addresses, Ziesler is distinctive in depending on 1 Cor. 8–10 and the situation in Corinth to structure his reading of the Romans passage. While he admits the possibility of what I shall argue, that Paul is simply adopting the nicknames "strong" and "weak" already in use among the Roman believers, he seems to favor the possibility that Paul imports the term "weak" from his experience in Corinth.[110] His work thus illustrates the results of reading Rom. 14.1–15.13 in light of 1 Cor. 8–10, a practice that must be balanced with a look at first-century Rome in its own right.

"Weak" are practicing Jews outside of the church

Mark D. Nanos[111]

Alone in this position is Nanos's work, which pictures the addressees of Paul's letter to be Jesus-believers still in the synagogue, in close contact with practicing Jews who are not attached to the Jesus movement. Nanos contends that past interpreters of Romans 14–15 have fallen into what he calls "Luther's trap." By this he means that the interpreters acknowledge Paul's dictum that the "strong" should not judge the "weak" (*sic*),[112] but then go on to

---

[107] J. Ziesler, *Paul's Letter to the Romans* (TPINTC, Philadelphia: Trinity Press International, 1989).

[108] Ibid., 324.

[109] Ibid., 324. On 326–27 he helpfully notes the possible influence of either a Jewish or pagan past on the "weak."

[110] Ibid., 326–27.

[111] Nanos, *The Mystery of Romans*.

[112] Actually the text seems consistently to command the "strong" not to despise

describe the "weak" in ways that violate Paul's command to respect them. This is because Nanos takes any description of the "weak" as immature or unenlightened in their Christian faith to be violations of Paul's commands for mutual respect.[113] A key presupposition that allows Nanos to spring "Luther's trap" on other Romans interpreters is his opinion that Paul thinks that the "weak in faith" should become "strong."[114] For Nanos, it is inconceivable that Paul would want Jewish believers to change their Torah-oriented diet or day observance.

Nanos notes that Paul calls the "weak" ones in Romans 14 the "weak in faith." He finds it significant that Paul does not label their practices of vegetarianism or day observance as "weak." "Weak in faith" for Nanos thus comes to mean that these Roman "weak" are practicing Jews whose faith Paul views as "weak" since they do not yet believe in Jesus. It is not their Jewish lifestyle that Paul views as "weak," but only their faith.[115] Thus Nanos avoids the "Luther's trap" he finds in other interpretations by emphasizing that it is not Torah observance that Paul considers "weak" or immature behavior. The "weak" are "weak in faith" only because they do not believe in Jesus, according to Nanos.

While Nanos writes generally of the significance that one's interpretation of Romans 14–15 has for one's reading of the whole letter,[116] I think that I can sharpen the implications of his interpretation: it points toward a very pro-Torah reading of Paul and Romans. After avoiding "the condescending trap that characterizes almost all interpretations of the 'weaknesses of the weak' as their failure to disregard the practice of the Law, as though the practice of the Law demonstrated a lack of faith," Nanos goes on to suggest that when Paul wrote Romans, he did not think that Jesus-believing Jews should abandon Torah and would have resisted anyone's proposal that he himself should abandon Torah.[117] Another point of significance that Nanos does acknowledge is that his reading contributes toward ecumenical understanding today between Jew and Christian.[118]

---

the "weak" and the "weak" not to judge the "strong" (Rom. 14.3, 10), but with this correction Nanos's caricature of the "trap" still stands.

[113] Nanos, *Mystery*, 87–95.   [114] Ibid., 154–57.   [115] Ibid., 103–15.
[116] Ibid., 91.
[117] Ibid., 91 (quotation); 153–54 (last half of my sentence).
[118] Ibid., 158–59.

Agnosticism toward an historical situation in Rome

While we examine the various options in one's approach to Rom.
14.1–15.13, those who understand Paul to be addressing a real
situation in Rome that cannot be identified may be mentioned:
Lietzmann, Dodd, and Nababan.

After discussing the prevalence of meat and wine abstinence in
antiquity, Lietzmann states, "Weil also diese Erscheinung so allge-
mein verbreitet war, ist es unmöglich, die 'Schwachen' unserer
Stelle auf Grund der Askese einer bestimmten Sekte zuzuweisen
oder einen speziellen Einfluß festzustellen."[119] C. H. Dodd similarly
views the Romans text as referring to an historical situation
occurring in Rome, but refuses to identify the ideological contours
of the divisive behavior.[120] Nababan thinks that Rom. 14.1–15.13
is addressed to a concrete situation, but since he finds the controversy represented so as to support general principles, he refuses to
specify the identities of "strong" and "weak."[121] The only recent
author similarly agnostic is Sampley.

J. Paul Sampley[122]

Sampley argues that Paul is oblique in his description of the
situation in Rome. His thesis is that Paul is vague and describes the
Romans' controversies in bigger than life terms in order to win a
hearing from both sides of the community. Sampley does not think
that "teetotalling vegetarians" were among Paul's audience, but
that Paul has shifted the issue of controversy from keeping Jewish
dietary laws (which Sampley assumes was a problem in Rome) to
the more general issue of vegetarianism.[123] Similarly, he notes how
Paul does not mention Sabbath (which Sampley assumes was
controversial in Rome), but talks generally about the observance of
days, since Roman society also had its calendar carefully con-

---

[119] Hans Lietzmann, *Einführung in die Textgeschichte der Paulusbriefe: An die Römer* (4th ed.; HNT 8; Tübingen: J. C. B. Mohr [Paul Siebeck], 1971), 115.

[120] C. H. Dodd, *The Epistle of Paul to the Romans* (MNTC; New York: Harper & Brothers, 1932), 211–12.

[121] Nababan, "Bekenntnis," 25.

[122] J. Paul Sampley, "The Weak and the Strong: Paul's Careful and Crafty Rhetorical Strategy in Romans 14:1–15:13," in *The Social World of the First Christians: Essays in Honor of Wayne A. Meeks* (eds. L. M. White and O. L. Yarbrough; Minneapolis: Fortress, 1995), 40–52.

[123] Ibid., 41–43, 46.

structed around days when business could and could not be performed.[124]

The value of Sampley's essay is that it takes seriously the way in which Paul's rhetorical situation in Romans must have affected the way that he portrays the controversy in Rome that he wants to address. Sampley emphasizes that Paul is addressing a real situation, while noting that our evidence for it is skewed by Paul's diplomatic aims in the letter. His point that Paul did not mean for the letter's readers to identify "strong" and "weak"[125] ignores evidence for "strong" and "weak" that Sampley does not mention, evidence that does make an identification of these groups possible.

Remaining challenges

The recent studies, like the past investigations in general, have focused on the abstinence from meat and wine as well as the observance of days to describe what was going on in Rome and to explain Paul's argument. In looking for a description of the "weak" group, they tend implicitly to assume that one ideology must explain both the dietary abstinence and the observance of days,[126] while the text does not necessarily indicate this.

Some parallels related to abstinence and day observance have been amply cited and repeated throughout the history of investigation. What is needed is a look at the picture Paul provides of "strong" and "weak" in light of the social life of Rome.

When this is done, it is seen that there was a variety of reasons to abstain from meat and wine and observe certain days in Rome. While the question of "weak" behavior does appear to contain Jewish influences, the investigations generally do not give an account of the plethora of forces at work in the Empire's capital that could give rise to the "weak" behavior described in Romans. The range of motives for vegetarianism is worth seeing, just so that one realizes what an attraction it would be for someone in first-century Rome.

Aside from the issue of the background of ritual practices, the investigations also lose sight of Rome in terms of the social composition of the city. It is amazing that no previous studies of Rom. 14.1–15.13 have mentioned the many *collegia tenuiorum* in

---

[124] Ibid., 42.   [125] Ibid., 48.
[126] So, e.g., Schneider, "Die 'Schwachen,'" 69, eliminates a Hellenistic background because for him it cannot explain the observance of days.

the Empire, or called attention to Roman authors' use of titles of strength to designate those on the upward end of a given social scale. When the use of such "weak" and "strong" terms is appreciated, one begins to see that Rom. 14.1–15.13 indeed fits with the Rome of the first century. The ancient Romans' suspicion of foreign religions, which they could view as superstitions, is also an element in the equation that not all who study the "strong" and "weak" catch.

The difference between the Christian "strong" and "weak" needs to be seen in the context of the status-conscious Roman society with its various levels of stratification. How did the "strong" and "weak" relate? What was at issue besides differences in consumption or day observance? These are questions that those who focus simply on the outward practices mentioned in Rom. 14.1–15.13 ignore. Past interpreters of this passage have sought to relate its description of the Roman churches to preceding passages in the letter,[127] and my study gains much from the relationships they have seen.

At the same time as past studies have focused on dietary abstinence and observance of days to the exclusion of the bigger picture in Rome, the same focus has occurred in an analogous way with Paul's evaluation and solution to the controversy. How does Paul's solution to the controversy fit with Roman social thought, especially its emphasis on obligation? Also, Paul's solution to the Romans' "strong" and "weak" controversy has not always been read in light of the letter as a whole.[128]

In general, then, we could say that past studies have centered on the surface phenomena in the text. In this volume, by focusing in an in-depth way on this limited section of Romans, I seek ultimately to extend the vista of Romans readers. I seek to answer the questions: "How does Paul's description of 'strong' and 'weak' and his response to them fit with first-century Roman society?" and "How does Paul's description of and response to 'strong' and 'weak' fit with the rest of the Romans letter?" These questions will help us form a response to the question with which this chapter began: "Where is Romans on the continuum between general treatise for all Christians and focused memorandum for Roman churches?"

---

[127] E.g., Watson, *Paul, Judaism and the Gentiles*, 88–181; Minear, *Obedience*, *passim*.
[128] L. William Countryman's unpublished paper "The Rhetoric of Purity in Romans" is certainly an exception to this generalization. I make use of it when relating Romans 14–15 to the letter as a whole in chapter 12 below.

2

ROMANS 14.1–15.13 REFERS TO AN HISTORICAL SITUATION IN ROME

haec pars philosophiae, quam Graeci paraeneticen uocant, nos praeceptiuam dicimus.. (Seneca, *Ep.* 95.1)

This branch of philosophy, which the Greeks call parenesis, we call praeceptiua

The boundaries of the "strong" and "weak" text in Romans

As we begin to look at the "strong" and "weak" passage in Romans, some reflection on its boundaries within the book is appropriate. Dunn makes a good case for breaking the section on "strong" and "weak" at 15.6 and viewing 15.7–13 as a fitting conclusion to the body of the letter.[1] But it must be noted that there are links between 14.1–15.6 and 15.7–13 – προσλαμβάνομαι in 14.1 and 15.7;[2] believing in 14.1 and 15.13; peace, joy, and the Holy Spirit in 14.17 and 15.13. No mention of believing, peace, joy, or the Holy Spirit is found in the preceding benediction of 15.5–6, making it more likely that an *inclusio* comes at 15.13 to conclude the section. Those who outline 14.1–15.13 as a unit include Sampley, Robert Jewett, Barth, Cranfield, and Fitzmyer.[3]

Walter Schmithals also breaks the "strong" and "weak" section at 15.6. According to Schmithals, a later editor took 15.7 from between 15.4a and 5, placed verse 7 into its present position as a transition to verses 8–13, and inserted 4b to round out the thought there.[4] His

[1] Dunn, *Romans*, 836, 844.
[2] This is noted by Sampley, "The Weak and the Strong," 51.
[3] Sampley, "The Weak and the Strong," 40–52; R. Jewett, "Ecumenical Theology for the Sake of Mission: Romans 1:1–17 + 15:14–16:24," in *Society of Biblical Literature 1992 Seminar Papers* (Atlanta: Scholars, 1992), 609; K. Barth, *The Epistle to the Romans* (trans. E. C. Hoskyns; 1933; reprint ed. Oxford: Oxford University Press, 1980), 502–505; Cranfield, *Romans*, 690–99; Fitzmyer, *Romans*, 688.
[4] *Der Römerbrief als historisches Problem* (SNT 9; Gütersloh: Gerd Mohn, 1975), 96, 157, 159–60.

commentary maintains the literary divisions presented in his earlier book.[5] But Schmithals's source criticism of Romans is unconvincing, and makes his division at 15.6 difficult to accept.

Heil draws the concluding boundary of the "strong" and "weak" section at 15.7, since it clearly forms an *inclusio* with 14.1. While he does admit that his distinct unit, 15.8–13, belongs closely with what precedes,[6] it would be better simply to include the latter unit within the "strong" and "weak" section. The γάρ in 15.8 ties it closely to the preceding verse, and the description of Jesus in 15.8 mirrors 15.3 too closely to warrant a break at 15.8.

Glad's decision to draw the ending boundary at 15.14 is due more to his desire to read that verse's δυνάμενοι καὶ ἀλλήλους νουθετεῖν back into the preceding discussion than to indications in the text that the unit ends at 15.14.[7] A clear break is made with the benediction at Rom. 15.13. If Glad must have verse 14 with the preceding section, he should at least include all of the unit it begins (verses 14–16), so that his boundaries would then be 14.1–15.16.

The relationship of Rom. 14.1–15.13 to 1 Cor. 8–10

It is commonly observed that Rom. 14.1–15.13 seems parallel to 1 Cor. 8–10. Given this relationship, is it legitimate to investigate Rom. 14–15 as descriptive of actual circumstances in the Roman church? Is it practical teaching that Paul would have written to any church, because he did not know what was going on in Rome? Or is it practical teaching that Paul wrote especially to Rome, because he did know what was going on there? These questions arise because of the similarity between Rom. 14.1–15.13 and 1 Cor. 8–10. The place to begin an investigation on the historical reference behind Rom. 14.1–15.13 is therefore with an examination of the relationship between this text and 1 Cor. 8–10.

Robert J. Karris's essay, "Romans 14:1–15:13 and the Occasion of Romans," is perhaps the strongest statement for reading this section as "general, Pauline paraenesis and not so many pieces of polemic from which a scholar may reconstruct the positions of the

---

[5] Ibid., 25–29.

[6] C. Heil, *Die Ablehnung der Speisegebote*, 243–44.

[7] C. E. Glad, *Paul and Philodemus: Adaptability in Epicurean and Early Christian Psychagogy* (NovT Sup 81; Leiden: Brill, 1995), 217. His teacher also follows this division, Stowers, *Rereading*, 320–23.

parties in Rome who occasioned this letter."[8] Karris's exegesis of Rom. 14.1–15.13 sees it as addressed only to an imagined situation similar to the actual state of affairs reflected in 1 Cor. 8–10.

I need to consider Karris's argument fairly and carefully as I begin a study that looks at parallels in language and behavior in first-century Rome to understand Rom. 14–15. Some scholars cite Karris's essay or the book in which it is found, *The Romans Debate*, as proof of the "bankrupt" value of searching for historical analogues to what Paul describes, or to conclude that Paul is not referring to an historical, or actual, situation when he addresses the "strong" and "weak" in Rome,[9] when in fact Karris has not proven his case. No one has published a detailed response to the verbal parallels Karris has aligned, so that is why I do so here.[10]

Karris's essay helpfully identifies parallels between Rom. 14.1–15.13 and 1 Cor. 8; 9; 10.23–11.1.[11] At the point where he lists the similarities between the texts, he presents them in translation and introduces them as "verbal parallels." In order for you to see the parallel relationship between these two Pauline texts, I have reproduced the parallels Karris presents, with his italics to show words he considers parallel. I have added the Greek text for at least the words that Karris has italicized. My evaluation follows each of the pairs.

Verbal parallels

Romans
14.1 As for the man who is weak in faith, welcome him, but not for *disputes over opinions* (διακρίσεις διαλογισμῶν).

1 Corinthians
10.25, 27 Eat whatever is sold in the meat market *without raising any question on the ground of conscience* (μηδὲν ἀνακρίνοντες διὰ τὴν συνείδησιν).

---

[8] "Occasion," 66. D. G. Bradley, "The Origins of the Hortatory Materials in the Letters of Paul" (Ph.D. dissertation, Yale, 1947), 142, 159 also presents this section of Romans as unrelated to the Roman situation and generalized instruction based on 1 Cor. 8–10. Glad interprets Romans 14–15 on the basis of 1 Cor. 8–10, though he assumes that Paul knew what was going on in Rome (*Paul and Philodemus*, 224–26).

[9] Sampley, "The Weak and the Strong," 40; Wayne A. Meeks, "Judgment and the Brother: Romans 14:1–15:13," *Tradition and Interpretation in the New Testament: Essays in Honor of E. Earle Ellis* (eds. G. F. Hawthorne and O. Betz; Grand Rapids/Tübingen: Eerdmans/J. C. B. Mohr [Paul Siebeck], 1987), 290–91.

[10] Donfried's response to Karris is well written, though his treatment of Karris's "verbal parallels" is relatively short ("False Presuppositions," 109).

[11] Ibid., 73.

It is certainly true that 1 Cor. 10.25, 27 parallel each other, but there are no verbal parallels between these verses and Rom. 14.1. This comparison allows us to note a key difference not mentioned by Karris: conscience plays a significant part in the argument in 1 Corinthians (*8.7*, 10; 10.25, 27, 28, 29*bis*), but it is not mentioned in Rom. 14.1–15.13.

> 14.6 He also who eats, eats in honor of the Lord, since *he gives thanks to God* (εὐχαριστεῖ γὰρ τῷ θεῷ) while he who abstains, abstains in honor of the Lord and *gives thanks to God* (εὐχαριστεῖ τῷ θεῷ).
>
> 10.30 If I partake *with thankfulness* (χάριτι), why am I denounced because of *that for which I give thanks?* (οὗ ἐγὼ εὐχαριστῷ;)

The verbal parallel consists of the shared use of the verb εὐχαριστέω. In the wider Pauline tradition, the idea that partaking of food with thanksgiving somehow renders that food acceptable is also found in 1 Tim. 4.3–4. Similarly, thanksgiving is presented in Col. 3.17 as a spiritual act that should accompany all actions. A key difference between Rom. 14.6 and 1 Cor. 10.30 is that in the former, Paul argues that when eating or abstaining is done for the Lord, either action is acceptable. By contrast, 1 Cor. 10.30 functions as a part of Paul's argument for abstinence. As Conzelmann observes with regard to the situation in Corinth, the "subjective conscience is not called upon at all, but the *status confessionis*, the 'situation of confession,' has arisen."[12]

> 14.13 but rather decide never to put *a stumbling block or hindrance in the way of a brother* (πρόσκομμα τῷ ἀδελφῷ ἢ σκάνδαλον).
>
> 8.9 Only take care lest this liberty of yours *become a stumbling block to the weak* (πρόσκομμα γένηται τοῖς ἀσθενέσιν).

Here the only verbal parallel is the word πρόσκομμα. ἐξουσία is a key concept in the 1 Corinthians passage (8.9; 9.4–6, 12, 18), but is entirely missing in Rom. 14.1–15.13.

---

[12] H. Conzelmann, *1 Corinthians: A Commentary on the First Epistle to the Corinthians* (Hermeneia, trans. J. W. Leitch; Philadelphia: Fortress, 1975), 179 (his italics).

14.14, 20 I know and am persuaded in the Lord Jesus that nothing is unclean in itself ... everything is indeed clean.

10.26 For "the earth is the Lord's, and everything in it."

In this pair there are no verbal parallels; the conceptual parallel that nothing God has created is unclean is only implied in 1 Cor. 10.26.

14.15 Do not let what you eat cause *the ruin of one for whom Christ died* (ἀπόλλυε ὑπὲρ οὗ Χριστὸς ἀπέθανεν).

8.11 And so by your knowledge this weak man is destroyed, the *brother for whom Christ died* (ἀπόλλυται γὰρ ὁ ἀσθενῶν ἐν τῇ σῇ γνώσει, ὁ ἀδελφὸς δι᾿ ὃν Χριστὸς ἀπέθανεν).

There is a verbal parallel here in the combination of ὑπὲρ οὗ/δι᾿ ὃν Χριστὸς ἀπέθανεν ("one for whom Christ died") with a form of ἀπόλλυμι ("destroy"). Christ dying on behalf of people or people's sins is found within Paul at Rom. 5.6, 8; 14.15; 1 Cor. 8.11; 15.3; 2 Cor. 5.15; 1 Thess. 5.10. Willis also identifies this parallel as a common element in Paul's argument in 1 Cor. 8–10 and Romans 14–15. The alternative to destroying "the one for whom Christ died" (1 Cor. 8.11–12; Rom. 14.15, 20) is coined in Paul's use of οἰκοδομέω (1 Cor. 8.1; 10.23; Rom. 14.19).[13] This pair also illustrates a significant difference between the two passages; 1 Cor. 8–10 emphasizes the γνῶσις that some have in Corinth, but Rom. 14–15 does not employ this term.[14]

14.16 So do not let *your good be spoken of as evil* (μὴ βλασφημείσθω οὖν ὑμῶν τὸ ἀγαθόν).

10.29bf. For why should my liberty be determined by another man's scruples? If I partake with thankfulness, why am I *denounced* because of that for which I give thanks?

---

[13] W. L. Willis, *Idol Meat in Corinth: The Pauline Argument in 1 Corinthians 8 and 10* (SBLDS 68; Chico: Scholars, 1985), 75–78.
[14] Cf. 1 Cor. 8.1, 2, 4, 7, 10, 11 with Rom. 14.14.

The value of this parallel hinges on whether τὸ ἀγαθόν in Rom. 14.16 is to be understood as the liberty that the "strong" have. Karris is aware of this.[15]

14.17 For the kingdom of God does not mean food and drink (οὐ γάρ ἐστιν ἡ βασιλέα τοῦ θεοῦ βρῶσις καὶ πόσις).

8.8 *Food will not commend us to* God. We are no worse off if we do not eat, and no better off if we do (βρῶμα δὲ ἡμᾶς οὐ παραστῆσαι τῷ θεῷ).

Here we note that there is a conceptual parallel, but not a verbal parallel.

14.20b Everything is indeed clean, but it is wrong for any one to make others fall *by what he eats* (ἀλλὰ κακὸν τῷ ἀνθρώπῳ τῷ διὰ προσκόμματος ἐσθίοντι).

8.9f. Only take care lest this liberty of yours somehow *become a stumbling block to the weak*. For if any one sees you, a man of knowledge, at table in an idol's temple, might he not be encouraged, if his conscience is weak, *to eat food offered to idols*? (... πρόσκομμα γένηται τοῖς ἀσθενέσιν ... εἰς τὸ τὰ εἰδωλόθυτα ἐσθίειν;)

The use of πρόσκομμα certainly is a verbal parallel in the texts above. Both texts describe eating as an act that could be a stumbling block for others. But as Gooch has noted, the material in Romans never specifies that it is meat offered to idols that is at issue.[16] We are left rather with the sense that the Roman "weak" are abstaining from all meat (14.2, 21).

14.21 it is right not *to eat meat or drink wine or do anything* ... (τὸ μὴ φαγεῖν κρέα μηδὲ πιεῖν οἶνον μηδὲ ἐν ᾧ ...)

10.31 So, *whether you eat or drink, or whatever you do*, do all to the glory of God (εἴτε οὖν ἐσθίετε εἴτε πίνετε εἴτε τι ποιεῖτε ...).

---

[15] Willis, *Idol Meat*, 74 n. 50. Dunn thinks that this ἀγαθόν "sums up all God's covenanted blessings" (*Romans*, 821). Cranfield argues convincingly that ἀγαθόν refers to the gospel (*Romans*, 717).

[16] P. D. Gooch, *Dangerous Food: 1 Corinthians 8–10 in its Context* (SCJ 5;

Both these texts mention eating and drinking, but in Romans Paul does not explicitly command that the church members should eat and drink to the glory of God. The actions that are to be performed for the glory of God in Romans are worship before the divine court of judgment (14.11) and corporate praise (15.6, 9).[17]

15.1 We who are strong *ought to bear with the failings of the weak*, and not to please ourselves (ὀφείλομεν . . . τὰ ἀσθενήματα τῶν ἀδυνάτων βαστάζειν).	9.22 *To the weak I became weak, that I might win the weak* (ἐγενόμην τοῖς ἀσθενέσιν ἀσθενής).

This pair does contain two cognate words, ἀσθένημα and ἀσθενής. While the language is the same, the text in Romans seems to concern harmony among church members, while the text in 1 Corinthians describes Paul's attempts to evangelize.[18]

15.2 Let each of us *please his neighbor for his own good, to edify him.*	8.1 "Knowledge" puffs up, but love *builds up* (οἰκοδομεῖ). 10.23–4: but not all things *build up*. Let no one seek his own good, but *the good of the neighbor.*
(ἕκαστος ἡμῶν τῷ πλησίον ἀρεσκέτω εἰς τὸ ἀγαθὸν οἰκοδομήν.)	(ἀλλ᾽ οὐ πάντα οἰκοδομεῖ. μηδεὶς τὸ ἑαυτοῦ ζητείτω ἀλλὰ τὸ τοῦ ἑτέρου.)

The verbal parallel that Karris draws between Rom. 15.2 and 1 Cor. 10.23–24 is closer in English than it is in Greek.[19] Karris is correct in noting a conceptual parallel here, even though there are

Waterloo, Ont.: Wilfrid Laurier University Press, 1993), 117–18 makes the point that Romans 14–15 does not concern εἰδωλόθυτα, but seems focused instead on *kashrut* laws.

[17] Since the acceptance shown by Christ was εἰς δόξαν τοῦ θεοῦ (15.7), there is the possibility that the mutual acceptance Paul commands at the beginning of the verse is also to be performed in order to glorify God.

[18] My analysis of the difference here assumes that the Roman "weak" are believing members of the Roman churches. For a discussion of why I hold this position, against Nanos, please see chapter 6, under the heading "Cultic Purity: Jewish or Jewish Christian?".

[19] Karris, "Occasion," 75. The italics are his.

few verbal correspondences. Both passages are based on common maxims concerning self-love as opposed to ἀγάπη and οἰκοδομή. Since such maxims are found elsewhere in Paul,[20] no compositional or textual divisions can be based on the parallel. "Neighbor" is the same word in Karris's English translation, but different words are used in Greek.

15.3 *For Christ did not please himself* (καὶ γὰρ ὁ Χριστὸς οὐχ ἑαυτῷ ἤρεσεν).	11.1 Be imitators of me as I am *of Christ* (Χριστοῦ).

While there is a conceptual parallel with regard to the example of Christ in Rom. 15.3 and 1 Cor. 11.1, no verbal parallel can found except Χριστός.

15.7 Welcome one another, therefore, *as Christ has welcomed you*, for the glory of God (καθὼς καὶ ὁ Χριστὸς προσελάβετο ὑμᾶς).	10.33–11.1 ... just as I try to please all men in everything I do, *not seeking my own advantage, but that of many, that they may be saved.* Be imitators of me, as I am of Christ (μὴ ζητῶν τὸ ἐμαυτοῦ σύμφορον ἀλλὰ τὸ τῶν πολλῶν, ἵνα σωθῶσιν).

The same evaluation can be made of this parallel as was made of the preceding pair, although in this case both texts also share the adverb καθώς. It is difficult to follow why Karris has italicized the words he has, since they are not parallel.

Of the fifteen "verbal parallels" Karris cites,[21] seven have been noted above as non-existent or questionable. The contention that "these parallels clearly indicate to what a great extent Rom. 14:1–15:13 repeats, rephrases, echoes the arguments of 1 Cor. 8; 9; 10:23–11:1"[22] does not seem to be as evident on the verbal level of the texts as Karris argues. The case for the Romans text's dependence on 1 Corinthians cannot stand on the basis of verbal

[20] 1 Cor. 13.4; 14.26; Gal. 5.13; 1 Thess. 5.11; Phil. 2.1–2.
[21] He links 1 Cor. 8.1 with 10.23f. and uses it as a parallel to Rom. 15.2 (Karris, "Occasion," 75). I am counting this alignment as two parallels, since different texts in 1 Corinthians are used.
[22] Karris, "Occasion," 75.

parallels. Indeed, several lacunae in a verbal comparison of the texts make the alleged dependence appear more uncertain.

The key imperative in Rom. 14.1–15.13 is formed from the word προσλαμβάνομαι. This word is not found in 1 Corinthians.[23] The stated difference in Romans seems to be centered around faith (14.1, 22, 23 *bis*). The word πίστις is not found in 1 Cor. 8.1–11.1. The word κοινός, which seems to indicate the main objection that Paul thinks the Roman "weak" had toward meat (14.14 *tris*), is not found in 1 Corinthians.

Conversely, key terms in the 1 Corinthians discussion of meat offered to idols are not found in Rom. 14.1–15.13. The role of conscience (συνείδησις) figures significantly in the argument of 1 Corinthians. Paul uses συνείδησις in Rom. 2.15; 9.1; 13.5, so he certainly considered it a legitimate word for his Roman audience. But it is not found in 14.1–15.13. The word for meat offered to idols, τὸ εἰδωλόθυτον, does not occur in Romans. Gooch concludes from this omission (already noted in our examination of Karris's verbal parallels), Paul's use of purity terms in Romans 14–15, and the "even-handedness" with which he treats "strong" and "weak" that while 1 Cor. 8–10 is about εἰδωλόθυτα as a food contaminated by idolatry, Romans 14–15 concerns a difference over *kashrut* laws.[24] Marcus notes that the Romans text's mention of people who eat vegetables (14.2) and the connection it makes between a special diet and the observance of days (14.5–6) are distinct from 1 Cor. 8–10. He argues that these differences point away from merely literary dependence and are more easily explained by the possibility that Paul has heard about a situation in Rome that he wishes to address.[25]

Parallels in argument

Despite the difficulties of linking the texts on the verbal level, one may also infer from the similarities in argument that the Romans passage is based on 1 Cor. 8–10, as Nababan does.[26] In his exegesis of 14.22–23, Nababan appeals to Rom. 2.15–16 to show that

---

[23] Of its five uses in Paul, four come in the Romans passage on "strong" and "weak" (14.1, 3; 15.7*bis*). The other instance is Philem. 17.

[24] Gooch, *Dangerous Food*, 117.

[25] J. Marcus, "The Circumcision and the Uncircumcision in Rome," *NTS* 35 (1989) 71.

[26] Nababan, "Bekenntnis," 102–103.

πίστις in Rom. 14.1–15.13 is used in a similar way to συνείδησις in 1 Cor. 8–10. He sees a connection between an eschatological reference shared by both of the Romans texts (14.23–κατακρίνω; 2.16 – ἐν ἡμέρᾳ ὅτε κρίνει ὁ θεός) and the verb διακρίνω in 14.23. Although it does not appear in Rom. 14–15 or 1 Cor. 8–10, the pair of terms that occurs within the description of final judgment – κατηγορέω and ἀπολογέομαι – appears in 2.15 along with συνείδησις. Nababan concludes that συνείδησις in 1 Corinthians and πίστις in Romans 14 are used synonymously.[27] From this conceptual link he draws two general implications: that the "weak in faith" in Romans 14–15 correspond with those who have a weak conscience in 1 Cor. 8–10, though they are not identical to them; and that Paul has made use of his experience with the Corinthians while dealing with the situation in Rome.[28]

While no one can contest that Paul uses his experience with the Corinthians when writing Rome, Paul's arguments to the two churches are not as close as Nababan portrays them. The common eschatological focus that Nababan sees between Rom. 14.22–23 and 2.15–16 is not transparent. κατακρίνω and its cognates do not necessarily refer to eschatological damnation in Paul, as 2 Cor. 7.3 shows. But since hopeless condemnation of others' destinies[29] might lie behind Paul's statements against judging in 14.4, it is likely that some of the judging Paul refers to is eschatological in nature. Still, an eschatological focus in both Romans and 1 Corinthians is not sufficient to show that conscience is at the forefront of Paul's mind as it is in 1 Cor. 8–10. A closer parallel (ignored by Nababan) to aid in understanding 14.22–23 is Rom. 4.20, which states of Abraham – εἰς δὲ τὴν ἐπαγγελίαν τοῦ θεοῦ οὐ διεκρίθη τῇ ἀπιστίᾳ ἀλλ᾽ ἐνεδυναμώθη τῇ πίστει, δοὺς δόξαν τῷ θεῷ.[30] When this is read together with the description of Christ confirming the promises in 15.8, one can see that Paul is not attributing simply a weak conscience to the Roman "weak." There is also a deficiency in their faith with regard to the significance of

---

[27] Ibid., 106–107.   [28] Ibid., 107.

[29] The eschatological focus of the judgment mentioned in 14.4 is held by Rauer, who relates the grief experienced by the "weak" (14.15) back to their opinion of others' fates (*Die "Schwachen,"* 84 n. 1).

[30] For the connection between 4.20 and the "weak in faith" of 14.1, see A. T. Lincoln, "Abraham Goes to Rome: Paul's Treatment of Abraham in Romans 4," in *Worship, Theology and Ministry in the Early Church: Essays in Honor of Ralph P. Martin* (eds. M. J. Wilkins and T. Paige; JSNT Sup 87; Sheffield: Sheffield Academic Press, 1992), 163–79.

Christ in salvation history. This points to a significant difference in the way the arguments progress in the two texts. Rom. 14.1–15.13 builds its argument on certain statements about Christ that are missing in 1 Cor. 8–10. It does so with no reference to the Jewish monotheistic confession, the *Shema*, central in Paul's argument to those who claim to have superior γνῶσις in Corinth.[31]

The following statements from Rom. 14.1–15.13 are not found in 1 Cor. 8–10:

(1) The Lord is able to make members on either side of the controversy "stand" (14.4);

(2) Both parties in the controversy perform their respective actions "for the Lord" (14.6);

(3) Christ died and rose in order to rule over all aspects of human existence (14.9);

(4) Paul knows "in the Lord Jesus" that nothing is unclean in itself (14.14);[32]

(5) Christ did not please himself (15.3);[33]

(6) Christ has accepted believers (15.7);

(7) Christ has "become a servant of circumcision" (15.8);

(8) Christ rules the nations and is the object of their hope (15.12, quoting LXX Isa. 11.10).

Except for the appeals to the example of Christ in both texts, these are differences in the arguments of Rom. 14.1–15.13 and 1 Cor. 8–10 that Karris does not treat. Besides the difference in Paul's argumentation in the two texts, possible differences in attitudes on the part of the "weak" in each community may also be suggested. The idea of the "weak" judging the "strong" that is so emphatically prohibited by Paul in Rom. 14.3–4, 10, 13 is not found in 1 Cor.

[31] N. T. Wright, *The Climax of the Covenant: Christ and the Law in Pauline Theology* (Minneapolis: Fortress, 1992), 126–30.

[32] A possible parallel might be Paul's quotation of LXX Ps. 23.1 (MT Ps. 24.1) in 1 Cor. 10.26–τοῦ κυρίου γὰρ ἡ γῆ καὶ τὸ πλήρωμα αὐτῆς. But this is an argument from creation while Rom. 14.14 seems to indicate that for Paul, Jesus in his coming did something to change dietary laws. Cf. Mark 7.19; Acts 10.15; 11.9.

[33] By juxtaposing 1 Cor. 9.22 with 11.1 one might approach a similar argument, but it is not conclusive. Cf. Karris, "Occasion," 80, who notes that Paul uses the example of Christ in both texts. This is certainly correct, but he fails to mention one crucial difference: the *imitatio Christi* mentioned in 1 Corinthians is mediated through the example of Paul (11.1); Paul does not use himself explicitly as an example in Romans (J. M. Bassler, *Divine Impartiality: Paul and a Theological Axiom* [SBLDS 59; Chico: Scholars, 1982], 164).

8–10, except for the incidental question in 10.29.[34] Nor is the suggestion that some "weak" were eating in doubt (Rom. 14.23) found in 1 Cor. 8–10.

This is not to affirm that the argumentation in the two texts is completely dissimilar. It is clear that the same author has written both texts. We have already seen a few verbal parallels and some conceptual parallels between the two. In argumentative strategy, Paul's studied avoidance of any persuasion directed to make the "weak" change their ways is also common to both texts.[35] Slogans from the more permissive group in each community seem to be repeated in both letters and then followed by Paul's qualifications (1 Cor. 10.23; Rom. 14.14, 20).[36] And since the texts are written by the same author, they share his presuppositions. In these ways one could say that there is a kind of literary dependence between the texts. But the differences in terminology and argument make it unlikely that Rom. 14.1–15.13 is a literary creation based on 1 Cor. 8–10, with no historical referent of its own. One must certainly admit that Paul uses his experience with the Corinthians to inform his argument in Romans,[37] but to conclude on the basis of parallels that Rom. 14.1–15.13 is derived primarily from 1 Cor. 8–10 does not fit with the evidence.

Differences between Rom. 14.1–15.13 and 1 Cor. 8–10

Beyond the question of verbal parallels, Karris uses the differences between Rom. 14.1–15.13 and 1 Cor. 8–10 to argue that the latter refers to an actual situation while the former does not. His basic strategy therefore becomes clear: similarities imply the literary dependence of Rom. 14.1–15.13 on the discussion of εἰδωλόθυτα in 1 Corinthians. This literary dependence is then taken as evidence that Paul is not directing his comments in Romans to an actual situation. Dissimilarities between the two texts are explained by the

---

[34] Related to my observation is J. C. Brunt's point that there is clearly a controversy, or dispute, in view in Romans. In 1 Cor. 8–10 this is lacking ("Paul's Attitude toward and Treatment of Problems Involving Dietary Practice: A Case Study in Pauline Ethics" [Ph.D. dissertation, Emory, 1978], 124–25).

[35] Willis, *Idol Meat*, 118–20. Cf. Stowers, *Rereading*, 322–23, and discussion at end of chapter 10 below.

[36] Nababan, "Bekenntnis," 100. Influenced by the direction of his essay, Karris ("Occasion," 75) maintains that in Romans Paul "has omitted references to the catchwords of the Corinthians" without noting the likely Roman catchwords found in 14.14, 20, as well as their nicknames, "strong" and "weak."

[37] Nababan, "Bekenntnis," 99.

proposed difference in historical reference. Whether the texts agree or disagree on various points, Karris makes them fit his picture.

Karris follows Leenhardt in noting that since most of the imperatives in 14.1–15.13 are either first plural or third singular in person, "Paul is not really addressing a particular group of people, whose concrete circumstances he is considering while pointing out their errors."[38] But it must be noted that the case is not as clear-cut as Karris and Leenhardt make it.[39] While ten out of the eleven imperatives in 1 Cor. 8–10 are second person,[40] six out of the thirteen imperatives in Rom. 14.1–15.13 remains a significant number of direct commands.[41]

Any argument about how Paul uses imperatives in this text must also take into account that it is addressed to a church he has never visited. Karris does not admit the possibility that the hortatory subjunctives and third singular imperatives may be used to soften the force of Paul's commands to a church previously outside of the sphere of his influence.[42]

Karris states that while 1 Cor. 8 has only one imperative verb, it has two "circumstantial 'if' clauses" (1 Cor. 8.10, 13) and 1 Cor. 10 has three such clauses (1 Cor. 10.27–30). These clauses indicate that the topic is rooted in a real situation, according to Karris. Since Rom. 14.1–15.13 has only one such clause (14.15)[43] in comparison to the four in 1 Cor. 8–10, Karris concludes that Paul is not dealing with an actual situation in the Roman church.[44]

But in his listing of these clauses Karris has overlooked Rom. 14.23, which clearly fits his "circumstantial 'if' clause" designation. If Karris had documented his syntactical presuppositions and defined a "circumstantial 'if' clause," his argument on conditionals would be more effective. As it stands, he does not acknowledge the

[38] F. Leenhardt, *Romans*, 345 as quoted in Karris, "Occasion," 72.

[39] Karris admits as much ("Occasion," 72 n. 42): "Leenhardt may go beyond the evidence in his evaluation of the meagreness of second person imperative (six in number), but his observation merits consideration."

[40] 1 Cor. 8.9; 10.14, 15, 18, 24, 25, 27, 28, 31, 32; 11.1. The third person imperative comes at 10.24.

[41] The imperatives occur at 14.1, 3*bis*, 5, 13*bis*, 15, 16, 19, 20, 22; 15.2, 7. Of these, the second person imperatives are at 14.1, 13, 15, 20, 22; 15.7.

[42] Hortatory subjunctives occur at 14.13, 19. Third singular imperatives occur at 14.3*bis*, 5, 16; 15.2. While third singular in form, the imperative in 14.16 functions as a second person imperative, since its object is second person – μὴ βλασφημείσθω οὖν ὑμῶν τὸ ἀγαθόν.

[43] I agree with Karris that the conditional clause in 14.8 cannot be considered circumstantial in nature ("Occasion," 72 n. 43).

[44] Ibid., 72.

difficulty involved in arguing from conditionals to the reality of a referent outside of the linguistic expression. While it may be suggested that εἰ with the indicative seems by NT writers to be used "with reference to a present or alleged reality,"[45] this is far from a consensus opinion.[46]

Given the tenuous case that can be made syntactically from Karris's "circumstantial 'if' clauses," however, it is still unclear how his argument functions. Is he stating that because 1 Cor. 8–10 has four as opposed to one (or two if he will admit Rom. 14.23) of these clauses, it is the more real? This argument becomes difficult when one examines 1 Thessalonians and Galatians, which are clearly addressed to actual situations but vary significantly in their use of "circumstantial 'if' clauses."[47]

The arguments Karris advances against the historical reference of Rom. 14.1–15.13 are therefore inconclusive. A final decision on whether the text relates to circumstances in Rome can only be made after parallels have been examined in chapters 3–9 of this monograph. At this point, however, the case against reading Rom. 14.1–15.13 as evidence of actual circumstances has been sufficiently questioned to allow the investigation to continue. We shall not understand Rom. 14–15 adequately if we merely acknowledge that the passage is different from 1 Cor. 8–10. A more specific question must be asked about the nature of the practical teaching in Rom. 14.1–15.13.

Is Rom. 14.1–15.13 general or focused practical teaching?

We know that the section on "strong" and "weak" is practical teaching. But might it simply be practical teaching in a general

---

[45] BDF, §371. Herbert Weir Smyth, *Greek Grammar* (rev. ed.; Cambridge, Mass.: Harvard University Press, 1956), §2298, describes the significance of such conditionals earlier in the language's development: "Simple present or past conditions simply state a supposition with no implication as to its reality or probability."

[46] Cf., e.g., M. Zerwick, *Biblical Greek Illustrated by Examples* (SPIB 114; Rome: Pontifical Biblical Institute, 1963), §308, who, after mentioning two reasons for using "real" conditions besides their correspondence to actual situations, states: "It is an astonishing fact that even scholars sometimes overlook what has just been said and seem to forget that, εἰ even in a 'real' condition still means 'if' and not 'because' or the like."

[47] 1 Thess. 3.8 seems to be the only such clause, as Karris has used the designation, in that letter. By contrast, Gal. 1.8, 9; 3.4; 5.2, 15; 6.1 are all instances of such clauses. Does this mean that the situation in Galatia was "more real" than in Thessalonica? See also Donfried, "False Presuppositions," 108–109 for other arguments against Karris's points on imperatives and "circumstantial 'if' clauses."

sense, without a connection to a situation in Rome? This is a distinction that scholars have made before in examining the nature of practical teaching in New Testament letters. Karris explains the verbal differences between 1 Cor. 8–10 and Rom. 14.1–15.13 identified above as arising from the "generalized adaptation of Paul's previous theological positions" that characterizes Rom. 14.1–15.13.[48] His point that the key terms from 1 Cor. 8–10 that are missing in Rom. 14.1–15.13 are distinctively Corinthian terms or slogans is right.[49] But this does not prove that the Romans passage is generalized and without historical reference. Karris's case for his reading of the passage is thus dependent on his view of the practical teaching in Romans.

In the section "The Nature of the Paraenesis in Romans 12–15" of his essay, Karris parts company with Dibelius, arguing that here in Romans, Paul's parenesis is influenced by his theological material earlier in the book. So far this is certainly correct, and I attempt, especially in chapter 12 below, to build on the theological-practical connections that Karris finds between chapters 1–11 and 12–15 in Romans. Here is Karris's conclusion on this question of the genre of 14.1–15.13.

> The above research into parallels between Rom. 12–15 and previous Pauline paraenesis and theologizing suggests that Rom. 14.1–15.13 be read as general paraenesis, not in Dibelius's sense that it has nothing to do with Paul's own theology. Rather it is paraenesis that is intimately connected with the theological principles of Paul, but at the same time it is general. It is addressed to possible situations within the Roman community or, if one accepts the hypothesis of Romans as an encyclical letter, within any Christian community.[50]

But Karris's discussion does not consider the relation between the practical teaching and what was happening in Rome, nor does he offer a complete picture of Dibelius's description of practical teaching in the New Testament.

Karris's discussion omits any consideration of features within the practical teaching that link it directly to the Roman situation. The section on obedience to authorities, Rom. 13.1–7, climaxes with repeated references to tax payment (verses 6–7). This seems to be a

[48] Karris, "Occasion," 76.   [49] Ibid., 75–76.   [50] Ibid., 83.

response to the clearly documented antipathy the Romans had toward their tax system in the early years of Nero's reign that resulted in Nero's tax reform.[51] Paul's three pairs of behaviors to avoid in 13.13 (μὴ κώμοις καὶ μέθαις, μὴ κοίταις καὶ ἀσελγείαις, μὴ ἔριδι καὶ ζήλῳ) also seem to fit with stereotypes of life in Rome.[52] Karris has not mentioned the reasons why vegetarianism was popular in first-century Rome, nor has he cited Josephus' account of Jews who remained vegetarians while in Rome.[53] The dismissal of history of religions as inadequate for our understanding of Rom. 14.1–15.13 seems premature, since it is based on a discussion of two secondary sources,[54] rather than on the primary texts that provide a window into the situation. The history of religions perspective when taken alone may be "bankrupt," as Karris claims. But when used to supplement exegetical and sociohistorical approaches to the text, it does play a valuable role.

Martin Dibelius and Philipp Vielhauer provide examples of how one might make a distinction within the practical teaching that the NT contains, a distinction left unmentioned by Karris. Vielhauer also applies this distinction to the book of Romans, allowing us to see him distinguishing between types of practical teaching in Romans 12–15, a section others treat uniformly.

Dibelius and Vielhauer draw a distinction between practical teaching that is applicable to any community, called parenesis, and practical teaching that is focused on a concrete situation in a specific community. The latter, according to Vielhauer, is addressed to a concrete situation, and hence is not parenesis in Dibelius's strictly applied sense.[55] Vielhauer seems to be making explicit what

[51] Tacitus, *Ann.* 13.50–51; Suetonius, *Nero* 10.1; see J. Friedrich, W. Pöhlmann, P. Stuhlmacher, "Zur historischen Situation und Intention von Röm 13, 1–7," *ZTK* 73 (1976) 131–66.

[52] See the discussion toward the beginning of chapter 4 on φαγεῖν πάντα and the relationship between Rom. 13.13 and 14.2.

[53] See chapters 4 (beginning at heading "Abstinence from Meat in First-century Rome") and 6 below, as well as Josephus, *Vita* 14.

[54] Karris, "Occasion," 66–69, rejects the descriptions of the "strong" and "weak" situation in Rome offered by Minear and Rauer. See also Donfried, "False Presuppositions," 110.

[55] Vielhauer follows Dibelius (Martin Dibelius, *Die Formgeschichte des Evangeliums* [3rd ed.; Tübingen: J. C. B. Mohr (Paul Siebeck), 1959], 234–65, esp. 239–42) in using *die Paränese* as a technical term for ethical teaching that may be appropriate for more than one community. While Vielhauer adopts this definition, he labels Rom. 12.1–13.14 as parenesis and 14.1–15.13 as simply another kind of ethical exhortation (Philipp Vielhauer, *Geschichte der urchristlichen Literatur* [2nd ed.; Berlin/New York: Walter de Gruyter, 1978], 49–50).

Dibelius implies in his parenthetical examples that come at the beginning of his section on Pauline parenesis.

> Paulus beschließt seine Gemeindebriefe häufig mit einem paränetischen Teil (Röm 12.13, Gal 5.13ff. 6, Kol 3.4, I Thess. 4.1ff. 5.1ff.).

> Paul often concludes his letters to communities with a parenetic section (Rom. 12.13; Gal. 5.13ff., 6; Col. 3, 4; 1 Thess. 4.1ff., 5.1ff.).[56]

The difference in types of practical teaching is crucial, because an implication of Vielhauer's definition of parenesis is that it cannot be used as historical evidence in reconstructing the contours of a given community.[57] While such a tight definition of parenesis is difficult to maintain,[58] it is noteworthy that Dibelius and Vielhauer do not present Rom. 14.1–15.13 as parenesis. Within the category of practical teaching, this passage is regarded as focused on a concrete situation by Vielhauer, who has divided up the practical teaching within Romans 12–15 as general material that could be addressed to any audience, and focused material that is specifically addressed to Rome.[59] Hence even in his view it does have value as historical evidence for the nature of the Christian community in Rome.

While I am not ready to include Rom. 13.1–7 as part of general parenesis as Vielhauer does,[60] his distinction between types of practical teaching is valuable for its admission that not every kind of practical teaching is generalized material that is unrelated to the readers' situation. Now scholars such as Popkes seem more ready to factor the historical element into the parenetic sections of the NT, recognizing that Paul was writing to a concrete situation about

[56] Dibelius, *Die Formgeschichte*, 239. He makes the same identification of parenesis in Romans again on 240.

[57] This is seen, e.g., when Vielhauer states that one cannot use vice lists to identify specific problems in a given church (*Literatur*, 57).

[58] One may note that even the selection of parenetic material in a given letter is conditioned by historical circumstances. Rom. 13.1–7 stands within Vielhauer's parenesis section, but this would not have been written if Paul had been writing to the Roman churches about nine years later, during the aftermath of the fire of 64.

[59] Dibelius, *Die Formgeschichte*, 239; Vielhauer, *Literatur*, 50, 176. See also Donfried, "False Presuppositions," 103–104, who argues that since every other Pauline letter addresses an actual situation in its audience, we should assume this of Romans.

[60] *Literatur*, 49–50. Tacitus, *Ann.* 13.50–51 is clear evidence that Roman tax policies were unpopular under Nero's reign.

which he was informed.[61] I mention Dibelius and Vielhauer to show that though Rom. 14.1–15.13 is often considered to be an integral part of the parenesis of Romans, it is regarded even by these scholars who exclude historical reference from their definition of parenesis to be related to the circumstances in Rome. Käsemann similarly begins his commentary's treatment of Rom. 14.1–15.13 with the comment that only in Romans "does special exhortation follow general exhortation."[62]

In the discussion to follow, I use the terms "practical teaching" or "protrepsis" to describe Rom. 14.1–15.13. Paul is clearly calling the believing communities in Rome to make changes, and following Stowers, it seems best to call this protrepsis.[63]

Beyond the precise classification of the nature of the practical teaching found here, we do well to ask, with Käsemann and Marcus, why Paul would spend so much space in this letter describing and addressing a situation that is only hypothetical. The best answer seems to be that it was not hypothetical, but was a church division occurring in Rome, of which Paul had been informed. The strategic placement of this section, right before the conclusion, also argues for its significance in Paul's mind, a significance that would be difficult to sustain if the situation were only hypothetical.[64]

The occasions behind Romans

We have examined the relationship between 1 Cor. 8–10 and Romans 14–15. The comparison of these texts does not prove that Romans 14–15 is a literary creation, based on the situation in Corinth. It appears to be practical teaching, focused on an actual situation in which Paul's first readers lived. It is therefore worth our

---

[61] W. Popkes, *Paränese und Neues Testament* (SBS 168; Stuttgart: Katholisches Bibelwerk, 1996), 36–37, 50. I only wish Popkes were more definite in distinguishing between what is recycled and what is tailor-made for the Roman audience in his coverage of our letter (ibid., 90–93).

[62] Käsemann, *Romans*, 364. For other remarks on the nature of Rom. 14.1–15.13 as practical teaching, cf. Karris, "Occasion," 81–84 and Donfried, "False Presuppositions," 110–11.

[63] S. K. Stowers, *Letter Writing in Greco-Roman Antiquity* (LEC; Philadelphia: Westminster, 1986), 92. See also D. Aune, "Romans as a *Logos Protreptikos*," in Donfried, *The Romans Debate*, 278–96.

[64] Käsemann, *Romans*, 366 and Marcus, "Circumcision," 71 both mention the length of the "strong" and "weak" section; Käsemann also notes its strategic placement within the letter.

while to pursue the nature of these "strong" and "weak" groups described in Paul's letter to Rome. In his rejoinder to Donfried, however, Karris has asked some trenchant questions that I must answer before we can proceed.[65]

First: "What are the criteria for distinguishing those sections in Romans which are comprised of 'sharing' and 'repeating insights gained in prior situations' and those which are addressed to 'a real situation'?"[66] In response I would first admit with Wedderburn that any reconstruction we do is hypothetical. Yet as Wedderburn also writes, differences in reconstructions of Paul's audience come from the sort of evidence we have, and do not prove that there is nothing to reconstruct, as though Paul were addressing hypothetical situations.[67] The different views of the universe since Ptolemy have led no one to conclude that it does not exist, or that it is futile to construct models of the universe. Now to the question: those sections of Romans should be read as addressed to a real situation, and not just sharing past insights, if they hit certain topics not dealt with in other Paulines (13.1–7), and/or refer to the Romans and their situation (6.17; 7.1). In addition, repeated clarifications or assertions must be answering something that Paul thinks that believers in Rome are hearing or saying about his gospel.[68]

Second: "By what criteria do we judge whether the situation behind Romans is a situation in the Roman church(es) or in the life of Paul (his missionary plans, summary of his gospel, journey to Jerusalem) or a combination of both?"[69] The criteria we use to answer this question are the same as those we use when listening to one side of a telephone conversation. If the person interjects abruptly or refers to something in the conversation partner's situation, we assume that the comment is elicited by the person on the other end of the telephone connection. Abrupt or unexpected changes of context[70] and explicit tags to the audience[71] therefore indicate an audience-based occasion for some sections of Romans.

---

[65] Karris's questions on methodology are answered here. In chapter 11 I shall deal with his penetrating questions on the theological situation in Rome and the contours of the "conflict" in 14.1–15.13 ("Response to Professor Donfried," 126–27).

[66] Ibid., 126.

[67] Wedderburn, *Reasons*, 63.

[68] Rom. 3.31; 7.12, 14; 13.8–10.

[69] Karris, "Response to Professor Donfried," 127.

[70] Rom. 13.1–7.

[71] Rom. 6.17, 21 focus that chapter on the Romans. Other examples are 7.1; 11.13; 13.6.

I admit that the diatribe style might prescind this criterion. Some contend that Paul uses the diatribe style because he is unfamiliar with the Romans' situation.[72] But I agree with others that the diatribe style is not a sufficient condition for labeling a passage "hypothetical" and that each instance of diatribe material needs to be individually examined before this label can be applied.[73] Also, while at this point we cannot state categorically that diatribe is a characteristic of Jewish literature,[74] we should do well to consider what Stowers called a "reasonable" (though not "highly probable or certain") thesis: "the style of the diatribe was mediated to early Christianity by hellenistic Judaism."[75] If this is so, Paul's use of diatribe in Romans might be due to his knowledge of an audience that included many Jewish believers, and not to his ignorance of their situation. Back to the criterion: we should relate a diatribe-like section of the letter to the Romans' situation if it fits what we know of early Roman Christianity, since the letter's first readers would hear material as addressed to them, rather than to the hypothetical interlocuter, if indeed it did match their situation. On the other hand, when Paul makes reference to his own situation, we should attribute the passage to the Pauline occasion.[76] Finally, Wedderburn's three criteria for judging the plausibility of reconstructed occasions behind Romans should be used to judge my work.[77]

In this chapter I have argued that Karris is mistaken to dismiss Rom. 14.1–15.13 as addressed to an hypothetical situation. I think it is occasioned mostly by a situation in Rome, as I will argue below. Most interpreters of Romans would agree that the letter arises out of both Paul's occasion and the Roman believers' occasion. The difference in how one reads the letter as a whole, or any section of it, lies in the weight one puts on one occasion or the other.[78]

[72] D. Aune, *The New Testament in its Literary Environment* (LEC; Philadelphia: Westminster, 1987), 201; J. Murphy-O'Connor, *Paul: A Critical Life* (Oxford: Clarendon, 1996), 334.

[73] Donfried, "False Presuppositions," 117–19; Karris, "Response to Professor Donfried," 126–27.

[74] But see D. W. Halivni's comment on the Jewish nature of diatribe in *Midrash, Mishnah, and Gemara: The Jewish Predilection for Justified Law* (Cambridge, Mass.: Harvard University Press, 1986), 144 n. 3.

[75] S. K. Stowers, *The Diatribe and Paul's Letter to the Romans* (SBLDS 57; Chico: Scholars, 1981), 41.

[76] Rom. 1.13; 3.8; 15.17–32.

[77] Wedderburn, *Reasons*, 64.

[78] Cf. J. Jervell, "The Letter to Jerusalem," in Donfried, *The Romans Debate*, 53–64 (totally Paul's occasion); Wedderburn, *Reasons*, 20–21 (both occasions, but weighted toward Paul's); Minear, *Obedience*, *passim* (totally the Romans' occasion).

In the next seven chapters of this book, I look for people and ideologies that lie behind the terms "strong" and "weak." You may disagree with the results of this endeavor, even with those of the next chapter, where I identify "strong" and "weak" as terms for social status in Roman society. But I think that you can agree with the main point of this chapter: on the question of historical reference behind Rom. 14.1–15.13, the burden of proof remains on those who would deny it.

3

"STRONG" AND "WEAK" AS TERMS OF
SOCIAL STATUS IN FIRST-CENTURY ROME

ut scis, potentissimorum hominum contumaciam numquam
tulerim. Cicero, *Att.* 6.3.6

As you know, I have never put up with defiance from
influential men.

Why does Paul refer to groups as "strong" and "weak" when
writing to Rome? Literary evidence for the presence of "strong"
and "weak" terms and ideology in first-century Rome place the
burden of proof on those who deny the existence of groups labeled
in that way by the Romans themselves. It makes sense to begin with
Paul's use of these terms in light of the sociology of first-century
Rome. Terms for "strong" and "weak" were common in first-
century Rome, and available evidence from the letter of Romans
indicates that these terms should be understood primarily as
designations of social status.

Indeed, previous commentators on this text have not adequately
considered the use of terms for "strong" and "weak" in Roman
society.[1] The terms, as Paul uses them, fit the Roman tendency to
define social hierarchies within various levels of early imperial
society and differentiate positions in a hierarchy on the basis of
status.

In identifying the "strong" and "weak" groups, the history-of-
religions approach may be limited, as Karris suggests,[2] but this is
because it has not been combined with a sociological look at
imperial Rome, not because it is "bankrupt." Since terms for
"strong" and "weak" were characteristic of Roman authors'

---

[1] I am indebted to my teacher Richard Saller for this approach. Stowers does
make the point that ἀσθενής/ἀσθένεια is a significant designation for "less mature"
people in Greek social philosophy (*Rereading*, 321).

[2] Karris, "Occasion," 66–70.

descriptions of imperial society, any discussion of what Paul meant by ἀδύνατος/δύνατοι and ἀσθενής must consider similar terms used by Latin authors.

Language and ideology of "strong" and "weak" in Rome

Terms for "strong"

Foremost among adjectives for "strong" applied to persons is the adjective *potens. Potens* in various forms was used to describe those with social power or influence in Rome. Thus Pliny mentions that an early case he argued was "contra potentissimos civitatis atque etiam Caesaris amicos" ("against the strongest ones of the city and even [against] the friends of Caesar").[3] Here we see that favor with Caesar contributes to the status of *potentissimi* ("the strongest ones").[4] The opinion of these powerful ones seems to have been a continual concern for persons in Rome. Seneca uses *vis* in connection with *potentes* to describe the damage that *potentes* can inflict on those of lesser status.[5]

Vis is the social force that the *potentes* exercised on others. So Tacitus writes: "Et propria vi Crispus incubuerat delatorem fratris sui pervertere" ("Crispus had used his own power to the uttermost to ruin the man who had informed against his brother").[6] *Vis* is used directly of political power in Suetonius, *Julius* 5.[7]

If *potentes* could show their superiority to those beneath them, so could people become liable to social slights from the *potentes* by

[3] Pliny, *Ep.* 1.18.3. Similarly, Cicero writes of the advantages of defending someone being oppressed by an influential person (*Off.* 2.51). On the use of the term *potentes* in the Republic, see J. Hellegouarc'h, *Le Vocabulaire latin des relations et des partis politiques sous la république* (Paris: Les Belles Lettres, 1963), 442–43.

[4] The Caesar is identified by A. N. Sherwin-White as Titus (*The Letters of Pliny: A Historical and Social Commentary* [Oxford: Clarendon, 1966], 128). A similar use of *potens* to designate those close to an emperor comes at Tacitus, *Dial.* 8.3.7.

[5] This example from Seneca (*Ep.* 14.4.1) comes in the context of the three objects of fear: "timentur quae per vim potentioris eveniunt" ("those things are feared that happen through the power of the strong ones"). See also *Ep.* 14.7.6; 14.8.8; 24.16.6; 76.33.4. Cf. fear of the Jews in Gal. 2.11–14 and fear of government in Rom. 13.1–7.

[6] *Hist.* 2.10 (*The Histories*, Vol. I, trans. C. H. Moore; LCL; London: William Heinemann, 1925).

[7] "auctores restituendae tribuniciae potestatis, cuius vim Sulla deminuerat, enixissime iuvit" ("He ardently supported the leaders in the attempt to re-establish the authority of the tribunes of the commons, the extent of which Sulla had curtailed"; trans. J. C. Rolfe; LCL; rev. ed.; London: William Heinemann, 1951).

offending them. Tacitus mentions that orators risk *potentiorum aures offendere* ("offending the ears/hearing of the stronger ones") when defending a friend.[8] Because of such concern, some were known to favor those with social influence and in so doing mistreat those with less influence.[9]

In the context of political strength (*potentia*) we meet the related characteristic of wealth.[10] Tacitus describes Calvia Crispinilla as *potens pecunia et orbitate* ("powerful in terms of money and having no heirs").[11] It is clear that wealth, and not simply membership in the senatorial order, allowed people to exercise social strength over others. The very fact that the aristocratic authors grated at the social power the servile members of the imperial household wielded shows that they recognized the latter to be *potentes* over them.[12]

The positions of social strength were not solely occupied by those of the senatorial order, nor were any positions invulnerable. The use of *potentes*, *inferiores*, and their functional synonyms was relative, so that anyone below the emperor in the social hierarchy of Rome might express concern about their *potentes*. The significance of this point for our study is that the "strong" described in Rom. 14.1–15.13 were not those of the senatorial order who wielded political influence in the city of Rome. They are rather to be understood as those of a much lower social order who held influence in the church life of Rome.[13]

Since the division of society into "strong" and "weak" occurred at all levels, a person at any level of society could take Seneca's advice to cultivate relationships that allow access to *potentes*: "amicitiae eorum, qui apud aliquem potentem potentes sunt" ("Have friends who have influence with someone among the strong ones").[14]

As a traditional Roman value, "strong" was applied as a

---

[8] Tacitus, *Dial.* 10.8.3.   [9] Pliny, *Ep.* 3.9.9.

[10] Sallust, *Cat.* 20.8, 12–13.   [11] Tacitus, *Hist.* 1.73.

[12] See P. Garnsey and R. P. Saller, *The Roman Empire: Economy, Society and Culture* (Berkeley: University of California Press, 1987), 122–23 on the "repugnant inversion of normal master–slave relationships" that occurred among imperial freedmen.

[13] I suggest in chapter 11 below that the "strong" in the churches probably included freedmen with significant social influence at the local level of Roman society.

[14] Seneca, *Ep.* 105.5.4. Paul turns this social strategy on its head when he asks the "strong" to change their lifestyle on behalf of the "weak" (Rom. 14.21) and support the "weak" (15.1).

designation of ability or competence in a variety of areas, physical and otherwise.[15] This concept is found in several other Latin words. The Romans were aware and concerned about who held *auctoritas* over whom. *Auctoritas* is a term that can denote social influence, or clout. It overlaps with our word "authority," for Cicero can use it to refer to the senate's authority.[16] But *auctoritas* may be nuanced from "authority" in that it is used in the sense of social influence[17] and respect or reputation in which something can be held.[18] This sense is applied in judging orators to denote the quality of making a deep or moving impression in one's speeches, as, for example, when Tacitus describes a speech by Corbulo: "multa auctoritate, quae viro militari pro facundia erat" ("all with a weight which in a professional soldier was a fair substitute for eloquence").[19]

The Roman value "strong" is also seen in the description of soldiers' values,[20] and since Rome was the seat of military and political power, terms for "power" or "strength" naturally became associated with one's identity as a Roman.[21] Such terms were no doubt used to describe the *auctoritas* of various persons.

People measured their worth in society by the people over whom they could exercise social power. Their positions of social power then inevitably involved public displays.[22] While verbal parallels to words for "strong" or "weak" are missing, the ideology behind this Roman ethos of social power is illustrated by the account of how the aedile L. Domitius Ahenobarbus (grandfather of Nero) forced the censor L. Munatius Plancus to make way on the street.[23]

Firmus is another word for "strong" that is well attested in pagan usage. It can refer to strength of character before opposition,[24] and

---

[15] Of course, the value placed on strength was not unique to Rome, being generally valued by other cultures as well.

[16] Cicero, *Phil.* 1.1; 6.3.   [17] Cicero, *de Orat.* 3.5.

[18] Pliny, *HN* 19.19.59.

[19] Tacitus, *Ann.* 15.26 (trans. J. Jackson; LCL; London: William Heinemann, 1937). See also Livy 24.28.8; Cicero, *Part.* 19; Quintilian, *Inst.* 8.3.3.

[20] Sallust, *Cat.* 7.6 – "virtus omnia domuerat" ("strength had conquered all").

[21] Note the lexical connection between Rome and the concept of "strength." J. Jüthner observes that the widespread use of the Greek language meant that the name "Rome" carried the meaning of its Greek homonym, ῥώμη, in *Hellenen und Barbaren: Aus der Geschichte des Nationalbewußtseins* (EA, n.s. 8; Leipzig: Dieterich, 1923), 75. See LSJ, s.v. "ῥώμη," "Ῥώμη."

[22] So Sejanus moved out of the city of Rome, so that the number of people at his *salutationes* would not become a social threat to Tiberius (Tacitus, *Ann.* 4.41).

[23] Suetonius, *Nero* 4.   [24] Pliny, *Ep.* 4.22.3.

is also used of such strength on the battlefield.[25] So Cicero declaimed that Gaius Caesar "firmissimum exercitum ex invicto genere veteranorum militum comparavit" ("collected a very stout army of the invincible class of veterans").[26] Since it is a word connoting a resolute bearing in the face of controversy, its occurrence in the Vulgate at Rom. 15.1 seems appropriate.[27]

Ideology of strength in Roman society

The language from the Principate is filled with words connoting strength. Whatever one thinks about whether Paul was addressing an actual situation when he wrote that the "strong" should support the "weak" (Rom. 15.1), one has to agree that Roman society distinctively used a variety of terms for strength to designate some people as especially powerful or influential.

From the Romans' use of words for "strength," several characteristics of their ideology of social strength may be noted. First, the criteria for the designation "strength" could range from physical strength to financial wealth to *auctoritas*. Second, the stratification of society occurred at every level, so there could be slaves who would be considered socially "strong" in comparison to other slaves. Third, common social strategy taught that it was to one's personal advantage to cultivate friendships or alliances with the "strong." Fourth, the "strong," especially those who were "strong" politically, were not viewed as invulnerable. Tacitus makes the parenthetical aside when describing the indictment against Vitellius: "adeo incertae sunt potentium res" ("so precarious are the fortunes of the mighty").[28]

Terms for "weak"

The focus on social strength in Roman society inevitably brought with it the use of another set of terms to designate social weakness. So the comparative adjective *inferior* could be applied to such

---

[25] Sallust, *Jug.* 51.5; Tacitus, *Agr.* 35.

[26] *Phil.* 3.3 (trans. W. C. A. Ker; LCL; London: William Heinemann, 1926).

[27] See *TLL*, s.v. "firmus," II.B.2, where the citations of *firmus* given above are listed with Rom. 15.1.

[28] *Ann.* 12.42.17 (trans. Jackson).

weakness in a legal sense.[29] But more significantly, *inferiores* is a term directly applied to people socially beneath others. So Marcellus includes Thrasea Paetus among the *inferiores* in his attack against Thrasea before the senate: "contumacia inferiorum lenitatem imperitantis deminui" ("The proud resistance of his inferiors was wearing at the mercy of the emperor").[30] And Cicero reflects what we would expect in this society that was so conscious of one's place on a vertical axis of status when he writes: "invident autem homines maxime paribus aut inferioribus" ("people are especially jealous of their equals, or those once beneath them").[31]

The adjective *tenuis* is another member within the social construction of "weakness" in Rome. This word is used to designate the mass of undifferentiated citizens who had low social standing in Rome.[32] While not the lowest social class, those called *tenuiores* were still considered needy recipients of aid, as Cicero's comment shows: "Atque haec benignitas etiam rei publicae est utilis, redimi e servitute captos, locupletari tenuiores" ("Ransoming prisoners from servitude and relieving the poor is a form of charity that is a service to the state as well as to the individual").[33] Such an understanding of this word continued into the Principate, for Trajan could write to Pliny that a certain *collegium tenuiorum* was approved as long as the contributions were *ad sustinendam tenuiorum inopiam utuntur* ("used to check the lack of the poor").[34]

Explicit proof that *tenuis* was used for those of limited means and not the completely destitute comes with the quotation of Iulius Paulus preserved by Aulus Gellius. Paulus' answer to a question regarding the meaning of *proletarius* is:

> "Qui in plebe," inquit, "Romana tenuissimi pauperrimique erant neque amplius quam mille quingentum aeris in

---

[29] "ad tris iudicum decurias quartam addidit ex inferiore censu, quae decenariorum vocaretur iudicaretque de levioribus summis" ("To the three divisions of jurors he added a fourth of a lower estate, to be called *ducenarii* and to sit on cases involving trifling amounts"), Suetonius, *Aug.* 32.3 (trans. J. C. Rolfe, *Lives of the Caesars*, Vol. I; LCL; London: William Heinemann, 1913).

[30] Tacitus, *Ann.* 16.28; my translation.

[31] *De Orat.* 2.209 (trans. E. W. Sutton and H. Rackham; LCL; rev. ed.; London: William Heinemann, 1948).

[32] Cicero, *Mur.* 47 uses the word as a parallel to *plebs*. Tacitus, *Ann.* 16.5.14, describes attendance at the theater during the Quinquennial Contest in Nero's reign: "Unde tenuioribus statim inrogata supplici" ("Hence, the lot of the humble was punishment, at once inflicted"; trans. Jackson).

[33] Cicero, *Off.* 2.63 (trans. W. Miller; LCL; London: William Heinemann, 1913).

[34] Pliny, *Ep.* 10.93.1.

> censum deferebant, 'proletarii' appellati sunt, qui vero nullo aut perquam parvo aere censebantur, 'capite censi' vocabantur, extremus autem census capite censorum aeris fuit trecentis septuaginta quinque."

> Those of the Roman commons who were humblest and of smallest means, and who reported no more than fifteen hundred asses at the census, were called *proletarii*, but those who were rated as having no property at all, or next to none, were termed *capite censi*, or "counted by head." And the lowest rating of the *capite censi* was three hundred and seventy-five asses.[35]

The fact that Paulus uses the adjective *tenuis* to refer to a group of people (*proletarii*) who had more wealth than the lowest group (*capite censi*) shows that the word does not connote absolute poverty.

By examination of the widespread *collegia tenuiorum*[36] we see that the term *tenuiores* carried the general meaning "the poor," though this will be qualified in the following paragraphs. I concede that the earliest reference which uses the phrase is from the jurist Marcian, who in the early third century CE uses it in his summary of past rescripts.[37] Still, as the reference above to Pliny's letter demonstrates, there is evidence that *tenuis* terminology was associated with some *collegia* earlier, and at least it shows us that Roman society did label as "weak" certain groups of people who regularly met together. The term *collegia tenuiorum* is a legal category for *collegia*, or associations, that were formed to help support those within Roman society who could not support themselves. This use of *tenuis* is therefore not necessarily depreciatory, but simply describes the financial situation of those freeborn poor or freedmen whose material insecurity forced them to band together. A couple of points are worth noting with regard to what sort of people would be called *tenuiores*.

The phrase *collegia tenuiorum* was used to describe *collegia* that included a cross section of the lower orders: slaves, freedmen/women, and freeborn. Despite Ausbüttel's suggestions

---

[35] Gel. 16.10.10–11 (*The Attic Nights of Aulus Gellius*, Vol. III, trans. J. C. Rolfe; LCL; London: William Heinemann, 1952).

[36] See, e.g., Pliny, *Ep.* 10.93.1.

[37] *Dig.* 47.22.1; 47.22.3.2.

to the contrary,[38] literary, epigraphical, and legal evidence combine to make it plain that slaves regularly participated in these *collegia*.[39] But all members were required to contribute of their property to the *collegium*.

When used to designate social class, *tenuis* does not describe those who had absolutely no financial resources. The expenses of the *collegia* indicate that the term *tenuiores* is applied to people with adequate resources for the regular dues of money, food, or wine to the *collegia*.[40] The costs of private graves which some *collegia* funded also imply that *tenuiores* in such associations held sufficient resources to provide for their graves. This is attested by the large number of grave inscriptions established by members of such *collegia*.[41]

It is surprising that no previous study of "strong" and "weak" in Romans has called attention to the widespread existence of *collegia tenuiorum* in the Roman world.[42] I shall return to this social institution in chapter 11 when portraying "strong" and "weak." For now we observe that later in the imperial period, Roman law codified an earlier label in the Roman social world that designated certain groups of people as "weak." The members of such groups were not completely destitute, but simply needed to pool their resources. Thus, the *collegia tenuiorum* are understood best to be voluntary associations of people with humble or modest means, rather than associations of the absolutely destitute.

It should also be noted that *tenuis* could be used for one's diet. The poet Horace uses the phrases *mensa tenuis* ("humble table") and *tenuis victus* ("humble food") in his presentations of the benefits of a simple life.[43] The use of weakness terminology for

---

[38] F. M. Ausbüttel, *Untersuchungen zu den Vereinen im Westen des römischen Reiches* (FAS 11; Kallmünz: Michael Laßleben, 1982), 40–42.

[39] J. A. Harrill, *The Manumission of Slaves in Early Christianity* (HUT 32; Tübingen: J. C. B. Mohr [Paul Siebeck], 1995), 147–52. Among the evidence Harrill cites are: Cicero, *Cat.* 1.27; 3.8; 4.4, 13; W. Dittenberger, *SIG*³ 985; *Dig.* 47.22.3.2.

[40] Harrill, *Manumission*, 46.   [41] Ibid., 43.

[42] J. C. Walters, *Ethnic Issues in Paul's Letter to the Romans: Changing Self-Definitions in Earliest Roman Christianity* (Valley Forge, Pa.: Trinity Press International, 1993), 15–16, describes *collegia tenuiorum*, but does not mention them in his discussion of "strong" and "weak" (84–92). Lampe, in *Die stadtrömischen Christen*, does not explicitly use the *collegia tenuiorum* phrase, but he does describe such *collegia* (e.g., 78) and does ask whether some Roman house churches functioned as *collegia* (313).

[43] Horace, *Carm.* 2.16.14; *Sat.* 2.2.53.

one's diet is thus already found in Latin literature the century before Paul penned Rom. 14.1–15.13.

As noted above for "strong" terms, the language of weakness also employed a variety of terms. Just as terms for "strong" could connote physical strength, the word *invalidus* could designate physical impotence, in the sense of inability to defend oneself. So Tacitus, in describing the prodigies of 51 CE, mentions how the "weak" were trampled by the crowd: "ac dum latius metuitur, trepidatione vulgi invalidus quisque obtriti" ("and as the panic spread, the weak were trampled underfoot in the trepidation of the crowd").[44]

Infirmus, the word for ὁ ἀσθενῶν at Rom. 14.1–2 in the Vulgate, was used in Rome to describe the social standing of people. Horace's account of a dialogue between two Romans, in which one refuses to converse at length because it is a Jewish Sabbath, includes the self-description *infirmior* of this person. It is surprising that commentators on the book of Romans have ignored this description of someone in Rome as a "weaker" person. Though this conversation is from a satire written in the first century BCE, the stereotyped "weaker one" in the conversation is valuable evidence for Roman perceptions of social weakness.[45] My quotation from the dialogue begins just after one person has reminded another that the latter had wanted to tell him something in private.

> "Memini bene, sed meliore tempore dicam; hodie tricesima sabbata: vin tu curtis Iudaeis oppedere?"
> "Nulla mihi," inquam, "religio est."
> "At mi; sum paulo infirmior, unus multorum. ignosces; alias loquar."
>
> "I mind it well, but I'll tell you at a better time.

---

[44] *Ann.* 12.43.

[45] It may be objected that satirists cannot provide reliable evidence for a sociological description of first-century Rome. This investigation proceeds on the basis that satirists' works have some historical value, once one recognizes that their works move within a triangle delimited by three points: attack, entertainment, and preaching. For a discussion of this approach to the satirists, see Niall Rudd, *Themes in Roman Satire* (London/Norman, Okla.: University of Oklahoma Press, 1986), 1–39. Rudd's text-oriented discussion of the various writers' positions within this triangle seems more balanced than Reekmans's judgment on Juvenal. Cf. Tony Reekmans, "Juvenal's Views on Social Change," *AS* 2 (1971) 161.

Today is the thirtieth Sabbath. Would you affront the circumcised Jews?"
"I have no scruples," say I.
"But I have. I'm a somewhat weaker brother, one of the many. You will pardon me; I'll talk another day."[46]

The passage is suggestive for our understanding of the Roman conception of "weakness" in several ways. It is most significant that the point of this self-reference of "weaker" by one of the dialogue partners simply functions as a way to conclude the conversation. I invite my readers to examine the larger context of this quotation, and see that Horace does not seem to be satirizing a group known as the "weak." It is used by one dialogue partner to describe himself, and thus is not primarily a term of derision or scorn here. We see that the self-confessed "weak" person labels himself so in opposition to his friend's assertion of irreligion. "Weakness" is therefore a quality that can be associated with the practice of a foreign religion.[47] In this case the foreign religion is Judaism.[48] The last phrase in his self-description, *unus multorum* ("one of the many"), seems to indicate at least that there were others of similar religious sentiment and therefore "weak" social presence. One may choose not to take the "many" as evidence for the size of such a group. But Horace ends the dialogue there, assuming immediate understanding on the part of the irreligious Roman within the dialogue. This at least shows that the person excessively observant of a foreign religion who fitted the "weak" caricature was known to Horace's audience. The exchange as a whole shows that the "weak" one's sensitivities resulted in a barrier to communication, a social consequence of "weakness" that also appears by implication in Rom. 14.1, 3, 10, 13; 15.7.

Other uses of *infirmus* are well attested in application to motives,[49]

---

[46] Horace, *Sat.* 1.9.68–72 (trans. H. R. Fairclough; LCL; rev. ed.; London: William Heinemann, 1929).

[47] It would be going too far to state that any religious practice was viewed as "weak," for Roman state religion was certainly viewed as a locus of social strength. Participation in imperial cult could actually help to identify the "strong," but this was not the case with religious performance in general.

[48] Though terms for "weakness" are not used (δειλίας πρόφασις is the nearest he comes in this context to "weakness"), Plutarch also depicts Judaism as "weak" when he describes how the Jews lost in battle because they refused to fight on the Sabbath (*Superst.* 169C).

[49] Gel. 5.3.7 (*The Attic Nights of Aulus Gellius*, Vol. I, trans. J. C. Rolfe; LCL; London: William Heinemann, 1946).

arguments,[50] or support.[51] These fit with its use in the Vulgate translation of Rom. 14.1–2 as applied to faith.[52]

Ideology of weakness in Roman society

The *inferiores* appear in the literature of the late Republic and early Empire to be those who were vulnerable to exercises of social power from those above them on the social ladder. While not a necessary component of the stereotype, the *inferiores* may have been associated with Semitic peoples living in Rome, as the quotation from Horace illustrates. Those who were socially "weak" were apparently known for their susceptibility to offense, as the line in Horace's dialogue, "Would you affront the circumcised Jews?," shows.

Significance of "strong" and "weak" language

A socially stratified society

Literary evidence of social description of Rome is filled with words for "strong" and "weak." This linguistic phenomenon is simply a reflection of the Roman social ideology that was preoccupied with one's place within a social hierarchy. When we read Paul's letter to the Romans in light of this ideology, we see that Paul's language fits with the socially stratified nature of Roman society. Is Paul simply using this language as appropriate for Rome, without any reference to what the Romans called the divided groups in their churches, or does Paul's language reflect the Romans' labels for these groups?

"Strong" and "weak" are Romans' labels

In the previous chapter I argued that the burden of proof is on those who argue that "strong" and "weak" groups are only literary identities constructed from Paul's knowledge of the Corinthian church. At this point I should like to press the argument a step

---

[50] Ibid., 5.11.4.

[51] Sallust, *Jug.* 85.4.

[52] The above citations are listed in *TLL*, s.v. "infirmus," I.B.2.a: "sub specie auctoritatis, efficaciae, fidei, virtutis sim." Reference to Vg Rom. 14.1–2 is missing in the whole entry.

further; "strong" and "weak" were most probably the very labels current in the Roman churches for the groups that divided their believing communities, used as self-designations by the members of these groups. Several considerations lead me to conclude that the labels "strong" and "weak" represent the Roman believers' names for their own groups within their church.

First, Paul uses these terms in an uncharacteristic way for his own writings. In 1 Cor. 4.10 Paul includes himself among the apostles who he says are "weak." This does not seem to be mere rhetoric on Paul's part, for he has already stated that God chose the "weak" things of this world (1 Cor. 1.27) and that he has become "weak" for the "weak" (1 Cor. 9.22; a balancing identification with the "strong" is missing!), and his practical response to the question of εἰδωλόθυτα is the same as the "weak" response.[53] But in Rom. 15.1 Paul identifies himself as one of the "strong," after already agreeing with the "strong" position on food consumption.[54] On the basis of his other letters,[55] we should not expect Paul to call himself "strong" if he were making up the labels here.

Second, from the limited evidence we have in Paul's other letters, he seems to write of divisive groups or persons in given churches in an informed way. His mention of the divided loyalties in Corinth is the clearest example (1 Cor. 1.12). But in all his other comments related to church divisions he seems to be writing from an informed perspective.[56] Paul's strategy seems to be that he writes to churches after learning what is happening in them, and not before.[57] Though Paul has not founded the believing communities in Rome, there is still evidence that he is writing the letter of Romans as an informed correspondent to believers who have heard about him.[58] Romans would be a different letter if Paul were writing to communities he

[53] Note 1 Cor. 10.14–22 with its implicit conclusion that all believers are weaker than the Lord. I agree with Gooch, *Dangerous Food*, 97: "Paul's objection to the Corinthian Christians' view of idol-food stems not from his concern over the consciousness of the weak but from his own consciousness and his own knowledge, which in turn were conditioned by his Judaism."

[54] Rom. 14.14, 20. Lincoln, "Abraham Goes to Rome," 172; Dunn, *Romans*, 798. Cf. Paul's vegetarianism in *Acts of Paul and Thecla* 25.

[55] Cf. the exchange of S. B. Andrews, "Too Weak Not to Lead: The Form and Function of 2 Cor. 11.23b-33," *NTS* 41 (1995) 263–76 and J. Lambrecht, "Strength in Weakness," *NTS* (1997) 285–90.

[56] Phil. 3.2; 4.2; Gal. 4.17; 2 Cor. 11.4, 12–13; cf. 2 Thess. 3.11–12.

[57] 1 Thess. 3.5–8; 2 Cor. 7.6–7.

[58] Paul is informed about the Roman believers (Rom. 1.8; 6.17; 7.1). They have heard about him (1.13; 3.8, 31; 6.1, 15; 15.22–23).

knew nothing about, and who knew nothing about him. In support of this point, the influence that the Roman church had (Rom. 1.8), and ease of communication between Rome and Corinth,[59] makes it likely that Paul knew what was going on in Rome.[60]

Third, it is hard to believe that Paul would label groups "strong" and "weak," thus risking a misreading or caricature of his addressees, in a church that he was trying to win for support (Rom. 1.11–13; 15.22–24). As this chapter has shown, the use of "strong" and "weak" terms in Roman society makes it likely that this is what groups within the Roman church were calling themselves. The nicknames "strong" and "weak" come with no introduction. One nickname does not seem to be positive, though it occurs in a letter where Paul wants to be positive about his audience (1.8, 12; 6.17; 15.14). Sampley, already committed toward viewing the divisive issues as *kashrut* and Sabbath observance, thinks that Paul has made an oblique approach to these issues by inventing the nicknames "weak" and "strong."[61] This still does not answer why Paul would begin, without explanation, with the imperative sentence that has thrown forward the "weak" for emphasis: Τὸν δὲ ἀσθενοῦντα τῇ πίστει προσλαμβάνεσθε. Nicknames in correspondence serve to confirm the understanding that author and audience already share.[62] Nicknames are particularly effective when an author can use one already coined by the audience.[63]

---

[59] On the evidence of the sailing records offered by the elder Pliny, a letter could reach Corinth from Rome in less than nine days (*HN* 19.1.3). Of course, time could be lost waiting for a trustworthy messenger, and the delivery time of Cicero's letters to his son in Athens (one took seven weeks; another only three) might be a better analogue for Rome–Corinth correspondence (L. Casson, *Travel in the Ancient World* [Toronto: Hakkert, 1974], 221). If there were believers in or near the *familia Caesaris* in Rome (Phil. 4.22; Rom. 16.10–11) and influential citizens in churches around Corinth (Rom. 16.1–2, 23), messengers were readily available.

[60] Cf. Murphy-O'Connor, *Paul*, 332 for the idea that Paul wrote Romans 1–12 generally and then added chapters 13–16 after receiving news from Rome. This is possible, though I think that already in 1.8; 3.5–8 and 6.1–17 we have evidence that Paul was cognizant and in conversation with developments and attitudes in Rome.

[61] Sampley, "The Weak and the Strong," 42, 46.

[62] See, e.g., Cicero's use of *calvum* ("baldhead") and *pulchellus puer* ("our little beauty"; *Att.* 1.16); βοῶπιδος ("Ox-eyes") and "Sampsiceramus" (*Att.* 2.14) as nicknames for others in his letters to Atticus (*Cicero: Selected Letters* [trans. D. R. Shackleton Bailey; London/New York: Penguin, 1986], 44, 46, 52). These nicknames are different from Cicero's use of people's *cognomena* and his occasional avoidance of people's names; cf. J. N. Adams, "Conventions of Naming in Cicero," *CQ* 28 (1978) 149–51, 163–64.

[63] "quae, ut tu soles dicere, νέκυια!" ("What an underworld, to use your favourite expression!"; *Att.* 9.18; Shackleton Bailey, *Selected Letters*, 152).

Since it is probable that there was an actual division in the church Paul was addressing, since terms for "strong" and "weak" were current in Roman social descriptions, and since these terms appear as nicknames for some in the audience whom Paul has never met, it follows that Paul is most likely using terms already used in the Roman churches. He does not apply "strong" and "weak" only from his own experience. He is using terms already used by the Romans themselves for groups in the divided Roman church called "strong" and "weak," or δυνατοί and ἀδυνατοί/ ἀσθενεῖς, or *potentes* and *inferiores*. Paul uses such terminology when addressing them because this is how they were already known within the Roman church. The letter to this church provides some clues as to the defining issue of status in these groups' identities.

Application of sociological theory on Rom. 14.1–15.13

In order to aid in the description of "strong" and "weak" groups, Weber's typology of social groups is used in the following discussion.[64] Though it is a typology of logically "pure" types and may not lend itself to categorizing every piece of evidence in given situations, it nevertheless forms a useful construct in describing the nature of the stratification in Rome. While Weber's typology is used here, an effort is made to avoid undue abstraction. The "strong" and "weak" are placed within the social hierarchy of Rome as the application of sociological theory proceeds through Weber's types. In the following description it will be seen that the "strong" and "weak" sides in the Roman church appear primarily to be status groups. However, some inferences may be made using the types of "party" and "class" as well.

---

[64] This typology is taken from the chapter, "Class, Status, Party," in *From Max Weber: Essays in Sociology* (trans. and eds. H. H. Gerth and C. Wright Mills; New York: Oxford University Press, 1946), 180–95. While much has been written since Weber, it is evident that his typology still forms the basis for investigations into group stratification. See E. Goode, *Sociology* (2nd ed.; Englewood Cliffs, N.J.: Prentice-Hall, 1988), 237: "What is now the 'mainstream' approach to stratification in the United States originated with Max Weber." See also the reference to Weber in W. A. Meeks, *The First Urban Christians: The Social World of the Apostle Paul* (New Haven/London: Yale University Press, 1983), 53 at the beginning of his section "Measuring Social Stratification."

Status groups and the language of honor

Sociologically, Rom. 14.1–15.13 provides ample evidence that there were at least two social "layers" within the Roman church, the "strong" and the "weak," although from such texts as Rom. 12.3–8, 16 it appears likely that there were more "layers" or divisions within the community than simply these two.

There is no clear evidence in Romans that "strong" and "weak" were distinguished primarily on the basis of social class, since nothing is explicitly stated about property. Indeed, to an outsider, both groups probably appeared to be in roughly the same social class among the lower population of Rome. And while the language of social power is present, the status indicators[65] that emerge in Paul's argument in Rom. 14.1–15.13 lead to the conclusion that the available evidence for "strong" and "weak" is best interpreted along the lines of Weber's typology for status. To use Weber's terminology, it appears that these groups are status groups because their situation "is determined by a specific, positive or negative, social estimation of *honor*."[66] In the case of a Roman, this "estimation of honor" was determined by those in one's social sphere.[67] The idea that the Roman "strong" and "weak" were essentially status groups fits with the role that honor and the avoidance of shame usually plays in more or less closed communities such as churches. J. G. Peristiany comments,

> Honour and shame are the constant preoccupation of individuals in small scale, exclusive societies where face to face personal, as opposed to anonymous, relations are of paramount importance and where the social personality of the actor is as significant as his office.[68]

---

[65] By allowing for other status indicators besides social class, I concur with Meeks, who notes that a person's level of status in a community is not found on a single continuum, but results from considering a person's positions on a number of continua that contribute to status. He lists "ethnic origins, *ordo*, citizenship, personal liberty, wealth, occupation, age, sex and public offices or honors" as categories in which status is assigned (*First Urban Christians*, 54–55).

[66] Weber, "Class, Status, Party," 187, his italic. See Rom. 14.1–3, 10, 13, 19; 15.1–3, 7 for evidence that the separation between the groups was an issue of honor, thus constituting "strong" and "weak" as status groups.

[67] Garnsey and Saller, *The Roman Empire*, 118.

[68] Introduction to *Honour and Shame: The Values of Mediterranean Society* (ed. J. G. Peristiany; Chicago: University of Chicago Press, 1966), 11.

In the context of status groups within the church, "honor" does not represent the civil positions that were officially bestowed in Roman society as a means of honoring persons.[69] It simply represents social recognition conferred on those within the community who were considered higher in status than others.[70] Through this insight we can also begin to understand why Paul includes himself among the "strong" in Rom. 15.1. He does so not simply because of his open view toward food consumption (14.14), but also because he is not ashamed of himself or his gospel, and those who are not ashamed in society are "strong."

With the suggestion that "strong" and "weak" are status groups, the question immediately arises: "In whose perspective is status determined?"[71] Though used in Roman society as a whole, the labels "strong" and "weak" as found in Romans are used as intra-communal designations, and aside from the prohibition against judging (14.4a,10a), Paul asks only the "strong" actually to change their behavior (14.13, 19, 21; 15.1).[72] These observations would imply that the status attached to the two groups mentioned in Rom. 14.1–15.13 originates from a reference group within the community, i.e., those who consume everything (14.2) and are known in the text as "strong." The superiority in status that the meat-eating "strong" enjoyed over the "weak" implies that the abstinence of the "weak" was not directly motivated by a desire to gain status, unlike cultures in which a group with high status is vegetarian.[73]

---

[69] Cf. the line in Trimalchio's epitaph: "Cum posset in omnibus decuriis Romae esse, tamen noluit" (Petronius, *Satyr.* 71.12). On *decuriis* in context see M. S. Smith, ed., *Petronii Arbitri Cena Trimalchionis* (Oxford: Clarendon, 1975), 198.

[70] Peristiany comments on the divisive function of honor: "Honour is at the apex of the pyramid of temporal social values and it conditions their hierarchical order. Cutting across all other social classifications it divides social beings into two fundamental categories, those endowed with honour and those deprived of it" (Introduction to *Honour and Shame*, 10).

[71] Ralf Dahrendorf, *Homo Sociologicus* (4th ed.; Cologne/Opladen: West-deutscher, 1964), 35, comments on R. K. Merton's use of the "reference group": "Er bezeichnet den Sachverhalt, daß ein Einzelner sein Verhalten an der Zustimmung oder Ablehnung von Gruppen orientiert, denen er selbst nicht zugehört. Bezugs-gruppen sind Fremdgruppen, die als Wertskalen individuellen Handelns fungieren; sie bilden das Bezugssystem, innerhalb dessen der Einzelne sein und anderer Verhalten bewertet." See also Meeks, *First Urban Christians*, 54.

[72] See consideration of the possibility that Rom. 14.1–15.13 includes a call for the "weak" to change at end of chapter 10 below.

[73] Cf. J. Goody on the rejection of food as "the other side of the hierarchical cuisine": "Abstinence and prohibition are widely recognised as ways of attaining grace in hierarchical societies such as China and India" (*Cooking, Cuisine and Class:*

If "strong" and "weak" were status groups, we have to ask how honor and deference were shown to the "strong." The first clue in Rom. 14.1–15.13 is Paul's repeated use of προσλαμβάνομαι. It appears that the social acceptance granted to the "strong" and denied to the "weak" was one way in which honor was used to distinguish these status groups. A second way that honor was used to differentiate between "strong" and "weak" was in the way that the former could force the latter into patterns of behavior the "weak" would otherwise shun. Julian Pitt-Rivers makes this clear: "Where there is a hierarchy of honour, the person who submits to the precedence of others recognizes his inferior status."[74] Thus, Paul's commands against forcing the "weak" to consume items considered forbidden[75] involve more than simply the issue of following one's conscience. These commands are meant to discourage the "strong" from emphasizing their higher status by forcing the "weak" to follow "strong" habits of consumption. I now offer preliminary descriptions of what these groups, "strong" and "weak," looked like in first-century Rome.

Descriptions of "strong" and "weak"

The "strong" are Roman citizens or foreign-born residents who display a proclivity toward things Roman.[76] Their appearance may be described as healthy, if not robust, since they eat everything (14.2a) and are "strong" (οἱ δυνατοί, 15.1). They exercise their *auctoritas* over those whom Roman society has placed below or equal to them in status (14.3a). They have material resources to appear more self-sufficient than others within their particular class and rank (15.1). Their place in the social hierarchy of Rome most likely corresponds to those freedmen who had risen in status, social influence, and property holdings above the freeborn within the

---

A Study in Comparative Sociology [Cambridge: Cambridge University Press, 1982], 116–17). Cf. also G. E. Ferro-Luzzi, "Food Avoidances at Puberty and Menstruation in Tamilnad: An Anthropological Study," in *Food, Ecology and Culture: Readings in the Anthropology of Dietary Practices* (ed. J. R. K. Robson; New York: Gordon and Breach, 1980), 97–98.

[74] J. Pitt-Rivers, "Honour and Social Status," in Peristiany, *Honour and Shame*, 23.

[75] Rom. 14.15, 20, 22–23.

[76] It is conceivable that some *peregrini* or their children who took pains to adopt as Roman a lifestyle as possible would also figure among the "strong."

lower population[77] of Rome. Within this population, such freedmen held relatively high status and significant social influence, and were materially independent.[78]

When we think about who the *potentes* may have been in the Roman church, two households who are identified in Romans 16[79] come to mind. These are the households of Aristobulus (verse 10) and Narcissus (verse 11). If this is the Aristobulus who was of the Herod family and a friend of Claudius,[80] then he may well have willed his property to the emperor and his slaves would thus pass into the *familia Caesaris*. Similarly, the designation "those of Narcissus" may indicate the slaves and freedmen of Tiberius Claudius Narcissus, the rich freedman in Tiberius' household, who also held much authority in the reign of Claudius. He was executed by Nero (at Agrippina's instigation) in 54; his own slaves and freedmen would have remained within the powerful imperial household.[81] Given the political power and social status of the imperial household at this time, if these names designate members of this household they would likely be among the *potentes* in the church.

The "weak" are those who are of foreign extraction or who

[77] I derive the term "lower population" from Lily Ross Taylor's article, "Freedmen and Freeborn in the Epitaphs of Imperial Rome," *AJPh* 82 (1961) 113, 131. She uses it to designate the freeborn and freedmen outside of the equestrian order and the servile class. Admittedly there were persons from this section of the population who surpassed equestrians in status, social influence, or property.

[78] By using "independent," I follow J. H. D'Arms's definition of the independent freedman: "a freedman released from the restricting controls of a former master and his *familia*, and in a position both to accumulate wealth in commercial and manufacturing ventures where success depended upon his own capacities, contacts, and initiative, and to establish and maintain social relationships which were largely of his own choosing," *Commerce and Social Standing in Ancient Rome* (Cambridge, Mass.: Harvard University Press, 1981), 148. See also P. Garnsey, "Independent Freedmen and the Economy of Roman Italy under the Principate," *Klio* 63 (1981) 359–71.

[79] On reading Romans 16 as an integral part of this letter to the Romans, see Murphy-O'Connor, *Paul*, 324–28; Lampe, *Die stadtrömischen Christen*, 124–35; W.-H. Ollrog, "Die Abfassungsverhältnisse von Röm 16," in *Kirche* (Günther Bornkamm Festschrift; eds. D. Lührmann and G. Strecker; Tübingen: J. C. B. Mohr, 1980), 221–24. Kurt Aland cautions against taking the silence of the early church fathers as evidence for the later addition of Romans 16 in "Der Schluß und die ursprüngliche Gestalt des Römerbriefes," in *Neutestamentliche Entwürfe* (Munich: Kaiser, 1979), 284–301.

[80] Josephus, *BJ* 1.552; 2.221–22; *AJ* 16.394; 20.104. This association of Aristobulus with the Herod family is made more likely by the occurrence of Herodion in verse 11, Paul's "kinsman," immediately after Aristobulus (Murphy-O'Connor, *Paul*, 325–26; F. F. Bruce, *Paul: Apostle of the Heart Set Free* [Grand Rapids: Eerdmans, 1977], 387).

[81] Murphy-O'Connor, *Paul*, 326; Bruce, *Paul*, 386–87.

sympathize with foreign religions and cultures. Some of the "weak" were *peregrini* without Roman citizenship. The "weak" include those of Jewish standing. But in light of the ascetic values within the early Principate, including vegetarianism,[82] the group cannot be limited to Jews. Their physical presence may be depicted along a continuum from unimpressive to sickly (14.2b; 15.1). They do not exercise their *auctoritas* over those placed below them in status by Roman society. They are scrupulous in religious observance (14.5a). Compared to the "strong" of their social class and rank, they have less property. While it is likely that there were also freedmen among the "weak," they did not enjoy the status of "strong" freedmen within the church.

These sketches cannot be proven. But the high incidence of "strong" (*potens, firmus, vis*) and "weak" (*inferior, tenuis, invalidus, infirmus*) terms applied to people in Rome show a society preoccupied with one's place on the vertical axis of social power. If this is what Roman society was like, we should expect some reflection of this social consciousness in the church. It is therefore likely that Paul's use of comparable Greek terms in his letter to the Romans is not done out of ignorance of their situation. If we have thought that Paul's Roman readers "recede curiously into the background" once Paul begins the argument of his letter, it may be because we have been reading the letter too much as scripture,[83] with our eyes closed to the traces of its first audience. We have been buyers of antique jewelry, concerned too much with how the gems will look on us, rather than how their first owners wore them. Paul's letter must therefore be seen as a viable piece of evidence for the social history of Roman Christianity under the Principate. It is to this letter's description of two Roman groups' habits of consumption that we now turn.

---

[82] See the discussion in chapter 4 below.

[83] Cf. R. B. Hays, *Echoes of Scripture in the Letters of Paul* (New Haven: Yale University Press, 1989), 5, 35.

4

"STRONG" AND "WEAK" EATING AND
DRINKING PATTERNS

quamobrem sit aliquis et his honos, neve auctoritatem
rebus vilitas adimat, cum praesertim etiam cognomina
procerum inde nata videamus, Lactucinosque in Valeria
familia non pudiuisse apellari.

Therefore let vegetables also have their meed of honour
and do not let things be robbed of respect by the fact of
their being common, especially as we see that vegetables
have supplied even the names of great families, and a
branch of the Valerian family were not ashamed to bear
the surname Lettuce.   Pliny, *HN* 19.19.59[1]

Paul's descriptions of consumption patterns

This chapter seeks to establish what Paul says about the eating and
drinking habits of his addressees in Romans 14–15. Our goal is
simply to understand the behaviors related to consumption that are
mentioned in the text. Then we check whether these behaviors fit
what we know of Roman consumption patterns. Does Paul's
advice to the Romans about a supposed difference in consumption
reflect what we know of eating and drinking habits in first-century
Rome? We can answer this question by examining what Paul says
about the eating and drinking habits of the Roman Christians in
his letter to them, and comparing this to what we know of
contemporary consumption patterns in Rome. The apparent asceticism among Paul's Roman addressees does seem to match ascetic
practices in first-century Rome, and there are indications elsewhere
in Romans that Paul is aware of an asceticism among his audience.

---

[1] *Natural History, Vol. V* (trans. H. Rackham; LCL; London: William Heinemann, 1950), 19.19.59.

Paul's descriptions of eating practices

προσλαμβάνεσθε *(Rom. 14.1; 15.7)*

The imperatives that bracket this section indicate that various church members were not welcoming one another. Since the description of a difference in eating immediately follows the first of these commands, we can infer that the Roman value of conviviality, in which people of different classes and orders could dine together,[2] was not followed among some of the believers to whom Paul wrote. The *convivium* was a distinctly Roman innovation, in that it could allow for "an astonishingly wide social range of participants, yet still retain at least something of the atmosphere of *symposia*."[3] While we must admit that because of the differentiation made in seating and menus for guests, these *convivia* did not exemplify social equality as we might conceive it, they were still valued as occasions when people of widely varying stations could eat together.[4] If Paul had any sense of how Romans were known to dine together in social contexts, he as the one obligated to proclaim his gospel to all levels of humanity (1.14–16) would think it unfortunate and indeed shameful (Rom. 14.16) that some in his audience were not eating together. Paul thus writes to resolve the social impasse and bring his audience out of a shameful position.

ὃς μὲν πιστεύει φαγεῖν πάντα *(Rom. 14.2a)*[5]

This is the first description that Paul gives of one group's eating habits within the Roman church. That those identified as the ones who eat everything are the "strong" is evident from the structure of 14.2. As those presented as opposed in practice to the "weak" who eat vegetables, those who eat everything must correspond with the "strong" mentioned in 15.1, who are to bear the "weaknesses of the weak." Also, the juxtaposition of ὁ ἀσθενῶν τῇ πίστει in verse 1 with ὃς πιστεύει in verse 2 indicates that the latter must be "strong." Paul Minear's identification in this passage of five distinct groups in the Roman church goes beyond the evidence. The doubter who does not eat according to faith (14.23) is more likely a

---

[2] J. D'Arms, "The Roman *Convivium* and the Idea of Equality," in *Sympotica* (ed. O. Murray; Oxford: Clarendon, 1990), 308–20.

[3] Ibid., 319.   [4] Ibid., 316–19.

[5] For an historical overview of overeating and gluttony, see R. Arbesmann, "Gefräßigkeit," *RAC* 9.345–90, but especially 368–69 for NT issues.

"weak" member, already called "weak in faith" (14.1), rather than Minear's representative of a distinct faction.[6] Rom. 14.1–15.13 as a whole, especially at 15.1, presupposes that there are two groups in the Roman churches, though of course these two groups serve as Paul's types for two termini on a continuum, between which some of the Roman believers lived.

φαγεῖν πάντα can mean: (1) eat every kind of food (without regard for its purity or impurity); or (2) eat all there is (in the sense of gluttony). The use of the object "everything" (πάντα) instead of "meat" (κρέα)[7] as the "strong" counterpart to the "vegetables" (λάχανα) of the "weak" in the contrasting part of the verse[8] hints that the controversial food in the "strong" diet included more than meat. This hint is confirmed by the open-ended dictum at Rom. 14.21–καλὸν τὸ μὴ φαγεῖν κρέα μηδὲ πιεῖν οἶνον μηδὲ ἐν ᾧ ὁ ἀδελφός σου προσκόπτει,[9] thus supporting the first option listed above, that πάντα refers to a removal of all dietary restrictions. The contrast with λάχανα and the epistolary situation eliminate the possibility that Paul is attempting a humorous description, as if the "strong" ate inedible objects. Just as we might say, "Martin drinks everything, while Katherine drinks water," and understand the contrast without taking "everything" literally, so we should read this verse. The conclusion in 14.21 also serves to indicate what the controversial items of consumption are, and thus should be used to help us understand the contrast in 14.2. The epistolary situation behind this letter offers Paul much more to lose by poking fun at his audience inappropriately than any gains he could make by a successful jab of humor here. I do not think that Paul is trying to be funny.

---

[6] Cf. Minear, *Obedience*, 8–15.

[7] Rom. 14.21 confirms that κρέας would be the expected antonym to λάχανον here.

[8] While 14.2 has two equally balanced parts, it does not meet the standard definition of a period (BDF §464). Indeed, since it begins with a relative pronoun linking it to the preceding sentence, it is rather written in the running (εἰρομένη) style more typical of Paul (BDF §458).

[9] The awkward μηδὲ ἐν ᾧ ὁ ἀδελφός σου προσκόπτει has received several emendations in the history of the text, but is best left as it stands. The conjectures by Hofmann (replacing ἐν with ἔν) and Mangey (adding ἔν so as to result in ἔν, ἐν), while providing an antecedent for the relative pronoun, use ἔν as an indefinite pronoun. This is extremely rare in Paul; 1 Cor. 11.5; 14.27 are the only instances where ἔν might function in this way. Michel's ground for accepting the additional variant ἢ σκανδαλίζεται ἢ ἀσθενεῖ is precisely the reason for rejecting it, when one sees that ἐν ᾧ ... προσκόπτει has already worked out the thought behind the two preceding clauses (*Römer*, 349 n. 2).

The φαγεῖν πάντα phrase in 14.2 also leaves open the possibility that the "strong" were known for eating in excess. A phrase in the immediately preceding context, μὴ κώμοις καὶ μέθαις (13.13), seems to support this possibility. But since Rom. 13.8–14 is not usually considered to reflect a knowledge of the community in Rome,[10] in the three paragraphs to follow I shall present the reasons why Rom. 13.8–14 should be taken into consideration when one is reading Rom. 14.1–15.13 and attempting to learn about Paul's first audience.

Romans 13 seems specifically focused on the situation in Rome. In 13.1–7 Paul addresses the problem of taxation, a pressing problem in Rome at this time.[11] The command to love in order to fulfill Torah (verses 8–10) fits with the picture the rest of the letter gives of a disunified community that includes an element concerned about Torah observance.[12] "Weapons of light" (ὅπλα τοῦ φωτός in verse 12) is unique in Paul[13] and may reflect his concern for Roman Christians' morality, a concern I shall address next.

There is some evidence for sexual immorality within the Roman community. In regard to κοίταις καὶ ἀσελγείαις, we see an emphasis on sexual vices in Rom. 1.26–27 and the repeated quotation of the seventh commandment at Rom. 2.22; 13.9, found in the Pauline corpus only in Romans. (Features that are uncharacteristic of Pauline writings in general may be present in Romans because of other factors than the situation in Rome, but that situation must be viewed as a strong candidate for the reason behind such features, whether or not they are integral to the argument of Romans.) Robert H. Gundry has suggested a sexual context for 7.7–25, although as the title of his essay shows, he does

---

[10] Cf. Ehrhard Kamlah, *Die Form der katalogischen Paränese im Neuen Testament* (WUNT 7; Tübingen: J. C. B. Mohr [Paul Siebeck], 1964), 38, who takes Rom. 13.12–14 as a catalog coming out of baptismal parenesis. Anton Vögtle does not consider either vice catalog of Rom. 1.29 or 13.13 to be situation-specific to Rome, *Die Tugend- und Lasterkataloge im Neuen Testament* (NTAbh 16.4–5; Münster: Aschendorff, 1936), 29, 44.

[11] See discussion in chapter 2.

[12] On the disharmony of the community see 1.7–πᾶσιν τοῖς οὖσιν ἐν Ῥώμη (connotes a plurality of congregations in the description of the addresses, cf. 1 Cor. 1.2, 2 Cor. 1.1, 1 Thess. 1.1); Rom. 2.1–ὦ ἄνθρωπε πᾶς ὁ κρίνων cuts beneath an abstracted diatribe partner to a problem in Rome; see 12.3–8 on humility and unity in social relations; and 14.3, 10 on judging and scorning. On Torah observance in Rome, see 2.1–3, 17–29; 3.19–31; 7.1.

[13] Cf. Rom. 6.13.

not consider the situation in Rome when making his argument.[14] Near the end of this chapter I suggest that Hebrews might offer us a vista of Roman Christianity; if this is so, one may note that Heb. 13.4 shows concern for avoiding adultery.

There is also some evidence for jealousy or strife in the community. In n. 12 above, I listed some texts that seem to indicate a disunified community in Rome. The letter of *1 Clement* is also concerned about ἔρις and ζῆλος, perhaps an indication that its authors were conscious of these problems through Roman Christianity's past experience.[15] Rom. 13.14 is most easily understood when one posits that Paul views the preceding vices as actually present in the community. Besides the contents of its context, the formal structure of the list in 13.13 suggests that it is not an abstracted list with no reference to the community. This is because an idealized list of virtues, the usual partner to abstract vice lists, is missing here.[16] While I generally agree with Moiser on the occasional nature of Romans 12–15, I cannot follow his assertion that Rom. 13.11–14 is in a "more general tone," based on pre-synoptic material found also in Luke 21. The parallels with Luke 21 are not convincing, and Moiser himself admits that Paul may have used this supposedly standard vice list "because of the peculiar appropriateness of the last two vices included: quarrels and jealousy."[17] Since the whole list in Rom. 13.13 repeats concerns found elsewhere in the letter, the list is probably crafted for Paul's audience in Rome. Many students of Romans today agree that Romans is definitely an occasional letter, but continue to read much of it as though it is a compendium of general theological truth. When we take seriously the probability that Rom. 14.1–15.13 is addressed to a specific situation in Rome, and then seek to relate that section to the rest of the letter, we begin to see that we are still infected by Melanchthon's virus.[18]

[14] "The Moral Frustration of Paul before his Conversion: Sexual Lust in Romans 7:7–25," in *Pauline Studies* (eds. D. A. Hagner and M. J. Harris; Devon: Paternoster, 1980), 228–45.

[15] ἔρις – *1 Clem.* 14.2; 54.2; ζῆλος – *1 Clem.* 4.7–13; 5.2, 4; 6.1–4; 14.1; 43.2; both terms – *1 Clem.* 3.2; 5.5; 9.1; and note emphasis on communal peace – *1 Clem.* 3.4; 54.2; 60.3–4; 65.1.

[16] Cf. Gal. 5.19–23 and H. D. Betz, *Galatians: A Commentary on Paul's Letter to the Churches in Galatia* (Hermeneia; Philadelphia: Fortress, 1979), 281–89.

[17] J. Moiser, "Rethinking Romans 12–15," *NTS* 36 (1990) 578.

[18] P. Melanchthon called the letter "caput et summa universae doctrinae christianae" ("head and summary of the complete Christian doctrine") in *Dispositio orationis in epistolam ad Romanos: Philippi Melanchthonis opera quae supersunt* (ed.

To return to φαγεῖν πάντα, though we cannot prove that Rom. 14.2 fits with 13.13, we do have evidence for gluttony in Rome and even in later Roman Christianity.[19] κώμοις καὶ μέθαις implies excess in terms of frequency and quantity of consumption.[20] The possibility that πάντα in 14.2 connotes this sort of excess is also supported by the slogan-like character of the phrase (including both eating and drinking) that Paul denies in 14.17, ἡ βασιλεία τοῦ θεοῦ βρῶσις καὶ πόσις,[21] and the reference to wine in 14.21. Perhaps some members of the Roman churches were living as if the kingdom of God were food and drink, and justifying their excessive consumption by this dictum.

"Eating in excess" as a behavior of the "strong" is also supported (but not proven) by the attention and communal disharmony that the abstinence of the "weak" seemed to evoke. The "weak" abstinence would not appear to be as divisive an issue if there were not a lifestyle that contrasted markedly with it. As Jack Goody has observed about food abstinence in other cultures, "Such a philosophy of rejection could develop only within the context of hierarchical society with its stratified cuisine, *since abstention only exists in the wider context of indulgence.*"[22]

The philosophical arguments and sociological implications behind the phrase "the one who has faith eats everything" are noted in the next chapter. The description in verse 2b of the weak person eating vegetables implies that at least meat consumption is dividing the community. But the phrases φαγεῖν πάντα in verse 2a, μηδὲ ἐν ᾧ ὁ ἀδελφός σου προσκόπτει in verse 21, and κώμοις καὶ

C. G. Bretschneider; Halle: Schwetschke, 1834–60) XV.445. In his *Commentarii in epistolam Pauli ad Romanos [anno 1532]*, he writes "continet enim praecipuos et proprios locos doctrinae christianae" ("for it contains outstanding and unique passages of Christian doctrine," ibid., XV.495), and in his *Loci communes, 1521* he calls it "doctrinae christianae compendium" ("compendium of Christian doctrine," in *Melanchthons Werke in Auswahl* II.1; ed. R. Stupperich; Gütersloh: Bertelsmann, 1952) 7. I learned of these references from Fitzmyer, *Romans*, 74.

[19] For Rome, see M. Corbier, "The Ambiguous Status of Meat in Ancient Rome," trans. R. P. Saller, *Food and Foodways* 3 (1989) 245, who describes with examples "the fascination that prodigious consumption of food (for example, extreme voraciousness for meat) held for the Romans." Juvenal, *Sat.* 3.234, on Roman residents sick with undigested food in their stomachs, seems to imply gluttony. For later Roman Christianity, see *Hermas Vis.* 3.9.3.

[20] Dunn, *Romans*, 789, thinks that the plurals show frequency. He also suggests that the phrase could be read as a hendiadys, "drunken revelry."

[21] Even if this were not a slogan, Paul's negation of the phrase in the section addressed to the "strong" points toward the likelihood that indulgence in food and drink was high on the agenda of the "strong."

[22] *Cooking, Cuisine and Class*, 117, my italic.

μέθαις in Rom. 13.13 make it possible that more than the eating of meat is at issue in the portrait Paul paints of the difference in "strong" and "weak" consumption. This possibility might fit with the description of those who work discord among the believers and serve their own belly (16.17–18). Paul can include himself among the "strong" (15.1), and write that the "strong" eat for the Lord (14.6). But perhaps there were some among the "strong" who were especially divisive,[23] whose gluttony prompted Paul to describe them as serving their belly.[24] If we accept these verses as integral to Romans, the letter in which Paul wants so desperately to compliment his audience,[25] they must arise from Paul's awareness of certain people in Rome and not from a hypothetical danger Paul sees.

ὁ δὲ ἀσθενῶν λάχανα ἐσθίει *(Rom. 14.2b)*

As the subject of the second half of this descriptive verse, the diet of this representative church member must be understood as being vegetarian. In contrast to the one who "eats everything" (14.2a), the one who "eats vegetables" is best understood as one who characteristically eats vegetables rather than meat.[26] Again, the prospect of reading this absolutely literally, as if this person eats only garden herbs, ignores the point of the contrast and Paul's epistolary situation. When we hear that "Martin drinks everything, while Katherine drinks water," we do not think that water is the only beverage Katherine drinks. So in this context, Paul is giving us a definition that is characteristic, rather than restrictive, of the "weak" diet. Vegetarians eat more than vegetables. The designation "weak" is linked to "the one who is weak in faith" of verse 1. At the same time, connotations of physical weakness cannot be eliminated from the description "weak."[27]

So far we have seen that in Paul's description, "strong" and "weak" differ at least over meat, possibly over other foods and quantity of consumption, but we know on the basis of 14.6 that both can thank God over whatever meal eaten. This leaves us

[23] Note that Paul places the primary responsibility for harmony in the communities on the "strong" (14.15–21; 15.1).

[24] See J. Lionel North, "'Good Wordes and Faire Speeches' (Rom. 16.18 AV): More Materials and a Pauline Pun," *NTS* 42 (1996) 600–14.

[25] Rom. 1.8, 12; 6.17; 15.14; 16.19.

[26] Cf. Rom. 14.21.

[27] See the discussion below on Celsus' connection of "strength" of food to "strength" of the one consuming it.

wondering what sort of meals are at issue. On the basis of Paul's commands to the "weak" to desist from judging the "strong" (14.3b, 4, 10a), Rauer makes a case for understanding the difference in consumption to occur in everyday meals, and not just on special occasions, such as the churches' love feasts. He states that the love feast itself would not be scandalous to conservative church members, i.e., the "weak." He also thinks that the controversy came out in everyday meals because the disunity of the church had already become known to those outside of the church (14.16–17).[28] Paul's directions in 14.21, especially the last clause, seem to me to confirm Rauer's point. καλὸν τὸ μὴ φαγεῖν κρέα μηδὲ πιεῖν οἶνον μηδὲ ἐν ᾧ ὁ ἀδελφός σου προσκόπτει most likely fits controversies that arose in daily life.

βρῶμα/βρῶσις *(Rom. 14.15, 17, 20)*

βρῶμα is the same word used for "food" in Paul's discussion of the Corinthian controversy. It is there used in Paul's general formulations of principle (1 Cor. 8.8, 13), consistently with its meaning that is more general than the technical term εἰδωλόθυτα or the word κρέας. Elsewhere in the NT, βρῶμα occurs in Heb. 13.9 as evidence that its author knew of the past practices of the community's "weak."[29] The phrase ἀπέχεσθαι βρωμάτων of 1 Tim. 4.3 reflects an asceticism already entrenched in a community familiar to the author. βρῶμα therefore functions as a term for the general area of foodstuffs within which various restrictions could be imposed. It is an appropriate term for the discussion here in Romans because while it can mean "meat," it can also mean "food" in a general sense,[30] and we have seen that the text does leave open the identification of the divisive food to more than meat.

Used nearly synonymously with βρῶμα, βρῶσις carries an additional sense of "eating."[31] Like βρῶμα, it can be used in the context

---

[28] Rauer, *Die "Schwachen,"* 96–97. Barclay, "'Do We Undermine the Law?'" 291, similarly takes the meals to be when the church members "attempted to share common meals."

[29] For a helpful summary of interpretations of Heb. 13.9, see Gerd Theißen, *Untersuchungen zum Hebräerbrief* (SNT 2; Gütersloh: Gerd Mohn, 1969), 76 n. 2, who opts for reading βρῶμα as food from the altar of Judaism.

[30] See LSJ, s.v. "βρῶμα," I.

[31] See LSJ, s.v. "βρῶσις," II. J. Behm states what we would expect: both βρῶμα and βρῶσις are used literally in Romans 14 to refer to physical food and the physical act of eating ("βρῶμα, βρῶσις," *TDNT* I [1964] 643).

of: food offered to idols (1 Cor. 8.4); dietary laws within some form of religious asceticism (Col. 2.16); and perhaps in a criticism of the value placed on eating by a "strong" faction (Heb. 12.16). Its grammatical character as a verbally formed noun suits it for the phrase in 14.17 in a way that βρῶμα could not fulfill, for the slogan there refers to characteristic activities of people in the kingdom of God: "The kingdom of God is not eating and drinking, but righteousness and peace and joy in the Holy Spirit."

So far, Paul's commands to the Romans seem derived from a view of the community in which there is a group known as "strong" who eat meat, are not bothered by restrictions on food, and may eat in excess. The "weak" are vegetarians. They may be bothered by other habits of the "strong" besides those of diet, as 14.21 suggests. The communal disunity mirrored by these commands fits with commands elsewhere in the letter, as does the possibility that one group ate in excess, or gluttonously.

Paul's descriptions of drinking practices

πόσις *(Rom. 14.17)*

A general term for "drinking,"[32] πόσις in 14.17 may connote excess in wine drinking (verse 21). But the word need not carry this negative connotation, as its eucharistic usage in John 6.55 shows.[33] In the phrase βρῶσις καὶ πόσις as used in Col. 2.16, the word seems only to specify the consumption of beverages; beyond that it cannot be pushed in specificity.

οἶνος *(Rom. 14.21)*

Suggestions that πιεῖν οἶνον in 14.21 rhetorically balances the preceding φαγεῖν κρέα and does not refer to actual disagreement over wine consumption ignores the preceding context[34] and the high incidence of wine abstinence occurring with variously

---

[32] Like βρῶσις, this substantive can denote both a beverage one drinks and the act of drinking (LSJ, s.v. "πόσις," I; Bauer–Aland places the Rom. 14.17 usage in the "Akt des Trinkens" category).

[33] Joachim Jeremias, *The Eucharistic Words of Jesus* (trans. N. Perrin; Philadelphia: Fortress, 1977), 107–108.

[34] Cf. Cranfield, *Romans*, 725. See the preceding sections in this chapter on κώμοις καὶ μέθαις in 13.13 and πόσις in 14.17.

motivated instances of vegetarianism.[35] Rauer's contention that actual wine abstinence is excluded because the "weak" must have participated in the eucharist ignores second-century evidence for water being used alongside wine, presumably as an option instead of wine, in the eucharist at Rome. Though he cites Justin, he does not disprove the possibility that these references show that water was used in the eucharist at Rome.[36]

On an initial reading there are two specific possibilities why the ascetic "weak" might lose confidence in wine drinking. Wine was so uniformly used in libations to the gods at communal meals in the Hellenistic world[37] that it may have become stigmatized for the "weak" as a pagan part of communal meals.[38] Second, drinking wine was such a common event at dinners[39] that the ascetics within the Roman church may have been reacting against practices they perceived as gluttonous in order to purify themselves. These possible reasons, along with the general observation noted above that ideologies that prompt meat abstinence often systemically prompt wine abstinence as well, lead me to accept the reference to abstaining from wine as just as tied to the situation in Rome, in Paul's perspective, as his commands related to eating.

So far we have examined Paul's statements about "strong" and "weak" consumption habits. The "strong" ate all foods, perhaps in a gluttonous and partying attitude. The "weak" were vegetarians and also abstinent from wine. Paul's descriptions allow us to see that the "weak" practices highlighted in Romans 14 seem to be ascetic in nature.

[35] Rauer recognizes this association (*Die "Schwachen,"* 98–99), but cites no examples beyond Jewish-Christian abstinence from sacrificial meat and wine. The following texts may be cited as evidence: Philo, *Cont.* 37 (Therapeutae); Hegesippus *apud* Eusebius, *HE* 2.23.5 (James); Porphyry, *Abst.* 4.6–7 (Egyptian priests). Note that Noah's wine drinking and shameful drunkenness (Gen. 9.21–24) are placed after the divine extension of the human diet to meat (Gen. 9.3). On the neo-Pythagorean association between meat and wine abstinence, see J. Haußleiter, *Der Vegetarismus in der Antike* (RVV 24; Berlin: A. Töpelmann, 1935), 300–301, 309–10.

[36] See Justin, *1 Apol.* 65.5; 67.5; A. von Harnack, *Brod und Wasser, die eucharistischen Elemente bei Justin* (TU 7/2; Leipzig: J. C. Hinrichs, 1891), 134–37. Cf. Rauer, *Die "Schwachen,"* 99–100.

[37] Dennis E. Smith, "Social Obligation in the Context of Communal Meals: A Study of the Christian Meal in 1 Corinthians in Comparison with Graeco-Roman Communal Meals" (Th.D. dissertation, Harvard, 1980), 13–15.

[38] See Diodorus Siculus 4.3.

[39] Smith, "Social Obligation in the Context of Communal Meals," 17: "it is difficult to imagine a meal, especially a formal one, where no drinking at all was done."

Asceticism in the Roman community

The "weak" behaviors mentioned in the preceding paragraph exemplify a form of asceticism, since they are cases of self-chosen abstinence. This is the definition that Jan Bergman offers in his contribution to the *TRE* article on asceticism. After commenting that a generally acknowledged definition of "asceticism" doesn't exist, he states,

> Askese bedeutet jedoch immer irgendeine Form selbstge-
> wählter Enthaltsamkeit ... Die Abstinenz gilt in milderer
> Ausformung gewissen von der Umwelt akzeptierten Gen-
> üssen, in strengerer Form der gewöhnlichen Befriedigung
> natürlicher Leibesbedürfnisse, wobei der Körper harter
> Zucht und schweren Prüfungen unterworfen wird.

> Nevertheless, asceticism means some form of self-chosen
> continence ... Abstinence in its milder manifestation cer-
> tainly permits the accepted pleasures from the world; in its
> stronger form [it permits only] the usual satisfaction of
> natural bodily requirements, so that the body experiences a
> harder discipline and difficult tests.[40]

It is true that the manifestations of asceticism vary in different cultures and ages.[41] But since abstinence from meat or wine was not the norm in the Judaisms[42] or Christian churches[43] of the first

---

[40] My translation of Jan Bergman's definition of asceticism; s.v. "Askese I," *TRE* IV.196. Since my goal is to cast the net as widely as possible in ascertaining the possible forces that gave rise to the practices and attitudes of the Roman "weak," I've chosen to use this definition of asceticism over narrower ones that limit the abstinence to that which is religious or ethical in character, e.g., H. Strathmann, *Geschichte der frühchristlichen Askese bis zur Entstehung des Mönchtums im religionsgeschichtlichen Zusammenhange* (Leipzig: A. Deichert, 1914), I.10.

[41] Bergman observes that within societies under Muslim or Buddhist influence, it would not be correct to describe abstinence from alcohol as a form of asceticism (*TRE* IV.196). This explains his use of the phrase "selbstgewählter Enthaltsamkeit" in his definition.

[42] On the variety within Jewish dietary and commensal practices, see A. Segal, *The Other Judaisms of Late Antiquity* (BJS 127; Atlanta: Scholars, 1987), 175. On the variety within first-century Judaisms, see also J. Z. Smith, "Fences and Neighbors: Some Contours of Early Judaism," in *Imagining Religion* (Chicago: University of Chicago Press, 1982), 1–18.

[43] The controversy addressed in Rom. 14.1–15.13, and especially Paul's statement in 14.14, is evidence that meat and wine abstinence were not universally practiced in Christian churches of the early Empire.

century, and since meat was available in Rome at this time,[44] such abstinence may legitimately be considered a form of asceticism.

The use of asceticism as a concept through which to examine Rom. 14.1–15.13 will be limited to those instances of asceticism that parallel terms or practices found in Paul's directions to the Roman church. I do not pursue such side-issues as the use of the terms ἄσκησις and ἐγκράτεια in antiquity, since they are not used in the text.[45] Similarly, ascetic practices besides meat and wine abstinence are bypassed in order to focus on the evidence at hand.

If we take Rom. 14.1–15.13 as evidence for actual patterns of consumption and asceticism in Roman churches, does such behavior match what was going on in first-century Roman society in general? The best way to answer this question is to examine meat and wine abstinence in first-century Rome.

Abstinence from meat in first-century Rome

In first-century Rome, limitations on consumption of food and drink were present both in the area of popular culture (including manifestations of these values in popular descriptions and also sumptuary laws) and in the area of philosophical/religious ideology. In general, a comparison of the evidence in Rom. 14.1–15.13 with the motives for abstinence found in these areas makes it difficult to argue that the situation assumed in the passage or the positions described are only hypothetical.[46] Such abstinence was simply too common in first-century Roman society for one to conclude on the basis of 1 Cor. 8–10 that the "strong" and the "weak" in Romans did not exist.

Consumptive abstinence in the Roman legacy

The Romans idealized their ancestors as living and eating simply. Thus Athenaeus quotes Poseidonius on ancient Roman values:[47]

---

[44] See Corbier, "Ambiguous Status," 224, for the availability of meat to the lower population of Rome in the late Republic and early Empire.

[45] They do appear elsewhere in the NT. Cf. Acts 24.16 (ἀσκέω). For ἐγκράτεια, cf. Acts 24.25; Gal. 5.23; 2 Pet. 1.6bis. Its cognates also appear, ἐγκρατεύομαι (1 Cor. 7.9; 9.25) and ἐγκρατής (Titus 1.8).

[46] Cf. Karris, "Occasion," 65–84; Sampley, "The Weak and the Strong," 42, 48.

[47] Athenaeus, The Deipnosophists (trans. C. B. Gulick; LCL; London: William Heinemann, 1929), 6.274A. In the next paragraph Athenaeus specifically mentions utensils and foodstuffs (Deip. 6.274B): κεράμεα δὲ καὶ χαλκᾶ τὰ διακονήματα

πάτριος μὲν γὰρ ἦν αὐτοῖς, ὥς φησι Ποσειδώνιος, καρτερία καὶ λιτὴ δίαιτα καὶ τῶν ἄλλων τῶν ὑπὸ τὴν κτῆσιν ἀφελὴς καὶ ἀπερίεργος χρῆσις.

As Poseidonius says, their ancestral traits used to be rugged endurance, a frugal manner of life, a plain and simple use of material possessions in general.

To focus on diet, the elder Pliny testifies to the vegetarian diet as a part of ancient Roman life.

Pulte autem, non pane vixisse longo tempore Romanos manifestum, quoniam et pulmentaria hodieque dicuntur.

It is clear however that for a long time the Romans lived on pottage, not on bread, since even today foodstuffs are also called "pulmentaria."[48]

Past heroes of Rome's armies became models for moderate asceticism in the Empire.[49] Even outside of military life, this image of austerity in consumption remained for Scipio, whom Horace describes as engaged in play while his meal of herbs boiled.[50] Some of Rome's heroes were glorified partially because of their ascetic practices. Classes of society were also differentiated on what they were allowed to consume. Cato would not furnish meat to his slaves, though his policy can scarcely be taken as indicative of all slaveowners' practice.[51] The traditional value of moderation led to a focus on the personal habits of emperors in consumption. Suetonius describes Tiberius as one who imposed by example the value of frugality on the people; Caligula as a glutton and otherwise

κομίζομεν κὰν τούτοις βρωτὰ καὶ ποτὰ πάντων ἀπεριεργότατα ("The utensils which we bring are of earthenware or bronze, and in them are the simplest foods and drinks in the world").

[48] Pliny, *HN* (trans. H. Rackham) 18.83. Similarly Varro, *L.* 5.105 – "de victu antiquissima puls" ("Of foods the most ancient is puls 'porridge'"; trans. R. G. Kent; LCL; London: William Heinemann, 1938).

[49] Corbier ("Ambiguous Status," 242, citing *SHA, Hadrian* 10.2) mentions how Scipio and Metellus were consciously adopted by Hadrian as examples of how to ration armies efficiently. Military heroes were known for limiting the ways their troops could prepare meat (Appian, *Ib.* 85; Frontinus, *Strateg.* 4.1.2).

[50] Horace, *Sat.* 2.1.71–74. See also H. J. Mette, " '*Genus tenue*' und '*mensa tenuis*' bei Horaz," *MH* 18 (1961) 136–39.

[51] Cato, *Agr.* 56. Corbier's use of Juvenal, *Sat.* 11.80–81 as a counterexample (a slave's dream of tripe he had earlier eaten in a cookshop) omits a significant point in its context: Juvenal's point is that Republican senators were more moderate in consumption than slaves of his own day. Still, she is right in affirming that Cato should not be taken as the norm ("Ambiguous Status," 226–27).

extravagant in consumption; Claudius as known for drunkenness and excessive eating; Nero as extreme in all forms of consumption.[52] Still, the value of frugality showed itself even in Nero, for he outlawed the sale of all but the most simply cooked food in the cookshops,[53] an example of the way this cultural value surfaced in the legislation of Rome.

Cultural value of abstinence in law

The legal manifestation of the popular value on frugality and moderation in consumption came in the sumptuary laws. While most investigations of Rom. 14.1–15.13 make no mention of them,[54] the fact that Rome had laws specifically limiting the consumption of meat must be considered in investigating the habits of the "weak." The connection between the value as seen in culture and law is made by Aulus Gellius in a programmatic beginning to his section on the sumptuary laws:

> Parsimonia apud veteres Romanos et victus atque cenarum tenuitas non domestica solum observatione ac disciplina, sed publica quoque animadversione legumque complurium sanctionibus custodita est.

> Frugality among the early Romans, and moderation in food and entertainments were secured not only by observance and training at home, but also by public penalties and the inviolable provisions of numerous laws.[55]

With a rising standard of living, people began to eat more meat in the last two centuries of the Republic.[56] In order to lessen lavish

---

[52] Suetonius, *Tib.* 34; *Calig.* 11; 37.1; *Claud.* 5; 33.1; *Nero* 27.2–3; 42.2; 51. Dio Cassius 61.4.3–4 notes how Nero became progressively wilder in his partying and drinking habits.

[53] Suetonius, *Nero* 16.2–"interdictum ne quid in popinis cocti praeter legumina aut holera veniret, cum antea nullum non obsonii genus proponeretur" ("the sale of any kind of cooked viands in the taverns was forbidden, with the exception of pulse and vegetables, whereas before every sort of dainty was exposed for sale" [trans. Rolfe]).

[54] The one exception is Brunt, "Paul's Attitude," 228, where he mentions "anti-luxury" as a theme in the Hellenistic world related to food consumption.

[55] *The Attic Nights of Aulus Gellius* (trans. Rolfe) 2.24.1.

[56] This statement is not to indicate the very beginning of Rome's sumptuary laws. Pliny, *HN* 14.12, mentions a Roman king who prohibited wine libations on funeral pyres, an early precedent for the sumptuary laws of the later Republic and Empire.

outlays and curb competition in consumption by the rich,[57] various sumptuary laws[58] were passed. The laws dictated not only the number of participants at mealtime, but even the menu.[59] One example is the *lex Fannia*, a sumptuary law passed in 161 BCE, which Pliny mentions in the context of describing the background of hen fattening. He states that the contents of the law were for:

> ne quid volucre poneretur praeter unam gallinam, quae non esset altilis, quod deinde caput translatum per omnes leges ambulavit.

> prohibiting the serving of any bird course beside a single hen that had not been fattened – a provision that was subsequently renewed and went on through all our legislation.[60]

While the law did allow one unfattened hen, it is easy to see how Haußleiter can find a vegetarian tendency within this law.[61] The legal tradition shows how firmly diet was fixed in Romans' minds as a moral question, an issue of *mores*. There seems to be a form of popular asceticism at work within the Roman ethos.

At the time when Paul wrote Romans, the city was under an emperor who, like the two before him, imposed severe laws on consumption but was personally extravagant. Of Nero, Cassius Dio writes:

> πάντα δὲ ὡς εἰπεῖν τὸν βίον ἐν καπηλικῇ διαίτῃ ποιούμενος ἀπεῖπε τοῖς ἄλλοις μηδὲν ἐφθὸν ἐν καπηλείῳ, πλὴν λαχάνων καὶ ἔτνους, πιπράσκειν.

> And though he spent practically his whole existence amid

---

[57] These are the reasons that Corbier offers for the sumptuary laws ("Ambiguous Status," 240). Cf. Jack Goody's comments on the sumptuary laws as typifying "a resentment virtually inherent in the existence of a publicly differentiated cuisine" (*Cooking, Cuisine and Class*, 103).

[58] I list them here to demonstrate the intensity of the Roman state's drive to limit consumption: *lex Oppia* (215 BCE), *Orchia de cenis* (181 BCE), *Fannia cibaria* (161 BCE), *Didia* (143 BCE), *Licinia* (between 113 and 97 BCE), *Cornellia* (81 BCE), *Aemilia* (78 BCE), *leges Juliae* (46 BCE). This list is from Haußleiter, *Der Vegetarismus*, 389. Most of the laws in this list are also mentioned in Gel. 2.24.

[59] Haußleiter, *Der Vegetarismus*, 389.

[60] Pliny, *HN* 10.139.

[61] Haußleiter, *Der Vegetarismus*, 389.

tavern life, he forbade others to sell in taverns anything boiled save vegetables and pea-soup.[62]

Thus, of course, it was not illegal to eat meat in one's home, but the tavern keepers were forbidden to serve it. The ruling of Nero is illustrative of the traditional Roman view that meat consumption was unnecessary and therefore needed to be controlled.

From such evidence we see that meat consumption was not absolutely prohibited in Rome, but that it was an object of imperial attention and legal control at the time of Paul's letter. There is no evidence in Romans that the "weak" abstinence was motivated by law. But the sumptuary laws do show that meat was a controversial subject in circles beyond the Christian community of Rome.

Meat, of course, was controversial long before the sumptuary laws were passed. Corbier notes the junction of Roman and Greek values leading to vegetarianism: "This Roman hierarchy of habits and preferences intersected with a long tradition in Greek philosophy favoring a vegetarian diet."[63] It is clear that philosophers in first-century Rome were writing in ways consistent with Romans 14–15. We see this both in Celsus' distinction between "strong" and "weak" foods and people and in popular vegetarians of the time. That an ascetic mindset toward food penetrated into the first-century Roman church is also confirmed by isolated references in early Christian literature.

Cultural value of abstinence among intelligentsia

Celsus on "strong" and "weak" foods, beverages, and people

Aulus Cornelius Celsus, the first-century Roman encyclopedist, compiled his books *On Medicine* during the reign of Tiberius (14–37 CE). His work preserved Greek medical thought and made it accessible to his Roman readers.[64] Celsus' distinctions between foods' physical properties are significant for our understanding of a description of people as either "strong" or "weak" in Paul's letter to Rome. Celsus divides foods and beverages into three classes of strength, based on the nourishment a given food provides. His

---

[62] *Dio's Roman History* (trans. E. Cary; LCL; London: William Heinemann, 1925), 62.14.2.

[63] Corbier, "Ambiguous Status," 247.

[64] L. Edelstein, "Celsus (2)," *OCD*, 2nd ed., 218.

"strongest" class of food includes pulses, grain-based breads, and meat from domesticated cattle.[65] His "weakest" class includes vegetable stems, whatever grows on stems, and all fruit.[66] From this distinction he makes the medical inference that the class of food one consumes should correspond to one's "strength," though he does not offer criteria for diagnosing someone's level of "strength."

> Itaque utendum est materiae genere pro viribus, modusque omnium pro genere sumendus. Ergo inbecillis hominibus rebus infirmissimis opus est: mediocriter firmos media materia optime sustinet, et robustis apta validissima est.

> Thus the quality of the food administered should be in accordance with the patient's strength, and the quantity in accordance with its quality. For weak patients, therefore, there is needed the lightest food; food of the middle class best sustains those moderately strong, and for the robust the strongest is the fittest.[67]

In his classification of "strong" to "weak" foodstuffs, Celsus lists raisin wine, fermenting wine, sweet wine, and very old wine among the strongest type (*valentissimi generis*). Of intermediate strength are wines several years old or those of inferior quality.[68] Because of this classification of wine as a drink with varying degrees of potency, Celsus recommends wine abstinence when ill.[69] He thinks that water is the weakest of all beverages.[70] Celsus states that "stronger" foods, including various meats and wines, are for stronger people and are more difficult to digest, though they bring more nourishment once digested.[71]

Still, excess of meat consumption (implied by φαγεῖν πάντα in 14.2) would be objectionable on medical grounds, according to Celsus. Having placed meat from domesticated cattle in his "strong" category of foods,[72] he later comments:

---

[65] Celsus, *On Medicine* (trans. W. G. Spencer; LCL; London: William Heinemann, 1935), 2.18.2.

[66] Ibid., 2.18.3.   [67] Ibid., 2.18.13.

[68] Ibid., 2.18.11.   [69] Ibid., 3.2.6.

[70] Ibid., 2.18.11. By contrast, Galen states that white wine passes through the body faster than water (*Nat. Fac.* 3.214). This distinction between the medical writers rests on the assumption that "stronger" beverages would take longer to digest and contain more bile.

[71] Celsus, *On Medicine*, 2.18.13.

[72] Ibid., 2.18.2.

Plus deinde aliquis adsumere ex levioribus potest: magis in iis, quae valentissima sunt, temperare sibi debet.

Finally, of the lightest foods more can be taken; it is rather with the strongest food that moderation should be observed.[73]

I have wondered whether these uses of "strong" and "weak" in contemporary medical terminology are worth considering, when our text begins by differentiating "strong" and "weak" on the basis of faith (14.1–2). If the "weak" to whom Paul refers were weak simply in faith, then it would seem misguided to examine a medical idea of physical weakness from contemporary Rome.

I concede that Celsus' medical basis for restricting the consumption of certain foodstuffs does not clearly exemplify asceticism. Abstinence from meat on a physician's recommendation is different from self-chosen abstinence on religious or philosophical grounds. But the significance of these medical distinctions for our study is that whatever the motive for ascetic practices, the physiological results of such practices are inseparable from them. As soon as one makes distinctions in foodstuffs (even when a diet is observed for philosophical or spiritual reasons), physiological distinctions among those who consume them inevitably follow.[74] Also, though an elitist mentality is widely found among ascetics,[75] physical weakness does often accompany asceticism. Commentators who exclude physiological considerations from the terms "strong" and "weak" in Rom. 14.1–15.13 are therefore limiting their appreciation of asceticism in Rome and its reverberations in this letter. This connection between the spiritual/ideological continuum of strength and its physiological counterpart may explain why Paul describes the condition of humanity in terms that register on either continuum.[76] Also, Paul's explanation in 15.13 of the strength by which he wanted the community to grow (ἐν δυνάμει πνεύματος ἁγίου) might indicate that he considered it necessary to clarify what sort of strength ought to be valued in a community with some members valuing physical strength. Finally, since this distinction between

---

[73] Ibid., 2.18.13.
[74] See, e.g., Dan. 1.15–16; LXX Esther 4.17x; 5.1b (ET 14.17; 15.5). Note also that the terms οἱ δυνατοί and ἀδύνατοί are used without qualification in Rom. 15.1, allowing at least the possibility that there is more to the distinction than faith.
[75] W. O. Kaelber, "Asceticism," *ER* 1.441.
[76] See Rom. 5.6; 6.19; 7.24; 8.3, 23, 26. Cf. Dunn, *Romans*, 837.

"strong" and "weak" foods and people was made in Rome within thirty years of Paul's letter to the Romans, it cannot be ignored, and should be included in the netful of evidence we gather in order to hear how this letter sounded when it was read in Rome. So, though Celsus on "strong" and "weak" foods does not exemplify asceticism, he considers it medically sound for certain types of people to abstain from certain types of food. This datum of medical science would have been in at least some of the Roman believers' minds as they participated in a community divided over consumption.

Famous vegetarians in first-century Rome

While a medical distinction between "strong" and "weak" foods and those who consume them had been made in Rome not long before Paul's letter, we also know that various forms of asceticism that included abstinence from meat were advocated in Rome before, during, and after the time that Paul wrote Romans.

Seneca and his teachers

The Stoic philosopher Attalus encouraged Seneca to be moderate in his consumption, causing Seneca to abstain from oysters, mushrooms, and wine.[77] Seneca mentions two other teachers in Rome who were clearly vegetarians, the philosophers Sotion and Quintus Sextius.[78] His testimony on vegetarianism is worth our attention, because his reasons for adopting and abandoning vegetarianism inform us about the philosophical and social dynamics of vegetarianism in first-century Rome.

Seneca describes how as a youth he was attracted to vegetarianism by his teacher Sotion, who passed on the health and moderation arguments for vegetarianism of Sextius, as well as the transmigration of souls argument of Pythagoras. He describes how he was a vegetarian for about one year, and felt more alert in his mind because of it. He abandoned the practice because he did not want to be associated with foreign religious practices that included

[77] Seneca, *Ep.* 108.13–16. This letter was already noted as a parallel for Rom. 14.2 by J. J. Wettstein, *Novum Testamentum Graecum* (1752; reprint ed., Graz: Akademischer Druck- und Verlaganstalt, 1962), 2.87.

[78] Seneca, *Ep.* 108.17–18, 20–21. See W. D. Ross, "Sextius (2), Quintus," and W. D. Ross, "Sotion (2)," *OCD*, 2nd ed., 983, 1005.

vegetarianism, which were beginning to be seen in Rome at this time, early in Tiberius' reign.[79]

Seneca's testimony shows us that in the Rome of Tiberius, not long before Paul wrote his letter, there were a couple of reasons that made vegetarianism appear preferable for educated people. We also see a clear link between vegetarianism and foreign religion in Rome, at least in popular consciousness. This is certainly a piece of evidence to consider in the identification of the "weak" group of vegetarians in the Roman church.

Musonius Rufus

The Stoic philosopher Musonius Rufus, also teaching in Rome in the first century, advocated vegetarianism. His influence during the early reign of Nero coincides with the time when Paul wrote Romans.[80]

Περὶ δὲ τροφῆς εἰώθει μὲν πολλάκις λέγειν καὶ πάνυ ἐντεταμένως ὡς οὐ περὶ μικροῦ πράγματος οὐδ' εἰς μικρὰ διαφέροντος: ᾤετο γὰρ ἀρχὴν καὶ ὑποβολὴν τοῦ σωφρονεῖν εἶναι τὴν σίτοις καὶ ποτοῖς ἐγκράτειαν ... τὴν μέντοι κρεώδη τροφὴν θηριωδεστέραν ἀπέφηνε καὶ τοῖς ἀγρίοις ζῴοις προσφορωτέραν. εἶναι δὲ ταύτην ἔλεγε καὶ βαρυτέραν καὶ τῷ νοεῖν τι καὶ φρονεῖν ἐμπόδιον· τὴν γὰρ ἀναθυμίασιν τὴν ἀπ' αὐτῆς θολωδεστέραν οὖσαν ἐπισκοτεῖν τῇ ψυχῇ.

On the subject of food he used to speak frequently and very emphatically too, as a question of no small significance, nor leading to unimportant consequences; indeed he believed that the beginning and foundation of temperance lay in self-control in eating and drinking ... he showed that meat was a less civilized kind of food and more appropriate for wild animals. He held that it was a heavy food (βαρυτέραν) and an obstacle to thinking and reasoning,

---

[79] Seneca, *Ep.* 108.17–22. See also Tacitus, *Ann.* 15.45 for confirmation of Seneca's short-lived abstinence.

[80] Περὶ τροφῆς, 18A, trans. Cora E. Lutz, "Musonius Rufus: 'The Roman Socrates,'" *YCS* 10 (1947) 113. In her introduction, Lutz states that Musonius Rufus "was at the height of his influence in the time of Nero" (14). Musonius was teaching in Rome at least until he followed Rubellius Plautus into exile *ca.* 60 CE (W. D. Ross, "Musonius Rufus," *OCD*, 2nd ed., 713).

since the exhalations rising from it being turbid darkened the soul.

Since there are ample examples of vegetarianism in Rome and known reasons for such asceticism, it is only responsible historiography to consider Romans 14–15 as probably reflective of an actual controversy over food that included vegetarianism as a point of disagreement. Since vegetarianism was popular in Rome, it probably had some adherents within Roman Christianity. But do we have clues regarding this Christianity outside of Romans 14–15 that point us in this direction? Evidence for Christian asceticism, including vegetarianism, may be gleaned from literature and accounts associated with early Roman Christianity.

Evidence from early Christian literature

Romans

Evidence for asceticism in the Roman church may first be found in Paul's letter itself. The term ἁγιασμός, which might give evidence of ascetic concerns, does occur earlier in Romans.[81] Romans 6 includes a description of the mind/body dualism that abstinence as a means of spiritual purity assumes. There is a mind/body dualism found elsewhere in Romans that may indicate that this viewpoint, characteristic of some ascetics, was operative among some in Paul's audience.[82] When one considers this dualism in relation to the description of those who abstain from meat (14.2, 21) and probably wine (14.21), an ascetic tendency based on dualism in the Roman church of the mid fifties seems possible.[83]

Hebrews

The NT letter called Hebrews contains evidence that its author and addressees alike valued asceticism. The description of past heroes'

---

[81] Rom. 6.19, 22. Its only other uses in Paul's uncontested letters are 1 Cor. 1.30; 1 Thess. 4.3, 4, 7. Cf. 2 Thess. 2.13; 1 Tim. 2.15; Heb. 12.14. καθαρός occurs at Rom. 14.20; then in the Pauline corpus broadly conceived: 1 Tim. 1.5; 3.9; 2 Tim. 1.3; 2.22; Titus 1.15.

[82] Rom. 1.24; 6.19; 7.23–24; 12.1–2. Jewett, *Anthropological Terms*, 400, notes how the language in Rom. 7.7–25 is unique in Paul. His suggestion of gnostic influence is difficult to prove.

[83] See the discussion below in chapter 6 on the motive of mystical purity for vegetarianism, which is based on anthropological dualism.

lifestyles in Heb. 11.37–38 and the command which occurs at Heb. 13.3[84] point to an ascetic consciousness, as does the strong purity language of Heb. 10.10; 12.10, 14; 13.4, 12–13. The enigmatic statement καλὸν γὰρ χάριτι βεβαιοῦσθαι τὴν καρδίαν, οὐ βρώμασιν ἐν οἷς οὐκ ὠφελήθησαν οἱ περιπατοῦντες of Heb. 13.9 may refer to vegetarian practice within the community.

I regard these texts in Hebrews to be worth consideration, because it is likely that the NT letter known as Hebrews was sent either to or from Rome.[85] Reference to an earthly city that does not last (Heb. 13.14) in contrast to a heavenly city (Heb. 11.10, 16; 12.22) fits best with a Roman address, since the city's reputation for permanence was impressed on Roman citizens' minds by the standard designation for the year – AUC (*ab urbe condita*). The greeting from "those from Italy" (13.24) also fits with a Roman destination. The parallels between Romans and Hebrews that may arise from the identity of the city addressed support Rome as this city.[86] Literary dependence that *1 Clement* has on Hebrews also argues for the latter's Roman destination.[87] The evidence of asceticism in the background of this letter that was noted in the preceding paragraph thus helps to confirm my argument in this chapter that the believing community in Rome was engaged in asceticism.

1 Clement

1 Clem. 20.4 reflects a vegetarian viewpoint, since it regards food from the earth as sufficient for all humans and animals, in accordance with God's decree:

γῆ κυοφοροῦσα κατὰ τὸ θέλημα αὐτοῦ τοῖς ἰδίοις καιροῖς τὴν πανπληθῆ ἀνθρώποις τε καὶ θηρσὶν καὶ πᾶσιν τοῖς οὖσιν ἐπ' αὐτῆς ζώοις ἀνατέλλει τροφήν, μὴ

---

[84] Μιμνήσκεσθε . . . τῶν κακουχουμένων ὡς καὶ αὐτοὶ ὄντες ἐν σώματι.

[85] Harold W. Attridge, *The Epistle to the Hebrews: A Commentary* (Hermeneia, Philadelphia: Fortress, 1989), 10, opts for a Roman address; Barnabas Lindars only identifies it as a major city in the diaspora ("The Rhetorical Structure of Hebrews," *NTS* 35 (1989) 403.

[86] Rom. 8.3 with Heb. 7.18; Rom. 5.6, 6.19, 8.26 with Heb. 4.15, 5.2, 7.28; Rom. 13.12 with Heb. 10.25c; Rom. 14.5b with Heb. 10.25b; Rom. 15.33 with Heb. 13.20.

[87] *1 Clem.* 9.3–4 on Heb. 11.5, 7; *1 Clem.* 12.1 on Heb. 11.31; *1 Clem.* 17.1 on Heb. 11.37; *1 Clem.* 17.5 on Heb. 3.2; *1 Clem.* 19.1–3 on Heb. 12.1–3; *1 Clem.* 27.2 on Heb. 6.18; *1 Clem.* 36.1–5 on Heb. 1.3–7, 13, 2.18, 3.1.

διχοστατοῦσα μηδὲ ἀλλοιοῦσά τι τῶν δεδογματισμένων ὑπ' αὐτοῦ.

The earth, bearing fruit in the proper seasons in fulfillment of his will, brings forth food in full abundance for both men and beasts and all living things which are upon it, without dissension or altering anything he has decreed.[88]

One wonders whether a strand of asceticism existed at Rome when one also reads,

Μιμηταὶ γενώμεθα κἀκείνων, οἵτινες ἐν δέρμασιν αἰγείοις καὶ μηλωταῖς περιεπάτησαν κηρύσσοντες τὴν ἔλευσιν τοῦ Χριστοῦ.

Let us be imitators also of those who went about "in goatskins and sheepskins," preaching the coming of Christ.[89]

It is worth while to consider what was involved in ascetic expressions in Rome contemporary to the composition of Rom. 14.1–15.13 when investigating the practices and attitudes described in that text.[90]

My suggestion that asceticism existed within Paul's audience is nothing new, since G. La Piana made the same observation earlier this century.[91] I hope that my survey of relevant texts has added new evidence for his claim. We have seen that there were cultural and political reasons to abstain from meat in first-century Rome. Famous teachers also advocated vegetarianism for philosophical reasons. Evidence that we have of first-century Roman Christianity does indicate that an ascetic element was present within the church. I think it likely that this ascetic tendency continued on into the second century, when Tatian adopted, in Rome, an asceticism that included abstinence from meat and wine.[92] It seems to be the more

---

[88] *The Apostolic Fathers: Greek Texts and English Translations of Their Writings* (eds./trans. J. B. Lightfoot and J. R. Harmer, 2nd ed., M. W. Holmes; Grand Rapids: Baker, 1992). This and all following English translations from *1 Clement* are from this edition.

[89] *1 Clem.* 17.1. The description of clothing comes from Heb. 11.37.

[90] Cf. Karris, "Occasion," 69–70. Further discussion on the relationship between Rom. 14.1–15.13 and the historical situation in Rome can be found in chapter 2 above.

[91] "La primitiva communità cristiana di Roma e l'epistola ai Romani," *Ricerche Religiose* 1 (1925) 211.

[92] Jerome, *Adv. Jov.* 1.3; Jerome, *Comm. in Amos.*

historically responsible option to take the statements of Paul in Romans 14–15 as reflective of actual ascetic practices, i.e., vegetarianism and wine abstinence, that were occurring in the church.

The ascetic practices under consideration would also account for the language in Romans that seems reflective of asceticism highlighted by others' excess in consumption, an asceticism that seems to partake of a mind/body dualism.[93] Most students of this letter today are ready to say that Romans is an occasional letter, but all they mean by this is that there is a real occasion behind 1.1–15 and 13.1–16.23. I suggest that if our best research indicates that Romans is an occasional letter, then we need to read the whole letter as such.

It remains for us to examine the motivation of such consumptive asceticism. This will then allow us to bring the "weak" church members among Paul's audience, and his letter itself, into clearer focus.

[93] See notes 76 and 82 in this chapter.

5

PAUL'S CLUES FOR IDENTIFYING THE ABSTINENCE OF THE "WEAK"

ἐν συμποσίῳ οἴνου μὴ ἐλέγξῃς τὸν πλησίον
καὶ μὴ ἐξουθενήσῃς αὐτὸν ἐν εὐφροσύνῃ αὐτοῦ.

Sirach 31.31

During a wine party, do not reprove your neighbor and do
not despise him in his mirth.

A look at the asceticism of first-century Rome shows us that there
were many reasons for its residents to follow abstinent lifestyles.
The direction in which the comparisons point is that while there
must have been Jewish Christians among the "weak," one cannot
say that Jewish purity concerns formed the exclusive background to
the abstinence practiced there.

Is Paul oblique in Rom. 14.1–15.13?

It must be emphasized at the outset of this section that Paul's
purpose in Rom. 14.1–15.13 is not to provide a complete description of the situation in the Roman church. And as Paul characteristically does not name his opponents,[1] so here he does not fully
explicate arguments of the differing parties in Rome.

Sampley has noted the incomplete description and stated that
Paul is intentionally "oblique" in describing the groups at odds
with each other in Rome. Sampley begins by asserting that Paul has
generalized the issue of *kashrut* to the neutral issue of vegetarianism, and the issue of Sabbath to the more neutral issue of
observing one day as special. A corollary of the oblique approach
that Sampley sees in Paul is his idea that Paul does not register any

---

[1] Morton Smith, "Paul's Arguments as Evidence of the Christianity from which
he Diverged," in *Christians among Jews and Gentiles* (K. Stendahl Festschrift; eds.
G. W. E. Nickelsburg and G. W. MacRae; Philadelphia: Fortress, 1986), 254–55.

"direct hits" with his Roman audience.[2] This evaluation of Rom. 14.1–15.13 as oblique, now followed by others,[3] is worth careful examination before we accept it. I am not sure that it accurately reflects what Paul is doing, or that the rhetorical model behind it is exegetically helpful.

There are three characteristics of the text that lead some to evaluate it as "oblique." First, nicknames: instead of a description like "household of Aristobulus that is concerned to keep Jewish dietary laws" we read simply "weak in faith" (14.1) or "weak" (14.2; 15.1).[4] Instead of "freedmen of the house of Narcissus who have no concerns about their consumption," we have "the one who has faith" (14.2) and "the strong" (15.1).[5] Second, Paul omits information we might want, for example, the precise motivation behind the abstinence of the "weak" or the observance of days. And third, Paul does speak somewhat generally; for example, the phrase μηδὲ ἐν ᾧ ὁ ἀδελφός σου προσκόπτει in 14.21c has a wide scope. At least the first two of these characteristics are more effectively explained by linking them to the occasion of Paul's letter, rather than to an oblique reference.

The surveys I have made in chapters 3 and 4 above have convinced me that the burden of proof has to be on those who think that Paul has invented the nicknames, and who think that "tee totaling vegetarians are not a reality among Roman believers."[6] The manner in which these nicknames are used does not arise out of a concern to be oblique or general, but to establish rapport by using terms already in use by the Roman believers.[7]

What we perceive as missing information must arise from shared information that is assumed between the letter writer and his audience. In a letter such as Romans that is designed to make a

---

[2] Sampley, "The Weak and the Strong," 42, 45.

[3] H. Gamble, Jr., *The Textual History of the Letter to the Romans* (SD 42; Grand Rapids: Eerdmans, 1977), 136, seems to be the first to have suggested that Romans has "an obliqueness of approach" instead of a "generality of content." Sampley, "The Weak and the Strong," has given it new life, and now J. L. Jaquette, *Discerning What Counts: The Function of the Adiaphora Topos in Paul's Letters* (SBLDS 146; Atlanta: Scholars, 1995), 133–35; Walters, *Ethnic Issues*, 86–89; and Barclay, "'Do We Undermine the Law?,'" 289, entertain the idea.

[4] The terms for "weak" are different: ὁ ἀσθενῶν τῇ πίστει in 14.1; ὁ ἀσθενῶν in 14.2; οἱ ἀδύνατοί in 15.1.

[5] The terms are ὃς πιστεύει in 14.2; οἱ δυνατοί in 15.1.

[6] Sampley, "The Weak and the Strong," 46.

[7] See discussion in chapter 3 on nicknames in correspondence.

favorable impression, the risks are too high for Paul to leave out information about the "weak" and "strong," unless both sides are clear about these references.[8]

The generalized cast to some of the material in this section is the one characteristic that could lead us to think that Paul is intentionally being oblique as he writes. If he is not being oblique, there must be some reason for him to be general in his approach, perhaps because there was more than one reason that prompted Roman believers to differ on consumption and day observance. The balance tips for me toward the latter when I consider the apology that comes at Rom. 15.14–16, following closely on the "strong" and "weak" section.[9] This apology suggests that Paul knew that his readers would recognize the people and practices he describes in 14.1–15.6. Paul does score direct hits in this section.[10] Apologies do not necessarily occur after oblique references, since the whole point of an oblique reference is to avoid close identification and the need for apology. If the description of "strong" and "weak" is oblique, it is oblique to us, but it is clearly not an oblique reference in its function in the letter. A helpful analogy may be Alan Greenspan's speech on December 5, 1996. In it he referred to "irrational exuberance," a phrase that seems quite oblique to most of us who do not understand the US stock market. But to those whom he was addressing, it was a clear signal. The markets immediately responded, and Greenspan's direct message was recognized and criticized as meddling.[11] So, Paul's description may seem general or oblique to us, but it was not so for his readers, since Paul needed to apologize. Indeed there are two reasons why the description of the situation seems general to us.

First, it is a general description because, as we have seen in the last chapter, there were many reasons for abstaining from meat in first-century Rome.[12] But this is different from saying that it is

---

[8] See 1 Cor. 7.26, where Paul's ἡ ἐνεστῶσα ἀνάγκη, while incomplete or oblique to us, is clearly not so for his Corinthian audience.

[9] On the status of these verses as an apology, see Cranfield, *Romans*, 753, Fitzmyer, *Romans*, 710–11, and Moo, *Romans*, 887–89, and discussion at end of chapter 10 on Stowers's take on these verses.

[10] Cf. Sampley, "The Weak and the Strong," 45; Rom. 14.4, 10, 15; 15.1 make perfect sense as direct hits.

[11] D. P. Goldman, "The Fed Giveth, the Fed Taketh Away," *Forbes* (December 30, 1996) 172; D. Foust, "Why Greenspan Should Keep Mum about the Market," *Business Week* (December 23, 1996) 35.

[12] Note that even Seneca, in describing his own experience, does not offer a single reason why he was abstaining from meat, *Ep.* 108.

oblique, especially since it is likely that Paul is using the Romans' own labels for the divided groups. Second, Lagrange's response to Sanday and Headlam, who see nothing in Rom. 14.1–15.13 on food consumption or day observance as referring to an actual situation in Rome,[13] seems just as appropriate for Gamble and Sampley's "oblique" label. Lagrange responds that for Paul, the issue is not what is happening in food consumption: the real issues are the doubting consciences of some church members, and the obligations owed to the scrupulous.[14] Paul's focus thus explains why we are missing information about the "weak" and "strong" behavior in the text. Lagrange's response has the advantage of fitting well with Rom. 14.14–21, which repeats the point that the real issue is not food consumption, but the spiritual equilibrium of other believers.

Gamble's idea that Paul is oblique because he has not visited there or exercised his authority there, nor have the Roman communities acknowledged his authority, is what Sampley has developed in his essay, by adding the rhetorical model that Paul steers a middle course between flattery and direct speech.[15] An unacknowledged weakness of this model is that the terms "frank speech" and "adverse criticism" are used to designate the same pole of the continuum.[16] Sampley has accurately noted that Paul does not address the Romans as he has addressed the Corinthians and the Galatians.[17] I wonder if a direct–oblique continuum has been conflated with an adversely critical–positively critical continuum. At least we can say that it is simplistic to read Romans only within the "figured speech" option of Demetrius' model. Paul evaluates his letter as being written τολμηρότερον in 15.15, which Sampley dismisses as reflective of "any intervention" Paul would make among the Roman believers,[18] and Paul uses some flattery in the letter as well.[19] Might the direct–oblique–flattering rhetorical

---

[13] Sanday and Headlam, *Romans*, 385, 401.

[14] Lagrange, *Romains*, 340, followed and expanded upon by Huby, *Romains*, 453–54.

[15] Gamble, *Textual History*, 136; Sampley, "The Weak and the Strong," 43–46.

[16] Sampley, "The Weak and the Strong," 44.

[17] Ibid., 44, 52.

[18] Ibid., 44. The concern for one's ethos that is found when one is using bold speech, which Sampley finds in 2 Cor. 1–7 (ibid., 43 n. 12), can also be found in Rom. 1.9–17; 3.1–2, 8; 6.1–2; 9.1–5; 15.15–32; 16.7c, 13b.

[19] Rom. 1.12; 6.17; 15.14. Sampley dismisses the first and last of these as being far from Plutarch's sense of flattery.

model, applied in an either–or way for the letter, be obscuring our sense of what is happening in the text?

I hope that we who read Romans can continue to proceed carefully in our use of the "oblique" label. There is clearly a sense that Paul leaves out information and is more general about the situation in Rome than we might wish. But his approach is not generalized so as to include groups different from those in Rome. (Why then the apology in 15.14–16?) Paul's approach is more easily explained as arising within a relationship in which he knew much more about the Romans than we do, including the variety of motives for abstaining from meat and observing days. Paul's desire to effect change among the Roman believers (1.11, 13), as well as his apology at 15.14–16, needs to be given due consideration. He is more direct than we think, because he and his first readers share information we lack. By inference from what Paul affirms and denies in the context of his argument, we can describe the attitudes of "strong" or "weak."[20]

Terminology of religious and social attitudes

ὁ ἐσθίων τὸν μὴ ἐσθίοντα μὴ ἐξουθενείτω (Rom. 14.3a)

The verb for "despise," ἐξουθενέω, denotes the social response of scorn that Paul prohibits the "strong" from showing toward the "weak."[21] It is used positively for the objects of God's call in 1 Cor. 1.28.[22] There Paul states that God has chosen the despised things of the world; human caricatures mean nothing before the inexorable call of God.

Other instances of the term in the Pauline corpus highlight its significance here. Its usage alongside ἀσθενής in 2 Cor. 10.10 shows us that as the "weak" of Rome experienced scorn from

[20] For a general introduction to the challenge of understanding the ideas of Paul and his audiences and opponents on the basis of the letters extant to us, see Morna Hooker, *A Preface to Paul* (New York: Oxford University Press, 1980), 7–20.

[21] See LSJ, s.v. "ἐξουδενόω"; Bauer–Aland, s.v. "ἐξουθενέω," 1. On the different spellings of the word and the possible distinction in meaning they imply, see BDF §33; §108(2). For our purposes the verb was used for "scorn" or "despise."

[22] καὶ τὰ ἐξουθενημένα ἐξελέξατο ὁ θεός.

[23] The link between weakness and being despised is also made in LXX Ps. 57.7. Cf. also LXX Ps. 59.14.

[24] See H. D. Betz, *Der Apostel Paulus und die sokratische Tradition: Eine exegetische Untersuchung zu seiner "Apologie" 2 Korinther 10–13* (BHT 45; Tübingen: J. C. B. Mohr [Paul Siebeck], 1972), 57.

others, so did Paul.[23] Its function there allows us to see that the word carries the sense of preconceived rejection.[24] Paul's use of the word in Gal. 4.14 shows that it designates an expected response to physical weakness.[25] This fits with what we would expect if the ascetic "weak" were viewed actually as physically weaker, a caricature that was likely held by the "strong."

The use of ἐξουθενέω as an expected response to something "weak" is illustrated by an important parallel, LXX Zech. 4.10–διότι τίς ἐξουδένωσεν εἰς ἡμέρας μικράς; ("For who has despised the day of small things?") In addition, we see it used with boasting in LXX Judg. 9.38 in the context of a scorn of other people expressed while drinking wine and feasting at a cultic meal (9.27). While it is impossible to locate precisely the origin of the scorn in the Roman community,[26] these parallels show us that the term fits the attitude of the "strong" toward the ascetic "weak" in Rome.

I cannot bypass a significant door into the whole letter of Romans that the prohibitions against despising in Rom. 14.3, 10 open. These prohibitions participate in the topos of "unashamed" statements that form the structural undergirding for the whole letter.[27] The link between shame and scorn can be seen in LXX Ps. 52.6c, a verse following those that Paul quotes in Rom. 3.11–12: κατῃσχύνθησαν, ὅτι ὁ θεὸς ἐξουδένωσεν αὐτούς.[28] The same link can be seen in LXX Ps. 30.18–19. In Rom. 5.5, Paul writes ἡ δὲ ἐλπὶς οὐ καταισχύνει, based on LXX Ps. 21.5–6 (ET Ps. 22.4–5). In this same psalm we read that God has not despised the prayer of the poor, presumably the same persona who has not been shamed earlier in the psalm: οὐκ ἐξουδένωσεν οὐδὲ προσώχθισεν τῇ δεήσει τοῦ πτωχοῦ.[29] The "unashamed" topos in Romans, which is clearly imported directly from Paul's scriptures,[30] must be broadened to include the closely related idea of not being scorned.

In Romans 14 we see that Paul considers it wrong to despise, or

[25] See Betz, *Galatians*, 225.

[26] It could have arisen simply out of perceived superiority to the ascetic lifestyle and apparent superstition of the "weak." On the other hand, some of the "strong" may have scorned the "weak" out of guilt from their perception of deeper religiosity on the part of the "weak."

[27] Rom. 1.16–17; 3.8; 5.5; 9.33; 10.11; 12.17; 14.16; 15.30–33. See discussion in the final chapter below.

[28] ἐξουδενόω is simply another spelling of ἐξουθενέω. See LSJ, s.v. "ἐξουθενέω."

[29] LXX Ps. 21.25a.

[30] See Hays, *Echoes*, 38–39. In addition to the texts Hays cites, see LXX Ps. 30.2.

shame, the "weak." This is because God has accepted this one
(14.3) and because this one will have to stand before divine
judgment (14.10), proving a human verdict of scorn to have been
mistaken or superfluous. Paul has already told us that he is not
ashamed of his gospel, because it contains God's power for salvation, another way of describing the divine acceptance seen at 14.3.
Also, the human's stance before a future, divine judgment is cited
by Paul as an integral part of his gospel as early as 2.16. There the
judgment functions as a discouragement to those who would judge.
The judgment aspect of Paul's gospel functions to discourage both
judgment and scorning in Rom. 14.10–12. So the prohibition
against scorning, or shaming, the "weak" is not an isolated part of
the practical teaching in Romans. Rather, because these "weak"
participate in Paul's gospel, they are not to be shamed, since Paul's
gospel is not shameful. The prohibitions are therefore integral parts
of the significant "unashamed" topos of Romans.

ὁ δὲ μὴ ἐσθίων τὸν ἐσθίοντα μὴ κρινέτω (Rom. 14.3b)

Most of the uses Paul makes of the verb κρίνω (verses 3, 4, 10, 13)
indicate that he was convinced that a judgmental attitude was
present within the community. The question in 14.10 assumes that
the attitudes denoted by κρίνω and ἐξουθενέω existed in the
Roman church. The adverb μηκέτι used along with the hortatory
subjunctive against judging in 14.13 also marks Paul's impression
that judging had been occurring in the community for a length of
time. κρίνω in 14.5 does not, of course, refer to the social attitude
of judgment. Here it is an act of cultic distinction, in which certain
days are regarded as religiously significant (verse 5a) or all days are
held as equally significant (verse 5b).

The disapproval connoted by the term κρίνω designates a rejection that the "weak" made of the behavior of the "strong" and a
resultant ruling by the "weak" on the eschatological status of the
"strong." This is evident in the way Paul argues against the
judgment occurring in the community. The differences in eating
and observing days form the basis of the judgment (14.2–3, 5–6).
In this sense the judgment was a rejection of the patterns of
behavior in the daily life of the community.

At the same time, this judgment also included a negative ruling
on the eschatological position of the "strong." Paul uses the future
passive σταθήσεται in 14.4 to show that God will finally establish

the "strong" party. The sense is that the identity of those who are actually "strong" will be established only at the last judgment.

Aside from the references to living, dying, and the final judgment (14.7–12), the description of the acceptance that God (14.3) and Christ (15.7) have given to members of the community also points to these members' disagreement on the eschatological significance of the divisive behavior. The portrait of Christ in his eschatological role (of uniting the Jews with the nations) as the object of hope[31] also fits with an eschatological interpretation of the judgment exercised by the "weak." The significance of this eschatological perspective in the judgment performed by the "weak" in considerations of the motive for their abstinence is not found in other discussions of their ideological or religious background.

When one compares a positive usage of the action of "judging" in the Hebrew Bible to the social attitude of the "weak" in Rom. 14.1–15.13, an ironic use of the term is evident. This is because judgment in its positive sense is something that is commanded to be exercised on behalf of the poor, or those who would in social categories be called "weak," in the Hebrew Bible.[32] Writing on the OT background to κρίνω, V. Herntrich comments,

> Yahweh's *mišpaṭ* is thus for an afflicted people. But this relationship of judgment to the needy and oppressed is something which can be seen from the very first, since it is materially implicit that the Judge should execute justice for those who have no rights.[33]

We should expect in the LXX usage of the term that those with social status (in the case of the Roman community, the "strong") would "judge" the "weak." Perhaps this thought is included behind Paul's statement at 15.1–ὀφείλομεν δὲ ἡμεῖς οἱ δυνατοὶ τὰ ἀσθενήματα τῶν ἀδυνάτων βαστάζειν.

κρίνω in our text is used predominantly in a negative sense.[34] It is probably intentional that the descriptions of divine judgment (14.12; 15.12) which highlight the positive function of judgment do not employ the term κρίνω. Since Paul plays on the word by using

[31] Rom. 15.9–12.
[32] V. Herntrich, "κρίνω," *TDNT* III (1965) 929–31. In addition to the texts cited there, see also Prov. 31.5b for another formulation of the same concept, using the noun *dîn*.
[33] Ibid., 929.
[34] See LSJ, s.v. "κρίνω," III:1, 2; see also BDB, s.v. "*šāpaṭ*," 3.c (2).

both negative and positive meanings in the same sentence (14.13), it is best if we affirm that the term carries its negative function when applied to the "weak," but still holds an ironic echo, because of its positive use in 14.13b.

The specific attitude of judgment highlights a characteristic of the foundational attitude the "weak" held toward food. Since the "weak" judgment extended to others not of their persuasion, we see that their general attitude to food and consumption was comprehensive in scope. It was not as if the "weak" felt that they were exercising one of several legitimate options; they felt that their position applied to the entire community. This point will be significant in considerations of the ideological background of the "weak" below.

The attitude of judgment held by the "weak" seems to fit with an ascetic mentality. The "weak" needed the "strong" to provide a justifying contrast to their asceticism, and it was then a short step from this comparison to a judgmental attitude. Such an attitude of social superiority is endemic to asceticism,[35] arising partially from the social tendency to defend one's practices when they differ so obviously from others'. But though judging from an assumed position of superiority, the ascetics were still the "weak," and their attitude can be called "weak," for they were influenced by the "strong." Aside from doubt within themselves (14.23), we see that they could be moved to offense (14.13, 20) and grief (14.15)[36] by the behavior of the "strong."

The prohibitions against judging in Romans 14 sound as a reprise to the main point of the diatribe in Romans 2. The judgment of God that removes any prerogative for human judgment of others is found in both Rom. 2.1–16 and 14.1–12.[37] One difference in these arguments against judgment, however, is that the inherent hypocrisy at work in human judgment is mentioned only in Rom. 2.1–3, 21–23. The κριν- words that are found throughout Romans 14[38] show us that this section is all about judgment: believers

---

[35] See, e.g., Philo, *Cont.* 40–60. This section is a lengthy description of the excesses of Hellenistic banquets and functions literarily as a foil for Philo's accounts of the Therapeutae that occur before and after this section.

[36] These attitudes are covered in chapter 9 below.

[37] Meeks, "Judgment and the Brother," 296–97.

[38] Bradley, "Origins of the Hortatory Materials," 159, 163 and Heil, *Die Ablehnung der Speisegebote*, 247, effectively present the recurrence of κριν- words in this section.

should not judge other believers (14.3, 10); believers should live in the light of God's judgment (14.10–12); believers should judge not to offend others (14.13); believers should not live so that they judge their own actions (14.23). Sampley is certainly right that 1.18–4.25 is not simply an "enunciation of doctrines of sin, grace, and faith for the sake for doctrinal clarity." It is clear that Romans 2, within this section, shows the common ground that believers in Rome share with one another, as Sampley argues.[39] Romans 2 also functions as Paul's opening salvo against judgment within the community, thus beginning a topos he concludes in Romans 14.[40]

ὁ λογιζόμενος τι κοινὸν εἶναι ... (Rom. 14.14a)

In the flow of Paul's argument, the clearest attitude underlying the abstinence of the "weak" seems to come in the phrase at the beginning of Rom. 14.14, quoted above. Since Paul and the "strong" do not share this attitude,[41] it becomes the most distinctive difference between "strong" and "weak," according to the evidence available from Rom. 14.1–15.13.

This phrase is used by Paul to describe a "weak" person who held certain foods to be profane. It is true that *ḥōl*, the Hebrew word behind the meaning of κοινός used for "profane," can refer in rabbinic literature to days other than Sabbaths or religious festivals.[42] But to include days within the reference of κοινός in 14.14 carries the logical difficulty of understanding how the more scrupulous "weak" would view more days as κοινός than the "strong" and two contextual difficulties. The only indications of what is regarded as κοινός point to foodstuffs (14.15, 17, 21), and there is no clear link of this usage of κοινός in 14.14 back to the question of days (14.5–6).

The use of λογίζομαι here is one of the minority of cases in this

---

[39] Sampley, "The Weak and the Strong," 50.

[40] For the function of Romans 2 within 1.18–3.20, see J.-N. Aletti, "Romains 2: sa cohérence et sa fonction," *Bib* 77 (1996) 165–77.

[41] Paul states in 14.14a that he recognizes nothing as unclean in itself. On the basis of 15.1 (ἡμεῖς οἱ δυνατοί), Paul's more open attitude can be ascribed to the "strong" party.

[42] Friedrich Hauck, "κοινός," *TDNT* III (1965) 791.

[43] The other instances are 2.3; 6.11; 8.13.

[44] λογίζομαι used with God as the actual or implied subject in Romans occurs at 2.26; 3.28; 4.3–6, 8–11, 22–24; 8.36; 9.8.

letter where the subject is a human person;[43] elsewhere it is used of God, often in a divine passive construction.[44] In this case it fits with the use in 6.11, illustrating Paul's contention throughout this letter that how one thinks is a direct sign of the status of one's faith.[45]

That κοινός as used here means "common" in the sense of "profane" or "unclean" is supported by 14.20, where Paul writes πάντα μὲν καθαρά to express the opposite of the "weak" view. κοινός is a term from Hellenistic Judaism used in discussions of purity laws. Indeed, the lack of non-Jewish sources using κοινός to mean "profane" is the strongest evidence in favor of viewing the abstinence of the "weak" as based on Jewish attitudes toward food.[46] It may also be observed that the emphasis on purity in Rom. 14.14, if descriptive of the "weak," is conceivably a logical outworking of the emphasis on purity and completeness behind the Jewish dietary laws.[47] While some take this as evidence for a Jewish background of the "weak,"[48] Rauer takes exception to such a judgment.

> Auch im Heidentum war nämlich, ebenso wie der Begriff καθαρός, auch der Begriff κοινός zur Zeit des Paulus-briefes bekannt, und in manchen Religionssystemen gab es "Unreinheit" von gewissen Speisen.

> Even specifically in paganism, equal with the concept καθαρός, the concept κοινός was also known in the time of the Pauline letters, and in many religious systems there was "uncleanness" of certain foods.

But though he cites examples from Philostratus' *Life of Apollonius*

---

[45] In addition to the texts listed above that use humans as the subject of λογίζομαι, see also Rom. 1.21, 28; 4.19–21; 12.2; 14.22.

[46] Hauck, "κοινός," 791. Lietzmann (*Römer*, 117) concurs that it appears to be "spezifisch jüdisch," but cites Plutarch, *Erot.* 751B – καλὸν γὰρ ἡ φιλία καὶ ἀστεῖον, ἡ δὲ ἡδονὴ κοινὸν καὶ ἀνελεύθερον ("For friendship is noble and charming, but pleasure is common and servile") – as a step toward the meaning of "profane."

[47] Mary Douglas, "Deciphering a Meal," in *Myth, Symbol, and Culture* (ed. C. Geertz; New York: Norton, 1971), 76–77.

[48] So Dunn, *Romans*, 818–"almost indisputable proof that the discussion moves within the context of distinctively Jewish concerns." Similarly, Käsemann (*Romans*, 374–75), Wilckens (*Römer*, 3.90–91), and more tentatively, Cranfield (*Romans*, 695). Although we have seen that Lietzmann (*Römer*, 117) writes that κοινός in the sense of "profane" appears to be specifically Jewish, he refuses to decide in favor of a Jewish background for the "weak" (115).

[49] Rauer, *Die "Schwachen,"* 105.

for καθαρός to support his contention, no examples are offered for κοινός.[49] In this way his argument is weakened.

Though Rauer's assertion does not hold, a second consideration against a simple identification of κοινός with Jewish concerns in Rome might lie in a consideration of Paul's background. One must remember that this may have been the easiest term for Paul as a Jew to use when writing of food considered unfit or inappropriate to eat.[50] It is therefore possible that Paul as a Jew would use a term from Jewish debates about table purity even though the "weak" attitudes toward food included views from non-Jewish quarters. But this consideration lacks argumentative force when one realizes that this is the only occurrence of the word in Paul. He therefore appears to be using it because it was a term in the controversy in Rome.[51]

κοινός in the sense in which it is used in this phrase follows Paul's own conviction, expressed in 14.14a – οἶδα καὶ πέπεισμαι ἐν κυρίῳ Ἰησοῦ ὅτι οὐδὲν κοινὸν δι' ἑαυτοῦ. If one accepts the variant αὐτοῦ in place of ἑαυτοῦ, Paul's statement in 14a allows less of a possibility of inferring what the distinctive view of the "weak" was, since αὐτοῦ refers back to Paul's own conviction in Jesus. Rauer states, with no examples, that many exegetes refer δι' αὐτοῦ to God the creator.[52] On external grounds, however, the witnesses א, B, and 1739 are especially strong on the side of ἑαυτοῦ. And on internal grounds, the antithetical pairing between οὐδὲν κοινὸν δι' ἑαυτοῦ/αὐτοῦ and ὁ λογιζόμενος τι κοινὸν εἶναι favors ἑαυτοῦ. The difference pivots around what something is in itself as opposed to what one thinks of something. I conclude that ἑαυτοῦ is the better reading, indicating Paul's affirmation that no food is essentially unclean.[53]

The link formed by the catchword κοινόν in 14a and 14b leads Rauer to assume that the "weak" were those who thought that certain foodstuffs were unclean in themselves, though the δι' ἑαυτοῦ is not found in 14b. He then contends that a Jew who was

---

[50] βέβηλος, the word most used by the LXX for *ḥōl*, is not found in the uncontested letters of Paul, occurring only in 1 Tim. 1.9; 4.7; 6.20; 2 Tim. 2.16. In these instances it does not refer to food, but cf. Heb. 12.16.

[51] Schneider, "Die 'Schwachen,'" 113, 129 n. 40.

[52] Rauer, *Die "Schwachen,"* 106 n. 1.

[53] See A. Schlatter, *Gottes Gerechtigkeit: Ein Kommentar zum Römerbrief* (2nd ed.; Stuttgart: Calwer, 1952), 374; Wilckens, *Römer*, III.92. For a succinct defense of limiting οὐδέν to things that are eaten rather than allowing it to refer to any action, see Cranfield, *Romans*, 713.

keeping Mosaic dietary laws could regard food as unclean, but not as unclean in itself. This is because the Jewish food laws were based on the command of God, while some pagans viewed certain foods as unclean if such items were thought to hinder the communication of the soul with the deity. In this sense Rauer thinks that a stigma of inherent uncleanness (κοινὸν δι' ἑαυτοῦ) more likely came from pagan rather than Jewish roots.[54]

It is worth noting here that though Rauer admits that there is secondary literature which combines explanations for the "weakness" in Rome, nowhere does he consider the breadth of possible combinations which evidence for the syncretism of first-century Judaism allows. He lists some commentators who see both a concern to avoid εἰδωλόθυτα and other contaminations of pagan life while keeping Mosaic law as some kind of nuanced combination of his categories. And he comments about the combination of motivations for Jewish abstinence,[55] but in his search for a background to the attitudes of the "weak" he uses a rigid Jewish versus pagan disjunction.

Methodological caution must be observed at this point. It seems clear that Paul's statement in 14.14, οἶδα καὶ πέπεισμαι ἐν κυρίῳ Ἰησοῦ ὅτι οὐδὲν κοινὸν δι' ἑαυτοῦ, is meant to render his own presupposition absolute, as οἴδαμεν ὅτι οὐδὲν εἴδωλον ἐν κόσμῳ καὶ ὅτι οὐδεὶς θεὸς εἰ μὴ εἷς does in 1 Cor. 8.4. It does not function to define, even in an antithetical way, the nature of the "weak" attitude regarding unclean foods. So Rauer's idea that the "weak" viewed food as unclean in itself (as opposed to viewing food as unclean on external grounds, namely, *kashrut* laws) cannot be accepted as conclusive. Even if Rauer's point is allowed to stand, one may still hold it possible that diaspora Jews could on religious grounds regard certain food as unclean in itself. His rigid Jewish versus pagan construct misses the fact that motives for

---

[54] Rauer, "Die 'Schwachen,'" 106. He recapitulates his conclusion on this point, along with other arguments against a Jewish-motivated abstinence, on 129–30.

[55] Ibid., 121, 128 n. 1, 129 n. 1. Cf. also C. Heil, *Die Ablehnung der Speisegebote*, 73–80 for a survey of texts related to Jewish food laws from the time around Paul's composition of Romans.

[56] See H.-F. Weiss, "Zur Frage der historischen Voraussetzungen der Begegnung von Antike und Christentum," *Klio* 43–45 (1965) 307–28, for the effects of diaspora Judaism on Early Christianity; and L. H. Feldman, "The Orthodoxy of the Jews in Hellenistic Egypt," *JSS* 22 (1960) 215–37, esp. 229–30, for "forerunners of Pauline antinomianism"!

Torah observance in diaspora Judaism cannot be conclusively determined.[56]

The issue is complex. Simply to exclude Jewish influence on Christian asceticism because such ascetic practices do not fit with the general picture of Judaism[57] ignores evidence of the syncretism in diaspora Judaism, as well as allegiance to "weak" elements in the Judaism pictured in Gal. 4.9–10.[58] And most devastating to Rauer's point is that though the phrase κοινὸν δι' ἑαυτοῦ is the central point in Rauer's argument against a Jewish and in favor of a gnostic background to the "weak," he cannot offer a single example of the word κοινός in a gnostic context.[59] Rauer's argument against viewing the "weak" as Jewish is consequently ineffective.

κοινός is clearly a term from Hellenistic Judaism. Its usage in this context does provide some indication as to the ideological background of the abstinence. But we shall suspend judgment on the origin of the "weak" attitude that certain foods or drinks were unclean (κοινόν) until comparisons are made with various motives for vegetarianism in the early Empire. Our goal in these comparisons is to identify points of continuity and discontinuity with contemporary attitudes toward consumption, thus allowing us to narrow the field of possibilities for an explanation of the attitude of the "weak."

[57] Cf. H. Strathmann, *Geschichte der frühchristlichen Askese*, 123, whose judgment rests on a presupposition that one can speak of Judaism in general at this time. But his own admission (124 n. 1) of another distinct form of Judaism, or a half-Jewish form of piety, makes a chimera of the "Gesamtbild" of early Judaism whose influence he eliminates from considerations regarding the background of Christian asceticism.

[58] See Betz, *Galatians*, 216.

[59] Schneider, "Die 'Schwachen,'" 92.

6

THE MOTIVATION BEHIND THE
ABSTINENCE OF THE "WEAK"

εἰ γάρ, φησὶν Ὅμηρος, μηδὲ σίτου ἐδεήθημεν μηδὲ
ποτοῦ, ἵν' ὄντως ἦμεν ἀθάνατοι.
Porphyry, *Abst.* 4.20; cf. Homer, *Iliad* 5.341

If only, as Homer says, we didn't need food or drink, so
that we might really be immortal!

We have seen in chapter 4 how the Roman emphasis on frugality
in consumption intersected long-standing traditions in Greek
philosophy that advocated vegetarianism.[1] Though Barclay considers it "inconceivable that Paul should be so accommodating to
scruples which derived from Pythagorean, Gnostic or other
Gentile convictions,"[2] we need to remember that some Judaisms
of the first century were quite syncretistic,[3] and we should thus not
exclude the possibility of syncretism within Roman Christianity.[4]
Yes, they are observing days and abstaining from food "for the
Lord,"[5] but if Seneca abstained from meat for more than one
reason, perhaps some early believers in Rome did so as well.[6]
Most investigations of Romans 14–15 seem to presuppose a rigid
Jewish versus pagan dichotomy for the "weak" behavior, a
dichotomy that cannot be superimposed onto the diaspora of the
first century. It is to these Greek traditions, expressed both in
philosophy and religion, that we now turn, in order to nail down
the abstinence of the "weak."

---

[1] Corbier, "Ambiguous Status," 247.
[2] Barclay, " 'Do We Undermine the Law?,' " 293.
[3] Philo, *Cont.* 11–12, 83–90; *Spec.* 2.15.56–59; Feldman, "Orthodoxy."
[4] Cf. *1 Clem.* 25.
[5] Rom. 14.6; Barclay, " 'Do We Undermine the Law?,' " 292.
[6] Cf. Seneca, *Ep.* 108.17–21.

Philosophical/religious arguments

The arguments for and against vegetarianism and wine abstinence range across philosophical schools and religions. Since philosophical/religious discussions of vegetarianism date from at least the seventh century BCE,[7] vegetarianism was no stranger to the Hellenistic world, and supporting ideas in arguments for its practice appear in a variety of configurations.

In first-century Rome there were at least three arguments from Greek philosophy that were advanced separately or in combination as rationales for vegetarianism: (1) arguments based on the metaphysical order of nature, that vegetarianism is the only moral course of action toward one's fellow creatures; (2) arguments based on various forms of primitivism, that vegetarianism is the preferable diet; and (3) arguments based on the spiritual value of purity, that vegetarianism allows one to approach the deity and therefore allows one successfully to pass into death and judgment by the deity.

Abstinence as response to the metaphysical order of existence

Arguments for vegetarianism based on the rationality of animals and on metempsychosis come under the rubric of the metaphysical order of existence.

Rationality of animals

The whole strategy of Porphyry in the third book of *De abstinentia* is to show that animals are rational and that therefore killing them for food is evil.[8] Rationality implies an ontological link between humans and animals; breaking this link by killing or harming animals is evil. Porphyry follows Pythagoras' teaching that animals have souls, and this leads to the belief that to kill and eat them is barbarism and morally evil.[9] Besides Pythagoras, Porphyry also

---

[7] Receiving its impetus in the Orphic religion, vegetarianism was then adopted by Pythagoras, whose school would long serve as its proponent (Haußleiter, *Der Vegetarismus*, 2). On Orphic vegetarianism, see ibid., 79–96.

[8] Though a look at Porphyry (232/3–*ca.* 305 CE) might seem anachronistic, his *De abstinentia* preserves many arguments that antedate Paul's letter to the Romans.

[9] This is assumed throughout the third book of Porphyry's *De abstinentia*; it is stated explicitly at 3.26. Included in the common characteristics between humans and animals is sensibility, which does not belong to plants (3.19).

appeals to the Egyptians for the view that animals are ensouled and therefore to be honored rather than eaten.[10] This argument is representative of one strand in the case for vegetarianism in antiquity, the rationality of animals.

Of course, this belief in animals' rationality is part of a larger issue, that of the superiority of animals.[11] This has a long history of discussion, beginning at least with Anaxagoras. The metaphysical position that views animals as ontologically equal or superior to humans is intimately associated with advocacy of a vegetarian diet.[12] This metaphysical position met with opposition from others who viewed humans as superior to animals on a metaphysical scale of existence. Since one's stance on vegetarianism indicates one's view of the place of humans on the earth, it became a shibboleth of one's position on this metaphysical question, and hence a controversial practice (on philosophical grounds) in its own right.

As the leading authority on animals, Aristotle could not be ignored by anyone who sought to compare humans to animals. Aristotle taught that since the human being was the first and most perfect of all creatures, the non-human creatures are appointed for human use.[13] Despite Aristotle's place as a meat-eater,[14] Porphyry

[10] Porphyry, *Abst.* 4.10. Herodotus also credited the Egyptians with the doctrine of human souls being reincarnated as animals (2.123). Franz Cumont thinks that they were only the intermediaries of this teaching as it spread from the Hindu eschatology of India to Greece (*After Life in Roman Paganism* [New Haven: Yale University Press; reprint ed., New York: Dover, 1959], 178).

[11] The following are basic works in this area: S. O. Dickerman, *De argumentis quibusdam apud Xenophontem, Platonem, Aristotelem obviis e structura hominis et animalium petitis* (Halle: Wischan & Burkhardt, 1909); Arthur O. Lovejoy and George Boas, *Primitivism and Related Ideas in Antiquity* (Baltimore: Johns Hopkins University Press, 1935; reprint ed., New York: Octagon, 1965), 389–420. See also George Boas, *The Happy Beast in French Thought of the Seventeenth Century* (Baltimore: Johns Hopkins University Press, 1933; reprint ed., New York: Octagon, 1966), 1: "The theoretical – if not psychological – basis of Theriophily is that the beasts – like savages – are more 'natural' than man, and *hence* man's superior" (his italic).

[12] Theophrastus' and Pythagoras' arguments in antiquity are preserved in Porphyry, *Abst.* 3.25–26. The modern animal-rights movement continues in this tradition. See, e.g., Roslind Godlovitch, "Animals and Morals," in *Animals, Men and Morals: An Inquiry into the Maltreatment of Non-Humans* (eds. S. Godlovitch, R. Godlovitch, J. Harris; New York: Taplinger, 1972), 156–72; R. M. Baird and S. E. Rosenbaum, eds., *Animal Experimentation: The Moral Issues* (Buffalo, N.Y.: Prometheus, 1991).

[13] Haußleiter, *Der Vegetarismus*, 236. On this page Haußleiter also helpfully suggests that Aristotle's lost works (listed in Diog. L. 5.25) *To the Pythagoreans* (Πρὸς τούς Πυθαγορείους) and *Concerning Pythagoreans* (Περὶ τῶν Πυθαγορείων) probably took issue with Pythagorean views on dietary abstinence.

[14] Timaios of Tauromenion, as preserved in Athenaeus, *Deip.* 8.342C, calls Aristotle a connoisseur of fine food (ὀψοφάγος). As Athenaeus presents it, the saying

uses Aristotle for his own purposes. Thus Porphyry mentions Aristotle as one who writes that animals have reason,[15] though Aristotle firmly held to the superiority of human over animal.

Aristotle's distinction between humans and animals on the basis of reason was carried on and emphasized even more strongly by the Stoics. They became the opponents of vegetarians in arguments related to consumption. While historically not in agreement with some members of the Academy on the philosophical status of animals, the Stoics did follow Aristotle's position that every living thing is made for human consumption.[16] The practical consequences of the ontological distinction between human and animal has not only the teleological implication on how animals are to be used; it also has a moral implication. Diogenes Laertius recounts the view of both Chrysippus and Posidonius:

> Ἔτι ἀρέσκει αὐτοῖς μηδὲν εἶναι ἡμῖν δίκαιον πρὸς τὰ ἄλλα ζῷα, διὰ τὴν ἀνομοιότητα.

> It is their doctrine that there can be no question of right as between man and the lower animals, because of their unlikeness.[17]

Thus the standard argument for vegetarianism based on the justice it involves toward animals is pointless for the Stoics.[18] While Chrysippus and his school were carefully observant of living in moderation, they nevertheless strongly supported meat consumption. Their position prompted vegetarian arguments like that of Plutarch, who writes against the position of Chrysippus, attacking the inconsistency of studied moderation in consumption while allowing meat:

refers to Aristotle's eating of fish, not the consumption of dainty food in general. See also LSJ, s.v. "ὀψοφάγος." In any case, in lifestyle and philosophy, Aristotle was firmly on the side of meat consumption.

[15] *Abst.* 3.6, 9.

[16] Haußleiter, *Der Vegetarismus*, 245–47, introduces the Stoic position on meat eating. See also 209–10, where Haußleiter discusses the argument between Carneades and the Stoics on the place of animals in their philosophical systems.

[17] Diog. L. 7.129. This and the rest of the selections from Diogenes Laertius come from *Lives of Eminent Philosophers* (trans. R. D. Hicks; LCL; London: William Heinemann, 1925).

[18] Of course, it is impossible to speak of a single Stoic tradition. Zeno, the founder of Stoicism, was known for his moderation and frugality and according to Haußleiter may have been an occasional vegetarian (*Der Vegetarismus*, 251). But it was not a vegetarianism based on concern for animals, as *SVF* 1 fr. 213 makes clear.

καὶ μὴν ἀκόλουθον ἦν αὐτοῖς, εἰ μύρον ἐξελαύνουσι καὶ πέμμα τῶν συμποσίων, μᾶλλον αἷμα καὶ σάρκα δυσχεραίνειν.

It would certainly be more consistent for them, since they banish perfume and cakes from their banquets, to be more squeamish about blood and flesh.[19]

The arguments of Heracleides and Clodius[20] that are cited in Porphyry's *Abst.* 1.13–26 have no parallel with evidence for the attitudes of the "strong" in Romans. The references to the healing properties of animals and the unlimited multiplication of animals and the argument based on the antiquity and sanction by the gods of sacrifice have nothing in common with what we read of the "strong" in Romans. Nonetheless, an understanding of the philosophical background to vegetarianism shows us how controversial this issue was in Greek thought. Meat consumption or abstinence was considered something worth debating in the Hellenistic age,[21] since it clearly showed one's stance on the metaphysical position of humanity in the universe.

Because of the prevalence of the view of animals' rationality, it is possible that this formed a part of the basis for vegetarianism among some of the "weak." The evidence for special consideration of animals as a motive behind the vegetarianism in the Roman

[19] Plutarch, *Esu carn.* 999A. This and following translations of Plutarch's *De esu carnium* are from *Moralia*, Vol. XII (trans. H. Cherniss and W. C. Helmbold; LCL; 1957; reprint; London: William Heinemann, 1968). Haußleiter, *Der Vegetarismus*, 253, suggests that this section is indeed directed against Chrysippus. The beginning of the paragraph in Plutarch confirms this, insofar as it mentions a difference with the Stoics.

[20] For the identification of Κλώδιός τις Νεαπολίτης (*Abst.* 1.3) see Jakob Bernays, *Theophrastos' Schrift über Frömmigkeit: Ein Beitrag zur Religionsgeschichte mit kritischen und erklärenden Bemerkungen zu Porphyrios Schrift über Enthaltsamkeit* (Berlin: W. Hertz, 1866), 10–12. He identifies this Clodius as the teacher of Mark Antony. Bernays also discusses the section Porphyry derived from Clodius and Heraclides on 141–43. He thinks it likely that Porphyry had direct access only to the work of Clodius, who in turn borrowed or adapted material from Heraclides. Haußleiter (*Der Vegetarismus*, 288–96) undertakes to separate what is from Heraclides and what is uniquely the material of Clodius. (*Abst.* 1.14, 16, 17, 22, 25 are taken as distinctly from Clodius.)

[21] See *Philonis Alexandrini De Animalibus: The Armenian Text with an Introduction, Translation, and Commentary*, ed. Abraham Terian (SHJ 1; Chico: Scholars Press, 1981). Philo, after hearing the case for animal rationality presented by his nephew Alexander (*Anim.* 10–71 [ed. Terian, 70–99]), refutes it (*Anim.* 77–100 [ed. Terian, 101–108]), and concludes: "To elevate animals to the level of the human race and to grant equality to unequals is the height of injustice" (*Anim.* 100 [ed. Terian, 108]).

church is slight within the text of Romans itself. There is only the mention of the exchange of God's glory for that of human, bird, cattle, and reptile (1.23) and the summary statement of 1.25 – οἵτινες μετήλλαξαν τὴν ἀλήθειαν τοῦ θεοῦ ἐν τῷ ψεύδει καὶ ἐσεβάσθησαν καὶ ἐλάτρευσαν τῇ κτίσει παρὰ τὸν κτίσαντα...

But strong evidence that such consideration of animals may have existed within the Roman church comes from *1 Clement*. Throughout the letter there is an emphasis on animals that is best explained by the presence of a view that sought to elevate the place of animals within the order of the world. *1 Clem.* 9.4 corrects Heb. 11.7 by stating that God used Noah to save the animals. It appears to be a deliberate attempt to show how the piety of Noah helped not only his household (Heb. 11.7), but the animal world as well:

> διέσωσεν δι' αὐτοῦ ὁ δεσπότης τὰ εἰσελθόντα ἐν ὁμονοίᾳ ζῷα εἰς τὴν κιβωτόν.

> Through him the Master saved the living creatures that entered into the ark in harmony.[22]

1 Clem. 33.3 states that the animals on the earth were created by God's distinct command. Other references to animals also confirm such an emphasis in *1 Clement*.[23] It is therefore entirely possible, especially when the *1 Clement* texts are carefully examined in light of the vegetarianism which we know was being practiced in the city of Rome, that some within the Roman community believed in the rationality of animals. We turn next to the related idea of metempsychosis.

Metempsychosis

A second argument under the metaphysical order of existence presented by some vegetarians is that of metempsychosis. It was considered to be not only unpleasant, but morally evil, to eat from

---

[22] *The Apostolic Fathers*. When one compares *1 Clem.* 9.2–13.4 with Heb. 11.1–12.3 and *1 Clem.* 36.1–6 with Heb. 1.3–7, it seems likely that *1 Clement's* authors knew Hebrews. Further discussion of *1 Clement's* literary dependence on Hebrews may be found in Attridge, *Hebrews*, 6–7.

[23] *1 Clem.* 20.10; 56.12 seem to fit an agenda of treating animals peaceably. The former text uses harmony in the animal kingdom as an example for the readers; the latter text is a verbatim quote of LXX Job 5.22b–23 – ἀπὸ δὲ θηρίων ἀγρίων οὐ μὴ φοβηθῇς· θῆρες γὰρ ἄγριοι εἰρηνεύσουσίν σοι ("Of the wild beasts you will not be afraid, for wild beasts will be at peace with you"). The description of the phoenix in *1 Clem.* 25 may also be cited as evidence of special attention to animals.

animals that might have held human souls from a previous existence. This type of vegetarian attitude is seen in Seneca's recollection of his teacher Sotion.

This teacher taught Seneca the Pythagorean argument of metempsychosis as a basis for vegetarianism. At the close of Seneca's recollection of his teacher's discourse we gain a sense of the complexity behind vegetarian attitudes in Rome. According to Seneca, Sotion hedged his appeal in order to persuade both those who accepted metempsychosis and those who did not.[24] It is worth noting that the logic behind Sotion's final appeal shows us something significant in the phenomenology of vegetarianism then. It had become an end in itself. Philosophical justification had given way to the practice of vegetarianism for its own sake. This point is missed by Haußleiter, who observes how Sotion had combined the Pythagorean rationale with the ethical-hygienic argument used by Sextius.[25] This characteristic of Sotion's appeal probably cannot be applied to the attitudes of the "weak." If they remained convinced that some foodstuffs were κοινός (14.14b) and that eschatological ruin awaited them if such abstinence was broken (14.20, 23), they did not practice vegetarianism as an end in itself.

Metempsychosis is hinted at in Plutarch's *De esu carnium* and softly affirmed in Porphyry's *De abstinentia*. The Persians are cited as practicing vegetarianism because of this belief in metempsychosis, as well as theologians, who abstain from animal food

> ἵνα ἀλλοτρίαις ψυχαῖς βιαίοις καὶ ἀκαθάρτοις πρὸς τὸ συγγενὲς ἑλκομέναις μὴ ἐνοχλοῖντο.

> in order that they might not be disturbed by alien souls, violently separated from the body and impure, and which are attracted to things of a kindred nature.[26]

There is no evidence that Paul or the Roman believers actually believed in metempsychosis. Yet from the parallels known from Orphic and Christian art[27] it is at least worth noting the points of

[24] Seneca, *Ep.* 108.20–21.

[25] Cf. Haußleiter, *Der Vegetarismus*, 261.

[26] *Abst.* 2.47. This and following translations of Porphyry are from Porphyry, *On Abstinence from Animal Food* (trans. T. Taylor, ed. E. Wynne-Tyson; n.p.: Centaur Press, 1965). Porphyry's reference to Persians is at *Abst.* 4.16. Plutarch's appeal to metempsychosis is in *Esu carn.* 998D–F.

[27] See R. Eisler, *Orpheus – the Fisher: Comparative Studies in Orphic and Early Christian Cult Symbolism* (London: J. M. Watkins, 1921), 51–128, though he overstates his case.

contact that one might see between Paul's argument to the "weak" in Rom. 14.1–15.13 and Orphism.

The statement in 14.7 relates to what a vegetarian who believed in metempsychosis would affirm – "For no one of us lives for himself, and no one dies for himself." The argument in 14.8–12 then shifts the train of thought in Paul's direction. While he agrees that one does not live or die for oneself, he refocuses the object of these stages of existence from another creature to the Lord. The climax of the argument emphasizes that all people are individually significant and accountable before God.[28] Reading Paul's argument in light of Orphism is highly speculative. Nothing is claimed here regarding the background of the "weak," except that there was a pool of ideas in Rome, including Orphism, that might have affected their beliefs at certain points. Rohde's comment on the anthropology behind the Orphic doctrine of transmigration reminds one of Rom. 6.23a and 7.24: "In expiation of 'guilt' the soul is confined within the body, the wages of sin is in this case that life upon earth which for the soul is death."[29]

The references to the scriptures in Romans that are unique in Paul[30] also might suggest to some that Paul is adapting himself to Christians who have come from an Orphic background that placed emphasis on their holy books.[31] We can imagine that there were perhaps some in the Roman church who had read Orphic literature, but again, there is no real evidence.

Finally, isolated descriptions of God in *1 Clement* are compatible with the doctrine of metempsychosis, most notably *1 Clem.* 59.3:

> μόνον εὑρέτην πνευμάτων καὶ θεὸν πάσης σαρκός ... τὸν παντὸς πνεύματος κτίστην καὶ ἐπίσκοπον.

> You alone are the Benefactor of spirits and the God of all flesh ... the Creator and Guardian of every spirit.[32]

---

[28] 14.10c – πάντες γὰρ παραστησόμεθα τῷ βήματι τοῦ θεοῦ; note the πᾶν γόνυ καὶ πᾶσα γλῶσσα in verse 11 (quoting LXX Isa. 45.23); and verse 12 – ἄρα οὖν ἕκαστος ἡμῶν περὶ ἑαυτοῦ λόγον δώσει τῷ θεῷ. Cf. also Heb. 9.27.

[29] E. Rohde, *Psyche: The Cult of Souls and Belief in Immortality among the Greeks* (trans. W. B. Hillis; London: Routledge & Kegan Paul, 1935), 343.

[30] References to scriptures include 1.2; 3.2; 4.3; 9.6; 15.4. The prescript's γραφαὶ ἅγιαι (1.2) is found only here in Paul; τὰ λόγια τοῦ θεοῦ of 3.2 is also unique in Paul. Cf. 16.26.

[31] W. K. C. Guthrie, *Orpheus and Greek Religion: A Study of the Orphic Movement* (New York: Norton, 1966), 171–79.

[32] *The Apostolic Fathers.* See also *1 Clem.* 60.1; 64.1.

But none conclusively indicate that such a view was espoused by the authors of the letter.

The examination of metaphysical arguments for vegetarianism has therefore left us with no hard evidence that the "weak" believed in the transmigration of the soul as a motive for their ascetic habits. We cannot accept this as a motive for their vegetarianism. But given the treatment of animals in *1 Clement*, a letter coming out of Rome less than forty years after Paul wrote Romans, it is possible that some "weak" church members believed that animals have souls, or ought to be treated as humanity's equals in this world. Now in our examination of possible motives behind the vegetarianism of the "weak" we move from ontology to a subset of the philosophy of history – the ideal of primitivism.

Arguments from primitivism

Chronological primitivism

Chronological primitivism may be defined as "a kind of philosophy of history ... as to the time – past or present or future – at which the most excellent condition of human life, or the best state of the world in general, must be supposed to occur."[33] Vegetarian arguments from chronological primitivism commonly picture a Golden Age in the past in which humanity was completely vegetarian. Humanity is then pictured to have been corrupted by the meat diet, by which it is contaminated to this day. In this way the pattern of history follows a finitist theory of decline.[34] It is thought that the Orphic writings contained a description of the Golden Age when humans were vegetarians.[35] Plato describes a Golden Age in which humans ate no meat, calling it an Orphic life.[36] Porphyry preserves

---

[33] Lovejoy and Boas, *Primitivism*, 1. Further literature on primitivism is cited in A. J. Droge, *Homer or Moses? Early Christian Interpretations of the History of Culture* (HUT 26; Tübingen: J. C. B. Mohr [Paul Siebeck], 1989), 2 n. 7.

[34] Lovejoy and Boas, *Primitivism*, 3–4. See also Judith N. Shklar, "Subversive Genealogies," in *Myth, Symbol, and Culture* (ed. Clifford Geertz; New York: Norton, 1971), 130: "Since Hesiod's day the myth of origins has been a typical form of questioning and condemning the established order, divine and human, ethical and political." Exceptions to this pattern fall under the category of anti-primitivism. Within the Hippocratic writings, e.g., we find a positive account of humanity's progress in diet from what animals eat to a better one (*VM* 3.26).

[35] Guthrie, *Orpheus and Greek Religion*, 197.

[36] *Laws* 782C.

accounts of this pre-history by Empedocles[37] and Dicaearchus of Messene[38] which include references to the simplicity and purity of humanity's original diet. Porphyry uses such accounts in a positive sense, i.e., considering the earliest humans who refused to eat meat, gaining nourishment only from the earth, as an example for his readers.[39] Plutarch also mentions Empedocles in a primitivistic argument:

> τὰ δὲ Πυθαγόρου καὶ 'Εμπεδοκλέους δόγματα νόμοι τῶν παλαιῶν ἦσαν 'Ελλήνων καὶ αἱ πυρικαὶ δίαιται.

But the precepts of Pythagoras and Empedocles were the laws for the ancient Greeks, along with their diet of wheat.[40]

From the positive depiction of a vegetarian diet in the Golden Age of the past, the finitist theory of decline also employs explanations on the origin of meat eating. Prominent in such explanations is the account of humanity's entrance into the custom of animal sacrifice and its connection to meat consumption. In these arguments, animal sacrifice is characteristically portrayed as an improper way to recognize the deity. Animal sacrifice is then shown to have led to meat consumption. This part of the argument is exemplified in Porphyry's presentation of Theophrastus' arguments against animal sacrifice, where he argues that even if animals are sacrificed, humans are not justified in eating them.[41] The meat diet is thus depicted as a result of an improper theology.

Theophrastus also provides an exception to this form of the chronologically primitive argument for vegetarianism. The ex-

---

[37] Porphyry, *Abst.* 2.21 (also in Diels–Kranz, I.362–63; Empedocles, fr. 128); 2.31.

[38] Porphyry, *Abst.* 4.2 (ET in Lovejoy and Boas, *Primitivism*, 94–96). See also E. H. Warmington, "Dicaearchus," *OCD*, 2nd ed.

[39] Porphyry, *Abst.* 2.31 (ancient people thought it unholy to slay animals that were beneficial to life); 3.27 (imitating those who lived in the Golden Age); 4.1 (quoting Hesiod on the earliest Greeks, who were vegetarian); 4.22 (descriptions in Draconian law on proper sacrifices conspicuously lack any reference to meat; Athenian lawmaker Triptolemus prohibited harming animals).

[40] *Esu carn.* 998A. On the significance of this work by Plutarch, see D. E. Aune, "De Esu Carnium Orationes I and II (Moralia 993A–999B)," in *PTWECL*, 301–16.

[41] *Abst.* 2.57. On the development of animal sacrifice see Walter Burkert, *Structure and History in Greek Mythology and Ritual* (SCL 47; Berkeley: University of California Press, 1979), 54–56, and Walter Burkert, *Homo Necans: The Anthropology of Ancient Greek Sacrificial Ritual and Myth* (trans. P. Bing; Berkeley: University of California Press, 1983), *passim.*

pected description of meat consumption resulting from animal sacrifice is assigned a second place to a converse formulation, that humans first tasted meat during times of famine and then came to offer it in sacrifice.[42]

It must also be noted that arguments from chronological primitivism are found among Jewish exponents of vegetarianism. Bleich describes how some authors argue for vegetarianism from *Sanh.* 59b, though he disagrees with their logic.[43] Rabbi Abraham Isaac Kook also inferred from antediluvian vegetarianism that in the eschaton, humanity will be vegetarian. But he was adamant that vegetarianism was not to be made into a norm in the present age.[44] It is thus worth while to note that Jews may be vegetarian for reasons other than observing *kashrut* in the diaspora.

Such primitivistic arguments may seem far removed from the question of the "strong" and "weak" in the Roman church. But when one notes Paul's direct borrowing of Hellenistic theories on the origin of religion[45] and proper service to the deity[46] and of terminology for sacrifice,[47] there is some basis for the suggestion that he was aware of this form of argument for vegetarianism in Rome.

Compared to meat abstinence, wine abstinence is not as fre-

[42] See Theophrastus, *Piet.* according to Porphyry, *Abst.* 2.9–10. Cf. Porphyry, *Abst.* 2.27, where the same order is used in the argument, with anthropophagy placed as an intermediate step between a vegetarian diet and one including animal meat. Porphyry himself does not seem to make this point concerning meat being tasted before animal sacrifice began; cf. *Abst.* 2.4. Bernays thinks that at places where Porphyry diverges from Theophrastus one may posit an unnamed source and also notes how Porphyry uses Theophrastus' *On Piety* to fit his own agenda (*Theophrastos' Schrift*, 60), but that Theophrastus presents meat consumption as both ground and consequence of meat used in sacrifice (118). The priority of eating meat to sacrifice is noted in M. P. Nilsson, *Geschichte der griechischen Religion*, Vol. II (2nd ed.; HKAW 5.2.1–2; Munich: C. H. Beck, 1961), 253.

[43] J. David Bleich, "Survey of Recent Halakhic Periodical Literature: Vegetarianism and Judaism," *Tradition* 23 (1987) 82–83.

[44] Ibid., 85–86.

[45] Rom. 1.18–32. Cf. Philo, *Praem.* 43; *Leg. all.* 3.97–99; *Spec. leg.* 1.35.

[46] In Rom. 1.22–25; 12:1–λογικὴ λατρεία; 14.18–εὐάρεστος τῷ θεῷ; 15.16 uses λειτουργός and ἱερουργέω. Religious performance that is acceptable to others, whether in or outside of the church, is also in view (14.18b; 15.31).

[47] Note the high incidence of sacrificial language in Romans among the uses found in the Pauline corpus: εὐάρεστος – Rom. 12.1, 2; 14.18 (cf. *1 Clem.* 35.5; 49.5); 2 Cor. 5.9; Phil. 4.18; Eph. 5.10; Col. 3.20; Titus 2.9; εὐπρόσδεκτος – Rom. 15.16, 31; 2 Cor. 6.2; 8.12; θυσία – Rom. 12.1; 1 Cor. 10.18; Phil. 2.17; 4.18; Eph. 5.2; θυσιαστήριον – Rom. 11.3 (quoting MT 1 Kgs. 19.10); 1 Cor. 9.13*bis*; 10.18. Other sacrificial language in Romans occurs at Rom. 3.24–25; 4.25; 5.6–11; 8.3, 32; 9.3; 15.16.

quently advocated on the basis of chronological primitivism. An argument for wine abstinence from accounts of the origin of wine libations is not clearly found in the sources. Theophrastus' work, Περὶ οἴνου καὶ ἐλαίου (*On Wine and Oil*) is now lost to us,[48] but his description of the introduction of wine into religious life fits with arguments for wine abstinence based on chronological primitivism:

> τὰ μὲν ἀρχαῖα τῶν ἱερῶν νηφάλια παρὰ πολλοῖς ἦν, νηφάλια δ' ἐστὶν τὰ ὑδρόσπονδα . . . τέλος δ' ἐπὶ πᾶσιν τὰ ὕστερον γεγονότα οἰνόσπονδα.

> Ancient sacrifices were for the most part performed with sobriety. But those sacrifices are sober in which the libations are made with water. Afterwards, however, libations were made . . . in the fourth and last place with wine.[49]

Though Ovid uses the phrase *tumidaeque in vitibus uvae* (grapes swollen on the vines), the only beverage of the Golden Age he actually describes is milk.[50] These are the closest we come to arguments for wine abstinence from chronological primitivism.[51]

Basic to the finitist theories of decline within chronological primitivism is the philosophical value of living according to nature (ζῆν κατὰ φύσιν).[52] The Cynics are credited with this motif early in Greek philosophy. Though Diogenes has been cited by vegetarians in their arguments, he cannot be considered to have been a thoroughgoing vegetarian, because of the anecdote that he had no qualms about stealing from temples or tasting animal

[48] This work is mentioned in Diog. L. 5.45. M. G. Sollenberger makes the plausible suggestion that references in Galen (*Simpl. med.* 2.5, 2.17, 4.3, 4.11, 4.14) and Plutarch (*Quaest. conv.* 676A–B) indicate that they were familiar with this work by Theophrastus ("Identification of Titles of Botanical Works of Theophrastus," in *Theophrastean Studies: On Natural Science, Physics and Metaphysics, Ethics, Religion, and Rhetoric* [Rutgers University Studies in Classical Humanities 3; eds. W. W. Fortenbaugh and R. W. Sharples; New Brunswick/Oxford: Transaction, 1988], 19 n. 18).

[49] Theophrastus according to Porphyry, *Abst.* 2.20. Wine libations are also mentioned by Theophrastus in Porphyry, *Abst.* 2.6.

[50] *Metamorph.* 15.77 (grapes), 15.79 (milk).

[51] Though Philo discusses the ancients' use of wine, he assumes its use even in the Golden Age he recalls (*Plant.* 154–64).

[52] On the background of φύσις in Greek thought in the time of the pre-Socratics, see F. Heinimann, *Nomos und Physis: Herkunft und Bedeutung einer Antithese im griechischen Denken des 5. Jahrhunderts* (SBAW 1; Basle: Friedrich Reinhardt, 1945), 89–109. Strathmann (*Geschichte der frühchristliche Askese*, 127–28) notes that Mosaic law and nature are not in opposition for Philo.

meat.[53] A later strand of Cynicism, begun by Crates of Thebes, did emphasize vegetarianism as part of its simple lifestyle.[54]

In the κατὰ φύσιν subset of vegetarian arguments, a return to the practices of the Golden Age is pictured as being most suitable, most healthful, and most reasonable for humans. This use of chronological primitivism therefore includes a direct appeal to the teleology of life forms. Thus Plutarch writes, ὅτι γὰρ οὐκ ἔστιν ἀνθρώπῳ κατὰ φύσιν τὸ σαρκοφαγεῖν, πρῶτον μὲν ἀπὸ τῶν σωμάτων δηλοῦται τῆς κατασκευῆς ("For that man is not naturally carnivorous is, in the first place, obvious from the structure of his body").[55] Musonius Rufus also describes a meat diet as more suitable for wild animals. This is related to his main teaching that a person's diet should be τὴν σύμφυλον ἀνθρώπῳ ("suitable for a human").[56] A corollary of this approach is an emphasis on the barbarity of meat eating. So we read of Musonius: τὴν μέντοι κρεώδη τροφὴν θηριωδεστέραν ἀπέφηνε καὶ τοῖς ἀγρίοις ζῴοις προσφορωτέραν ("On the other hand he showed that meat was a less civilized kind of food and more appropriate for wild animals").[57] Musonius' attitude that some foods are suitable while others are not comes from the Stoic use of the philosophical value that one should live κατὰ φύσιν,[58] an obligation that for the Stoics is based first on moral considerations.

While the expression παρὰ φύσιν is used in Rom. 1.26, any indication that the "weak" judged the "strong" for so living is missing in Rom. 14.1–15.13.[59] At the same time, Musonius Rufus' arguments, delivered as they were around the time when Paul's

---

[53] Diog. L. 6.73. For a discussion of vegetarian interpretations of the Diogenes testimonia, along with considerations of his practice of eating raw meat (Diog. L. 6.34, 76) see Haußleiter, *Der Vegetarismus*, 167–77.

[54] Haußleiter, *Der Vegetarismus*, 181–82.

[55] Plutarch, *Esu carn.* 994F. Note also the following argument in 994F–995B. Cf. Theophilus, *Ad Autol.* 2.16 on the disobedience of carnivorous animals to the divine pattern of vegetarianism. On Theophilus' use of chronological primitivism related to diet, see Droge, *Homer or Moses?*, 108–10.

[56] Musonius Rufus 18A. In the same discourse he also uses the phrases σύμφυλον ἡμῖν ("suitable for us") and σύμφαλα ἀνθρώπῳ ("things suitable for a human").

[57] Musonius Rufus 18A (*Reliquiae*, ed. Hense [Leipzig: B. G. Teubner, 1905], 95.10–11) and similarly Plutarch, *Esu carn.* 993B, 994F.

[58] See Marcus Aurelius, *Med.* 2.9; 5.1. On the Stoic view of ζῆν κατὰ φύσιν see J. M. Rist, *Stoic Philosophy* (Cambridge: Cambridge University Press, 1969), 6–10; 214–22.

[59] Elsewhere in Romans, the uses of παρὰ φύσιν and κατὰ φύσιν (11.21, 24) are linked to Paul's metaphor of the olive tree and therefore provide little evidence for the ideological background of the Roman community.

letter arrived in Rome, could easily be followed "for the Lord" (Rom. 14.6c). Such arguments could fit with the Bible's picture of a postdiluvian introduction of meat into the human diet (Gen. 9.3). Arguments for vegetarianism on the basis of its value for moral development, especially non-violence, are also found within Jewish circles,[60] and could also be practiced by believers "for the Lord."

The claim that a diet κατὰ φύσιν is bound up with the human's proper end (τέλος) leads to the philosophical appeal to health as a motive for vegetarianism.[61] As the healthful diet, vegetarianism is pictured as the spur toward physical purity. Porphyry preserves such arguments from physical purity for vegetarianism. In a section in which he is using an Epicurean source, Porphyry includes an argument for vegetarianism from health considerations:

> ἔτι δὲ οὐδὲ πρὸς ὑγείαν τὰ κρέα συντελεῖ, ἀλλὰ μᾶλλον τῇ ὑγείᾳ ἐμποδίζει ... ἀνακτᾶται δὲ διὰ τῆς λιτοτάτης καὶ ἀσάρκου διαίτης, ὥστε καὶ ταύτῃ ἂν συμμείνειεν.

> Again, neither does animal food contribute, but is rather an impediment to health ... But [health] is recovered through a most slender and fleshless diet; so that by this also it is preserved.[62]

He combines considerations of health with a reference to the ancient Greeks, stating that their health was due to abstaining from food too strong for them.[63] He also advocates purity in what kind of food one eats, for defilement comes from mixing foods.[64]

On the other hand, wine consumption rather than wine abstinence is normally represented as healthful in ancient texts. Arrian assumes that the athlete in training will abstain from cold water but

---

[60] Roger T. Beckwith, "The Vegetarianism of the Therapeutae, and the Motives for Vegetarianism in Early Jewish and Christian Circles," *RevQ* 13 (1988) 409, mentions Philo, *Prov.* fr. 2, 69–70 as representative of this motivation. Similarly, Bleich cites the medieval scholars Rabbi Isaac Abarbanel and Rabbi Joseph Albo, "Vegetarianism and Judaism," 84–85.

[61] Vegetarianism is not advocated in Plutarch's *De tuenda sanitate praecepta* (*Guidelines on Staying Healthy*), though he does suggest eating very little after one has consumed much meat (129F).

[62] *Abst.* 1.52. Porphyry refers to his Epicurean source at 1.48.

[63] *Abst.* 4.2 (cf. discussion of Celsus, *Med.* 2.18.13 above in chapter 4). Porphyry also refers here to the ancient physicians' belief that the less excrement a body produces the healthier it is, another health consideration for vegetarianism.

[64] Porphyry, *Abst.* 4.20. Material from Dicaearchus (according to Porphyry, *Abst.* 2.21) may also be placed in this category of arguments for vegetarianism based on health.

drink wine moderately.[65] Though Clement of Alexandria assumes that water is the natural drink for humanity, he argues in the same context for a moderate use of wine, rather than abstinence.[66] Athenaeus mentions certain wines as nutritious, aiding in one's physical growth, productive of blood, and aiding in digestion.[67] Kircher mentions how wine drinking was performed for health reasons within the Asclepius cult.[68] One exception is Philo's advocacy of wine abstinence in the context of a description of wine's harmful effect as a drug on the mind.[69] From the evidence available, therefore, it is unlikely that the "weak" were grounding their wine abstinence in health considerations.

The Golden Age so wistfully imagined by chronological primitivists is presented as an age of purity. Vegetarianism is then advocated as a cause of physical purity, both with reference to one's digestive system and with reference to sexual purity. Vegetarians are often described in terms of both dietary and sexual abstinence, leading to an association between self-control in diet and a celibate[70] or continent lifestyle. This is seen most clearly in Sextus, *Sent.* 240: ὡς ἂν γαστρὸς ἄρξῃς, καὶ ἀφροδισίων ἄρξεις ("As you control your stomach, so you will control your sexual desires").[71] The connection in lack of self-control between diet and sex is made elsewhere in the *Sententiae* as well.[72] Sociologically, we do need to be careful not to subsume self-control in either area under the other. While Goody can state that "The breaking of prohibitions on food and sex clearly run in parallel lines; they defined the boundaries of the civilised, or rather of the *domesces*, the familiar," he also qualifies the statement with a warning against an easy equation between the two sorts of breach in prohibition.[73]

Though the deeply seated association between meat consumption

---

[65] *Ench. Epictetus* 29.

[66] *Paed.* 2.

[67] *Deip.* 1.32C–33A.

[68] K. Kircher, *Die sakrale Bedeutung des Weines im Altertum* (RVV 9.2; Gießen: A. Töpelmann, 1910), 92–94.

[69] Philo, *Cont.* 74.

[70] Goody refers to Brahmins and some Benedictine monks as examples of celibate vegetarians (*Cooking, Cuisine and Class*, 144).

[71] *The Sentences of Sextus* (eds. and trans. R. A. Edwards and R. A. Wild; SBLTT 22; Chico, Calif.: Scholars, 1981).

[72] See Sextus, *Sent.* 108a–b, 428, 435 and note Henry Chadwick's comment on the *Sententiae*: "The mastery of the belly is only second in importance to the mastery of sex" (*The Sentences of Sextus: A Contribution to the Early Christian History of Ethics* [Cambridge: Cambridge University Press, 1959], 101).

[73] Goody, *Cooking, Cuisine and Class*, 145, 228 n. 51.

and overt sexual expression may in part be due to frequent use of bovines in ancient fertility cults,[74] this cannot be proven. What is clear is that the idea that meat consumption leads to sexual activity, and its obverse – that vegetarianism allows for control or inhibition of one's sexuality – is seen throughout history. Theißen has drawn a connection between meat eating and perceived sexual promiscuity in the Corinthian church.[75] Later evidence for the association between a tendency to eat what others would consider prohibited and sexual immorality comes from descriptions of various gnostics.[76] Tertullian associates gluttony with promiscuity because of the proximity of belly to pudenda.[77] Concerns for sexual purity were behind the development of vegetarian foods by more recent vegetarians: Graham crackers by Sylvester Graham (1794–1851) and cornflakes by John Harvey Kellogg (1852–1943).[78] The association between meat eating and sexual fervor seems to span various cultures. Ferro-Luzzi describes the reason for abstinence from meat by non-vegetarian women of a certain area of India: "They were at heart convinced that non-vegetarian food was impure and passion-raising ... and therefore to be avoided during pollution periods."[79] This connection between meat eating and sexual activity is, however, not the same as the link made between consumption of certain foods and increased health or strength of one's sexual organs.[80]

One reason for the "weak" abstinence in consumption may then have been a reaction against both sexual (13.13b) and consumptive (13.13a; 14.2a) excesses that the "weak" perceived in the behavior

---

[74] F. J. Simoons, "The Sacred Cow and the Constitution of India," in Robson, *Food, Ecology and Culture*, 120.

[75] G. Theißen, *The Social Setting of Pauline Christianity: Essays on Corinth* (ed. and trans. J. H. Schütz; Philadelphia: Fortress, 1982), 133.

[76] Irenaeus, *Adv. haer.* 1.26.3 on Nicolaitans (adultery and eating εἰδωλόθυτα are ἀδιάφορα to them; cf. Rev. 2.6, 14 and Hippolytus, *Adv. haer.* 7.24) and 1.28.2 on the followers of Basilides and Carpocrates (criticized for the same perspective as the Nicolaitans).

[77] Tertullian, *Ieiun.* 1.

[78] P. Gardella, *Innocent Ecstasy: How Christianity Gave America an Ethic of Sexual Pleasure* (New York/Oxford: Oxford University Press, 1985), 44–46.

[79] "Food Avoidances," 98. See also the account of the vegetarian George Bernard Shaw and his paramour in M. Holroyd, *Bernard Shaw, Vol. 2: 1898–1918, The Pursuit of Power* (New York: Random House, 1989), 311: "His advances could have led to love-making if – 'if only you'd eat red steaks and drink beer your spirit would be meet, I mean meet to mate – no I dont [sic] mean that ...' But she did mean it, even if she might not have wanted it."

[80] Cf. Athenaeus, *Deip.*1.5C–D.

of the "strong." Of course, besides abstinence from meat, abstinence from expensive food[81] or all food[82] as a means toward sexual purity is also attested. But simply in terms of abstinence from meat, we see that in addition to contextual arguments,[83] common associations in vegetarian ideology confirm an hypothesis that the "strong" who ate everything were also considered sexually promiscuous by the "weak."

Parallels between vegetarian arguments related to eating "according to nature" (κατὰ φύσιν) and Rom. 14.1–15.13 come with the purity language of 14.14, 20. But the sense of this terminology, κοινός in 14.14 and καθαρός in 14.20, seems to be more cultic than hygienic. The word κοινός that Paul uses to characterize the attitudes of the "weak" toward their avoided foods (14.14) could reflect a Jewish understanding of hygienic impurity. But still the gravity with which the "weak" held the violations of their consumptive guidelines is unparalleled in evidence for vegetarianism motivated by concern for physical purity. We are forced by the use of such terms as πρόσκομμα,[84] σκάνδαλον,[85] and κατακρίνω[86] to conclude that the attitude of the "weak" toward food involved more than considerations of hygiene. Also, Paul's statement at verse 14b, εἰ μὴ τῷ λογιζομένῳ τι κοινὸν εἶναι, ἐκείνῳ κοινόν, is more easily linked to matters of conscience than to hygienic concerns. If one takes καθαρός (14.20) as evidence for health-related concerns, its balancing member in verse 20, κακός, must be explained with a sense not found elsewhere in Paul.[87]

Related to the motive of living according to nature (ζῆν κατὰ φύσιν) is the teaching that vegetarianism is the more rational mode of life for humans. Both the idea that such a lifestyle is simply a wiser course of behavior and the claim that vegetarians have

[81] Philo, *Cont.* 74.

[82] See Chrysostom, *Hom. 2 Thess.* 1 (fasting is the beginning of chastity) and the descriptions of analogous tribal practices in Ernest Crawley, *Studies of Savages and Sex* (ed. T. Besterman; New York: Dutton, n.d.), 40–41.

[83] See the discussion above in chapter 4 on the relationship of Rom. 13.13 to the descriptions of the "strong."

[84] Rom. 14.13, 20 and also προσκόπτω in 14.21.

[85] Rom. 14.13.

[86] Rom. 14.23.

[87] Cf. Rom. 1.30; 2.9; 3.8; 7.19, 21; 12.17*bis*, 21*bis*; 13.3, 4*bis*, 10; 16.19; 1 Cor. 10.6; 13.5; 15.33; 2 Cor. 13.7; Phil. 3.2; 1 Thess. 5.15*bis*; Col. 3.5; 1 Tim. 6.10; 2 Tim. 4.14; Titus 1.12. Nor is κακός with a reference to physical health found among the five headings Walter Grundmann attaches to the term for its usage within the NT as a whole, s.v. "κακός," *TDNT* III (1965) 479–81.

greater mental capacity than meat-eaters are included here. Thus Musonius states that the meat diet casts a shadow over the mind, Sextus that the vegetarian diet is the more rational, and Porphyry that it makes one more fit for understanding.[88] While we do not see evidence within Rom. 14.1–15.13 for such a basis for vegetarianism, there is evidence for an emphasis on the place of human reason over the body in the letter of Romans. References to the ἀδόκιμος νοῦς (1.28),[89] the responsibility of the mind to consider itself victor over sin (6.11), the self trapped in a body (7.24), and the rational presentation of one's body to God (12.1–2) all constitute evidence for such an emphasis.

It must also be noted that the claim to humanity's eating habits in its earliest history has also been made by those who advocate a meat diet. The argument for eating according to nature appears in both those who favor vegetarianism and those against it.[90] Epicurus, whom Haußleiter considers to have practiced only an "occasionally vegetarian lifestyle,"[91] also valued eating according to nature.[92]

Theories of decline within chronological primitivism sometimes appear with the prediction that humanity will return to practices of its primeval past in some future age.[93] Thus, for example, Lactantius writes of a new world in which animals will not feed on each other.[94]

---

[88] Musonius Rufus 18A. Sextus, *Sent.* 109: ἐμψύχων ἁπάντων χρῆσις μὲν ἀδιάφορον, ἀποχὴ δὲ λογικώτερον ("The eating of any animal is a morally indifferent act, but it is more in accord with reason to abstain"); Porphyry, *Abst.* 4.20: a mind uncontaminated by foreign flesh πρὸς σύνεσιν ἑτοιμοτέρα ("is more prompt for intellectual energy"). See also Plutarch, *Esu carn.* 995E, and note David Aune's remark that the desire to clear one's mind in order to contemplate and think clearly is a motive behind fasting and asceticism in general ("De esu carnium orationes I and II," 312).

[89] Rom. 1.28. The δόκιμος νοῦς (fit mind) is a Stoic theme which carries the idea of the reason ruling over the body. On the Stoic idea of τὸ καθῆκον (the proper/appropriate), which also seems to be echoed in this verse, see M. Aurelius 6.22 and Rist, *Stoic Philosophy*, 97–111.

[90] Diogenes' regular practice of eating raw meat and his consumption of a raw octopus exemplify a carnivore who sought to live according to nature (Diog. L. 6.73, 76).

[91] *Der Vegetarismus*, 281. On understanding the alternate accounts of Epicurus' lifestyle, i.e., Timocrates' negative comments on Epicurus' excesses in consumption (Diog. L. 10.6–7) along with Diocles' and Athenaeus' positive accounts of his frugality (Diog. L. 10.11–12), see Haußleiter, *Der Vegetarismus*, 280.

[92] Diog. L. 10.130; see also Seneca's use of Epicurus' emphasis on eating frugally, *Ep.* 25.4.

[93] Lovejoy and Boas, *Primitivism*, 3, call this "the Theory of Decline and Future Restoration."

[94] *Div. inst.* 7.24.

Deems suggests a distinctive synthesis behind early Christian asceticism which partakes of such a "Theory of Decline and Future Restoration."

> The early asceticism of the Christian groups, then, was caused by the central hope (the immediate return of the Messiah) which led to renunciation of the things of this world, and by the early implantation and adoption of a Hellenistic dualism, requiring a cosmic struggle between the Christian and the demonic powers (to conquer which no sacrifice, whether of food or sexual enjoyment, could be too great), and heightened by the social conflict between rich and poor.[95]

Little evidence is available from the text of Romans for the factors that Deems cites as significant in the synthesis of Christian asceticism. The use of κοινόν in 14.14 may connote a drive for purity. References to forces or powers (8.38) and Satan (16.20) provide passing evidence that Paul shared his contemporaries' belief in the occult world, but we see no evidence for this as a motive behind the ascetic abstinence of the "weak."

Slight evidence that the argument of chronological primitivism may have been used in Rome occurs with Paul's presentation of human decline (Rom. 1.21–32) and his account of the origin of sin (Rom. 5.12–19). But in neither case is any reference made to a primeval lifestyle to which some ascetics might advocate a return. *1 Clem.* 20.4 remains our best piece of evidence for chronological primitivism used as an argument for vegetarianism in Rome.[96]

Since no direct appeals to pre-history occur in Rom. 14.1–15.13 we are left there only with the suggestion noted above that Paul's argument in 14.14 goes outside of *kashrut* laws and back to a pre-Noahic perspective on creation.[97] This suggestion holds that Paul is deftly wielding the appeal to pre-history, a weapon usually used only by the vegetarians[98] and perhaps by the "weak" in Rome, on

---

[95] M. M. Deems, "The Sources of Christian Asceticism," in *Environmental Factors in Christian History* (Shirley Jackson Case Festschrift; eds. J. T. McNeill, M. Spinka, and H. R. Willoughby; Chicago: University of Chicago Press, 1939), 158.

[96] It is quoted above, near the end of chapter 4.

[97] Dunn, *Romans*, 830.

[98] Gen 1.29–30 is usually cited as evidence that according to Genesis, humanity was vegetarian before the flood. Gen. 9.3 is then the text that contains divine sanction for humanity to eat meat. But cf. Edmund Leach's view that from creation "everything else, including the meat of the animals, is for Man's use (i. 29–30)"

behalf of the meat-eating "strong." He could do this not by describing the actual diet, but by proposing that before Noah there was no distinction between profane and sacred. Again, Paul's argument is only indirect evidence of the "weak" position, but the suggestion has been made before that the asceticism of the "weak" derives from a desire to get back to the pre-historical state of human existence.[99]

Given the references to pre-history in 1.21–32 and 5.12–19, the possible reference to it in 14.14, and the vegetarian cosmology of *1 Clem.* 20.4, the possibility remains that some sort of appeal to an early diet of humanity was being made in the Roman community. This possibility is all the more likely when one considers how Greek thought went back to descriptions of pre-history to support a vegetarian lifestyle. A decision on whether such an appeal occurred in isolation or was philosophically or religiously motivated must be suspended until other common arguments for vegetarianism are compared with the text of Romans.

Cultural primitivism

Cultural primitivism may be defined as:

> the discontent of the civilized with civilization, or with some conspicuous and characteristic feature of it. It is the belief of men living in a relatively highly evolved and complex cultural condition that a life far simpler and less sophisticated in some or all respects is a more desirable life.[100]

Practices that seem roughly similar to the abstinence of the Roman "weak" also occur in arguments of cultural primitivism. Philo's reference to the Therapeutae clearly falls into this category of cultural primitivism. His writings contain evidence for an idealized strain of asceticism within Judaism. Philo's asceticism is based on an anthropological dualism in which sensation (αἴσθησις) is set in

("Genesis as Myth," in *Genesis as Myth and Other Essays* [London: Jonathan Cape, 1969], 13).

[99] Godet, *Romans*, 453–54, 467, thinks that the "weak" were believers influenced by a form of Jewish primitivism; Rauer, *Die "Schwachen,"* 167–69, sees a non-Jewish form of gnostic primitivism behind the "weak."

[100] Lovejoy and Boas, *Primitivism*, 7. This form of primitivism points to specific exemplars and need not be chronologically separate from one's present point of comparison (ibid., 8).

opposition to mind (νοῦς), with the result that denials of physical appetites are viewed as instrumental in one's ethical development.[101] This ascetic emphasis appears throughout Philo's writings,[102] but is best seen in his *De vita contemplativa*.[103] Philo writes disparagingly of excess in banquets and favorably describes the Therapeutae as the paradigm of temperance. The colony of Therapeutae described there are described in favorable terms for their diet of bread, salt, hyssop, and spring water.[104] Their vegetarianism was practiced as an expression of their Judaism. The motivation offered for such a diet includes deference to the priests of the Jerusalem temple. Wine abstinence likewise is followed because the priests do not serve while consuming wine.[105] Although little can be said about Christianity in Egypt at the time when Paul wrote Romans,[106] its adoption of an anthropological dualism not unlike that seen in *De vita contemplativa* may account for the later rise of Christian asceticism in Egypt. But neither the reasons related to temple worship nor the thoroughgoing dualism evident in the description of the Therapeutae are reflected in Paul's discussion of the "weak" attitudes and practices in Rome.

The argument of cultural primitivism is not clearly found in Romans. It is possible that ascetic groups like the Therapeutae provided a model for ascetics living in Rome, but no definite

[101] Strathmann, *Geschichte der frühchristlichen Askese*, 134–35, 142.

[102] *Abr.* 52–53 and *Sacr.* 64, 81 describe Jacob as the model of ἄσκησις; see also *Praem.* 27.

[103] The case against Philonic authorship is made by P. E. Lucius, *Die Therapeuten und ihre Stellung in der Geschichte der Askese* (Strasburg: C. F. Schmidt, 1879), who places the writing as composed at the end of the third century as an apology for spreading asceticism (198). His arguments against Philonic authorship (summarized on 133) are in general hindered by too narrow a conception of diaspora Judaism (129). For a discussion of the Philonic authenticity of this work, see Paul Wendland, *Die Therapeuten und die philonische Schrift vom beschaulichen Leben* (Leipzig: B. G. Teubner, 1896), 720–31, and Strathmann, *Geschichte der frühchristlichen Askese*, 148–50. Wendland's use of the work as evidence of Hellenistic Judaism is cognizant of the varieties of Judaism in the diaspora (*Die Therapeuten*, 767).

[104] On excess in banquets, *Cont.* 48–56; on the temperance of the Therapeutae, *Cont.* 37.

[105] *Cont.* 74. Strathmann, *Geschichte der frühchristlichen Askese*, 154, takes these motivations as "urphilonisch," holdovers from the Judaism in Egypt before Philo. Nevertheless, he accepts as historical the account of the practice of such abstinence as an expression of Judaism in an Egyptian community (154–57).

[106] See C. H. Roberts, *Manuscript, Society and Belief in Early Christian Egypt* (Schweich Lectures, 1977; London: Oxford University Press, 1979), 54–58, on the dearth of evidence for Christianity in first-century Egypt. On Egypt as a fertile environment for the rise of Christian asceticism from the third century on, see Deems, "The Sources of Christian Asceticism," 165–66.

evidence can be found to establish this. There are continuities in descriptions of the "weak" in Romans and Therapeutae in *De vita contemplativa*. Both exhibit a lifestyle driven by a desire for spiritual purity.[107] Of all Paul's writings, Romans comes closest to an anthropological dualism[108] as pronounced as that in Philo. It is possible that Paul was using the language of dualism used by ascetics within the Roman church. Like the Therapeutae, the "weak" in Rome may have shared in ascetic tendencies to venerate holy books, as Paul's unusual comment on the purpose of scripture may indicate.[109] We see enough continuities between the Roman "weak" and ascetic appeals to primitivism to suggest that the "weak" may have used some sort of primitivism to defend their practices.

These continuities lack the specificity necessary to prove actual dependence on particular ascetic cultures by the "weak" in the Roman church.[110] Nor is the derivation of the "weak" asceticism as simple as a decision between Jewish and Gentile asceticism, for Jewish practices had become somewhat of a trend in the early Empire within Rome. At this point what we can say is that since vegetarianism was so common in antiquity, and since arguments for it are not too dissimilar to language in Romans that is distinctive within the Pauline corpus,[111] it is likely that Paul knew of an ascetic group among the Roman Christians that practiced vegetarianism. We now proceed to another motive for vegetarianism in antiquity, the desire for spiritual purity.

Abstinence as a means of spiritual purity

While the primitivistic arguments for vegetarianism on the basis of health include a regard for physical purity, there was also a spiritual

---

[107] See the following discussion in this chapter.

[108] Strathmann, *Geschichte der frühchristlichen Askese*, 156–57; Rom. 6.12–13; 7.18–24; 8.5–11; 12.1–2; 13.14.

[109] Rom. 15.4. Such a tendency is not limited to Jewish asceticism, however. We have already noted in this chapter a similar tendency within Orphism.

[110] Unlike clear arguments of cultural primitivism, Rom. 14.1–15.13 contains no reference to named individuals or groups as exemplars of ascetic behavior. Cf. Alexis according to Athenaeus, *Deip.* 4.161B on the Pythagoreans as the only ones who drink no wine or Clement, *Paed.* 2.1 that the apostle Matthew is cited as a virtuous vegetarian.

[111] To summarize: these sections include appeals to pre-history (Rom. 1.18–32; 5.12–21); mind/body dualism (Rom. 6.11; 7.24; 12.1–2); and the idea of pollution through eating meat (Rom. 14.1–2, 14, 21).

side to the quest for purity, including both mystical and cultic conceptions of purity.

Mystical purity

In certain religious traditions, asceticism in consumption was practiced as a temporary measure before initiation into a mystery. So, for example, Apuleius states that in his initiation he was commanded "decem continuis illis diebus cibariam voluptatem coercerem neque ullum animal essem et invinius essem" ("to restrain my pleasure in food for the next ten days, not to partake of animal food, and to go without wine").[112] Deems comments on the general motive of mystical purity that prompted temporary ascetic measures in the mystery religions:

> Union with deity, to accomplish which one must free himself from bodily demands, was a familiar conception in ancient Greece, in cults of Pythia, Athene, Demeter, and others, and in the first century of the Christian Era the idea was widespread through the mystery religions ... The mysteries, with their emphasis upon blessed immortality, would tend to disparage the things of this world. But union with deity was the end sought, and purity of life the means. Therefore, the explanation of their prohibitions of foods and sexual intercourse during specified periods was to rid the body of all possible demonic infection and to prepare it for attainment to deity.[113]

While Rom. 6.3–23 contains parallels with initiatory language,[114] there is no evidence from Rom. 14.1–15.13 that the "weak" were abstaining out of a desire to prepare themselves for baptism.[115] Their asceticism discernible in this section seems to be permanently maintained, rather than adopted temporarily before certain rites.

[112] Apuleius, *Metamorphoses* (trans. J. A. Hanson; LCL; Cambridge, Mass.: Harvard University Press, 1989), 11.23.

[113] Deems, "The Sources of Christian Asceticism," 151.

[114] A. J. M. Wedderburn, *Baptism and Resurrection: Studies in Pauline Theology against its Graeco-Roman Background* (Tübingen: J. C. B. Mohr [Paul Siebeck], 1987).

[115] If one wished to argue this, the declaration Ἀνθρώπινον λέγω διὰ τὴν ἀσθένειαν τῆς σαρκὸς ὑμῶν of 6.19 might be emphasized, but the ties between asceticism of the "weak," contemporary asceticism in preparation for initiation rites, and the use of ἀσθένεια in Rom. 6.19 (near Paul's discussion of baptism) are too tenuous for indicating that the Roman "weak" abstained in preparation for baptism.

Closely linked to ascetic measures observed in preparation for initiatory rites is the motive of preparation for the reception of a vision. Evidence for such asceticism appears in Judaism and various cults, but there is no evidence from Romans that ascetic measures in that community were followed out of visionary motivation.[116]

Apart from occasions when mystical purity motivated temporary ascetic measures, the ascetic theme that those who maintain a certain lifestyle are closer to the deity is found in a variety of ascetic expressions. This proximity to the deity is the main argument for abstinence from meat in Porphyry's *De abstinentia*. The emphasis on spiritual purity assumes a strict mind/body dualism, so that we read of fattening the mind rather than the body, an emphasis that is closely akin to the theme that vegetarianism allows one to subjugate the body and so become more like an incorporeal deity.[117]

The exact connection between an ascetic diet and an approach to deity varies, allowing a number of expressions of mystical purity. Musonius Rufus writes of the foods of the gods, and how it is best that one follow their example in consumption.[118] In mythic categories this seems to be related to what Leach notes about the creation account: those foods that contain their own seeds, cereal, fruit, and grass (as opposed to meat) are in the area of "perfect ideal categories"[119] and thus suited to the gods and those who wish to approach them.

With this teaching on inner purity and the individual's approach to the deity we see a particular emphasis in asceticism: that of the individual singly approaching the deity. Thus Porphyry can write of the self-sufficiency that moderation brings and its ability to make one like the deity, or of the individual's lone ascent to the deity.[120]

---

[116] Dan. 1.8, 12, 16–17; 10.3 give evidence for this phenomenon within an apocalyptic form of Judaism, though in this case it may be combined with a drive for cultic purity as well. Cf. Gal. 1.8; Col. 2.19, 23. Such hints at visionary experiences within a congregation are missing in Romans.

[117] Porphyry, *Abst.* 4.20.

[118] Musonius Rufus 18A. According to Musonius, since vapors and water satisfy the gods, foods most like these should also be human fare.

[119] Leach, "Genesis as Myth," 20. This idea of foods that contain their own seeds, though not suggested by Leach, may relate on a mythical level to the emphasis (already observed in this chapter) on vegetarianism as a means of maintaining sexual purity.

[120] On self-sufficiency, see Porphyry, *Abst.* 1.54. On ascending alone to the deity, he mentions a philosopher who is also a priest μόνος μόνῳ δι' ἑαυτοῦ θεῷ προσιέναι σπουδάζων ("earnestly endeavouring to approach through himself alone to the alone God"), ibid., 2.49.

Seen much earlier in Orphism,[121] the ascetic emphasis on the individual's approach to the deity leads to solitude in lifestyle. In its doctrinal outworking there is a responsibility placed on the individual for effecting their own approach to the divine, without reliance on social or any other means external to the soul.[122]

It is significant in Rom. 14.1–15.13 that Paul accepts an emphasis on the individual's approach to God, at least in terms of its social isolation. Such statements as those in 14.5b, 12, 14b, 20b, 22 are uncharacteristic of Paul in the latitude given the individual for determining their own approach to God. When one considers them in light of the communal language elsewhere in Paul,[123] this individual emphasis is all the more noteworthy. The objection that this emphasis is only a byproduct of Paul's diatribe style[124] misses the content of the text. Paul actually recognizes that individuals with different convictions can simultaneously be serving God (14.6). This emphasis fits with Rom. 12.3, which is not a prime example of Paul's diatribe style, and therefore hints that the recognition of the individual is more than stylistic in this letter. It does appear possible, then, that an ascetic emphasis on individual purity and responsibility to approach the deity, paralleled in Orphic and Pythagorean theology,[125] was current among the ascetic "weak" and accepted by Paul. While this mystical motive among the "weak" may not have involved a quest for visions, it does appear that they sought individually to reach God.[126]

[121] Guthrie in *Orpheus and Greek Religion*, 201, describes Orphism as "the height of individualism. Any religion which involves the doctrine of transmigration, with its absorption in 'soul-history,' is almost bound to be."

[122] On the social isolation of the truly spiritual, Porphyry cites the Stoic Chaeremon as his authority in a description of the solitude in which Egyptian priests lived, *Abst.* 4.6. See also 1.31 for the metaphor of the naked athlete as an indication of how one approaches the divine.

[123] Cf. Gal. 1.6–9; 5.2–3; Phil. 3.15–16 for Paul's usual tendency to direct others' approach to God, making it a public matter. If the individual's approach to the deity is tied to spiritual purity, as seen in ascetic texts such as Porphyry's *De abstinentia*, then we can at least state that κοινόν in the context of Rom. 14.14 includes a sense of spiritual impurity that impedes one's approach to God.

[124] Stowers, *Rereading*, 102.

[125] It is impossible to decide how direct this influence on the individual's approach to the deity was in the Roman situation. It may have been mediated through Judaism, since the Hellenistic world did have a profound effect on Jewish asceticism. A Platonic mindset seems to have influenced Jewish asceticism in the Hellenistic period to emphasize the individual's practice of piety as significant for salvation (J. Maier, "Askese III," *TRE*, 201).

[126] Besides the texts from Rom. 14.1–15.13 cited above, see also Rom. 2.9–πᾶσαν ψυχὴν ἀνθρώπου; 3.19–πᾶν στόμα; 7.7–25 (individualism of the ἐγώ).

One may also note that a concern about death seems to be present in the community. This concern would be present in people who believed in metempsychosis or those who focused on purity as a requirement for the individual's approach to God. The language in 14.7–8 may indicate that the "weak" were afraid of death. At least the final statement, ἐάν τε οὖν ζῶμεν ἐάν τε ἀποθνῄσκωμεν, τοῦ κυρίου ἐσμέν, seems to be directly addressing a fear of death that was present within the community. This fits both with our knowledge of the significance that death had as a social force in imperial Rome[127] and with the treatment in Romans of death as a theologoumenon to an extent unmatched elsewhere in the Pauline corpus.[128] The probability that the "weak" were afraid of death also matches the stereotypical behavior of superstitious people who appeared scrupulous about food consumption and feared death.[129] Jaquette's explanation for Paul's references to death here in Romans 14 is not convincing. What makes the varieties of behavior acceptable in 14.6 is that they are undertaken for the Lord, as also living and dying should be (14.7–9). The link between various forms of day observance or consumption and living or dying does not clearly seem to be that they are *adiaphora*; the link is rather that all activities of human existence should be performed for the Lord.[130]

Wine was also associated with death in antiquity. Kircher offers a variety of links between wine usage and the dead: he notes that unmixed wine in Greek usage was almost only used to show respect for the dead; the ἀγαθὸς δαίμων, to whom wine libations were offered at the end of meals, was honored in relation to the ancestral cult; wine libations over a tomb were considered fortunate or respectful; and wine was used in Greek magic to entreat the dead.[131] It is conceivable that if the meat abstinence was somehow

---

[127] On the ever-present reminders of death in and near the city of Rome, see K. Hopkins, *Death and Renewal* (SSRH 2; Cambridge: Cambridge University Press, 1983), 201–10. See also Heb. 2.15.

[128] Consider the frequent occurrence of words describing death in Romans: ἀποθνῄσκω – Rom. 5.6, 7*bis*, 8, 15; 6.2, 7, 8, 9, 10*bis*; 7.2, 3, 6, 10; 8.13, 34; 14.7, 8*tris*, 9, 15; θάνατος – Rom. 1.32; 5.10, 12*bis*, 14, 17, 21; 6.3, 4, 5, 9, 16, 21, 23; 7.5, 10, 13*bis*, 24b; 8.2, 6, 38; θανατόω – Rom. 7.4; 8.13, 36.

[129] Dale B. Martin, *The Corinthian Body* (New Haven/London: Yale University Press, 1995), 114, 156.

[130] Jaquette, *Discerning*, 129–30.

[131] Kircher, *Die sakrale Bedeutung des Weines*, unmixed wine (27, 84); the ἀγαθὸς δαίμων (30–31); libations over a tomb (12); magical entreaties (13).

motivated by a fear of death, then the wine abstinence of 14.21 would also have arisen from that concern.

But once again, the precise nature of this concern for death is irretrievable, and we are left unable to infer that there was any relation between the fear of death Porphyry mentions[132] and a concern for death that may have existed in the Roman church. Beyond the mystical manifestations that the motive of spiritual purity takes, there is also a cultic manifestation.

Cultic purity

"Cultic purity" here designates a purity defined by religious considerations that do not include explicit reference to ascent to the deity. Cultic purity usually requires the continuing observance of a prescribed form of asceticism. Asceticism in consumption due to a desire for such cultic purity was known in Greek[133] and Roman religion.[134] Other religions could be cited, but direct influence from them to the practice of the "weak" is unlikely, because of the description ὁ μὴ ἐσθίων κυρίῳ οὐκ ἐσθίει in 14.6. This description indicates that the only religion from which abstinence due to cultic purity might directly be traced is Judaism.

While it is generally stated that Judaism is not an ascetic religion,[135] we do see in it instances of self-chosen abstinence based on cultic purity. Central to the consideration of cultic purity as a motive for first-century Jews and Christians is the connection between pagan sacrificial rites and the meat eating that inevitably followed.

The link between meat eating and sacrifice to deities seems

---

[132] In *Abst.* 1.53–54 Porphyry mentions the fear of death as a motive for both those who abstain from meat and those who indulge in it.

[133] The basic works here are Theodor Wächter, *Reinheitsvorschriften im griechischen Kult* (RVV 9.1; Gießen: Töpelmann, 1910), and Robert Parker, *MIASMA: Pollution and Purification in Early Greek Religion* (Oxford: Clarendon, 1985). See Wächter, *Reinheitsvorschriften*, 76–115, for purity laws related to animals and plant foods.

[134] Plutarch, *Quaest. Rom.* 109–10. See Georg Wissowa, *Religion und Kultus der Römer* (HKAW 5; Munich: C. H. Beck, 1902), 100–13, for discussion of the Jupiter cult.

[135] So, e.g., M. Burrows writes: "Judaism, by and large, was never an ascetic religion, and John the Baptist was condemned for his austerity (Mt. 11.18; Lk. 7.33)" ("Old Testament Ethics and the Ethics of Jesus," in *Essays in Old Testament Ethics* (J. Philip Hyatt Festschrift; eds. J. L. Crenshaw and J. T. Willis [New York: Ktav, 1974], 229). Also H. Strathmann comments that asceticism played only a small role among Israelites and Jews (s.v. "Askese I," *RAC* I.750).

present in each culture relevant to this investigation. Lexically, this can be seen in the Hebrew noun which is used both for sacrifices and for meals eaten in sacrificial settings.[136] For Greeks, a close association existed between the sacrifice and the sacrificial meal of meat.[137] The connection between meat sacrifice and consumption carried over into the Roman setting. Juvenal writes of practices in the Republic, in which one might be served fresh meat if a recently made sacrifice happened to be available.[138] Corbier's statement is fitting:

> Meat at Rome remained characterized in its vocabulary, hierarchy of qualities, methods of preparation, rites of sharing, and occasions of consumption, by the place that it came to occupy early, perhaps from the beginning, in cults devoted to the gods and in funerary ceremonies.[139]

Avoidance of perceived contamination by foodstuffs (meat or wine) offered to other deities was a motive for abstinence among some Jews and Christians and must be considered here as a possible explanation for the abstinence of the "weak."

A motive of cultic purity, perhaps unrelated to sacrifice, seems to be behind Philo's statement that the Therapeutae do not drink wine because priests are not permitted to drink it when serving in the temple.[140] This is the closest that Philo gets to ascribing a motive of Torah observance to the dietary asceticism of the Therapeutae. Elsewhere he writes as if self-control is its main motive.[141]

The motive for dietary abstinence among Jews was intensified by

---

[136] See BDB, s.v. "*zebaḥ*," I, II.

[137] See, e.g., Homer, *Odyssey* 3.455–65, 470. Kircher, *Die sakrale Bedeutung des Weines*, 48, describes a meat offering without a sacrificial meal as unthinkable, and states that every animal slaughtered was a sacrifice. Kircher also notes the sacred and cultic significance that the Greeks saw in the death of any animal (7). See also P. Stengel, *Die griechischen Kultusaltertümer* (3rd ed.; HKAW 5.3; Munich: C. H. Beck, 1920; reprint ed., New York: Arno, 1975), 95–155, for an examination of sacrificial rites in Greek religion.

[138] Juvenal, *Sat.* 11.82–85.

[139] Corbier, "Ambiguous Status," 224–25.

[140] Philo, *Cont.* 74. For Talmudic parallels to wine abstinence, Jeremias, *Eucharistic Words*, 213 n. 4, cites Ned. 6.7–9; 8.1, 5; 9.8; Naz. 2.3. These are explicitly identified in the text as from "late Judaism," so they can only be used as illustrative parallels.

[141] Philo, *Cont.* 34. Similarly Josephus gives reasons from Hellenistic asceticism rather than the Torah in his account of Daniel's abstinence (*AJ* 10.194). Schneider states that Josephus' explanation is a concession to his Hellenistic audience ("Die 'Schwachen,'" 103). I am not convinced that all diaspora Jews who practiced or admired various expressions of asceticism did so on the basis of cultic purity within

their desire to keep *kashrut* laws. Segal describes Jewish practices in the Hellenistic world.

> Not stated explicitly in the mishnaic laws but an implication of the discussion is that, whenever there is a question, many Jews would entirely avoid eating with gentiles, as Cephas himself does, or, as a lesser safeguard, limit eating with gentiles to vegetable, bread, and fish, (assuming that the other laws could be observed). Since "ritual vegetarianism" avoids issues of slaughter and possibly even some of the issues of tithing, which had specific implications for produce of Israel's land, vegetarianism continues to be a natural choice available to some pious Jews in a similar situation today. The New Testament seems to bear out that this common ritual strategy was also in use in the Christian community, in discussing the difficulties between the "strong" and the "weak."[142]

Josephus provides evidence for Jewish abstinence from meat in Rome when he writes of Jewish priests imprisoned in Rome, *ca.* 61 CE, who subsisted on figs and nuts in order to maintain cultic purity.[143] The case for an hypothetical or imagined situation behind Romans 14–15 becomes all the more tenuous when we see this example of vegetarianism in Rome that occurred about five years after Paul wrote Romans.

The clearest example of a Jewish Christian who maintained a vegetarian lifestyle is James.[144] It appears quite possible that Jewish Christians in Rome modeled themselves after James, the preeminent Jew also associated with the Jesus movement.

The Jewish ideal of vegetarianism from this time period is also preserved in the *Testament of Isaac* 4.5, which describes Isaac as a

Judaism. See Feldman, "Orthodoxy," 233–37. Surely many would abstain from certain foods for reasons common throughout the Hellenistic world.

[142] A. F. Segal, *The Other Judaisms*, 177. His reference to Cephas is from Gal. 2.11–13. Segal's point may also be illustrated by Luke's depiction of the Jerusalem church leaders' accusation against Peter in Acts 11.3b – εἰσῆλθες πρὸς ἄνδρας ἀκροβυστίαν ἔχοντας καὶ συνέφαγες αὐτοῖς.

[143] Josephus, *Vita* 14. For Josephus it is clear that their abstinence was due to their observance of Judaism: καίπερ ἐν κακοῖς ὄντες οὐκ ἐπελάθοντο τῆς εἰς τὸ θεῖον εὐσεβείας, διατρέφοιντο δὲ σύκοις καὶ καρύοις ("Even in affliction, they had not forgotten the pious practices of religion, and supported themselves on figs and nuts"; trans. H. St. J. Thackeray; LCL; London: William Heinemann, 1926).

[144] Eusebius, *HE* 2.23.5 preserves Hegesippus' testimony on the meat and wine abstinence of James.

vegetarian who abstained from wine. Though dated to the second century CE, this might demonstrate that Judaism under the early Empire included such ascetic tendencies.[145]

Beyond these parallels, there is lexical evidence for viewing abstinence of the "weak" as motivated by Jewish concerns. In Hellenistic Judaism κοινός came to designate those items which were cultically impure. As mentioned above,[146] Paul's use of it in Rom. 14.14 is one of the strongest pieces of evidence for tracing the "weak" abstinence to a Jewish background. It is difficult to know what significance κοινός carried in a diaspora church with a mixture of Jewish and hellenized Christians,[147] but certainly for the Jewish Christian recipients of Romans, κοινός would be understood on the basis of cultic purity laws.

Now that comparisons have been made, the parallels and lexical evidence bring us back to the possibility of Jewish influence among the "weak." Such concerns would surely fit in a diaspora community such as that in Rome. Insofar as there were Jews in the Roman church, there were probably Jewish concerns operative among the "weak." Indeed, as mentioned in the first chapter, Nanos sees Jewish concerns among the "weak" in that they are Jews who do not believe in Jesus. This is an appropriate place for an evaluation of this possibility.

Cultic purity: Jewish or Jewish Christian?

Mark Nanos argues that commentators who see the "weak" in Romans as Jewish Christians who abstain from certain foodstuffs in order not to violate their *kashrut* laws necessarily fall into Luther's trap. Nanos springs this trap on commentators who see Jewish Christians as the "weak," and identify this weakness as arising from their loyalty to *halakhot* that uphold Torah. The trap snaps on the inconsistency of endorsing the call for full acceptance and avoiding judgment on others' opinions in 14.1 and then in fact

---

[145] W. F. Stinespring, "Testament of Isaac," in *Old Testament Pseudepigrapha*, Vol. I: *Apocalyptic Literature and Testaments* (ed. J. H. Charlesworth; Garden City, N.Y.: Doubleday, 1983), 903–904, considers this work a Christianized version of a Jewish testament.

[146] See discussion above in chapter 5.

[147] See H. Braun, *Spätjüdisch-häretischer und frühchristlicher Radikalismus* (BHT 24; 2 vols.; Tübingen: J. C. B. Mohr [Paul Siebeck], 1957), II.65–66 n. 7. He shows through gospel traditions how questions of purity remained important for Jewish Christians, while "die Wundertopik" replaced this focus for Hellenistic Christians.

judging the "weak" as somehow defective in their faith because of Torah loyalty.[148]

A couple of assumptions contribute to the tensive qualities of this trap. First, Nanos assumes that Paul wants the "weak" to change and become "strong." If this is so, then the inconsistency of juxtaposing 14.1 with Paul's supposed goal of moving the "weak" into the "strong" position allows Nanos to spring his trap. If Paul wants "weak" to become "strong," or "able," as Nanos also translates δυνατοί, it cannot mean that Paul wants them to give up acts of Jewish piety. Instead, for Nanos, it must mean that Paul wants those Jews who are unable to believe in Jesus to become able to do so.[149] In support of this point, Nanos draws a dichotomy between faith on the one hand and opinions and behavior on the other. He points out that it is only a group's faith that is called "weak," not their opinions or behavior, as if Paul had no problem with the opinions or behavior of the "weak."[150] Second, Nanos assumes that Paul coins the terms "strong" and "weak." If this is so, then a portrait of the "weak" as those Jewish Jesus-believers who cannot give up their dietary habits grates on Nanos's picture of a Paul who continued to follow Torah and all the accompanying marks of first-century Judaism, including the dietary laws. It also makes it difficult to understand why Paul would name them "weak" and call himself "strong," when they both follow the same dietary habits. Nanos's way out is to say that Paul's term "weak in faith" is "a highly nuanced and respectful reference to the Jews in Rome who were not Christians."[151] It is not pejorative, but is rather Paul's "euphemism" for those who had not seen that Jesus was Israel's Messiah.[152]

Nanos's book is helpful in calling Christian readers of Romans back to the Jewish roots of this letter's audience. Nevertheless, the argument that the "weak" were Jews who did not believe in Jesus does not convince me. It is not clear to me that Paul wants, or imagines, that the "weak" ever will become "strong." Nanos is correct in emphasizing the respect that Paul wants shown to the "weak." In fact, the respect is such that there is no clear evidence

---

[148] Nanos, *Mystery*, 91–94.
[149] Ibid., 154.
[150] Ibid., 103, 119.
[151] Ibid., 155.
[152] Ibid., 157. While Tomson thinks that the "weak" are believers in Jesus, his translation of ἀσθενής as "delicate" is a preliminary move in the direction Nanos has followed (Tomson, *Paul and the Jewish Law*, 194–95, 243).

that Paul wants the "weak" to change. The supporting dichotomy between faith and opinions or behavior cannot be made, for the "weak in faith" are immediately described in terms of behavior, and behavior has been and continues to be definitive in describing Jewish faith.[153] Similarly, though Paul asks the "strong" to welcome the "weak" and not squelch their opinions (14.1), opinions and cognition are clearly included within "faith" in this letter.[154] Paul asks the "strong" to adopt the behavior (14.21) and respect the thoughts (14.14b-15) of the "weak." More is at issue here than adding a belief in Jesus to one's religious faith.

With regard to the second assumption, the "strong" and "weak" language of Rome summarized in chapter 3 above makes it very difficult for me to believe that Paul coined the term "weak in faith" as a respectful euphemism. Why risk a misunderstanding with such a negatively loaded adjective? We can retrace Paul's steps in this letter most easily if we conclude that he is using a nickname current among the Roman communities of believers. If Paul is therefore using the Roman communities' terms, asking that the "strong" not trounce the opinions of the "weak," and not trying to change the "weak" ones' opinions, behavior, or faith,[155] I don't think that Paul, or we his readers, are falling into Luther's trap. I shall now explain why I think the "weak" are believers in Jesus.[156]

Nanos's strongest argument for understanding the "weak" to be those Jews who do not believe in Jesus seems to be his juxtaposition of the section on Abraham in Romans 4 with the descriptions of the "weak" in Romans 14.[157] Since Paul uses strength and weakness language in describing Abraham's faith, Nanos argues that the "strong" in faith are "those who recognize God's righteousness as did Abraham ... they believe in the faithfulness of God to keep his promise in spite of appearances to the contrary ... in Abraham's 'seed' (Jesus the Christ)."[158] But there is one discontinuity in

---

[153] Rom. 14.1–2; J. D. Levenson, *Sinai and Zion: An Entry into the Jewish Bible* (San Francisco: Harper & Row, 1985), 86; cf. Jas. 2.14–26.

[154] Rom. 12.3 and M. Reasoner, "The Theology of Romans 12:1–15:13," in *Pauline Theology*, Vol. III: *Romans* (eds. David M. Hay and E. Elizabeth Johnson; Minneapolis: Fortress, 1995), 291.

[155] For more discussion on whether Paul is asking the "weak" to make any changes, see the end of chapter 10 below.

[156] I used the term "believers in Jesus" to avoid the anachronism and connotations of the word "Christian," which might not have been used in Rome when Paul wrote this letter. With this admission, I ask my readers' permission to allow me to use the term in the following four paragraphs in order to avoid repeated circumlocutions.

[157] Nanos, *Mystery*, 139–43.   [158] Ibid., 142.

comparing Abraham's "strong" faith in Romans 4 with the "strong" in faith of Romans 14. In Rom. 4.19–20, Paul writes that Abraham did not weaken in faith, but grew "strong" in faith, giving glory to God. Paul seems to assume that if he were "weak" in faith, he would not have given glory to God. But in Romans 14–15, both "strong" and "weak" give glory to God, for both thank God (14.6), and Paul blesses them in a way that assumes that the "weak," as they are, will glorify God along with the "strong" (15.5–6). The juxtaposition of chapters 4 and 14 as an argument to prove that the "weak" are those who do not believe in Jesus does not work, for the verbal parallels do not reflect conceptual parallels.

The letter of Romans is addressed to Christians (1.6). Romans 4 begins in a way that might lead us to think that it is addressed to non-Christian Jews (4.1), but by the end of the chapter it is clearly Jewish and Gentile Christians who are being addressed (4.23–25).[159] Within Rom. 14.1–15.13, the strongest evidence for viewing the "weak" as Christians is that their distinctive behavior is understood as being done "for the Lord" (14.6). While Nanos considers the use of "Lord" and "God" in 14.1–8 alongside the omission of "Christ" as "inclusive of non-Christian Jewish faith,"[160] he does not see that 14.9 seems to define the κύριος of the preceding verse as a Christ who has already died and risen. Bousset has argued that κύριος clearly refers to Jesus in early Christian communities of the diaspora.[161] This seems to be confirmed in Romans, where except for the quotations from Paul's scriptures, almost all of the instances of κύριος must be taken as referring to Jesus.[162] The activity that Paul wants to be performed within the community, οἰκοδομή (Rom. 14.19; 15.2), is elsewhere character-ized by Paul as something that happens within the Christian community, and not as evangelism.[163]

The minimization of the Claudius edict that Nanos uses to

---

[159] J. S. Siker, *Disinheriting the Jews: Abraham in Early Christian Controversy* (Louisville: Westminster/John Knox, 1991), 57–58.

[160] Nanos, *Mystery*, 113.

[161] W. Bousset, *Kyrios Christos* (trans. J. E. Steely; Nashville: Abingdon, 1970), 147.

[162] The OT quotations in Romans that use κύριος to refer to God are: Rom. 4.8; 9.28–29; 10.13, 16; 11.3, 34; 12.19; 14.11; 15.11. Of the twenty-five other uses of κύριος outside of Rom. 14.1–8 in the letter (not counting 16.24), the only two that could refer to God are 10.12 and 12.11, though the context in both cases indicates Jesus. All others must be taken as referring to Jesus.

[163] 1 Cor. 3.9; 14.3, 5, 12, 26; 2 Cor. 5.1; 10.8; 12.19. Similarly, Eph. 2.21; 4.12, 16, 29. Paul does use the verb οἰκοδομέω once for evangelism, in Rom. 15.20. Otherwise

support his picture of Paul's audience as still within the synagogue community does not convincingly show why we must take Cassius Dio and Suetonius as referring to the same event.[164] I think it more likely that since Claudius inherited the problem of Jewish unrest from Caligula and had to deal with it repeatedly, it is best to take the divergent testimonies of Cassius Dio and Suetonius as referring to two different events.[165] Nanos uses Acts 28.21–22 to argue that the Jewish and Christian communities of Rome were not as polarized as some think, on the basis of "the edict of Claudius construct" that portrays a complete break between synagogue and church occurring after the Claudius edict. It is an argument from silence that questions why Luke doesn't present the Jewish leaders as more familiar with Christianity and negative toward it.[166] While we might question Nanos's use of Acts 28.21–22 as historical evidence, all that these two verses picture is some Jewish leaders in Rome who do not know Paul but know that Christianity is ubiquitously in ill repute claiming that they want to hear Paul. Luke is painting with broad strokes here. The portrait could fit a situation of complete polarization, or one in which Christians are still in the synagogue ambit. While Nanos' dismissal of "the edict of Claudius construct" is not convincing to me, it should highlight for us the limits of historical reconstruction based on this edict.

Instead we need to return to the text of Romans. There we find plenty of evidence that Christianity is separate from Judaism, though Paul wants his Christian readers to remember the Jewish roots of their faith and the Jewish place in God's plan. Such texts as Rom. 2.17–29; 3.1–3; 9–11; 15.30–31 not only indicate a theological distinction between Jews and Christians; they indicate a social distinction as well. Nanos's presentation that shows how Paul uses the same language to address either "Christians" or "non-Christian Jews" does not note how Paul qualifies his reference

it also is only used in an intra-Christian sense (1 Cor. 8.1; 10.23; 14.4, 17; 1 Thess. 5.11) or neutrally (1 Cor. 8.10; Gal. 2.18).

[164] Dio Cassius, *Hist.* 60.6.6; Suetonius, *Claudius* 25.4. The possibility is dismissed with a good question, "Why would [Dio] note what did not happen when writing the history of what did happen unless he was challenging another version of the event(s) at this point?" (Nanos, *Mystery*, 381 n. 31). I answer that he was distinguishing this event, which happened in 41 CE, from other expulsions of the Jews (cf. Dio Cassius, *Hist.* 57.18.5).

[165] Ben Witherington, "Claudius, Jews, and a *Religio Licita*," 1996 SNTS paper (material also to be found in his forthcoming Acts commentary); Fitzmyer, *Romans*, 32; Dunn, *Romans*, xlix.

[166] Nanos, *Mystery*, 375–76.

to his unbelieving Jewish brothers (9.3). All the references to parallel language for Jews come from chapters 4, 9, and 11,[167] sections in which Paul highlights the theological heritage that Jews and Christians share, in order to support his gospel. Nowhere do these common terms of address seem to indicate the inclusion of Christians within the synagogue. Indeed, Paul's pathos at the beginning of chapter 9 makes most sense if some sort of separation, much as we regret it today, has already happened between synagogue and church. The "weak," as far as I can tell, were Christians. It remains for us to summarize our understanding of the motivation behind their abstinent diet in Rome.

Final analysis on motivation of "weak" abstinence

With regard to the abstinence occasioned by the attitude toward certain foodstuffs as κοινός, the following arguments may be cited on the side of viewing the abstinence in meat and wine as a particularly Jewish function: (1) The usage of κοινός to designate something as "profane" was almost exclusively Jewish; (2) Differences in eating habits between Jew and Gentile were apparently inevitable, as indicated, for example, in 1 Cor. 10.32; (3) The Jew/Gentile pairing that occurs in Rom. 15.8–12 points toward (but does not necessitate) a division in the community that was somehow related to Jewish distinctiveness; (4) The description of a controversy within the church is easily interpreted in light of the Jew/Gentile distinction that runs throughout the letter.[168] Whether one agrees with Joel Marcus's suggestion on the exact epithets Jew and Gentile in Rome used to insult one another, his article at least illustrates the probability that disunity in the Roman churches stemmed from ethnic strife;[169] (5) We have clear examples from the first century of Jewish vegetarianism in Rome and a Jewish Christian who was a vegetarian;[170] (6) If one assumes the Roman provenance of the book of Hebrews,[171] Heb. 13.9 indicates that there was a group in Rome which thought that a certain diet gave it some sort of spiritual advantage. The following verse makes it

[167] Ibid., 110–13.
[168] See Rom. 1.16; 2.9–10, 17, 28–29; 3.1, 9, 29; 9–11; 15.25–27, 31. Possible evidence may be gleaned from the use of συγγενής in 9.3; 16.7, 11, 21.
[169] "Circumcision," 67–81.
[170] On Jewish vegetarianism in Rome, see Josephus, *Vita* 14. The Jewish-Christian vegetarian was James (according to Hegesippus in Eusebius, *HE* 2.23.5).
[171] See discussion near end of chapter 4.

likely that this diet was somehow linked to Judaism, for a comparison is made to the altar from which those who served in the tabernacle ate.[172] These factors combine to make a background of diaspora Judaism, with all of the syncretism it inevitably involved, the best candidate for the asceticism of the "weak."

Against viewing the background of the "weak" attitudes as limited to Judaism, three arguments may be listed: (1) The sheer number of reasons for vegetarianism and its popularity in the Greco-Roman world, as well as the profound influence that Hellenistic thought had on Jewish asceticism,[173] make one hesitate to label the "weak" abstinence as particularly Jewish in motivation. Roman Jews may have abstained from meat for different reasons. Romano Penna helpfully emphasizes the variety within the Jewish communities of first-century Rome. The Jews in Rome were not as organized or unified a body as those in Alexandria;[174] (2) Some similarities exist between the "weak" attitudes toward dietary consumption and what we know of pagan Greek thought in relation to the drive for purity and an approach to the deity through asceticism; (3) No reference is made to Torah or to the Jews in connection with the description of the attitudes of the "weak" or "strong." This is certainly the weakest of the arguments, since Paul may have had another reason for remaining silent about Torah here, i.e., pacifying those in the implied audience who accuse him of shamefully countenancing antinominianism and immorality.[175] But the lack of a distinct Jew/Gentile reference, admittedly an argument from silence, is conspicuous in a letter that elsewhere does not hesitate to mention the Jew/Gentile distinction.[176]

The abstinence of the "weak" in the Roman community must therefore be identified as a composite of Jewish and pagan values current in first-century Rome. Since the "weak" abstained "for the Lord" (Rom. 14.6b) and probably used the term κοινός to apply to unclean food, it is likely that there was Jewish influence in their practices. But given the variety of reasons to abstain from meat in first-century Rome, the popularity of Jewish customs among Romans who remained outside of Judaism and the Hellenistic

---

[172] M. B. Isaacs, "Hebrews 13.9–16 Revisited," *NTS* 43 (1997) 282, takes "food," "camp," and "city" as representative not "of Judaism *per se* but the Mosaic cult."

[173] In addition to literature already cited, see J. Z. Smith, "Wisdom and Apocalyptic," in *Map Is Not Territory*, 67–87.

[174] 'Les Juifs à Rome au temps de l'apôtre Paul," *NTS* 28 (1982) 327–28.

[175] Cf. Rom. 3.5–8; 6.12–23; 7.12, 14.

[176] Rom. 2.1–16; 11.13–24.

influences within diaspora Judaism, one cannot say that the meat abstinence was exclusively motivated by Jewish concerns.[177] That Jews were open to association of their practices with pagan philosophers is seen in Josephus.[178] Such syncretism was entirely possible within first-century Judaism or Christianity.

The number of reasons for people in first-century Rome to abstain from meat and wine is sufficient to place the burden of proof on those who state that Rom. 14.1–15.13 addresses an hypothetical situation. Eclectic asceticism within a religious community in Rome appears expected when the variety of attitudes that could lead to dietary abstinence among first-century Romans is realized. In terms of consumption, it appears that the "weak" contained a Jewish element, though they must not be identified as exclusively Jewish. We begin to see the "weak" as clearly a product of their environment, a city that was wary and yet fascinated by the religions of the East.[179]

We have also identified a range of possible motives behind the abstinence of the "weak." If the more likely of these motives are accepted, our understanding of the variety within early Christian attitudes is enriched. We consider this variety in the next two chapters in relation to the observance of days.

[177] Here I am in agreement with Watson, *Paul, Judaism and the Gentiles*, 95, who states that the "weak" may have had proselytes to Judaism in their number, and some ethnic Jews could have been among the "strong." Similarly, Robert Jewett, *Christian Tolerance: Paul's Message to the Modern Church* (Philadelphia: Westminster, 1982), 28.

[178] Josephus, *AJ* 15.371; *C. Apion.* 162–65. Tomson is on the right track in looking both to rabbinic and Cynic parallels in his investigation of our passage; *Paul and the Jewish Law*, 246–48. But his use of the loan word ἀσθενής in *m. Yoma* 3.5 as the guiding indicator for its significance in 1 Cor. 8–10 and Romans 14–15 misses the differences between the rabbinic usage (sick, infirm) and its NT usage (careful, scrupulous; *Paul and the Jewish Law*, 195).

[179] Cf. Seneca, *Ep.* 108.22; Horace, *Sat.* 1.9.68–72; and Juvenal, *Sat.* 3.62 – "Iam pridem Syrus in Tiberim defluxit Orontes" ("Long since the Orontes of Syria has flowed into the Tiber"), *Juvenal and Persius* (trans. G. G. Ramsay; LCL; London: William Heinemann, 1940).

7

THE OBSERVANCE OF DAYS IN ROMANS 14.5-6

Διὰ τί ἡμέρα ἡμέρας ὑπερέχει,
    καὶ πᾶν φῶς ἡμέρας ἐνιαυτοῦ ἀφ᾽ ἡλίου;
ἐν γνώσει κυρίου διεχωρίσθησαν,
    καὶ ἠλλοίωσεν καιροὺς καὶ ἑορτάς: Sirach 33.7-8

Why does a day surpass other days,
    though all a year's daylight comes from the sun?
By the Lord's knowledge they were distinguished,
    and he differentiated seasons and feasts.

Terminology of practice

ὃς μὲν γὰρ κρίνει ἡμέραν παρ᾽ ἡμέραν, ὃς δὲ κρίνει
πᾶσαν ἡμέραν (Rom. 14.5ab)

This sentence indicates that some in the community considered certain days to be significant. Their understanding of the calendar was motivated by religious concerns, i.e., certain days were observed as religiously significant, as verse 6a makes clear. We certainly cannot say that *everyone* in the "weak" group of vegetarians invested certain days with religious significance. But if we follow Paul in seeing that there are primarily two groups in the church, "strong" and "weak," then the one who "judges[1] one day above another day" is probably one of the "weak."

Rauer thinks that 14.1-12 describes one point of controversy in the church. In this reading, verses 5-6 describe from a new angle

---

[1] Though κρίνω here in 14.5 means "observe" or "regard" because of the parallel use of φρονέω in the next verse, it is helpful to retain "judge" as our translation of κρίνω, since it functions as a Stichwort in this section, usually meaning "judge" (Bradley, "Origins of the Hortatory Materials," 159, 163).

the disagreement over food already mentioned in verses 1–2. For Rauer, "to judge a day" in verses 5–6 means to fast from meat on that day. This leads him to conclude that the one who observes all days equally is the "weak" one, who always abstains from meat. According to Rauer, the "strong" fasted (or abstained) from meat only on certain days, so they are the ones who made religious distinctions between days.[2]

But in other cases where a scrupulous or "weak" habit of observing days is mentioned, it is always the case that certain days are selected above others as more important. Theophrastus' "religious person" (δεισιδαίμων) observes the fourth and seventh days each month.[3] Most telling against Rauer's view is the dialogue between two Romans that Horace records, in which the one who is observing a special Sabbath calls himself *infirmior*, a "weaker one."[4] People who *abstain* from food are more prone to observe certain days as important than are people who eat everything. And one who makes distinctions in foods is more likely to make distinctions in days than to treat them all the same.

If one accepts the ὃς μέν-ὃς δέ construction of 14.5 as a second indication of difference between "weak" and "strong" groups,[5] an identification of the "weak" one as the person mentioned in 14.5a (ὃς ... κρίνει ἡμέραν παρ' ἡμέραν) necessarily leads to linking the person mentioned in verse 5b who views all days equally with the "strong."

Not as many parallels from contemporary sources exist for those who treat all days equally as compared to the parallels for observing special days. Those who observe days as especially important are understandably considered more noteworthy than those who make no distinction in days. Perhaps the best examples from a Roman context of people observing all days alike are descriptions of leaders leaving for battle on days religiously unfit for such action.[6] With regard to the "strong," then, we conclude that their basic attitude was to regard all days as equal in religious significance.

[2] Rauer, *Die "Schwachen,"* 180–83.

[3] Theophrastus, *Char.* 16. 10.

[4] Horace, *Sat.* 1.9.68–72. See quotation on pp. 53–54 above.

[5] Against Rauer, *Die "Schwachen,"* 182–83, who at 14.6 sees the completed description of three groups: (1) ὁ φρονῶν τὴν ἡμέραν (one who fasts on selected days); (2) ὁ ἐσθίων (one who never fasts); (3) ὁ μὴ ἐσθίων (= ὃς κρίνων πᾶσαν ἡμέραν, the "weak" one who always fasts).

[6] Cicero, *Div.* 1.29.

ὁ φρονῶν τὴν ἡμέραν κυρίῳ φρονεῖ (Rom. 14.6a)

"Observe" (φρονέω) as used in Paul carries in every other case the general connotation of thinking. No connotation of fasting or any other activity besides thinking is given in the other instances of φρονέω.[7] Bertram offers the sense of "to observe" for φρονέω in 14.6, but then goes too far when he states, "The point is that we are not to observe cultic rules and customs but to see to it that decision is made in responsibility to the Lord."[8] This statement overlooks the indicative mood of φρονεῖ in 14.6. Paul is not telling one group of believers to observe certain days for the Lord; they are already observing days for the Lord, as the text indicates. This point is helpful in eliminating pagan designations of certain days as the background for the observance mentioned here.

φρονέω in Rom. 15.5 is used in the usual NT sense of "think." Its use there reveals that the challenge the "weak" present for Paul is that they do not think in what he perceives to be a proper way.[9]

Significance of day observance in first-century Rome

Observance of days as a religious boundary marker

The issue of food as an indication of social power is not necessarily related to the observance of days, though humans mark significant days by the meals customarily prepared on them.[10] In the observance of days practiced by one group of Roman believers, we therefore encounter a second means of drawing a boundary marker,[11] for a group's designation of certain days serves to give it a sense of order and distinguish it from those who do not observe such days.

---

[7] Aside from the two instances of φρονέω in 14.6, the other occurrences in the greater Pauline corpus are: Rom. 8.5; 11.20; 12.3*bis*, 16*bis*; 15.5; 1 Cor. 13.11; 2 Cor. 13.11; Gal. 5.10; Phil. 1.7; 2.2*bis*, 5; 3.15*bis*, 19; 4.2, 10*bis*; Col. 3.2.

[8] G. Bertram, "φρήν, κ.τ.λ.," *TDNT* IX (1974) 233.

[9] Cf. Plutarch, *Superst.* 165D, on the irrational state (τὸ ἀλόγιστον) that comes with superstitious fear.

[10] See Douglas, "Deciphering a Meal," 62.

[11] Against Sanday–Headlam (*Romans*, 386), who do not view the difference in observance of days as actually occurring in Rome, and Rauer (*Die "Schwachen,"* 183), who views the mention of it here as part of Paul's strategy to bring unity over the issue of diet rather than a separate issue of contention in the church. Sampley, "The Weak and the Strong," 42, considers Rom. 14.5–6 to be Paul's generalized treatment of a difference over Sabbath observance.

The religious function is evident at the surface of the text, for 14.6a reads, ὁ φρονῶν τὴν ἡμέραν κυρίῳ φρονεῖ. Given the fact that the observance of days was a religious activity, we look first at how observance of days functions in religion in general.

After commenting on the interplay of eternity and temporality within "sacred time," Gerardus van der Leeuw states, "He who is celebrating, so to say, controls time; he attempts to dominate it."[12] The idea of controlling time is close to the notion of power. This connection is confirmed in van der Leeuw's continuing discussion, for he summarizes, "The calendar, then, indicates clearly which instants of time have value and possess power; each period, each instant, has specific individuality and its own potency." The distinction of days within religion is therefore a means of defining and gaining power amid the phenomena of one's world.[13] The implications for a group called "weak" who did observe days beside one called "strong" who did not is best explained after we have noted the general significance of day observance in the late Republic and early Empire.

The Roman tendency to categorize days

We have already seen that Paul presents the observance of days as an act of piety,[14] and this is consonant with Roman religion in general.

In Rome, a detailed religious calendar was observed, since the observance of specific days was essential in Roman state religion.[15] Nor is it fully accurate to state that only certain days were religiously significant. Since the Roman calendar had a notation for every day of the year, we see that every day was assigned a value in relation to its place in religious observance. The calendrical designations, *F*, *C*, or *N* provided the Roman citizen with guidelines for what activities could be performed on a given day, though these

---

[12] G. van der Leeuw, *Religion in Essence and Manifestation* (trans. J. E. Turner; 1963; reprint ed., Gloucester, Mass.: Peter Smith, 1967), II.385.

[13] Ibid., II.386.

[14] See Rom. 14.6a.

[15] See the discussion in Georg Wissowa, *Religion und Kultus der Römer*, 50–54, and the calendars provided there, 491–515. On the Roman calendar in ancient times and the Republic, see Theodor Mommsen, *Die römische Chronologie bis auf Caesar* (2nd ed.; Berlin: Weidmann, 1859).

were supplemented by other designations on some calendars.[16] Some religious days were invested with significance beyond the basic *nefastus* designation, as, for instance, the *dies atri*.[17]

But given the nature of Roman religion, it would be mistaken to confine a discussion of the Roman calendar to the category of "religion," as such a category is perceived today. In modern categories, a distinction in observance of days within Roman society constituted more than a religious statement. It also served as a claim for social influence on others.

This is illustrated in the difficulty of separating religion and politics, at least in regard to Roman state religion. Beard and Crawford helpfully explicate this difficulty:

> In contrast to the modern Western stress on private manifestations of religious commitment, religious observance in Rome consisted primarily in public or communal rituals and the interests of the gods were perceived to lie above all in the business of the state, in political and military action.[18]

With regard to our understanding of Rom. 14.1–15.13, therefore, it is necessary to stress that factors both of religious expression and church administration were at work in the observance of days mentioned there. But the identification of such factors is not meant to signify that such a distinction was present in the minds of the Roman Christians who differed on this issue. It is rather to help readers today understand the dynamic behind observance of days for Romans under the early Empire.

The observance of religious days had been used as a political tactic in the late Republic.[19] Religious significance was proclaimed

---

[16] *F* = *fas* or *fastus*, meaning that business could be conducted freely. *C* = *comitiales*, meaning that the *comitia* were allowed to convene on these days; business could also be conducted if no other prohibition was stated. *N* = *nefastus*, meaning that the day was religious; business could not be conducted on it. The significance of calendrical designations is detailed by W. Ward Fowler, *The Roman Festivals of the Period of the Republic: An Introduction to the Study of the Religion of the Romans* (London: Macmillan, 1908), 8–10.

[17] These days occurred on the days following the *Kalends*, *Nones*, and *Ides* of each month. No religious rites of state could be performed on them. H. H. Scullard, *Festivals and Ceremonies of the Roman Republic* (Ithaca: Cornell University Press, 1981), 46.

[18] Mary Beard and Michael Crawford, *Rome in the Late Republic* (London: Duckworth, 1985), 30.

[19] See L. R. Taylor, *Party Politics in the Age of Caesar* (SCL 22; 1949; reprint ed., Berkeley: University of California Press, 1961), 78–84.

for certain days, in order to delay or block legislation and other political moves. Though the actual operation of the government was different in the Principate, we still see the conjunction of religious and political significance in the observance of days. For example, Tacitus records that the charges Nero used against Thrasea Paetus include failure to observe the Juvenalia days[20] as one in his order (senator and quindecimviral priest) was expected and failing to take the vows that priests in his position were expected to take at the beginning of each year.[21]

Given the fact that the observance of days was a means of exerting influence on others by those in government posts, the possibility remains that day observance was a significant arena for maintaining order in other groups,[22] including the church. It now remains for us to focus on the sociological implications of observance of days in regard to the community depicted in Rom. 14.1–15.13.

Sociological significance of observance of days

The controversy over observance of days in our text seems to indicate a struggle for social control in the church(es). This is because observance of days in the climate of the late Republic and early Empire represents an appropriation of the power somehow associated with certain days. Making others observe certain days then confirms one's influence over them.

As those with political influence in the state were expected to perform religious activities on certain days, it is likely that leaders in the Roman church would also be expected to observe certain days in a manner appropriate to the Christian religion. The failure of the "strong" to distinguish between days (14.5b) would be viewed by the "weak" as neglect in the role of the "strong" as church leaders.[23] The "weak" observance of days emerges then as a pious means of asserting some level of political power within the

---

[20] Tacitus, *Ann.* 16.21.

[21] Ibid., 16.22; cf. 4.17. Such oaths seem to be similar to the consular oaths of the Republic; see Scullard, *Festivals and Ceremonies*, 52–54.

[22] Cf. the prescribed dates on which dinners are to be held for the burial club in *CIL* XIV 2.112. They are associated with the birthdays of patrons and family members of patrons. Those with influence determined which days were "special."

[23] Assuming a Roman destination for Hebrews, the author might be siding with the "weak" on this issue, against Paul's more neutral stance: μὴ ἐγκαταλείποντες τὴν ἐπισυναγωγὴν ἑαυτῶν, καθὼς ἔθος τισίν (Heb. 10.25a).

church. Despite the "weak" label and "weak" tendency to be affected by the actions of the "strong" in matters of consumption (14.15, 20–21, 23), the observance of days remained an arena in which the "weak" attempted to exercise political power in the church. It now remains for us to examine the motivation behind the observance of days in the Roman churches.

8

THE IDENTIFICATION OF DAY
OBSERVANCE IN THE ROMAN CHURCHES

Ne Iudaeus quidem, mi Tiberi, tam diligenter sabbatis
ieiunium servat quam ego hodie servavi.

Not even a Jew, my Tiberius, observes the Sabbath fast as
scrupulously as I observed it today.   Augustus[1]

Comparative analysis of day observance

Day observance in Rom. 14.1–15.13 and Hellenistic
religion

A background check on the observance of days in any religious
group in the Mediterranean world must consider the significance of
designating certain days in Hellenistic religion. Such observance is
one of the religious practices included in the later additions to
Hesiod's *Works and Days* and is an indication of increased concern
that humans live justly in relation to the gods.[2] The rules on this
kind of day observance had a Delphic background,[3] and remained
a definite part of Hellenistic religion. When someone followed these
injunctions excessively or in a fearful way, the person was considered superstitious. Thus both Theophrastus and Plutarch include
the observance of days in their caricatures of superstitious people.
Theophrastus' δεισιδαίμων, who is very scrupulous on the fourth
and seventh days of each month,[4] must be read in light of Hesiod's
teaching, Πρῶτον ἔνη τετράς τε καὶ ἑβδόμη ἱερὸν ἦμαρ τῇ
γὰρ Ἀπόλλωνα χρυσάορα γείνατο Λητώ ("To begin with, the first,

---

[1] Augustus *apud* Suetonius, *Aug.* 76.
[2] Martin P. Nilsson, *A History of Greek Religion* (2nd ed.; trans. F. J. Fielden;
Oxford: Clarendon, 1949; reprint ed., Westport, Conn.: Greenwood, 1980), 186–89.
[3] Ibid., 188–89.
[4] Theophrastus, *Char.* 16. 10.

the fourth, and the seventh – on which Leto bare Apollo with the blade of gold – each is a holy day").[5] Plutarch's example of Nicias' fearful inactivity during a lunar eclipse[6] may be usefully compared with the importance Hesiod accords the moon.[7] This shows us how superstition is an outgrowth of a pious desire to please the gods, especially since Plutarch also uses Hesiod's *Works and Days* positively at *Superst.* 169B.

It is unlikely that the day observance of the Roman church members was directly influenced by Hellenistic day observance, since the text says ὁ φρονῶν τὴν ἡμέραν κυρίῳ φρονεῖ (Rom. 14.6a). But in a history-of-religions perspective, the concern the Christian "weak" showed in observing days as a necessary part of religious practice no doubt had its background in observance of the Hellenistic calendar. Piety that included day observance could easily be baptized into a piety that observed days "for the Lord."[8]

Day observance in Rom. 14.1–15.13 and Roman religion

The view that the "weak" attitude toward days was based on direct observance of the Roman calendar with its auspicious and inauspicious days[9] is also rendered unlikely by Paul's statement in 14.6a.[10] Käsemann states that "Christians are in view who are convinced that days stand under lucky or unlucky stars."[11] His suggestion does open the possibility that the observation of days by the "weak" was astrologically based. There is ample evidence that astrology was viewed by some as superstitious and so could be

---

[5] *Hesiod: The Homeric Hymns and Homerica* (trans. H. G. Evelyn-White; LCL; London: William Heinemann, 1936), *Works and Days* 770.

[6] Plutarch, *Superst.* 169A.

[7] Hesiod, *Works and Days* 772, 780; *Ad lunam* 3–5.

[8] Cf. Hesiod, *Works and Days* 826–27, on the εὐδαίμων τε καὶ ὄλβιος ("happy and lucky" one) who follows the preceding instructions and therefore ἐργάζηται ἀναίτιος ἀθανάτοισιν ("does his work without offending the deathless gods"). The basic study on the Greek context of observance of days is M. P. Nilsson, *Die Entstehung und sakrale Bedeutung des griechischen Kalenders* (Lund: Gleerup/ Leipzig: Otto Harrassowitz, 1918).

[9] On the Roman calendar, see Wissowa, *Religion und Kultus der Römer*, 365–81 (discussion), 491–515 (monthly charts of the calendar); Georges Dumézil, *Archaic Roman Religion* (trans. Philip Krapp; 2 vols.; Chicago: University of Chicago Press, 1970), I.333–40.

[10] Rauer, *Die "Schwachen,"* 179.

[11] Käsemann, *Romans*, 370. He cites only Billerbeck and Lagrange after this suggestion.

considered "weak."[12] But the connection between astrology and the "weak" observance of days mentioned in Rom. 14.5–6 also, because of the general dearth of evidence for Christians who practiced some form of astrology,[13] makes this view tenuous at best, and most likely off the mark.

It has been suggested that the "weakness" in the Roman church was a matter of food offered to idols (εἰδωλόθυτα) in which the "weak" attitude toward days involved a change of lifestyle on the pagan feast days so as to avoid contamination.[14] Such an interpretation is certainly possible, but the place of εἰδωλόθυτα as the central concern in the Roman controversy cannot be proven.[15] The difficulties with Greek, Roman, astrological, and sacrificial contamination motivations for the day observance lead us to a consideration of Sunday observance as the possible background for the day observance of the "weak" in Rome.

Day observance in Rom. 14.1–15.13 and Christian Sunday

The suggestion may also be made that the observance of days that the "weak" observe is specifically Christian in background. The tendency for Christians to distinguish their special days from those of Judaism is exemplified in *Did.* 8.1, which refers to fasting on days other than when followers of Judaism fast. Earlier attestation for Christian observance of days, Sunday observance, occurs in the New Testament.[16] Since Sunday is called κυριακὴ ἡμέρα in Rev.

[12] See Tacitus, *Ann.* 6.20–21, where Tiberius' use of astrology is recounted; Tacitus' own reservations on the art follow in 6.22. For astrology in Rome around the time of the composition of Romans, see F. H. Cramer, *Astrology in Roman Law and Politics* (MAPS 37; Philadelphia: American Philosophical Society, 1954), 115–31; 241–43. For further information (including a list of astrological references in the *SHA*) and perspective on the place of astrology in the Empire, see Ronald Syme's chapter, "Astrology in the Historia Augusta," in his *Historia Augusta Papers* (Oxford: Clarendon, 1983), 80–97. On "astral immortality" in Pythagoreanism, see Walter Burkert, *Lore and Science in Ancient Pythagoreanism* (trans. E. L. Minar, Jr.; Cambridge, Mass.: Harvard University Press, 1972), 350–68.

[13] Cramer, *Astrology*, 78, mentions that Pope Gregory I believed in catasterism (*Moralia* 17.16; *PL* 76.21–22), but instances are hard to find beyond that.

[14] Rauer, *Die "Schwachen,"* 179–80. He apparently bases this interpretation on the analogy of *Aboda zara* 1.1 concerning Jewish response to pagan feast days (180 n. 1). No commentators are cited.

[15] Ibid., 180. Rauer admits that this explanation stands or falls with whether one can find in the text a fear of contamination from meat offered to idols (εἰδωλόθυτα). We have already seen above in chapter 2 that this term does not occur in Rom. 14.1–15.13.

[16] Acts 20.7; 1 Cor. 16.2; Rev. 1.10. See also *Did.* 14.1.

1.10, it does seem possible that the day Paul describes as observed κυρίῳ (Rom. 14.6a) is Sunday.

Rauer rejects the Christian holiday of Sunday as the "weak" observance because of the fact (undocumented in his text) that it does not fit with our knowledge of the early church.[17] Zahn states that the churches in the sphere of Paul's influence show unmistakable signs of Sunday observance.[18] While we might object that the churches of Rome are outside of Paul's influence when he writes his letter, the people there whom Paul seems to know, according to Romans 16, indicate that they may have moved in Paul's circles. It is probable that some Roman believers were observing Sunday as the Lord's day.

Another objection to a consideration of Sunday as being behind the special day observed in the Roman churches is that if the Lord's day observance was quite common by this time, it is unlikely that this would have been the point around which the attitudes toward days differed. Along with this argument, one might object that 14.6a becomes awkwardly tautologous if the attitude Paul is describing has primary reference to the Lord's day. But these objections are not sensitive to the milieu of day observance in first-century Rome. If one were baptized into the believing community from a Roman background that held all days religiously significant, the observance of a special Christian day could very well be considered superstitious. And Paul's description of the motive in 14.6a, though perhaps tautologous, could well be a necessary reminder that however superstitious the day observance appears, it is done for the Lord. The observance of days to which Paul refers has become a Christian observance in the minds of the "weak" (Rom. 14.6a).

Thus far in the survey of possible interpretations of the attitude toward days that the "weak" held, the Christian observance of the Lord's day, supported as it is by the κυρίῳ of Rom. 14.6a and evidence outside of Romans for the early practice of believers' gatherings on Sunday, makes Sunday observance a much more likely possibility than Greek or Roman day observance. We turn now to examine the Sabbath as a possible background to the special day of Rom. 14.5–6.

[17] Rauer, *Die "Schwachen,"* 176.
[18] T. Zahn, *Geschichte des Sonntags vornehmlich in der alten Kirche* (Hanover: Carl Mener, 1878), 22.

Day observance in Rom. 14.1–15.13 and Judaism

Sabbaths[19] and new moon festivals are the holidays usually cited as possible Jewish festive days over which observance in the community differed.[20] Further evidence that the attitudes toward days might have included the notion of Sabbath observance comes in extant evidence of what Romans thought about the Sabbath. The frequency of references to the Sabbath, both in the legal and literary sources for the early Empire, combines with our knowledge of a populous Jewish community in Rome[21] and traditions of a Jewish element within the Roman church to place Sabbath observance as a logical possibility when we read ὃς μὲν γὰρ κρίνει ἡμέραν παρ' ἡμέραν in Rom. 14.5. If a person were conspicuous for a unique attitude toward days in the early Empire, the legal and literary evidence shows that the Jewish attitude toward the Sabbath would be one of the prime targets for attention, and in some cases, scorn.

The Jews had received imperial permission for observance of the Sabbath.[22] Philo comments that when the grain dole fell on a Sabbath, some was set aside in order to allow the Jews to collect their grain on the following day.[23]

While the satirists scorned Sabbath observance, there is clear evidence that some Romans thought it fashionable to observe the Sabbath. Ovid describes the Sabbath as a good day to meet women, perhaps because some women associated with the senatorial order allowed themselves to socialize more on that day: "Nec te praetereat Veneri ploratus Adonis, cultaque Iudaeo septima sacra Syro" ("Nor let Adonis bewailed of Venus escape you, nor the

---

[19] On Sabbath observance see Emil Schürer, *The History of the Jewish People in the Age of Jesus Christ (175 B.C.–A.D. 135)*, Vol. II (eds. M. Black, F. Millar, and G. Vermes; rev. ed.; Edinburgh: T. & T. Clark, 1979), 467–75.

[20] See, e.g., Cranfield, *Romans*, 694–95, 705; Wilckens, *Römer*, III.83; Dunn, *Romans*, 805. But cf. Lietzmann, *Römer*, 115, who refuses to place it definitely in a Jewish background.

[21] H. J. Leon, *The Jews of Ancient Rome* (Philadelphia: Jewish Publication Society of America, 1960), 257; Jean Juster, *Les Juifs dans l'Empire romain: leur condition juridique, économique et sociale* (2 vols.; Paris: Paul Geuthner, 1914; reprint ed., New York: Burt Franklin, 1965), I.209.

[22] Josephus, *AJ* 14.226–27, 242–43, 246, 258, 261, 263–64; 16.163, 173; 20.13. See Juster, *Les Juifs*, I.354–57, for the Jewish Sabbath in Roman law; for Roman allowance of Jewish feasts, II.121–22.

[23] Philo, *Legat.* 158.

seventh day that the Syrian Jew holds sacred").[24] Augustine quotes Seneca's generalization that no doubt includes the fad of Sabbath observance: "victi victoribus leges dederunt" ("The subjects have given laws to their captors").[25] Indeed, it appears that the Jewish Sabbath was popular among some of the upper levels of Roman society.[26] But like Rome's attitude toward other foreign ideas, its faddish interest in the Sabbath was accompanied by scorn in some quarters.

Seneca writes critically of the practice of lighting lamps at the beginning of the Sabbath, as if it is an instance of misguided superstition:

> Quomodo sint di colendi, solet praecipi. Accendere aliquem lucernas sabbatis prohibeamus, quoniam nec lumine di egent et ne homines quidem delectantur fuligine.

> Precepts are commonly given as to how the gods should be worshipped. But let us forbid lamps to be lighted on the Sabbath, since the gods do not need light, neither do men take pleasure in soot.[27]

Persius also writes critically of the Sabbath as an outward form of the Judaism he knows.[28] Juvenal describes how a son may follow a father in holding the Sabbath in special regard. The practice is associated with disrespect for Roman law and idleness or sloth.

> Romanas autem soliti contemnere leges Iudaicum ediscunt et servant ac metuunt ius ... sed pater in causa, cui septima quaeque fuit lux ignava et partem vitae non attigit ullam.

> Having been wont to flout the laws of Rome, they learn and practise and revere the Jewish law ... For all which the

---

[24] Ovid, *The Art of Love (Ars Amatoria)* (trans. J. H. Mozley, 2nd ed. rev. G. P. Gould; London: William Heinemann, 1979), 1.75–76.

[25] Augustine, *CD* 6.11.

[26] See R. Goldenberg, "The Jewish Sabbath in the Roman World up to the Time of Constantine the Great," *ANRW* II.19.1 (1979), 441–42: "Jewish ritual thus entered the world of upper-class Rome primarily as a fad."

[27] *Seneca: Ad Lucilium epistulae morales*, Vol. III (trans. R. M. Gummere; LCL; London: William Heinemann, 1925), *Ep.* 95.47. Note also Goldenberg's comment on this passage: "The kindling of lamps at the onset of the Sabbath was apparently one of the first Jewish customs which non-Jews would adopt, and Seneca was anxious to keep the practice from spreading" ("Jewish Sabbath," 434).

[28] Persius, *Sat.* 5.179–84, portrays a Sabbath dinner in a way that makes it appear strange for Roman sensibilities. See also Goldenberg, "Jewish Sabbath," 435, on this passage.

father was to blame, who gave up every seventh day to idleness, keeping it apart from all the concerns of life.[29]

Similarly, Tacitus' statement on the Sabbath principle shows both the Roman caricature of laziness and the uncertainty of its origin.

> Septimo die otium placuisse ferunt, quia is finem laborum tulerit; dein blandiente inertia septimum quoque annum ignaviae datum.

> They say that they first chose to rest on the seventh day because that day ended their toil; but after a time they were led by the claims of indolence to give over the seventh year as well to inactivity.[30]

Aside from sloth, Plutarch characterizes it as a fearful superstition.

> ἀλλ' Ἰουδαῖοι σαββάτων ὄντων ἐν ἀγνάμπτοις καθεζόμενοι, τῶν πολεμίων κλίμακας προστιθέντων καὶ τὰ τείχη καταλαμβανόντων, οὐκ ἀνέστησαν ἀλλ' ἔμειναν ὥσπερ ἐν σαγήνῃ μιᾷ τῇ δεισιδαιμονίᾳ συνδεδεμένοι.

> But the Jews because it was the Sabbath day, sat in their places immovable, while the enemy were planting ladders against the walls and capturing the defences, and they did not get up, but remained there, fast bound in the toils of superstition as in one great net.[31]

These caricatures of Sabbath observance as idleness or cowardice are significant because they show how such day observance could be treated: it was not simply considered socially anomalous; it was scorned.[32] Philo's explicit defense of the Sabbath against the charge of idleness is also evidence that the Sabbath suffered bad press in the Hellenistic world.[33] That the Sabbath was observed "for the Lord" (14.6a) could well be a defense that Paul is giving on behalf of the "weak," to dissipate such scorn. The criticism that Sabbath

---

[29] Juvenal, *Sat.* 14.100–101; 105–106.

[30] Tacitus, *The Histories*, Vol. II (trans. Moore) 5.4.

[31] Plutarch, *Moralia*, Vol. II (trans. F. C. Babbitt; LCL; London: William Heinemann, 1928), *Superst.* 169C. Morton Smith cites Rom. 14.5 under his category of "Christian attacks on sabbath observance" in the context of his treatment of this section in Plutarch ("Superstitione," *PTWECL*, 30).

[32] Cf. Synesius' description, *Ep.* 4, of a Jewish ship captain who abandoned the helm in a storm, because it was the Sabbath (*Epistolographi Graeci*, ed. Rudolph Hercher; Paris: A. F. Didot, 1873), 641.

[33] Philo, *Spec.* 2.60–61.

observance could receive in Rome fits with caricatures of the "weak" as superstitious and foreign, caricatures that Paul wanted the "strong" to replace with respect.

By far the best-known passage of the Roman satirists on the Sabbath, and also most significant for this investigation, comes from Horace, *Sat.* 1.9.67–72, in which he describes a conversation he had with Fuscus Aristius while trying to rid himself of a tagalong.[34]

While Horace's phrase *tricesima sabbata* (thirtieth Sabbath) is difficult to explain,[35] the passage is useful in providing evidence for popular Roman interest in foreign attitudes toward days.[36] Horace describes how Fuscus, as a Roman, excuses himself from speaking on the basis of the Jewish convention of Sabbath observance. As the preceding context indicates, Fuscus is presented as joking with Horace and therefore the text does not necessarily imply that he is a devout Sabbath observer: "male salsus ridens dissimulare; meum iecur urere bilis" ("The cruel joker laughed, pretending not to understand. I grew hot with anger").[37] But the fact that Horace could place the claim of Sabbath observance in the mouth of a Roman combines with the selections from Seneca and Juvenal above to show that Sabbath observance was catching on among non-Jews in Rome. If this was the case, it would explain why Paul does not describe the controversy over the observance of days simply as a Jew versus Gentile issue in Rom. 14.5–6a.

It is also significant that Jewish Sabbath observance had reached the point in social caricatures by the time when Horace was writing that it is associated with a term for "weakness": "sum paulo infirmior, unus multorum" ("I'm a somewhat weaker brother, one of the many").[38] This dialogue in Horace also mentions avoiding

---

[34] See pp. 53–54 above for the complete quotation.

[35] Goldenberg ("Jewish Sabbath," 437–38), offers no conclusive suggestion on what "the thirtieth Sabbath" might mean. T. C. G. Thornton thinks that this phrase "very probably refers to a Jewish New Moon festival" ("Jewish New Moon Festivals, Galatians 4.3–11 and Colossians 2.16," *JTS* 40 [1989] 97). Most convincing is P. LeJay, "Le Sabbat juif et les poètes latins," *RHLR* 8 (1903) 329, who argues that the phrase means it was both the Sabbath and the new moon.

[36] E. Fraenkel notes that the Jews are the only population group mentioned in this satire, evidence of the Roman curiosity about the Jews, piqued by their distinctive lifestyle (*Horace* [1957; reprint ed., Oxford: Oxford University Press, 1970], 116).

[37] Horace, *Sat.* 1.9.65–66. LeJay thinks that Fuscus is simply placing two excuses (Sabbath and new moon) together ("Le Sabbat juif," 329).

[38] Horace, *Sat.* 1.9.71.

an insult to the Jews on the matter of Sabbath observance: "vin tu curtis Iudaeis oppedere?" ("Would you affront the circumcised Jews?")[39] exemplifies the same response that Paul fears the "strong" are effecting in the "weak."[40]

Paul's portrait of "weak" people in Rome with unique attitudes toward the observance of days is therefore in line with the social commentary of a Roman satirist who preceded him by less than a century. The argument that the day observance among the "weak" in the Roman community was Sabbath observance fits with Horace's association of Sabbath observance with the "weak"; the fascination that some Romans had for Sabbath observance – enough to make it a divisive issue in the church; the scorn that the same observance incurred by the more Roman element in imperial society, just as Paul warns against scorn in Rom. 14.10b; and the Jewish element within the "weak," seen also as the best possibility for explaining vegetarianism among the "weak."

But the Sabbath explanation for the day observance of the "weak" is not airtight. Rauer rejects the interpretation that 14.5–6a means that "weak" were observing Sabbaths while "strong" were not, because he notes the fervor with which the Sabbath was observed in the diaspora. He thinks that there must have been Gentile proselytes, who though not within the camp of the "weak," still observed the Sabbath.[41] He is correct in mentioning the practice of Sabbath observance in the diaspora. But Rauer displays no sensitivity to the historical difficulty of saying anything about the mode or intensity of Sabbath observance when the sources in Jewish law follow Paul's composition of Romans by at least four centuries. In Goldenberg's discussion of the Talmudic development of Sabbath law he pinpoints the anachronism: "This elaborate legal development characterizes only the fully mature rabbinic tradition. There is no ground for presupposing that a similar situation prevailed in earlier Jewish communities, or in those of the distant diaspora."[42] Besides the problem of historical anachronism in using

[39] *Sat.* 1.9.69. Cf. Rom. 14.3a, 10b. Horace's *oppedo* does overlap semantically with *sperno*, the Vulgate's word for ἐξουθενέω here.

[40] Rom. 14.13, 21.

[41] Rauer, *Die "Schwachen,"* 175.

[42] Goldenberg, "Jewish Sabbath," 424. In n. 50 on the same page he draws the relevant implication: "It may be observed in passing that most surveys of the Jewish world in New Testament times presuppose exactly this ... To use these materials [Jerusalem Talmud; Babylonian Talmud; "non-halakhic *midrashim*"] for a descrip-

the sources, there is also the problem of geographical disparity in expressions of Sabbath observance.[43]

Rauer makes the tacit assumption here that those who are "weak" in attitude toward eating must be identified with the "weak" in attitude toward days. He concludes that since there must have been members of the Roman church who observed the Sabbath but were not among the "weak," Sabbath observance is to be rejected as a possible referent of the attitude described in 14.5a.[44] While the texts cited by Rauer may indicate that Sabbaths were observed in early Jewish Christianity,[45] they do not eliminate the possibility that there was disagreement over the way in which observant attitudes toward the Sabbath were expressed. From the evidence of the Pauline corpus, Sabbath observance was more controversial than Rauer makes it out to be.[46]

Wilckens argues explicitly that the ὃς μέν–ὃς δέ construction of verse 5 and the alignment of day observance and eating habits in verse 6 show that the same groups of "strong" and "weak" are in view in verses 2–3 and 5.[47] Unlike Rauer, however, he does not move from this to eliminate the possibility of Sabbath observance as a trait of the "weak." The exact association of those "weak" in attitudes toward eating and "weak" in attitudes toward days cannot be pressed. It is true that 15.1 seems to indicate that there were recognizable boundaries for "strong" and "weak" groups. In that sense I can agree with Rauer and Wilckens that there was one group of "strong" and one group of "weak," broadly defined. Yet

tion of ... 'the Jewish world in the time of Jesus'... is a dangerous proceeding indeed."

[43] Ibid., 429. Note that according to some sources the Jews fasted on the Sabbath (Suetonius, *Aug.* 76; Martial, *Epig.* 4.4.7); according to others they ate fish (Persius, *Sat.* 5.183) or got drunk (Plutarch, *Quaest. conv.* 4.6.2). This comparison is made by Goldenberg, "Jewish Sabbath," 441. For evidence of differences of Sabbath observance among earlier Jews in the land, see *1 Macc.* 2.29–38.

[44] This assumption and the argument that follows from it are seen in Rauer's statement that the Sabbath must have been kept by proselytes to Judaism who then joined the Roman churches. He does not think that Sabbath observance could have been a distinguishing mark of the "weak," since so many church members in Rome probably observed the Sabbath (*Die "Schwachen,"* 175–76).

[45] Ibid., 177 n. 1, cites *Const. Ap.* 2.59; 7.23; *Can. Ap.* 68.

[46] Though ἡμέρας παρατηρεῖσθε in Gal. 4.10 is part of a caricature of those viewed as "religiously scrupulous" (Betz, *Galatians*, 217), the phrase may include an attitude of honoring the Sabbath as a part of τὰ ἀσθενῆ καὶ πτωχὰ στοιχεῖα of the preceding verse. The strand of Pauline tradition preserved in Col. 2.16 treats Sabbath observance as "weakness," a sign of unenlightened religious practice, though no term for "weakness" is explicitly given.

[47] Wilckens, *Römer*, III.83.

14.21 remains as proof that the "weak in faith" could be identified in a variety of ways, any one of which was sufficient to place that person among the "weak."

Besides the Sabbath, others suggest that other festive days of the Jewish calendar might have been in view. On the basis of the singular word "day" (ἡμέρα), used in an expression that assumes that one can choose a single day, Rauer rejects this suggestion.[48] Wilckens more reasonably refuses to exclude the possibility of calendrical observance as a whole, but states that Sabbath and fast days are more likely, since these would be more likely to account for the character of the conflict as it appears in the text, occurring in the everyday life of the community and not on the occasional feast day.[49] If Paul's brief expression of attitudes toward days possibly includes the Jewish calendar in its scope, then the diaspora observance of new moon festivals[50] would also be in view. But there is not enough evidence clearly to confirm or eliminate this possibility.

One might think, with Lietzmann and Rauer, that Judaism is not behind the "weak" attitude toward days, because of Paul's mild response to the difference in observance of days within the church.[51] But this judgment, based on the common perception of Paul's attitude toward the Judaizers in Galatians, ignores the differences in Paul's own situation and that of the addressees at the times of composition of Galatians and Romans. Second, if the faddish adoption of Sabbath observance was occurring in some segments of first-century Roman society, as argued in this chapter, Paul would not be able to treat such practices simply as a religious threat to his gospel.

What activities did the controversial observance of days involve? It might have included fasting, as Rauer contends. But we should not limit our understanding of this observance to fasting, as he does. Against Rauer's view that the observance of days refers exclusively to fasting and not to Sabbath observance in

---

[48] He argues that since the Jewish religious calendar offered its adherents no choice but to observe all its festive days, the expression does not appear to match (Rauer, *Die "Schwachen,"* 176). In n. 2 on the same page he refers to Gal. 4.10 and Col. 2.16, noting the unique use of the singular here in Rom. 14.5–6. But one should also note that in these other texts, several terms are used serially to provide the sense of adherence to a religious calendar.

[49] Wilckens, *Römer*, III.114.

[50] See Thornton, "Jewish New Moon Festivals," 97–100.

[51] Lietzmann, *Römer*, 115; Rauer, *Die "Schwachen,"* 177.

general,[52] four arguments may be noted to extend the reference of day observance to include other Sabbath observances, such as rest and social gatherings, also. (1) Paul does not state here that the attitude toward days comprises a form of fasting, though elsewhere he is ready to write about fasting.[53] Given the prevalence of fasting in religions of antiquity,[54] the practice Paul describes as observance of days may easily include fasting, but to limit such observance to that activity ignores the breadth of interpretation Paul leaves open with his expression in verses 5–6a. (2) Sabbath observance was closely connected with fasting in the minds of some writers of this period,[55] so Rauer's decision to interpret the observance as fasting unrelated to the Sabbath seems ill-advised. (3) If the judgment language of Romans 14 does parallel Romans 2,[56] then those who do observe days may be identical with those accused of judging. This would then fit with the understanding of the "weak" attitude toward days as having some background in Judaism, making a reference to Sabbath likely. (4) If the Roman provenance of Hebrews is accepted,[57] then the reference to the Sabbath in Heb. 3.16–4.11 shows that the Sabbath was indeed a controversial issue in the Roman community. Hebrews may then reflect a shift from actual observance of the Sabbath by Roman Christians to a spiritualized understanding of its significance. Given early Christianity's rejection of Sabbath observance, such a shift must have occurred at some point in the early communities that arose in the matrix of Jewish Christianity.[58] Zahn's description of how early Christians believed that the Sabbath could be fulfilled by abstaining

[52] Rauer, *Die "Schwachen,"* 180–84.

[53] νηστεία – 2 Cor. 6.5; 11.27.

[54] For example, on pagan fasting see P. R. Arbesmann, *Das Fasten bei den Griechen und Römern* (RVV 21.1; Giessen: Töpelmann, 1929). On one form of Christian fasting see Jacob Vellian, "Lenten Fast of the East Syrians," in *A Tribute to Arthur Vööbus: Studies in Early Christian Literature and its Environment, Primarily in the Syrian East*, ed. Robert H. Fischer (Chicago: Lutheran School of Theology at Chicago, 1977), 373–74, for a chart and list of fasts of east Syrian Christianity. References to fasting abound in ECL, e.g., *1 Clem.* 55.6; *Did.* 8.1; *Herm. Vis.* 3.1.2.

[55] Strabo 16.2.40; Suetonius, *Aug.* 76.

[56] Note the similarities between Rom. 2.1 and 14.4, 23 and see discussion on 14.3b in chapter 5.

[57] See discussion at end of chapter 4.

[58] For this connection I am indebted to Morton Smith's citation of Heb. 4.1–13 in a listing of texts he takes as "evidence for early *Christian observance of the sabbath*" ("Superstitione," *PTWECL*, 30). Evidence for difference over the observance of days in Roman Christianity also comes at Heb. 10.25 (ἐγκαταλείποντες τὴν ἐπισυναγωγὴν ἑαυτῶν, καθὼς ἔθος τισίν), which seems to undermine Paul's acceptance in Rom. 14.5c of those who do not observe days.

from all sin, continuing in good works, in the freedom of a good conscience and in the hope of an eternal Sabbath, may be similar to an interpretation current among the Roman "strong."[59]

It is best to be evenhanded with the evidence and state that if the attitude toward days involved fasting, it very likely had the appearance of a Jewish practice to those outside of the church. Paul's tersely worded formulation certainly can include fasting. It seems best to allow social gatherings and rest on the Sabbath, as well as fasts, as possible referents for the "weak" attitude of judging one day above another.

Identification of the observance of days

The following results emerge from our examination of the attitude of the "weak" toward days. Any observance of days, whatever its origin, would be controversial in first-century Roman society, which had its own system of registering a religious value to every day. Though brief in length, Paul's description in Rom. 14.5–6a fits with common stereotypes of the superstitious person. The phrase in 14.6a – ὁ φρονῶν τὴν ἡμέραν κυρίῳ φρονεῖ – is particularly significant in identifying the contours of this attitude. It shows that whatever its origin, the attitude toward days was being maintained as something Christian. While not eliminating the possibility of survivals from other religions, it at least shows that the practices could be interpreted in a Christian way. The observance of "the Lord's day" is possible, on account of the evidence for such practice in early Christianity, as well as the use of κύριος in Paul's description of the day observance. From our knowledge of the impressions with which Sabbath observance was held in the early Empire, and the prevalence of fasting as a form of religious expression, these two activities seem to be the best candidates for the nub of the dispute over days that is reflected in 14.5–6a.

Further discussion on the actual background of the observance of days would obscure the point of Paul's argument. His interest is not in the background of the "weak" observance of days, but in the scrupulous attitude with which they observed them. Both to the "strong" and to Roman society outside of the church, Paul knew that the "weak" appeared to be superstitious people who took offense at variations from their own conception of proper religious conduct.

[59] Zahn, *Geschichte des Sonntags*, 36.

9

SUPERSTITION IN ROME AND IN ROMANS 14-15

> Habebant inter se scandala: illi illos quasi carnales iudicabant, et illi illos tanquam stultos irridebant et superstitiosos putabant.
>
> They had stumbling blocks among themselves: some were judging others as carnal, just as those were mocking them as silly and considering them superstitious.
>
> Sedulius Scottus[1]

Now that we have examined the vegetarianism, wine abstinence, and day observance mentioned in Romans 14-15, we are able to see the social implications of the controversial issues in this church. The issues themselves and Paul's advice to the church lead to the conclusion that the "strong" regarded the "weak" as superstitious. While this stereotype led to disharmony in the church, Paul was also concerned lest the Roman churches as a whole be regarded as superstitious and this stigma mar the church's standing in Roman society. To see that this is so, we begin by examining what it meant to be called "superstitious" in first-century Rome.

The best working definition for the first-century use of *superstitio*, the Roman word for superstition, is a religion, "either native or imported, that posed a threat to the stability of the state or to the fabric of family life."[2] It is true that *superstitio* did carry positive connotations in its earlier usage,[3] but we are concerned here with

---

[1] *Sedulii Scotti collectaneum in apostolum 1. In Epistolam ad Romanos* (VLGLB 31; eds. H. J. Frede and H. Stanjek; Freiburg: Herder, 1996), 286 (at Rom. 14.3).

[2] Robert Hodgson, Jr., "Superstition," *ABD* VI.240. On the Greek term for "superstition," see P. J. Koets, Δεισιδαιμονία: *A Contribution to the Knowledge of the Religious Terminology in Greek* (Purmerend: J. Muusses, 1929). On the Latin term, see Salvatore Calderone, "*Superstitio*," *ANRW* I.2 (1972) 377–96 and Denise Grodzynski, "*Superstitio*," Revue des études anciennes 76 (1974) 36–60.

[3] See Morton Smith, "*Superstitio*," in *Society of Biblical Literature Seminar Papers* 20 (ed. K. H. Richards; Chico, Calif.: Scholars, 1981), 349–50. Smith cites

Roman descriptions of Christianity as *superstitio*, which always used the word in à pejorative sense.

The Roman use of *superstitio* is distinct from its Greek counterpart (δεισιδαιμονία) in that by the time of Paul, *superstitio* often carried a foreign connotation. A *superstitio* could be a foreign religion that included habits of worship considered strange by Roman society in general, and a threat to its structure.[4] The Latin *superstitio* and Greek δεισιδαιμονία are also distinct in that the latter word originally had a positive meaning when it was used to connote simply being religious in the ways considered socially acceptable.[5] From the composition of Theophrastus' portrait of the δεισιδαίμων, δεισιδαιμονία increasingly connoted the negative idea of excessive fear of the gods and the strange behavior that accompanied it.[6] Though these words' semantic fields did not always overlap, then, we can carefully use them as we try to understand what it meant to label a person "superstitious" in first-century Rome.

The negative connotation of the Greek word for superstition, δεισιδαιμονία, does provide a general background for the caricature of a superstitious person in Hellenistic thought. Theophrastus provides a picture of the religious person who has this excessive fear of the divine in chapter 16, Δεισιδαιμονιάς, of his *Characters*. Some sections of this short chapter describe actions that seem close to what we read of the "weak" in Rome. Theophrastus describes how the superstitious person observes the fourth and seventh day each month as religiously significant, and sacrifices on those days (10). The superstitious person is also very concerned about impurity, considering himself defiled by a tomb, a corpse, or a woman giving birth (9). The concern for purity means that he continually purifies his house (7). While this portrait is better taken as a stock piece for entertainment than a technical definition of superstitious behavior,[7] it illustrates the common caricature of a superstitious person in the Hellenistic world.

uses of *superstitio* in a positive sense, from the second and first centuries BCE: Plautus, *Curculio* 397; *Amphitruo* 323; *Rudens* 1139; Ennius, *Alexander*, fr. 8 (ed. Vahlen); Cicero, *Div.* 1.66; and perhaps the original context of Cicero's quotation in *Div.* 2.115 used *vox superstitiosa* positively.

[4] Livy, 39.16.5–11; Tacitus, *Ann.* 15.44; Pliny, *Ep.* 10.96.
[5] Polybius 6.56.7; Acts 17.22.
[6] Theophrastus, *Char.* 16; Morton Smith, "*Superstitio*," 350–51.
[7] Here I am following Robert Hodgson, Jr., in an unpublished essay he sent me in April, 1990, "*Superstitio* and *Deisidaimonia*."

It is impossible for us to recover the exact attitude of the "strong" toward the "weak" or the attitude of Romans outside of the church toward the church there. But from what we see in the text, it appears that both ideas – excessive fear of the divine realm (a negative connotation of δεισιδαιμονία) and a foreign cult with strange practices (a connotation of *superstitio*) – seem to be behind the label "weak" within the churches and the image that the churches were presenting to those outside. Before I examine relevant sentences and terms in Romans 14, perhaps it would be wise to consider whether it is really likely that Roman Christianity, or a segment of it, was labeled a superstition in the first century.

Superstitio as Christianity's label in first-century Rome

Everyone knows that Roman writers outside of the church called Christianity a superstition.[8] I admit that these writers date from two generations after Paul wrote Romans, but it is worth noting that two of the three uses are describing Christianity in the reign of Nero, precisely when Paul is writing his letter. From the perspective of Suetonius and Tacitus, then, Christianity carried the malodorous stigma of *superstitio* during Nero's reign. Since it was this emperor who finally did exploit Christians as his scapegoats for the fire of 64,[9] it is likely that the perception of Christianity as a superstition was growing and nervously watched by Paul and other Christians in those years. This would explain why Paul tells Christians to submit to the emperor in Rom. 13.1–7.[10] More light is available on the question of Christianity and superstition when we consider the religion from which Christianity grew.

Roman authors also called Judaism a superstition.[11] Given the Jewish presence within Roman Christianity and the difficulty the Romans had in distinguishing Judaism from what we now call Christianity,[12] it is likely that Jewish practices within the churches of Rome made Romans only more prone to label Christian

---

[8] Pliny, *Ep.* 10.96.7, 12; Tacitus, *Ann.* 15.44; Suetonius, *Nero* 16.2.

[9] Tacitus, *Ann.* 15.44.

[10] I owe this connection to Hodgson ("Superstition"), who writes that "Rom. 13:1–7 is a short-term strategy for survival" from charges and prosecutions of *superstitio* in Rome.

[11] Cicero, *Flac.* 67; Valerius Maximus 1.3.3; Horace, *Sat.* 2.3.281–95; Plutarch, *Superst.* 169C. On circumcision as a sign of superstition, see Horace, *Sat.* 1.9.69–71; Juvenal, *Sat.* 14.99, 104.

[12] See Lampe, *Die stadtrömischen Christen*, 5–6.

churches "superstition." When Tacitus refers to Christianity as a *superstitio*, he mentions its origin in Judaea,[13] a fact that shows that Christianity was perceived in Rome as a foreign, strange religion.

In discussing Christianity under Nero, we have already noted a desire to evade the label *superstitio*, which may lie behind Rom. 13.1–7. Other features of this letter also fit the picture of a church with a public relations problem related to superstition.

The task of introducing and defending his gospel that Paul undertakes in Romans allows him at certain points to come very close to the Roman *religio–superstitio* distinction.[14] Descriptions of both pagan and Jew as responding inappropriately to the supernatural begin the letter. For Paul, the pagan suppression of the truth (Rom. 1.18) leads ultimately to a superstitious belief in the religious value of animals (1.23), what is for him an invalid response to the supernatural.[15] Paul's description of unbelieving Jews is close to contemporary treatments of superstitious people, in its criticism of an undue value placed on possession of Torah, the name "Jew," and the rite of circumcision (2.12–29). Throughout the letter, Paul is concerned to highlight for his Roman audience the proper ways, according to his gospel, to worship and live before God.

I cannot go so far as to say that Paul is defining his gospel as religion, because I do not find evidence in this letter that he is dealing at that abstract a level. His gospel is not shameful and it is worth spreading, according to this letter, but I am not sure that the letter explicitly defines his gospel as religion.[16] Paul offers focused definitions to disassociate himself, his gospel, and its followers from the "superstitious" label, but he does not define his gospel as *religio*.

Rom. 12.1–2 defines reasonable worship (λογικὴ λατρεία), and describes God's will as the good, acceptable, and perfect – attributes a Roman would consider characteristic of *religio* instead of *superstitio*. How does this desire to distinguish Christianity from superstition work out in Rom. 14.1–15.13?

---

[13] Dieter Lührmann, "*Superstitio* – die Beurteilung des frühen Christentums durch die Römer," *TZ* 42 (1986) 202; Tacitus, *Ann.* 15.44.

[14] See H. D. Betz, "Christianity as Religion: Paul's Attempt at Definition in Romans," *JR* 71 (1991) 337; Lührmann, "*Superstitio,*" 193–213.

[15] On the tendency of superstitious beliefs to include that of ensouled animals, see Rieß, "Aberglaube," *PW* Sup 1.30–31.

[16] Cf. Betz, "Christianity as Religion," 315–44.

Paul's concern about superstition in Rom. 14.1–15.13

Though fear is not mentioned in Rom. 14.1–15.13, Paul's argument in this text allows one to consider a fear that would appear superstitious as a workable explanation for some symptoms of the "weak" party. Rom. 14.4 is written as if the "weak" were afraid that very few people in the community would reach standards that allowed them to be "established" before God. The significance of death is another issue in the complex of attitudes within superstition, and in 14.8 it appears again that Paul is addressing a group afraid of separation from the deity at death. Hence the phrase there, ἐὰν τε οὖν ζῶμεν ἐὰν τε ἀποθνῄσκωμεν, τοῦ κυρίου ἐσμέν.[17] The references to peace and joy (both occur in 14.17 and 15.13), encouragement (15.4, 5), and hope (15.4, 13)[18] fit with the possibility that the "weak" in Rome held some sort of anxiety or fear[19] about God, a central trait of superstition. Another instance of φόβος that appears consistent with this hypothesis comes at Rom. 8.15 – οὐ γὰρ ἐλάβετε πνεῦμα δουλείας πάλιν εἰς φόβον.

A controversy related to eating as seen in Rom. 14.1–15.13 fits in the sphere of superstition. In his article on superstition, Rieß states that the table where eating occurs is holy, invested with religious significance for the superstitious person.[20] It is plain that the "weak" were attaching religious significance to food that others in the community thought was religiously insignificant (14.14). The possibility of destroying a brother (14.15) shows the gravity with which the "weak" viewed the foodstuffs in question. For the "strong" such a perspective was superstition, and what appeared on the surface to be only a difference in eating became an ethical difference also (14.20).

Though we can locate eating as a concern within the realm of superstition, we must also note that motives behind superstitious practices are very complex. In Rieß's survey of some of the attitudes behind superstitions, at least three of them could be involved in

---

[17] Cf. Heb. 2.15.

[18] On hope as contained in a proper view of the deity (as opposed to a superstitious view) see Plutarch, *Superst.* 169C: ἀρετῆς γὰρ ἐλπὶς ὁ θεός ἐστιν, οὐ δειλίας πρόφασις.

[19] The other uses of φόβος in Romans are positive in character: Rom. 3.18 (quoting LXX Ps. 35.2), 11.20; 13.3–4, 7. δειλία is not found in Romans.

[20] Rieß, "Aberglaube," 30.

motivating someone to abstain from meat.[21] Therefore, while an identification of superstition as a factor in the community's attitudes will help us trace Paul's arguments in relation to contemporary Roman society, a single motive behind the practices and attitudes observed may not be recoverable from the text.[22] Still, this look at superstition in Rome is helpful in broadening our perception of the regard with which the "weak" were held in the churches of Rome. From the commands not to scorn them (14.3, 10) or allow them to be grieved (14.15), it appears that the "strong" applied the Roman society's evaluation of superstition on this group within their community. The "strong" probably thought that the "weak" were superstitious, and so despised or shamed them.

The reference to observance of days (14.5–6a) also fits with the image of superstitious behavior in antiquity. Theophrastus, Horace, and Plutarch mention the designation of certain days as religiously significant in their presentations of the superstitious person.[23]

While the remarks about living and dying certainly do not prove that there was a superstitious group in the Roman church, they fit with such an hypothesis. This is because the areas of birth and death are especially conducive to superstition[24] and because the discussion of living and dying (14.7–9) is unique in Paul. The statements that Paul makes on living and dying for the Lord come in the paragraph addressed to the "weak." Nowhere else does Paul suggest that the reason for Christ's existence and death was to reign over dead and living.[25] Paul's word order ("in order that he might reign over *dead* and living") suggests that he was responding to a concern that the "weak" had with the dead.[26] With these general comments on the stereotype of superstition in Romans 14–15, it

---

[21] These categories are: omitting or abstaining from certain things (Rieß, "Aberglaube," 34–35); "Sympathie und Antipathie" in various parts of the natural world (ibid., 36–37); and the motive of avoiding that which is against nature (ibid., 37).

[22] On the mindset of superstitious people in the context of religion, see Conrad Zucker, *Psychologie de la superstition* (trans. François Vaudou; Paris: Payot, 1972), 193–207.

[23] Theophrastus, *Char.* 16.10; Horace, *Sat.* 1.9.68; Plutarch, *Superst.* 169C.

[24] See the discussion with examples in Rieß, "Aberglaube," 91–93.

[25] The uniqueness of this statement also tells against Jaquette's idea that Paul is simply applying his life and death *adiaphora* topos here. See Jaquette, *Discerning*, 130 and see discussion on pp. 127, 208 here.

[26] Cf. Theophrastus, *Char.* 16.9–καὶ οὔτε ἐπιβῆναι μνήματι οὔτ' ἐπὶ νεκρὸν ... ἐλθεῖν ἐθελήσας ("Set foot on a tomb he will not, nor come nigh a dead body" [*sic*]); trans. J. M. Edmonds; LCL; London: William Heinemann, 1953).

remains for us to look in detail at several sentences and terms used there.

Μηκέτι οὖν ἀλλήλους κρίνωμεν· ἀλλὰ τοῦτο κρίνατε
μᾶλλον, τὸ μὴ τιθέναι πρόσκομμα τῷ ἀδελφῷ ἢ
σκάνδαλον (Rom. 14.13)

While the terms for offense or stumbling[27] are used in the context of the "weak" response to the eating practices of the "strong," such a response is related more to the scrupulous or superstitious attitudes of the "weak" than to the actual habits of asceticism. Stählin takes "stumbling block" (πρόσκομμα) here as a causal noun meaning "hindrance to faith," or "cause of spiritual ruin."[28] It is precisely because of the superstition of the "weak" that there is a danger of the "strong" placing a πρόσκομμα before them.

The use of the prepositional phrase διὰ προσκόμματος in 14.20 is taken by Stählin not to mean an actual fall from faith, but rather an "offense of conscience." He opts for this because it seems to parallel διακρίνομαι (14.23) as an issue of conscience rather than connoting actual behavior, as διάκρισις (14.1) seems to connote. Stählin also cites Rom. 2.15 as a parallel text to illumine 14.21.[29] While I agree with his conclusion that the use of διὰ προσκόμματος fits somehow with the wounding or pollution of conscience mentioned in 1 Cor. 8.7, 12,[30] he has not gone far enough. The postulation of his two options (conscience versus behavior) for the διὰ προσκόμματος phrase[31] is in a sense a false dichotomy, for while it is very likely that the social and spiritual phenomenon Paul describes includes damaged consciences of the "weak," it is also clear that he writes of spiritual ruin actually

---

[27] On the variants that omit πρόσκομμα and ἤ, see Cranfield, *Romans*, 712 n. 1.

[28] Gustav Stählin, "προσκόπτω," *TDNT* VI (1968) 747. Bauer–Aland seem to agree with the category of *nomen causae* in their classification of πρόσκομμα for Rom. 14.13 under the heading "die Gelegenheit, Anstoß zu nehmen oder einen Fehltritt zu tun" (s.v. "πρόσκομμα," 2.b).

[29] Stählin, "προσκόπτω," VI.756–57.

[30] Ibid., VI.757.

[31] Ibid., VI.757 (his own quotation marks are used to note his paraphrases of the text) – (1) "falling in faith; this takes place when a man acts contrary to his conviction and thus betrays it"; when eating this means that "he stumbles inwardly"; or (2) "The reference may be to offence of conscience: 'It is bad for a man if he eats and offends his conscience by his act,' i.e., 'with a disturbed, resisting, bad conscience.'"

occurring on the part of the "weak."[32] Paul and the "weak" consider πρόσκομμα to be more than simply a wounded conscience; they consider it to be spiritual ruin, i.e., losing one's link to the divine.

The cognate verb προσκόπτω in 14.21 similarly refers to the superstitious "weak" who stumble by following the "strong" and therefore experience not only the wounding of their consciences, but also spiritual ruin. One is reminded of the language of bondage so common to descriptions of superstitious people[33] when reading Stählin on 14.21.

> The ἐξουσία [authority] ... of the strong, which is legitimate as such and which Paul himself shares, becomes a πρόσκομμα to the weak with their as yet unconquered bonds, 1 C. 8.9; R. 14.21.[34]

This confirms the appropriateness of using the πρόσκομμα/ σκάνδαλον concept to inform our understanding of the "weak" as superstitious. While a verbal parallel does not exist, the conceptual parallels of the "weak" one stumbling (i.e., being bothered by things that do not bother others) is a common theme in descriptions of the superstitious person.[35] The parallel word to "stumbling block," σκάνδαλον, also deserves comment.

In its LXX uses, σκάνδαλον is primarily used to translate words from the yāqōš word group, meaning "ensnare" or "entrap." There are cases, however, where σκάνδαλον and cognates are used to translate words from the kāšal word group ("stumble"), usually associated with προσκόπτω.[36] Thus there is some overlap between the terms. The addition of σκάνδαλον in 14.13 serves only to intensify the demand Paul places on the "strong." Special significance for the term comes only insofar as it is associated with

---

[32] Like Plutarch (*Superst.* 166C), Paul realizes that superstitious people live in their own world, and therefore he works within their own set of scrupulous presuppositions.

[33] See Plutarch, *Superst.* 169C on the Jews being enmeshed in the net of their superstition.

[34] Stählin, "προσκόπτω," 6.753.

[35] Theophrastus, *Char.* 16.2–8; Plutarch, *Superst.* 168C–D. Both these texts portray the δεισιδαίμων as seeing divine and grave significance in matters that routinely occur in the course of life.

[36] Gustav Stählin, "σκάνδαλον," *TDNT* VII (1971), 340–41. He cites Lev. 19.14 and 1 Sam. 25.31 as cases where σκάνδαλον is used in place of an expected πρόσκομμα to translate *mikšôl*.

πρόσκομμα; it is unlikely that Paul makes an intentional differentiation between πρόσκομμα and σκάνδαλον.

Very significant for our understanding of the whole letter is the
association between stumbling and being ashamed. This association
is found in the combination of Isa. 8.14 and Isa. 28.16, two texts
which Paul has juxtaposed in Rom. 9.32–33. Paul's request that the
"strong" not despise, or shame, the "weak" (14.3, 10) runs parallel
to his command that the "strong" not cause the "weak" to stumble
(14.13, 20). Since Paul's gospel is not shameful (1.16), those who
follow it are not to shame other believers, but welcome them
instead (14.1; 15.7).

εἰ γὰρ διὰ βρῶμα ὁ ἀδελφός σου λυπεῖται, οὐκέτι κατὰ
ἀγάπην περιπατεῖς (Rom. 14.15a)

On a surface reading, the likelihood that the "weak" were emotion-
ally grieved by the eating habits of the "strong" is supported by
references to hope (15.4, 13) and joy (14.17; 15.13), dispositions
that Paul wishes to flourish in the community. But an examination
of the background of the term λύπη and cognates allows one to see
that more than emotional disturbance may be in view here.

If the asceticism of the "weak" was based on a view of what was
proper to a human diet by nature,[37] then when φύσις was violated
by meat-eaters, λύπη would be the expected result.[38] Such grief,
caused by a rupture in the metaphysical construct of the "weak"
vegetarians, need not exclude the idea of physical pain. It is "food"
(rather than the "eating" of the "strong"; cf. verse 17) which Paul
uses as the occasion of this pain. Given the usage of λυπέω and
λύπη for physical pain,[39] and the fact that what is in view is an
actual difference in diet for habitual vegetarians, we cannot exclude
the conjecture that Paul includes the connotation of physical pain
on the part of the "weak" who join the "strong" in their eating
habits.

Paul's use of the passive voice (λυπεῖται) may hint that it is the

[37] See discussion in chapter 6 above.
[38] Cf. Plato, *Phileb.* 31E–32B. Aristotle refers to this and gives it a more nuanced
treatment (*EN* 10.3.6; 1173b7–8). Elsewhere he inverts the relationship between a
deficient nature and λύπη in that he states that λύπη destroys the nature of its
possessor (*EN* 3.12.2; 1119a23–24).
[39] LSJ, s.v. "λυπέω," 2; "λύπη," 1; Plato, *Phileb.* 31C.

"weak" who are allowing grief or pain to affect themselves[40] by means of the "strong" food. But Paul is addressing the "strong" as if it is their responsibility when the "weak" are grieved. Dunn helpfully describes the significance of the passive λυπεῖται here:

> Paul is implying that it is not simply a matter of the strong's intention in the matter; they might have had no thought, far less purpose, so to upset the weaker brother. What matters, however, is whether the brother actually was upset in any particular event.[41]

The active verbs in verses 15b and 20a also confirm that Paul is placing primary responsibility on the "strong" for this λύπη. In the context, these verbs also help to define what Paul means in verse 15a.

In the social writers of the day, λύπη is a standard quality in the caricature of the superstitious person. Given the description of one with a burden of religious scruples among the Roman Christians, the use of λυπέω here fits perfectly. The absence of λύπη or λυπέω in 1 Cor. 8–10 shows us that this portrait of the "weak" as superstitious is distinctive of the Roman community. Taken in association with the description of the observance of days, it appears most likely that the "weak" in Rome carried the stigma of being superstitious in the community prior to the composition of Romans. The original application of this label of superstition to the abstaining and day-observing group may therefore be traced primarily to the "strong" and then to the Roman church as a whole, not to Paul, although his hints concerning this label are undoubtedly intentional.

While Paul is concerned to avoid the "superstitious" label for himself and his gospel (14.14a), he is willing to work with the presuppositions of those who appear to be superstitious (14.14b).[42] He does therefore present his gospel as a mediating, balanced approach to religious life and not superstitious, though I do not think that we can say that he is explicitly defining his gospel as *religio*, or what would be considered proper religion for the

---

[40] See BDF §314 on the passive for "to allow oneself to be ..." Bultmann cites Sophocles, *Aj.* 260ff. and *OT* 1230f. on how the worst pain is that which we cause ourselves ("λύπη, λυπέω," *TDNT* IV [1967], 314). He also mentions *SVF* 1.85.18f. and 3.94.39ff. on how difficult it is to be rid of λύπη (ibid., IV.315).

[41] Dunn, *Romans*, 831.

[42] I examine the arguments of those who think that Paul is trying to change or enlighten the "weak" toward the end of the following chapter.

Romans.[43] It is a helpful insight to note that this letter deals with definition, but Paul defines his gospel primarily to show that it is not shameful, rather than to offer a presentation of it as *religio*. Thus, λογικὴ λατρεία in Rom. 12.1 might connote the reasonableness of Paul's gospel, which avoids the "superstitious" label,[44] as well as indicating the appropriate fulfillment of the obligation to respond to God's mercies.

μὴ βλασφημείσθω οὖν ὑμῶν τὸ ἀγαθόν (Rom. 14.16)

This command shows that Paul has a public relations concern that those outside of the churches not stigmatize the Christian faith. Paul does not want disturbances within the community based on issues of food consumption or observance of days to accentuate Roman society's tendency to call Christianity a superstition.

This verse warns against the consequences of offending a "weak" believer. Our understanding of verse 16 hinges on what is meant by τὸ ἀγαθόν and on whether μὴ βλασφημείσθω refers to an event within or without the community.

Among Paul's uses of ἀγαθός[45] the nearest parallels are Rom. 2.10; 12.9, 21; 13.3b; 15.2; 16.19; Gal. 6.10; 1 Thess. 5.15. In these texts we see that τὸ ἀγαθόν is described as activity characteristic of the one living in divine favor (Rom. 2.10). The connection between τὸ ἀγαθόν and the fruit of the Spirit (as opposed to the "works of the flesh")[46] fits well in the context of Romans 14 also. The whole discussion here in Romans is over a difference in faith, identified in Gal. 5.22 as part of the Spirit's fruit. Love, joy, and peace share this identification in Gal. 5.22 and also figure significantly in the discussion in Romans (14.15, 17; 15.13). Reference to the Spirit is also made in 14.17 and 15.13. To prepare for the fruit of the Spirit, the believer is to give no forethought for the flesh (13.14) so that its desires will not be satisfied.[47] We can conclude, then, that τὸ

[43] Cf. Betz, "Christianity as Religion," 317. See also the last paragraph of the following section on 14.16.

[44] Betz, "Christianity as Religion," 337.

[45] Cf. Rom. 2.7, 10; 3.8; 5.7; 7.12, 13*bis*, 18, 19; 8.28; 9.11; 10.15; 12.2, 9, 21; 13.3*bis*, 4; 14.16; 15.2; 16.19; 2 Cor. 5.10; 9.8; Gal. 6.6, 10; Phil. 1.6; 1 Thess. 3.6; 5.15.

[46] See Betz, *Galatians*, 311.

[47] This is confirmed by the construction of Gal. 5.16, which shows us that for Paul, the antithesis of living according to such desires is "walking according to the Spirit."

ἀγαθόν here signifies for Paul the qualities of behavior that he calls "fruit of the Spirit," in which orbit he expects Christians to live.[48]

This τὸ ἀγαθόν can be observed by those within the community (Rom. 15.2) as well as by those without (Rom. 13.3). Explicit mention is made of both groups in 1 Thess. 5.15 and Gal. 6.10. The order of reference in 1 Thess. 5.15 (τὸ ἀγαθὸν διώκετε [καὶ] εἰς ἀλλήλους καὶ εἰς πάντας), when read alongside ἐργαζώμεθα τὸ ἀγαθὸν πρὸς πάντας, μάλιστα δὲ πρὸς τοὺς οἰκείους τῆς πίστεως in Gal. 6.10b, seems to indicate that in those verses the primary reference is to those inside of the community. In Romans, further support for the intra-communal nature of τὸ ἀγαθόν is the entire focus of the paragraph thus far in Romans 14.[49] Paul primarily expresses concern for the life of the community.

But at Rom. 14.18b with δόκιμος τοῖς ἀνθρώποις there is a reference to those outside of the community. This is consistent with Paul's command in Rom. 12.17b. Clearly Paul is concerned that the churches of Rome not unnecessarily offend society at large with "the good" they possess in their believing communities. It is most likely that "Let not your good be blasphemed" in Rom. 14.16 leads up to this phrase in verse 18b.[50] And as evidence for an outside reference of Paul's command in verse 16, one may note with Käsemann that usually non-Christians are designated as the subject of the verb βλασφημέω in the NT.[51] In 1 Cor. 10.30, the blasphemy seems to be occurring from another Christian,[52] but Paul's self-description in verse 33, μὴ ζητῶν τὸ ἐμαυτοῦ σύμφορον ἀλλὰ τὸ τῶν πολλῶν, ἵνα σωθῶσιν, refers most naturally to unbelievers outside of the community. One must also remember that Paul is writing to the Roman community with its reputation among the churches of the Mediterranean world in mind (1.8). When one is

[48] Dunn's statement (*Romans*, 821) that τὸ ἀγαθόν "sums up all God's covenanted blessings" is too general for the immediate context.

[49] Cf. the use of ἀδελφός in 14.10, 13, 15 and other descriptions of one's fellow member in 14.4, 15.

[50] Dunn's reconstruction (against Sanday and Headlam) makes sense of verse 16 as follows: "What is in view is the likelihood that such insensitive conduct will cause such hurt to 'the weak' and disharmony among the Roman congregation(s) that the gentile onlookers and casual acquaintances will gain a low opinion both of the community who claim to be recipients of this covenanted good and of the God they claim to serve" (*Romans*, pp. 821–22).

[51] Käsemann, *Romans*, 377, following Nababan, "Bekenntnis," 95. This fits with Rom. 12.14, 17–21, where it appears that Paul is writing to encourage the church in the face of an external threat. See also *1 Clem.* 1.1; 47.7; Ign. *Trall.* 8.2; Ign. *Eph.* 10.2, which refer to blasphemy occurring outside of the community.

[52] εἰ ἐγὼ χάριτι μετέχω, τί βλασφημοῦμαι ὑπὲρ οὗ ἐγὼ εὐχαριστῶ;

identifying what Paul means by "your good being blasphemed," then, the potential blasphemy is best pictured as occurring outside of the community, including both non-Christians and believers elsewhere. This reading fits also with the opening concern of the section, which is to avoid controversies (14.1b).[53]

Given the balance of evidence it seems best to conclude that in Rom. 14.16 Paul does not want the Christian qualities of behavior (τὸ ἀγαθόν) to be called "superstition" by anyone outside of the community. Beyond this the evidence does not permit us to go.

Now that we have seen that 14.16 has this external reference, we see that it fits with a significant number of imbricate statements in Romans, aligned with the main current, or topos, of this letter. There are repeated references in this letter that Paul's gospel and those who believe it are without shame (1.16; 5.5; 9.33; 10.11). Instead of shame, those who follow this gospel can boast in it and in God, since both are glorious and powerful (1.17; 5.2–3; 11.13; 15.18–20). Along a parallel line, Paul and those who follow his gospel should not be blasphemed (3.8; 6.1; 14.16), since this gospel brings righteousness (1.17; 3.21–26; 4.13, 20–25; 5.1; 6.13–16; 14.17), is consistent with the scriptures (1.2; 3.21; 4.3; 11.25–27; 15.3–4, 9–12; cf. 16.26), respectable before society in general (12.17b; 13.7; 14.1, 16), and worthy of bold expression (15.15).

ὁ διακρινόμενος (Rom. 14.23)

Doubt is a characteristic attitude of the superstitious person. Since this phrase is used in 14.23 as the opposite of ὁ μὴ κρίνων ἑαυτὸν ἐν ᾧ δοκιμάζει with respect to the exercise of one's faith before God (verse 22), it is evident that the attitude of doubt is more than amoral uncertainty; it is a doubt sharpened by the moral consequences perceived to follow an action. This is confirmed by the conclusion of verse 23 – πᾶν δὲ ὃ οὐκ ἐκ πίστεως ἁμαρτία ἐστίν. ὁ διακρινόμενος refers to the "weak" one who engages in action while uncertain of its moral legitimacy. The questionable action in view is at least the eating of meat, since the phrase ἐὰν φάγῃ immediately follows. Since verse 23 concludes with a general statement of principle, it is best to infer that Paul applies this

---

[53] Cf. Francis Bacon, "Of Unity in Religion," *Essays* (ed. R. F. Jones; New York: Odyssey, 1937), 9, "When atheists and profane persons do hear of so many discordant and contrary opinions in religion; it doth avert them from the church, and maketh them 'to sit down in the chair of the scorners.'"

principle to those who doubt in the observance of days (14.5–6),[54] consumption of wine (14.17, 21), and any other issues of possible controversy (14.21c). It is significant in this survey of terminology to note that for Paul, an attitude of judgment against others (14.3–4, 10) is inseparable from an attitude of self-judgment (14.22–23).[55]

From the word's only other occurrence in Romans, it is clear that διακρίνω signifies a lack of faith. Rom. 4.20 describes Abraham: εἰς δὲ τὴν ἐπαγγελίαν τοῦ θεοῦ οὐ διεκρίθη τῇ ἀπιστίᾳ ἀλλ' ἐνεδυναμώθη τῇ πίστει, δοὺς δόξαν τῷ θεῷ. (Note other terms of this description that show verbal parallels with Rom. 14.1–15.13: ἐπαγγελία–15.8; οἱ δυνατοί–15.1; δοξάζω–15.6, 9.)

The word διακρίνω is not used in the "strong" and "weak" passage of 1 Corinthians; nor is there any description there of the "weak" eating in doubt. The possibility emerges that Paul was specifically informed of this attitude of doubt held by the Roman "weak."[56] If so, this doubt, like λύπη, fits perfectly with the stereotype of the superstitious one in Rome.

An investigation of the language and concepts used in Rom. 14.1–15.13 in light of contemporary Hellenistic and Roman stereotypes of the superstitious person reveals that the "weak" were likely looked at, at least in their habit of day observance and in their reaction to the eating habits of the "strong," as superstitious. The gravity with which they viewed any departure from their religious observances is evidence in itself that they were unable to step outside of their reality structure and consider "strong" habits of consumption or day observance to be legitimate.

In terms of practice, what the "strong" regarded as superstition showed itself in both the scrupulous observance of days and diet by the "weak" and by the "weak" reaction of offense at "strong" conduct. The possibilities of Sabbath observance and fast days remain as the actual behavior of the "weak"; the text does not allow further specificity. In terms of attitude, the superstition of the

---

[54] The command in 14.5b, ἕκαστος ἐν τῷ ἰδίῳ νοῒ πληροφορείσθω, indicates that Paul perceived the observance of days to be a matter of doubt for some in the community, since it follows directly upon a description of the difference in such observance.

[55] The principle is articulated in 2.1 – ἐν ᾧ γὰρ κρίνεις τὸν ἕτερον, σεαυτὸν κατακρίνεις.

[56] On the parallels to Rom. 14.23b in Latin literature, see M. Reasoner, "Theology of Romans 12:1–15:13," 297–98.

"weak" showed itself in anxious fear of God, grief, doubt, and offense at the behavior of the "strong."

The "strong" group's response to the practices and attitudes of the "weak" fits with the general scorn evident in first-century society of those caricatured as superstitious. Paul's use of the verb ἐξουθενέω in a prohibition and question directed to the "strong" (14.3, 10) is evidence of such scorn.[57] While this scorn was also a response to the ascetic practices of the "weak," it fits with what we would expect of a response to the superstitious attitudes of the "weak." The strength of such anti-superstitious scorn is seen in Seneca's comment that he gave up his vegetarian diet so as not to be associated with a *superstitio*.[58]

There is also evidence that the "strong" flaunted their enlightened understanding of religion before the "weak." The following statements in Paul's argument are addressed to the "strong" and suggest such a reaction to the superstition of the "weak": the prohibition against placing πρόσκομμα or σκάνδαλον before a fellow member (14.13); the warning that they do not walk in love if a neighbor is grieved (14.15); the command to pursue peace[59] and the upbuilding of one another (14.19); the maxim against doing anything to cause another to stumble (14.21); the command to hold one's faith before God (as opposed to displaying the liberties one's faith allows before others – 14.22a); and the command to please not oneself but one's neighbor who is ἀδύνατος, for the good of the community (15.1–2).

It is unquestionable that for those outside of the Christian community in Rome, the community as a whole could be called superstitious.[60] It is also entirely possible that within the Pauline sphere of first-century Christianity, the Roman church had a reputation for distinctive, and therefore perhaps what others considered to be superstitious, expressions of faith (Rom. 1.8; 6.17).

What difference does the label of superstition make in interpreting Rom. 14.1–15.13? The parallels that it brings to the text

---

[57] See discussion at beginning of chapter 5 above on ἐξουθενέω.

[58] Seneca, *Ep.* 108.22–"sed inter argumenta superstitionis ponebatur quorundam animalium abstinentia" ("abstinence from certain kinds of animal food was set down as a proof of interest in the strange cult"; *Seneca: Ad Lucilium epistulae morales*, Vol. III, trans. Gummere.

[59] See also Rom. 12.18; Heb. 12.14a.

[60] This is due to the Roman tendency to label every religion non-Roman in origin or unfamiliar in Roman society as *superstitio*. See, e.g., Livy 39.9–19; Tacitus, *Ann.* 15.44.

support the case for an historical controversy in the church of Rome. When we realize the xenophobic scorn that Roman society invested in its label *superstitio*, we begin to understand why religiously motivated distinctions of consumption or day observance would lead to scorn (not seen in 1 Cor. 8–10) and the danger of a falling reputation for the church in the outside community (14.16). Outsiders' impressions that the Jesus-believers in Rome were a part of a superstition also meant that they were considered shameful,[61] a reputation that Paul is working throughout his letter to remove from himself, from his gospel, and from the believers he addresses in Rome. The presence of perceived superstition within the community and Paul's acceptance of such "weak" practices allow us to see how open-minded he is in dealing with the "weak," highlighting Paul's view that his gospel is inclusive of both those who seem superstitious and the enlightened.

To return to the question we tabled in chapter two, the evidence we have examined regarding the nicknames "strong" and "weak," asceticism in diet, scrupulous day observance, and the "superstitious" label all indicate the probability that Romans 14–15 is addressed to an actual situation in first-century Rome. We now turn to Paul's response to this situation.

---

[61] Tacitus, *Ann.* 15.44. In the same sentence in which he calls Christianity a *superstitio*, he includes it among the *atrocia aut pudenda* (awful or shameful) things that reach Rome.

10

OBLIGATION: PAUL'S SOLUTION TO THE CONTROVERSY

> omnibus te precibus oro et obtestor, ut in tuis maximis
> curis aliquid impertias temporis huic quoque cogitationi,
> ut tuo beneficio bonus vir, gratus, pius denique esse in
> maximi beneficii memoria possim.

> I beg and implore you with all my heart, to spare amid
> your grave preoccupations some time to consider how by
> your kindness I may meet the claims of honour, gratitude,
> and loyalty in the remembrance of a signal obligation.
>
> Cicero to Caesar[1]

Paul's solution to the controversy between the enlightened
"strong" and the superstitious "weak" is to inform the "strong"
that they are obligated to support the "weak" – ὀφείλομεν δὲ
ἡμεῖς οἱ δυνατοὶ τὰ ἀσθενήματα τῶν ἀδυνάτων βαστάζειν (Rom.
15.1). While obligation no doubt functioned through the patronage
relationships of Corinth, we do not see explicit references to
obligation in 1 Corinthians, as we do in Romans.[2] Why does Paul
state here that the "strong" church members are under obligation?
He does so because Roman society was held together by cords of
personal obligation. We begin to see not only that the difference
over meat and days is something that would be expected in first-
century Rome, but also that Paul's response fits Roman social
thought.

---

[1] Cicero, *Att.* 9.11A; trans. Shackleton Bailey, 150.
[2] On patronage in Corinth, see John K. Chow, *Patronage and Power: A Study of
Social Networks in Corinth* (JSNT Sup 75; Sheffield: JSOT, 1992). For the language
of obligation in Romans, see 1.14; 8.12; 11.35; 13.8; 15.1; 16.2 and the discussion in
the latter half of this chapter.

The background of obligation

As a working definition, we define obligation as the ethic of reciprocity[3] that motivates the exchange of goods and services between persons. Several parts of this definition call for clarification, based on the use of relevant terminology.[4]

Ethic: obligation as a moral issue

With the first word of the definition the question of obligation is placed in the realm of morality.[5] The Romans' use of the term *officium*, whose usage includes the concept of obligation in view here, makes this clear. This term, usually translated as "duty,"[6] receives its classic exposition in Cicero's *De officiis*.[7] On the basis of a book by the Stoic Panaetius, Cicero fills out the duties necessary to reach four virtues: knowledge of the truth; organized society; courage; and temperance.

It is with the second virtue of an organized society that we find the *officia* related to the "reciprocity ethic" central to the notion of obligation in view here. This virtue is realized, according to Panaetius, by the pursuit of two subsidiary virtues, justice and

---

[3] "Ethic of reciprocity" is taken from R. P. Saller, *Personal Patronage under the Early Empire* (Cambridge: Cambridge University Press, 1982), 19. Since I am using "ethic" in the sense of a "moral code" (R. Abelson, "Ethics, History of," *The Encyclopedia of Philosophy*, ed. Paul Edwards [New York: Macmillan/The Free Press, 1967], III.81), one can say that obligation is an "ethic of reciprocity" because reciprocity is an element of the moral code of many cultures.

[4] See also G. W. Peterman, *Paul's Gift from Philippi: Conventions of Gift Exchange and Christian Giving* (SNTSMS 92; Cambridge: Cambridge University Press, 1997), 51–89.

[5] In using the term "morality" here, I am not drawing a distinction between "ethic" and "morality." I use "morality" in the sense of the area in which "the faculty by which we distinguish between moral right and wrong" is operative (E. Sprague, "Moral Sense," *Encyclopedia of Philosophy*, V.385).

[6] In the following discussion I use "obligation" as a subset of "duty," rather than keeping the two completely separate, as some jurists have done (H. L. A. Hart, "Duty," *IESS* IV.321).

[7] The basic work on the ethics of the *De officiis* is Gred Ibscher, *Der Begriff des Sittlichen in der Pflichtenlehre des Panaitios: Ein Beitrag zur Erkenntnis der mittleren Stoa* (Munich: R. Oldenbourg, 1934). Other works worth consulting are: Max Pohlenz, *Antikes Führertum: Cicero De Officiis und das Lebensideal des Panaitios* (Leipzig: Teubner, 1934); Willibald Heilmann, *Ethische Reflexion und römische Lebenswirklichkeit in Ciceros Schrift De Officiis: Ein literatursoziologischer Versuch* (Wiesbaden: Franz Steiner, 1982); A. Schmekel, *Die Philosophie der mittleren Stoa in ihrem geschichtlichen Zusammenhange* (Berlin: Weidmann, 1892), 18–29.

generosity.[8] Justice involves a use of property according to nature:

> in hoc naturam debemus ducem sequi, communes utilitates in medium afferre mutatione officiorum, dando accipiendo, tum artibus, tum opera, tum facultatibus devincire hominum inter homines societatem.

> In this direction we ought to follow nature as our guide, to contribute to the general good by an interchange of acts of kindness, by giving and receiving, and thus by our skill, our industry, and our talents to cement human society more closely together, man to man.[9]

It also involves the maintenance of good faith (*fides*) with others.[10] The references to obligation to exchange goods and services with those from whom one has received them in the context of these virtues thus show that such obligation involves the repayment of debt.[11] Of course, friendship relationships also carry with them obligations,[12] and in these the metaphor of debt may function at varying levels of consciousness. It is this notion of debt that makes obligation a moral issue, and not simply a question of etiquette or utility.[13]

The morality of obligation is also seen in discussions of the word *beneficium*. Seneca shows this in his exhortation to imitate the gods in matters of gift-giving.[14] Originally used for "gift," the term can be used in place of *officium* in the context of exchange.[15] Gift-giving occurred in both public[16] and private contexts.[17] A return gift or

---

[8] Cicero, *Off.* 1.20.

[9] Cicero, *De officiis* (trans. W. Miller), 1.22. All translations of this work in this chapter come from this edition.

[10] Ibid., 1.23.

[11] This is supported by F. Hauck, who offers the primary definition of ὀφείλω as "to owe someone something" ("ὀφείλω," *TDNT*, V [1967] 559).

[12] S. N. Eisenstadt and L. Roniger, *Patrons, Clients and Friends: Interpersonal Relations and the Structure of Trust in Society* (Cambridge: Cambridge University Press, 1984), 2.

[13] On *utile* itself, see Cicero, *Off.*, book 2, *passim*; on decisions between the *utile* and the *honestum*, ibid., 3.11–120.

[14] Seneca, *Ben.* 1.1.9.

[15] Saller, *Personal Patronage*, 17–20.

[16] On this sort of public benefaction, see Paul Veyne, *Le Pain et le cirque: sociologie historique d'un pluralisme politique* (Paris: Seuil, 1976), 21; 214–17; 251–53.

[17] The discussions of benefaction in Cicero's *De officiis* and Seneca's *De beneficiis* mainly relate to interpersonal exchange in private (as opposed to public) life.

service was viewed as obligatory in cases after an initial gift or honor was bestowed.[18] One example of the moral constraints upon one to return a *beneficium* is Cicero's decision in 49 BCE to side with Pompey.[19] Though the obligation that drove the exchange of gifts was perceived as a moral issue, this obligation was not always used in ways consonant with conventional morality.[20]

Foundational to the reciprocity ethic is the attitude in which such beneficent acts were to be received – "nullum enim officium referenda gratia magis necessarium est" ("For no duty is more imperative than that of proving one's gratitude").[21] The term *gratia* was used to denote the goodwill incumbent upon the reception of a benefit.[22] Its occurrence with verbs used for repayment confirms its place as an expected part of relationships of obligation.[23] This goodwill could include the expression of thanks to the benefactor for a good or service received. The place of thanksgiving in the context of obligation is illustrated by the meaning of εὐχαριστέω in the third century BCE –"'to do a good turn to' (someone), 'to oblige.'"[24] In the ethics of reciprocal exchange, then, a foundational obligation for anyone in society, according to the sources, is the expression of gratitude, thanksgiving, when a favor has been received. Indeed, Seneca exaggerates the significance of the attitude

[18] See Marcel Mauss, *The Gift* (trans. I. Cunnison; Glencoe, Ill.: Free Press, 1954), 5. After describing a variety of "ideas and principles" in an exchange system he observes: "The most important of these spiritual mechanisms is clearly the one which obliges us to make a return gift for a gift received."

[19] Cicero, *Att.* 9.5. Cf. P. A. Brunt, "Cicero's *Officium* in the Civil War," *JRS* 76 (1986) 26–31. Brunt seems to conclude (against Cicero's protests to the contrary in *Att.* 9.19.2) that the ultimate cause of Cicero's emphasis on Pompey's *beneficium* and decision to join Pompey was his political stance that had more in common with Pompey than with Caesar (30).

[20] Cf. Josephus, *AJ* 18.67.

[21] Cicero, *Off.* 1.47. See also J. H. D'Arms's comment on how "the notion of reciprocity is grounded in the Latin language," "Control, Companionship, and *Clientela*: Some Social Functions of the Roman Communal Meal," *Echos du monde classique* 28 (1984) 331.

[22] See A. Stuiber, "Geschenk," *RAC* X.694–97, for gift-giving practices in Hellenistic and Roman culture and law.

[23] Saller, *Personal Patronage*, 21. Formal expressions of thanks also took place in political contexts as a return for services rendered (Tacitus, *Ann.* 15.20.6), but our attention remains on the attitude of *gratia* as displayed at the level of interpersonal exchange.

[24] Peter T. O'Brien, "Thanksgiving within the Structure of Pauline Theology," in *Pauline Studies* (F. F. Bruce Festschrift; eds. D. A. Hagner and M. J. Harris; Grand Rapids: Eerdmans, 1980), 51, citing Moulton and Milligan, 267, and T. Schermann, "Εὐχαριστία und εὐχαριστεῖν in ihrem Bedeutungswandel bis 200 n. Chr.," *Philologus* 69 (1910) 376.

in which gifts are received when he claims that "qui libenter beneficium accipit, reddidit" ("he who receives a benefit gladly has already returned it").[25]

Exchange: the continuing mutuality of obligation

The use of "obligation" in discussions of exchange[26] occurs in the context of goods and services that are extended in both directions between relevant parties. There is no relationship of obligation that involves only the unilateral extension of goods or services between members. No matter how different in status the two members of the relationship are, if obligation is present in their relationship there is an expectation that goods or services must be extended from each side to the other in a continuing relationship.

In the idealized discussions of Cicero and Seneca, the exchange is to be continuing. No relationship is pictured as simply coasting in neutral, with obligations on both sides completely satisfied. Seneca discusses what happens even after paying a friend what one owes: "debeo enim, cum reddidi, rursus incipere, manetque amicitia" ("The bond between us still holds; for just when I have finished paying it, I am obliged to begin again, and friendship endures").[27]

A conscious attempt at leaving the value of goods or services unquantified is what gives obligation its durative force in interpersonal relations. Since neither partner would presume to quantify the value of a specific favor, its recipient could never be sure exactly when something was repaid.[28] But this tendency to leave *officia* unquantified does not mean that partners did not consider the worth of material exchanged. It is precisely because the recipient considers the worth of a benefit that a return of comparable value will be made. The tension between a stated disregard of value and an actual preoccupation with it is easily illustrated.

On the one hand, Seneca can deny the quantification inherent in

---

[25] Seneca, *On Benefits (De Beneficiis)* (trans. J. W. Basore; LCL; London: William Heinemann, 1935), 2.30.2. The overstatement here is apparent when one compares this statement with *Ben.* 5.11.1, in which Seneca writes that in returning *gratia* one ought to expend something. Cicero's letters (e.g., *Fam.* 13.9.3) also make it clear that more than an attitude was expected in actual expressions of *gratia*.

[26] On the significance of exchange in society in general and its theological implications, see Günter Bader, *Symbolik des Todes Jesu* (HUT 25; Tübingen: J. C. B. Mohr [Paul Siebeck], 1988), 105–35, on "Der Tausch."

[27] Seneca, *Ben.* 2.18.5.

[28] Saller, *Personal Patronage*, 16–17.

an accounting metaphor of obligation: "Nemo beneficia in calendario scribit nec avarus exactor ad horam et diem appellat" ("No one enters his benefactions in his account-book, or like a greedy tax-collector calls for payment upon a set day, at a set hour").[29] On the other hand, there is ample evidence that the worth of *officia* or *beneficia* was quantified in daily life.[30] This can be seen on both sides of obligation exchanges. Cicero can write of becoming "good calculators of duties" in the context of determining to whom one most owes a duty in differing circumstances.

> Haec igitur et talia circumspicienda sunt in omni officio et consuetudo exercitatioque capienda, ut boni ratiocinatores officiorum esse possimus et addendo deducendoque videre, quae reliqui summa fiat, ex quo, quantum cuique debeatur, intellegas.

> Such questions as these must, therefore, be taken into consideration in every act of moral duty and we must acquire the habit and keep it up, in order to become good calculators of duty, able by adding and subtracting to strike a balance correctly and find out just how much is due to each individual.[31]

The accounting metaphor was also used with respect to receiving from others what one was due. Thus, when standing for office, Cicero was enjoined by his brother to calculate exactly how deeply others were obligated to him, and then call up these obligations in full.[32]

When asking Sosius Senecio to promote Varisidius Nepos to military tribune, Pliny states, "obligabis me, obligabis Calvisium nostrum, obligabis ipsum, non minus idoneum debitorem quam nos putas"("It will be an obligation to me, to our good Calvisius, and to himself, who is as solvent a debtor as you reckon me to be"). This statement is made in the context of the ability both Pliny and

---

[29] Seneca, *Ben.* 1.2.3; see also *Ben.* 3.31.3.

[30] Seneca writes in a moralistic tone about how people regard the worth of *beneficia* conversely to what is proper in *Ep.* 81.28.1–3.

[31] Cicero, *Off.* 1.59.

[32] Quintus Tullius Cicero, *Comm. pet.* 5.19. While I admit that this letter may not have been written by Q. Tullius Cicero, it still illustrates the manner in which a Roman could calculate obligations others owed and make the most of them. For a brief discussion and citation of relevant literature on the authorship of the *Commentariolum petitionis*, see J. P. V. D. Balsdon, "Cicero (2), Quintus Tullius," *OCD*, 2nd ed., 239.

Nepos have to repay favors, clear evidence that some form of accounting is present in the request.[33]

We see, then, that precise quantification of exchanged goods and services was resisted, giving the relationships lasting force. At the same time, a consciousness of the certainty and worth of a reciprocation[34] ensured that such relationships continued.

Between persons: obligation as dynamic behind patronage

A standard legal definition of *obligatio* that reflects earlier Roman understanding shows cognizance of the relationships of obligation that existed on an interpersonal plane:

> Obligationum substantia non in eo consistit, ut aliquod corpus nostrum aut seruitutem nostram faciat, sed ut alium nobis obstringat ad dandum aliquid uel faciendum uel praestandum.

> The essence of obligations does not consist in that it makes some property or a servitude ours, but that it binds another person to give, do, or perform something for us.[35]

Our consideration of obligation deals mainly with these interpersonal duties.[36] This is appropriate for an ensuing comparison with Rom. 14.1–15.13, where the relationships which concern Paul are clearly personal in nature. If this is the area in which obligation is being considered, we must also ask about its extent.

Panaetius and Cicero teach that *officia* are owed to everyone in one's social sphere. This can be seen by Cicero's citation of the duties one owes toward those who have wronged one.[37] Similarly, Cicero approves of "foedera, quibus etiam cum hoste devincitur fides" ("treaties in which good faith is pledged even to the

---

[33] Pliny, *Letters* (trans. W. Melmoth; rev. W. M. L. Hutchinson; LCL; London: William Heinemann, 1915), 4.4.2.

[34] For the relationship between reciprocal exchange and the practice of hospitality in modern Greece, see Michael Herzfeld, "'As in Your Own House': Hospitality, Ethnography, and the Stereotype of Mediterranean Society," in *Honor and Shame and the Unity of the Mediterranean* (ed. David D. Gilmore; AAA 22; Washington, D.C.: AAA, 1987), 78–86.

[35] *The Digest of Justinian* (eds. Theodor Mommsen and Paul Krueger; trans. and ed. Alan Watson; Philadelphia: University of Pennsylvania Press, 1985), 44.7.3.

[36] *Officium* also functioned as a technical term for government posts under the Empire. See A. E. R. Boak, "*Officium*," PW XXXIV.2045–56, which examines the term only in this sense.

[37] Cicero, *Off.* 1.33.

enemy"),[38] the last person with whom one would expect a duty to obtain. Duties owed to the lowest members of society,[39] including the burial of corpses, were commonly maintained in cultures throughout the Mediterranean world.[40] These duties must be seen as a distinct subset of the all-encompassing *officium* Panaetius teaches, the duty to act virtuously.[41] But this comprehensive scope of duty[42] is not viewed as burdensome. It is simply the nature of human existence, according to Panaetius. The payment of obligations, occurring as it does in the *fides* relationship, is a moral issue.[43]

Within the scope of one's obligations, a ranking can also be made as to the relative significance of obligations owed to others. Panaetius provides a catalog of *officia* when he itemizes the "gradations of duty."

> In ipsa autem communitate sunt gradus officiorum, ex quibus, quid cuique praestet, intellegi possit, ut prima dis immortalibus, secunda patriae, tertia parentibus, deinceps gradatim reliquis debeantur.

> Moreover, even in the social relations themselves there are gradations of duty so well defined that it can easily be seen which duty takes precedence of any other: our first duty is to the immortal gods; our second, to country; our third, to parents; and so on, in a descending scale, to the rest.[44]

This recognition of a continuum of duties lessened the gravity of offenses committed against certain persons. If it became known that such offenses occurred only in the line of repaying an obliga-

---

[38] Ibid., 3.111.

[39] For *officia* toward one's slaves, see Cicero, *Off.* 1.41.

[40] See Hendrik Bolkestein's discussion of these duties in his section "Ein Fall von sozialethischen Synkretismus" in *Wohltätigkeit und Armenpflege im vorchristlichen Altertum* (Utrecht: Oosthoek, 1939; reprint ed., Groningen: Bouma, 1967), 435–37.

[41] This duty is based on the very presence of virtue, as indicative grounds imperative (Ibscher, *Der Begriff des Sittlichen*, 139).

[42] Cicero himself admits that after the knowledge of the truth, the category of *officia* that are *latissime patet ea ratio, qua societas hominum inter ipsos et vitae quasi communitas continetur* ("most extensive in its application is the principle by which society and what we may call its 'common bonds' are maintained") – *Off.* 1.20.

[43] Cf. Pliny, *Ep.* 1.18.4, for his insistence that maintaining the *fides* of a client is more important than loyalty to *patria*. On the religious background of *fides* and the duties related to it, see Bolkestein, *Wohltätigkeit*, 291–92.

[44] Panaetius according to Cicero, *Off.* 1.160.

tion to someone higher in one's scale of *officiorum*, the offenses would be excused.[45]

While the texts used to describe obligation are mostly from the elite of Rome, it is evident from Cicero's and Seneca's works that they understood obligation to function at any level of Roman society.[46] It is therefore not inappropriate to apply the concept of obligation as seen in these sources to the lower population of Rome, which probably included the church members to whom Paul wrote.

The ethic of reciprocity, while idealized as continuing, may not always have kept people in a relationship of exchange that lasted over a period of time. The normative descriptions of obligation show us an ideal that was not always realized. Some exchanges or favors may have resembled commercial transactions in that no obligation existed after the exchange occurred or favor was given. Tiberius' payment of the praetorian Marius Nepos' financial debts provides such an example. Seneca interprets Tiberius' manner of disposing of the debts as calculated to prevent others from making similar requests for financial assistance, and remarks:

> liberavit illum a creditoribus, sibi non obligavit. Aliquid Tiberius secutus est; puto, noluit plures esse, qui idem rogaturi concurrerent.

> Tiberius freed him from his creditors, but failed to attach him to himself. Yet Tiberius had his purpose; he wished to prevent others, I suppose, from rushing to him in order to make the same request.[47]

It is also obvious that exchanges occurring in the context of actual friendship between persons of equal status contained elements of obligation.[48] But our ultimate aim in examining obligation is to understand how Paul meant it to function in the relationship of "strong" and "weak," groups who differed in social status, and for whom the language of friendship is not used.

[45] Tacitus, *Dial.* 10.7.

[46] In Cicero, see his arguments that foreigners and the very poor have rights one ought to recognize (*Off.* 3.28–31). In Seneca, see the illustrative account of how to help a poor person (*Ben.* 2.9.1); how slave may place master under obligation (3.28.1); and the lengthy discussion of benefits between fathers and sons (3.29–37). These writers thus show that benefits are exchanged and obligations incurred at all levels of society.

[47] Seneca, *Ben.* 2.7.2.

[48] Cicero, *Att.* 2.1.7; Pliny, *Ep.* 1.4.2.

In cases in which obligation did motivate exchanges of some duration in a personal context between persons of unequal status, the ensuing relationship is known as patronage.[49] This social institution forms an outward manifestation of the "ethic of reciprocity."

Patronage may be defined as a reciprocal exchange of material items or service. It is personal in nature and conducted over a period of time. This relationship exists between persons of unequal status with different commodities of exchange.[50] The difference in status that is an essential part of this definition may be illustrated by Proculus' statement in *Dig.* 49.15.7.1 that one's clients are free, though they are inferior in authority, dignity, or strength.

> hoc enim adicitur, ut intellegatur alterum populum super-
> iorem esse, non ut intellegatur alterum non esse liberum: et
> quemadmodum clientes nostros intellegimus liberos ess,
> etiamsi neque auctoritate neque dignitate neque uiri boni
> nobis praesunt, sic eos, qui maiestatem nostram comiter
> conseruare debent, liberos esse intellegendum est.

> It has to be added that that other people is to be under-
> stood to be superior, not that [the federated] people is not
> free; and insofar as we understand our client [states] to be
> free, even if they are not our equals in authority, dignity or
> power, so also those who are bound to preserve our
> *majestas* with good will are to be understood to be free.[51]

On an interpersonal level, the *clientes* were often called *amici* (friends),[52] though it would still be clear by attendance at the *salutatio*[53] and other acts of deference within continuing exchanges that such people actually were clients.

It is important to realize that the institution of patronage characterized some relationships that are not described explicitly

---

[49] Patronage is a specific type of reciprocal exchange; see the definition to follow in the next paragraph of text.

[50] Saller, *Personal Patronage*, 1. On contexts of patronage in Republican Rome, see Eisenstadt and Roniger, *Patrons, Clients and Friends*, 52–64.

[51] This example is from Richard Saller, "Patronage and Friendship in Early Imperial Rome: Drawing the Distinction," in *Patronage in Ancient Society* (ed. A. Wallace-Hadrill; London/New York: Routledge, 1989), 51. The editors of the *Digest* have indicated that this statement applies to client states, but the same principle applies in interpersonal relationships.

[52] Saller, *Personal Patronage*, 12, 29, 120.

[53] See, e.g., Tacitus, *Ann.* 4.41 and E. Badian, "*Salutatio*," *OCD*, 2nd ed., 948.

with patronage terms. Such descriptions avoided "patron" or "client" out of a desire to soften the social inequality in the relationship. The absence of explicit reference to patronage does not keep us from identifying patrons and clients where other evidence is available.

Besides evidence from the early Empire which shows patronage linking the aristocratic orders with freedmen who engaged in trade,[54] early Christian sources show how patronage extended into the lower levels of society. A case can be made from 1 Corinthians that the church of Corinth was held together by patronage.[55] Whether influenced by Rom. 15.1 or not, *1 Clem.* 38.2 points to the obligation that was supposed to exist within the church and even includes the language of reciprocity:

> ὁ ἰσχυρὸς τημελείτω τὸν ἀσθενῆ, ὁ δὲ ἀσθενὴς ἐντρεπέσθω τὸν ἰσχυρόν· ὁ πλούσιος ἐπιχορηγείτω τῷ πτωχῷ, ὁ δὲ πτωχὸς εὐχαριστείτω τῷ θεῷ, ὅτι ἔδωκεν αὐτῷ, δι' οὗ ἀναπληρωθῇ αὐτοῦ τὸ ὑστέρημα.

> The strong must not neglect the weak, and the weak must respect the strong. Let the rich support the poor, and let the poor give thanks to God, because He has given him someone through whom his needs may be met.

This tendency continued on into the second century, as the *Shepherd of Hermas* shows.[56] Carolyn Osiek comments on this tendency:

> A Jewish or Christian paraenesis for the rich would be unthinkable without stressing the obligation of the rich toward the poor. Even in the second *Similitude* the essential insight of mutual complementarity that is developed necessitates the involvement of the poor, even if the real focus does not rest on them.[57]

Sometimes the care of the poor by the rich is noted, without regard to any sort of reciprocity.[58]

---

[54] D'Arms, *Commerce and Social Standing in Ancient Rome*, 20–47.

[55] Chow, *Patronage and Power*.

[56] *Herm. Vis.* 3.9.3–6; *Herm. Man.* 2.4–6; 8.10; *Herm. Sim.* 2.5–10.

[57] Carolyn Osiek, *Rich and Poor in the "Shepherd of Hermas": An Exegetical-Social Investigation* (CBQMS 15; Washington, D.C.: CBA, 1983), 133.

[58] Cf. L. William Countryman, *The Rich Christian in the Church of the Early Empire: Contradictions and Accommodations* (TSR 7; New York/Toronto: Edwin

Lucian of Samosata tells how the Christians designated Pere-grinus as a patron,[59] and so gives us a view of patronage within second-century Christianity. One might find a reciprocal exchange in comparing Peregrinus' teaching of the people with their material support for him.[60] This support is described in later accounts of how the Christians waited on the imprisoned Peregrinus: bringing him food; reading to him; sitting with him.[61] Upon his release Peregrinus was able to travel with the material support of the Christians, who provided for him handsomely.[62]

Though a caricature, this description does provide evidence that Christians did support their leaders materially and provide for their needs.[63] The description of Peregrinus gaining wealth at the expense of church members cannot be wholly imaginary, since such an occurrence is confirmed by the command to honor prophets materially, while being wary of being swindled by them.[64] There is evidence, therefore, that exchanges with varying sorts of reciprocity existed in Christian communities. The exchanges could be financial support of the poor by the rich in return for respect for the rich, or financial support of leaders by members in return for their teaching. While not identical to the instances of patronage evident in the pagan sources, the evidence from Christian communities at least shows that some sort of obligation obtained within the community.

Given this background of obligation and the function of obliga-tion within Christian communities, we turn to Paul's argument in Rom. 14.1–15.13.

Mellen, 1980), 160, who notes that the primary role of rich people in the early church was to provide buildings for churches and food, clothing, and burials for the poor.

[59] προστάτην ἐπεγράφοντο (Lucian, *Peregr.* 11). On the historical value of this text, see M. J. Edwards, "Satire and Verisimilitude: Christianity in Lucian's *Peregrinus*," Historia 38 (1989) 89–98.

[60] Edwards, "Satire and Verisimilitude," 89–98.

[61] Lucian, *Peregr.*, 12.   [62] Ibid., 16.

[63] H. D. Betz, *Lukian von Samosata und das Neue Testament: Religionsgeschicht-liche und paränetische Parallelen: Ein Beitrag zum Corpus Hellenisticum Novi Testamenti* (TU 76; Berlin: Akademie, 1961), 9–10, takes Lucian's description of the support of Peregrinus in prison as consonant with the practices of early Christianity, as well as a leader's profiting from the naive generosity of church members (11).

[64] *Did.* 11.9, 12; 12.1–2; 13.1–7; 15.1. In the context of the Peregrinus episode narrated above, Lucian describes how Christians shared their property so that some did take advantage and profit materially from them (*Peregr.* 13). See Betz, *Lukian*, 112–14, for parallels in Lucian and the NT against the gathering of wealth by religious leaders. 1 Thess. 2.9 is also early evidence of concern over inordinate gain by those in ministry.

Obligation in Rom. 14.1–15.13

The use of obligation in this letter does not appear for the first time in Romans 14. From Romans 1 on, the readers see that Paul is making ample use of this social force, so understandable to them as Romans. Paul introduces himself as one who is obligated to civilized and uncivilized, learned and ignorant (1.14). The obligations humanity is to show toward the deity are assumed at 1.21. Paul frames the believer's ethical orientation in terms of obligation in 8.12. In the benediction at the end of Romans 11, Paul includes a quotation from Job 41.3a (ET 41.11a) that shows that God is obligated to no one (Rom. 11.35).[65] Then with 12.1–2, Paul begins to spell out the obligations that church members in Rome have toward each other (12.3–21), toward their government (13.1–7), and to society in general (13.8–14). The command in Rom. 13.8, μηδενὶ μηδὲν ὀφείλετε εἰ μὴ τὸ ἀλλήλους ἀγαπᾶν, is worked out in the section on "strong" and "weak," which develops how one should live κατὰ ἀγάπην (14.15) and how one group is obligated to another (15.1–2), concluding with the command, προσλαμβάνεσθε ἀλλήλους (15.7).[66] So when Paul turns to the controversy dividing the Roman church (14.1–15.13), he presents his solution in terms of obligation.

It is clear that Rom. 14.1–15.13 contains a repeated progression in each of the major sections of Paul's argument. First he mentions social obligations that members of the community owe one another (14.1–4; 14.13–15.2; 15.7). Then he presents an activity of Christ as the basis for the obligation (14.9; 15.3; 15.8–12).[67] Each section then ends with the description of how the performance of the obligation, along with Christ's past activity, leads to the fulfillment of the ultimate obligation, worship to God (14.10–12; 15.5–6; 15.13). The example of Christ provides the summation of Paul's argument in Rom. 15.8–12. Hays's comment on Paul's use of LXX

---

[65] I am indebted to Steven E. Enderlein for pointing out Rom. 11.35 in this regard to me.

[66] Tomson, *Paul and the Jewish Law*, 238, makes clear how "the whole of 13:8–14 appears to be an introduction to our passage" with the links shown above.

[67] See the incisive explanation of Paul's use of the psalms in his presentation of Jesus as model for the Romans in R. B. Hays, "Christ Prays the Psalms: Paul's Use of an Early Christian Exegetical Convention," in *The Future of Christology: Essays in Honor of Leander E. Keck* (eds. A. J. Malherbe and W. A. Meeks; Minneapolis: Fortress, 1993), 122–36.

Ps. 17 in Rom. 15.9 includes the idea of the obligation to follow Christ's example.

> The Messiah, the seed of David who has been delivered by the hand of God from all his enemies, has won this victory – Paul contends – precisely for the purpose of "welcoming" Israel and Gentiles together, as shown in the psalm's concluding words of praise; *therefore*, Jew and Gentile, weak and strong, should also welcome one another for the glory of God, joining in the chorus of praise created by Paul's climactic *florilegium*.[68]

Barrett has stated that a problem is made explicit in Romans: the problem of motivating humans to live morally when salvation is presented as unilaterally effected by God.[69] In the examination that follows it is evident that Paul solves the problem by emphasizing an obligation arising from the benefits of Christ as his basis for morality in Romans.[70]

While the concept of obligation has been applied to the NT in a variety of ways, its place in Romans has not been fully explained. Danker's work from benefaction-related inscriptions as a way of informing our reading of the NT is suggestive,[71] but his case is not proven from the inscriptions used.[72] Nor does his work directly address the question of obligation between "strong" and "weak," for from our passage he mentions only Rom. 14.18 and 15.8, texts that do not concern the horizontal exchange within the community that Paul advocates.[73] Stephen C. Mott's article is helpful for describing how obligation functioned in Hellenistic society in general, but he does not address the NT.[74] Gerd Theißen is also

---

[68] Ibid., 135 (his italic).

[69] C. K. Barrett, *Freedom and Obligation: A Study of the Epistle to the Galatians* (Philadelphia: Westminster, 1985), 54. For Barrett, the concept of obligation in Galatians functions primarily between the believer and God. In that letter, Paul has a personal obligation to God (1.15; Barrett, 53) as do the Galatians in general (5.13; Barrett, 71).

[70] This thesis is already found in H. D. Betz, "Das Problem der Grundlagen der paulinischen Ethik (Röm 12,1–2)," *ZTK* 85 (1988) 208–16.

[71] Frederick W. Danker, *Benefactor: Epigraphic Study of a Graeco-Roman and New Testament Semantic Field* (St. Louis: Clayton, 1982).

[72] David E. Aune, review of *Benefactor*, by Frederick W. Danker, *Interp.* 38 (1984) 421–25.

[73] Danker, *Benefactor*, 383, 385, 442.

[74] "The Power of Giving and Receiving: Reciprocity in Hellenistic Benevolence," in *Current Issues in Biblical Interpretation* (M. C. Tenney Festschrift; Grand Rapids: Eerdmans, 1975), 60–72.

sensitive to issues of obligation in his sociological reading of the NT. The "love-patriarchalism" he finds at Corinth[75] may be helpful for the situation as depicted in 1 Cor. 8–10, but it does not include the element of reciprocity that Paul commands for the "strong" and "weak" of Rome. Glad helpfully mentions obligations incumbent on members of the Roman churches,[76] but as I argue at the end of this chapter, I cannot follow Glad's idea that Paul sanctions continuing mutual correction in this section. I can agree with Westerholm's distinction between the universal human obligation to the good that Paul sees and its particular instantiation among Jews as obligation to Mosaic law.[77] The obligations that Paul calls for between "strong" and "weak" and the various statements within the obligation topos that are evident elsewhere in Romans are simply specific cases of this general obligation to the good.

This chapter on obligation within the Roman churches fits with John Chow's application of patronage and "social networks" to 1 Corinthians,[78] G. W. Peterman's application of social reciprocity to Philippians,[79] and E. A. Judge's descriptions of obligation at work in the communities depicted in the NT, both in their relationships to outside institutions[80] and as an important force within the communities themselves.[81] My suggestions on the way in which Paul uses obligation in Romans 14–15 seem especially to fit with Judge, who acknowledges that Paul used the social forces bound up in patronage for his churches, while adapting them to fit with the love command.[82] I also fully agree with Sampley's seminal statement, "Each believer has the obligation to welcome and nurture

---

[75] Theißen, *Social Setting*, 138–40.

[76] Glad, *Paul and Philodemus*, 218, 225.

[77] S. Westerholm, *Preface to the Study of Paul* (Grand Rapids: Eerdmans, 1997), 117–19.

[78] *Patronage and Power*.

[79] Peterman, *Paul's Gift from Philippi*.

[80] *The Social Pattern of Christian Groups in the First Century: Some Prolegomena to the Study of New Testament Ideas of Social Obligation* (London: Tyndale, 1960). For example, he mentions "the acute sensitivity to public opinion" as a motive for keeping one's obligations to those without the church (73).

[81] While he can write such statements as "It was only within the intimacy of the Christian associations themselves, untrammelled by past history or ulterior objects, that free expression could be given to the principles of the fraternity" (ibid., 76), Judge does acknowledge that first-century churches did employ obligation as an internal, cohesive force (E. A. Judge, "Cultural Conformity and Innovation in Paul: Some Clues from Contemporary Documents," *TynBul* 35 [1984] 3–24).

[82] Judge, "Cultural Conformity and Innovation," 23.

others,"[83] and seek to develop that idea by examining our passage in light of obligation.

Obligation in Rom. 14.1–12

This paragraph is mainly directed to the "weak." While Paul mentions the obligations of "strong" to accept "weak" (verse 1) and desist from scorning "weak" (verses 3a, 10b), the rest of the paragraph argues that the coming judgment of God makes all human judging (the activity of the "weak") superfluous. The "weak" practice of judging is first countered by the relationship between each believer and Christ (verse 4).[84] Since everyone in the community has a distinct relation with the Lord, judging a fellow believer is actually usurping the place of the Lord (verse 4a). The obligation to desist from judging is intensified further by the Lord's ability to establish each believer (verse 4b). After a second description of "strong" and "weak" (verse 5), there follows a second reason to desist from judging.

The second reason is an argument from fulfilled obligation. One sign of the individual link each member shares with Christ is the act of thanksgiving.[85] Paul states that each believer is already fulfilling this major obligation of humanity to express thanksgiving[86] to the deity,[87] for in verse 6 he notes that both eater and non-eater express thanks to God. Since this obligatory act toward the deity is being performed already, he has only commendation for the practice. In so doing he uses this fulfilled obligation as an argument to bring both groups closer to performing unfulfilled obligations necessary for communal harmony.

The individual connection between believer and Christ is then

---

[83] Sampley, "The Weak and the Strong," 48.

[84] This argument is appropriately reversed when Paul addresses the "strong." There is an obligation to avoid offending the "weak," since the latter are those for whom Christ died and the work of God (14.15, 20).

[85] O'Brien, "Thanksgiving," 62, states that Paul's use of thanksgiving is "always a *response* to God's saving activity in creation and redemption" (his italic). As such it clearly occurs within the context of obligation. On the obligation to show thanksgiving, see pp. 178–79 above.

[86] See Peter Krafft, "*Gratus animus*," *RAC* XII.732–52.

[87] Cf. Rom. 1.21. Paul Schubert's suggestion that the thanksgiving mentioned in 14.6 may refer to "a general pagan custom" (*Form and Function of the Pauline Thanksgivings* [BZNW 20; Berlin: A. Töpelmann, 1939], 85) offers the possibility that Paul is working with the obligation to express *gratia* to the deity that was common in antiquity.

broadened in scope to include the gamut of human existence. Thus one belongs to the Lord whether one lives or dies (verse 8). The basis for this individual connection and its correlative obligation to desist from judging is then given: by dying and living, Christ has won the right to rule over every person, placing every human in his debt. It is in this conceptual context that Paul's teaching about the divine calling (κλῆσις) is significant.[88] On the basis of the Christ event[89] God's power works to call even the "weak" and despised to himself (1 Cor. 1.27–28). The calling functions as an essential step in God's appropriation of the obligations owed him, according to Paul.

The scripture proof in 14.11 functions in Paul's argument from obligation in two ways. First, it highlights the sense of individual accountability before the deity, which Paul makes explicit in 14.12. The obligation that this relationship of accountability implies is that one must not judge or scorn another community member. To do so is to interfere in that person's relationship before Christ's place as ruler of all and God's role as judge. Second, the proof emphasizes what is for Paul the inevitable result of salvation history. The primary obligation to glorify the deity will be accomplished, regardless of minor differences within churches. For Paul, the means of ensuring that present obligations of social harmony in the church are fulfilled is by remembering the eschatological obligation to glorify God. The use of the glory of God as a goal here is remarkable. Jewett notes OT texts in which divine glory is pictured as the result of one segment of humanity completely conquering another. Throughout our passage, however, the obligation to glorify God is presented as something that will be accomplished not by the victory of "strong" over "weak" or *vice versa*, but by these groups' peaceful coexistence.[90]

Obligation in Rom. 14.13–15.6

Primarily addressed to the "strong," this section presents the obligation that the "strong" have to support the "weak" and so work toward the upbuilding of the community. This obligation is first presented in a negative way: the "strong" are not to offend the "weak" (14.13). Then in verse 15 Paul extends the responsibility of the "strong" beyond a fixed set of activities to avoid; the love

---

[88] See 1 Cor. 1.26–31.
[89] See ὁ λόγος τοῦ σταυροῦ of 1 Cor. 1.18.
[90] Jewett, *Christian Tolerance*, 40–42. See also Rom. 15.7.

command obligates them to live in such a way that "weak" members are not grieved.

Like the argument in the preceding section, the obligation of the "strong" to avoid offending the "weak" is presented by Paul as based on the relationship that already obtains between this "weak" one and Christ (14.15). Because of this relationship, the "weak" one can be called τὸ ἔργον τοῦ θεοῦ (14.20),[91] a description that calls for the respect of others in the community. The priority of the relationship that obtains between believers and Christ makes one's treatment of fellow believers actually a form of service to Christ.[92] This service pleases God first,[93] and only secondarily is "acceptable to people."[94] When the obligation of the "strong" is summarized in 15.1 as one of support, the basis is again not the horizontal relationship between "strong" and "weak" but the vertical relationship between Christ and humanity (verse 3). Paul's direction for "strong" to support "weak" in this context would cause some tension with how Roman social values usually worked out in convivial situations: "the brisk exchange of *officia* and *beneficia* can be assumed to have flowed continuously, along with the wine and conversation."[95] A sympathetic reader in Paul's audience would have to redefine the *officia* and *beneficia* they would expect at a meal of the believing Roman community.

The call to deny self and please neighbor as Christ did is based on Paul's understanding that believers are obligated to a mimesis of Christ. Hays's explanation of Rom. 15.1–3 is clear:

> Paul's point seems to be simply that Christ endured suffering and blame *vicariously*: he was innocent but incurred reproaches. Thus, the powerful, rather than pleasing themselves, should likewise be willing to suffer if necessary for the sake of others.[96]

[91] The "weak" one is called this on the basis of Christ's power to establish each believer (14.4) because of his death (14.15). The parallelism between verse 15c and verse 20a leads me to identify τὸ ἔργον τοῦ θεοῦ as a "weak" member instead of Käsemann's interpretation of the phrase as the whole community (*Romans*, 378).

[92] Rom. 14.18 – ὁ γὰρ ἐν τούτῳ δουλεύων τῷ Χριστῷ . . .

[93] εὐάρεστος τῷ θεῷ; see 12.1–2; 15.16, 31 for other sacrificial language in Romans.

[94] We note that for Paul, one is obligated to live in a way that meets with human approval. See Rom. 12.3, 17b; 1 Cor. 11.28; 2 Cor. 13.5; Gal. 6.4.

[95] D'Arms, "The Roman *Convivium* and the Idea of Equality," 319.

[96] "Christ Prays the Psalms," 131. An extreme form of the mimesis of Christ is seen in Ign. *Rom.* 6.3– ἐπιτρέψατέ μοι μιμητὴν εἶναι τοῦ πάθους τοῦ θεοῦ μου.

As Christ's acts of dying and living were used to ground the obligation Paul placed on the "weak," so here the act of Christ's death[97] is used to ground obligation for the "strong."[98]

In verse 4 we come to the first of three references to hope (15.4, 12, 13), all of which fit in the context of reciprocal obligations. Obligatory gratitude was expressed or duties performed for a benefactor often in the hope that further benefactions would occur. Philo mentions, in the context of how one must express gratitude to the deity, that one should not neglect to request from God in a thankful manner, even if one has no hope of return benefits for such thanksgiving.

> μηδεὶς οὖν τῶν ἀφανεστέρων καὶ ταπεινοτέρων εἶναι δοκούντων ἐλπίδος ἀπογνώσει τῆς ἀμείνονος ἀποκνησάτω ἱκέτης εὐχάριστος γενέσθαι θεοῦ, ἀλλ' εἰ καὶ μηδὲν ἔτι προσδοκᾷ τῶν μειζόνων, ὑπὲρ τούτων ὧν ἔλαχεν ἤδη κατὰ τὴν ἑαυτοῦ δύναμιν εὐχαριστείτω.

> Let none then of the lowly or obscure in repute shrink through despair of the higher hope from thankful supplication to God, but even if he no longer expects any greater boon, give thanks according to his power for the gifts which he has already received.[99]

We know that the basic obligation of both "strong" and "weak" is to offer themselves in self-sacrifice to God (Rom. 12.1) on the basis of the divine benefits. In Romans Paul sees the believer as primarily under obligation to God, on the basis of the divine benefits that God has shown in Christ (Rom. 6.12–8.39). The obligation that is owed Christ (14.8–9) is a means of expressing the basic obligation to God (14.12; Phil. 2.11). The hope in which this obligation is to be performed includes the thought of future benefits.[100] This is

[97] I follow Dunn (*Romans*, 838), who takes 15.3 to refer specifically to the death of Christ. In addition to Dunn's arguments, the references to the death of Christ in the preceding context (14.9, 15) make it unlikely that the self-emptying in the incarnation (Lietzmann, *Römer*, 119) or the incarnation as a whole (Cranfield, *Romans*, 732) are in view in 15.3.

[98] See Wolfgang Schrage, *Die konkreten Einzelgebote in der paulinischen Paränese: Ein Beitrag zur neutestamentlichen Ethik* (Gütersloh: Gerd Mohn, 1961), 151, on what it means for the "strong" to bear weaknesses of the "weak."

[99] *Mut.* 222. Philo (Vol. V; trans. F. H. Colson and G. H. Whitaker; LCL; London: William Heinemann, 1934). On Philo's tendency to see God as the ultimate benefactor, see Peterman, *Paul's Gift from Philippi*, 49.

[100] See Rom. 12.11–12, where τῇ ἐλπίδι χαίροντες follows immediately upon a reference to serving the Lord. See also Rom. 8.18–25; 1 Cor. 9.10; 1 Thess. 5.8–10.

especially confirmed in the next section by the eschatologically oriented scripture proofs of 15.9–12. They are concluded by Paul's wish "that you may overflow in hope" (verse 13). Here the thought of future benefits from the relationship are picked up only in the references to endurance (verses 4–5) and an eschatological allusion to the final state of praise to God (verse 6). As elsewhere in Romans,[101] hope here is not exclusively eschatological in focus. It includes an expectation for further divine benefits in this life. In Rom. 15.4, 13, hope retains its dual function for Paul. Theologically it is both a presupposition and a goal of one's spiritual orientation and existence.

As with the obligation to support the "weak" (verse 1), the obligation to think κατὰ Χριστὸν Ἰησοῦν (verse 5) is similarly built on the mimesis of Christ. This pattern of thought leads naturally into a reference to united worship of God. As at the end of the preceding section (14.11), Paul situates the obligation of the "strong" as a means toward the ultimate obligation of glorifying God (15.6).[102]

Obligation in Rom. 15.7–13

The shared obligation for thought "according to Christ Jesus" (15.5) results in a common obligation for action, expressed in the "welcome one another" (προσλαμβάνεσθε ἀλλήλους) command of 15.7. Here the vertical dimension in the rationale for the obligations between "strong" and "weak" receives its final statement. Christ's acceptance of the believer forms the basis for the obligation to accept a fellow member.[103] The details of Christ's acceptance are explicated in verse 8. Paul's description of him as a "servant of the circumcision" in the context of confirming the promises of the fathers must refer to the historical Jesus' Jewish identity. This is confirmed by two other references in Romans that are uncharacteristic of Paul and point to an interest in the Jewishness of Jesus.[104] The goal of the acceptance of Jesus is given as the glory of God in

---

[101] See Rom. 5.4; 8.24–25.

[102] See Käsemann, *Romans*, 383–84, on the picture Paul presents here of a chorus praising God.

[103] The καθώς is causal (Cranfield, *Romans*, 739). Since Christ has accepted the believers, they must accept one another.

[104] Rom. 1.3; 9.5.

verse 7b, with intermediate steps provided in verses 8–9.[105] Christ's service confirmed the promises of the fathers, causing the nations to glorify God. Following Christ in his acceptance of others is therefore depicted as a way to fulfill one's fundamental obligation to glorify God (verse 7b). Like the preceding two sections, the horizontal obligation within the community receives its basis in an act of Christ. The end result of the horizontal obligation and the act of Christ in all three cases is portrayed as the glory of God.

At least in the case of the Roman "strong" and "weak," then, Paul's social ethics are based primarily on a divine–human relationship, rather than on a mere respect for one's fellows. The basis which Paul gives for the obligations of behavior and thought between "strong" and "weak" is primarily the relationship that obtains between the individual and Christ. This vertical dimension behind Paul's understanding of obligation makes his directions to the Roman churches different from how social obligation usually worked out in Roman society.[106]

Instead of endorsing the "strong" patrons' right to live as they please in regard to "weak" clients, Paul directs the "strong" to support the "weak" (15.1), to give up some rights in order not to offend the "weak" (14.21), all so that each side may welcome and accept the other (15.7). These directions run against the typical dynamic between those of "strong" and "weak" status in Rome. But it is not as though this vertical dimension affected only the responsibilities of the "strong."

Paul's rhetorical question in 14.4 asks the "weak" why they judge another's servant (the "strong"). Since the fate of this servant is the concern of the servant's master, all human judgment is superfluous. The obligation to desist from judging is therefore based on the prior relationship that obtains between the "strong" (whom the "weak" want to judge) and the Lord.[107]

The obligation to desist from judging (14.4) and the obligation for mutual acceptance (15.7) indicate the only changes that Paul is

---

[105] The Jewish cast to this catena may be seen in Paul's selection of at least one quotation from each section of the *TaNaK*: Law (LXX Deut. 32.43 in verse 10); Prophets (LXX 2 Sam. 22.50 in verse 9; LXX Isa. 11.10 in verse 12); Writings (LXX Ps. 17.50 in verse 9; Ps. 117.1 [LXX Ps. 116.1] in verse 11).

[106] My point here on obligation in the Roman churches fits with John Chow's conclusion that in Corinth, Paul's commands "carried subversive implication for vertical patron–client ties in the church" (*Patronage and Power*, 190).

[107] Peterman also notes how Paul has brought God into the reciprocity construct, *Paul's Gift from Philippi*, 159.

asking the "weak" to make. Stowers seems open to the idea that the "weak" were to be gently instructed by the "strong," since this fits within his idea of "psychagogic practices" that he thinks Paul is fostering in this section. By understanding ἀσθενής to overlap with our adjective "sick," and by a literal reading of 15.14 as a conclusion to the "strong" and "weak" section, Stowers thinks that Paul is asking "weak" and "strong" to adapt to one another.[108] Because of Stowers's favorable references to his student's dissertation, we may fill in what sort of "mutual evaluation and criticism"[109] and adaptation he thinks Paul advocates by looking at Clarence Glad's monograph.

Glad contends that Paul prohibits the "weak" from judging the "strong" in the sense of condemning their status before God or considering them unacceptable, and that Paul prohibits the "strong" from judging the "weak" in the sense of disqualifying them from membership in their circles of friendship.[110] This definitely seems to be an accurate reading of the text. But Glad also states that "in Paul's view mature members should evaluate their erring co-members"[111] and that Paul is not trying to terminate all judging that the "strong" do.[112] He asserts this on the basis of a distinction he draws on the nature of judging that Paul prohibits. While Paul outlaws a judgment that breaks friendships and pronounces on another's standing before God,[113] he does, according to Glad's literal reading of 15.14, continue to advocate a kind of mutual "education that makes use of rebuke and censure," including "behavior modification and attitude change through admonition and blame in the reformation of others."[114] But Rom. 15.14 comes within an apology, and functions, like 1.12, as a *captatio benevolentiae*. I did not find in either Stowers or Glad an argument to move me from Lietzmann's position on Rom. 15.14. Lietzmann considers the verse a polite return to 1.12, and writes that if Rom. 15.14 were to be taken literally, it would make 12.1–15.13 superfluous.[115] Rom. 15.14 therefore cannot be taken as

[108] Stowers, *Rereading*, 320–23.
[109] Ibid., 322.
[110] Glad, *Paul and Philodemus*, 217–24.
[111] Ibid., 217. But cf. his statement on 226: "Instead of evaluating the beliefs of the weak, the powerful should rather 'decide' (κρίνατε) not to put an offense in front of 'a brother' (13b)."
[112] Ibid., 222.   [113] Ibid., 224.
[114] Ibid., 232–33.
[115] Lietzmann, *Römer*, 120.

indicative of Paul's sanction for a continuing relationship of mutual correction or "behavior modification and attitude change."

Glad's position also ignores the force of Paul's statement in 14.14b – εἰ μὴ τῷ λογιζομένῳ τι κοινὸν εἶναι, ἐκείνῳ κοινόν. The spiritual ruin that Paul perceives will happen to the "weak" (14.15, 20) shows how seriously he takes their preoccupation with purity. It is unlikely that Paul, concerned about his upcoming reception in Jerusalem, is actually trying to dissuade believers from an abstinence that might have roots in Judaism, or to persuade them out of observing certain days "for the Lord."[116] I therefore disagree with Glad's idea that Paul wants some sort of continuing education between "strong" and "weak."

Barclay argues that while Paul writes for an acceptance of the "weak" on the surface, he indeed introduces the seeds of their position's dissolution.[117] This seems to be a variation of Watson, who reads this letter as Paul's attempt to unite disparate congregations in Rome, while allowing for difference in practice.[118] I agree with Watson and Barclay that Paul has an edge toward Torah in this letter, though I am not sure that Paul is trying to move the "weak" from their distinct perspectives and practices.

Barclay's perspective can only be taken now if we read this letter first as scripture,[119] in light of the outcome of the rivalry between the Jesus movement and Judaism in the early Empire. If we wish to "read Romans afresh as a letter from the Greco-Roman world of the first century CE,"[120] we must recognize that Paul is the underdog. He has no hope of changing the Jewish establishment's view on dietary laws and their powerful hold on diaspora Jews throughout the Empire, no doubt adopted by some followers of Jesus. He is rather focused on gaining a positive hearing for his

---

[116] So I am in agreement with Rauer, *Die "Schwachen,"* 97, who states that Paul considers it purposeless to try to change the "weak" behavior. Willis, *Idol Meat*, 120, cites Rom. 14.17 in defense of his argument that Paul does not attempt to change the Corinthian "weak"; presumably he would argue the same in the Roman case. Schrage, *Die konkreten Einzelgebote*, 151, mentions how Paul regards both "strong" and "weak" positions as legitimate.

[117] Barclay, " 'Do We Undermine the Law?,' " 305–308.

[118] Watson, *Paul, Judaism and the Gentiles*, 97–98. Dunn's judgment (*Romans*, lvii), "Had Watson argued that the likely *effect* of Paul's advocacy was a polarization of synagogue and church, as Jewish Christians found it increasingly difficult to maintain the twin loyalties to law and faith, he would have been on stronger ground," could function as a starting point for Barclay's essay.

[119] On the necessity of reading Paul's letters first as "not-Scripture," see Hays, *Echoes*, 5.

[120] The phrase is from Stowers, *Rereading*, 6.

gospel and a positive evaluation on his life (15.30–32). Paul simply wants to make room in the Roman communities for both "strong" and "weak" positions on consumption and day observance. Paul's imperative that includes the idea of "weak" welcoming "strong" (15.7)[121] does not contradict Torah in Paul's framework (3.31; 13.8–10; 15.7–12), because of the emphases Paul finds in the Torah on the love command and on an eschatological vision of Jew and Gentile worshiping together. Barclay's statement that Paul's rejection of the clean/unclean distinction in 14.14, 20 "constitutes nothing less than a fundamental rejection of the Jewish law in one of its most sensitive dimensions"[122] is true in the sense that Paul no longer holds to a clean/unclean distinction in consumption as he once undoubtedly did. Surely we err if we ignore the radical departure from a mindset espoused by some Judaisms contemporary to Paul that Rom. 14.14 signals. But note that this departure is made on the basis of what Paul knows "in the Lord Jesus" (14.14). He is reading Torah now through lenses that regard Jesus as Torah's goal (10.4–10) and the Spirit as a gift from the God of the Torah (8.2). So while that aspect of Torah that dealt with food seems to have been undermined on the basis of the historical Jesus' authority,[123] Paul writes not as though he has undermined a static Torah but as one who has seen a dynamic Torah's completion in Christ (3.21). I agree with Barclay against Nanos and Tomson that Paul did not keep the dietary laws. But I disagree with Barclay that Paul is undermining the Torah here. An analogous assertion would be to say that Lincoln's emancipation proclamation undermined the United States' constitution.

Paul in this text is not towing a Trojan horse into the Romans community.[124] Rather, he is simply waving a flag for a truce in the Roman churches, in order to make room for both his "strong" approach to diet and the "weak" approach. The ways in which Paul's truce flag has been used by later interpreters is, of course, another question.

Paul's directions would not work without the use of obligation

---

[121] See Barclay, " 'Do We Undermine the Law?,' " 306–307.

[122] See ibid., 300.

[123] The unusual beginning to 14.14, οἶδα καὶ πέπεισμαι ἐν κυρίῳ Ἰησοῦ, most probably introduces material Paul knew of from traditions similar to those preserved in Mark 7.15–19 (Dunn, *Romans*, 819; cf. T. J. Deidun, *New Covenant Morality in Paul* [AnBib 39; Rome: Pontifical Biblical Institute, 1981], 221; 2 Cor. 5.16).

[124] See Barclay, " 'Do We Undermine the Law?,' " 308.

throughout Roman society as a means of defining relationships. But he superimposes the relationship of the believer to Christ onto the controversy between those with and without status in the Roman churches, and this changes the way that relationships are to work out between "strong" and "weak."

11

PORTRAITS OF THE "STRONG" AND "WEAK"

ἐὰν δὲ δῆμος ἢ φράτορες ἢ ἱερῶν ὀργίων ἢ ναῦται ἢ
σύσσιτοι ἢ ὁμόταφοι ἢ θιασῶται ἢ ἐπὶ λείαν οἰχόμενοι ἢ
εἰς ἐμπορίαν, ὅτι ἂν τούτων διαθῶνται πρὸς ἀλλήλους,
κύριον εἶναι, ἐὰν μὴ ἀπαγορεύσῃ δημόσια γράμματα.

If the inhabitants of a city district or precinct be in
association for the purpose of holding religious feasts or of
dining together or to provide for their burial or if they be
members of the same club or they combine to engage in
some enterprise or for profit, anything that they agree
between themselves will be valid unless forbidden by public
statutes.   Solon[1]

After looking at the "strong" and "weak" section of Romans in
light of first-century ascetic practices, the stigma of superstition,
and the social value of obligation, I am now ready to offer portraits
of these groups in the believing communities of Rome. Before I do
so, however, I need to answer two more of Robert Karris's helpful
questions. First, he asked what the "theological situation" in Rome
was when Paul wrote this letter.[2]

The theological situation was one in which Gentiles dominated.
As the opening to chapters 9–11 makes most sense if we understand
Paul's pathos to be concerned with real Jews he knew, so these
chapters' conclusion makes most sense if there were real Gentiles
who boasted in their theological priority over Jews (11.13–23).
These Gentiles emphasized that they were not under Torah
(6.14–15), and somehow used this to justify immoral behavior
(6.1–21; 13.12–14). To choose one of Karris's options, I shall call

---

[1] Solon *apud* Gaius, XII Tables, Book 4 *apud Dig.* 47.22.4 (eds. and trans.
Mommsen, Krueger, and Watson). The editors suggest ἢ ἱερῶν ὀργίων θύται instead
of ἢ ἱερῶν ὀργίων ἢ ναῦται.
[2] Karris, "Response to Professor Donfried," 125–26.

these Gentile believers "antinomians."At the other pole of this theological situation were some Jewish believers in Jesus. These believers were pro-Torah and concerned that Paul was anti-Torah and anti-Semitic. This is the most satisfying explanation for why Paul seems so concerned to identify positively with Torah, Jews, and Judaism in this letter (3.2, 31; 7.12, 14; 9.1–5; 13.8–10). Karris might object that perhaps this positive identification springs only from Paul's own occasion,[3] i.e., his anticipation of a hostile reception in Jerusalem (15.30–32). I would respond that this possibility ignores direct address to his actual audience (4.1; 7.1; 16.7, 11), and uncharacteristic expressions (1.3; 4.6) where the Jewish dimension predominates.[4] The positive identification with Torah, Jews, and Judaism in this letter arises mostly from Paul's audience in Rome, about whom Paul is informed (1.8) and whom Paul regards as his mission field and potential sending base (1.11–13; 15.22–24), and is only secondarily due to Paul's personal occasion, the public relations challenge he faces in Jerusalem.[5] Paul was familiar with some of the teaching that was current in this church (6.17). He finds it theologically deficient in its doctrine of judgment (2.16; 3.6; 14.10–12). He also thinks that there is confusion on both sides regarding the place of Torah in the *ordo salutis* and in the believer's life (3.21, 31; 6.12–18; 7.1–8.4; 10.4–13; 13.8–10). Now we move to Karris's next question about a possible "Jewish–Gentile conflict" reflected in Rom. 14.1–15.13: "Does such a conflict exist? If so, what are its contours?"[6]

There is a conflict, actually occurring in Rome, that is reflected in Rom. 14.1–15.13. One group, nicknamed in Rome "weak," are concerned about dietary purity and are scornfully shamed by another group, nicknamed in Rome as "strong." The "weak" appear to be superstitious to the "strong" and to those outside of the community, since they are perceived as being excessively concerned about food and the consequences its consumption has for the afterlife.[7] The vegetarian "weak" include some Jewish believers who are abstaining over concerns to maintain the *kashrut* laws and

---

[3] Ibid., 127.

[4] Romans 2 belongs as evidence here, but since our guild is hypnotized by its identification as "diatribe," I did not list it, for fear that it would be thrown out of court.

[5] See Jacob Jervell, "The Letter to Jerusalem," in Donfried, *The Romans Debate*, 53–64.

[6] Karris, "Response to Professor Donfried," 127.

[7] Rom. 14.7–9, 14; Martin, *Corinthian Body*, 114, 156.

to avoid the contamination they think might come by eating with those who eat everything. Among the "weak" there were probably some Gentiles, since first-century Rome had teachers who were aggressive in espousing vegetarianism. Since their philosophical arguments for vegetarianism were not antithetical to Christianity, it is very possible that they joined the "weak" and were abstaining "for the Lord" (14.6). A native Italian believer, who formerly studied with Musonius Rufus, could abstain "for the Lord." Paul, viewing this person's abstinence alongside that of some Jewish believers, would say that the Italian considered meat to be κοινόν (14.14). The "strong" were predominantly Gentiles, but included some Jews (15.1) who were not concerned about what they ate. Some of the "strong" were gluttonous eaters (13.13; 16.18).

The communities of Jesus-believers in Rome are as whole groups shamed by their inability to eat peacefully together. The Roman value of *convivium* is not followed, because the believers are scorning or judging one another for what they eat (14.16). Paul is convinced that his gospel is not shameful, and thinks that it can speak directly to believers who shame brothers and sisters at the risk of bringing the whole Jesus movement in Rome into shame. Paul writes to change behavior among his audience, so that they can live, as he does, without shame.

We saw in the third chapter that the Romans used words for "strong" and "weak" to designate one's place on the social hierarchy of status.[8] Since Paul tells the Roman believers to welcome one another (14.1; 15.7), and tells the "strong" not to despise the "weak," it seems likely that there was a difference in status between these groups that kept them apart. The evidence fits Watson's suggestion that there were really two congregations who received Paul's letter.[9] Indeed, given the Jewish association with Roman Christianity and the number of Jewish synagogues in Rome,[10] Paul may have had more than two Roman congregations in mind when he wrote this letter. The time is ripe for us to use the plural – "Roman *churches*" – in our discussion of this letter's audience.

---

[8] See pp. 45–63 above.

[9] Watson, *Paul, Judaism and the Gentiles*, 94–98.

[10] On the Jewish roots of the Roman churches, see George La Piana, "La primitiva communità cristiana di Roma," 209–11. Philo, *Legat.* 155, gives us a sense of the size of the Jewish community in first-century Rome. On synagogues in first-century Rome, see Penna, "Les Juifs," 327–30 and Lampe, *Die stadtrömischen Christen*, 53–56, 367–68.

Comparison by order, class, and status

So there must have been one congregation, the "strong," who had higher status relative to the other groups of believers in Rome. And there must have been at least one congregation of lower status, the "weak." Paul's goal was to bring these groups to the point where they could worship together.[11] What held them apart? While these groups can be differentiated primarily with the category of status, we also look at the "strong" and "weak" through two other categories used in first-century Rome. These portraits of "strong" and "weak" therefore describe them in terms of order, class, and status.

Order

There is no clear indication that any of the Roman churches' members were of senatorial or equestrian orders. Though this study does not depend on accepting Romans 16 as part of the letter, we can suggest that some of the *potentes* had significant contact with these orders if we do assume that Paul wrote chapter 16 to Rome.[12]

Contact with the senatorial order

There is a good possibility that two households mentioned in Romans 16 were well placed within Roman society. These are the households of Aristobulus (verse 10) and Narcissus (verse 11). If this is the Aristobulus who was of the Herod family and a friend of Claudius,[13] then he may have willed his property to the emperor and his slaves would thus pass into the imperial household (*familia Caesaris*). Similarly, the designation "those of Narcissus" may indicate the slaves and freedmen of Tiberius Claudius Narcissus,

---

[11] Watson, *Paul, Judaism and the Gentiles*, 97, helpfully citing 15.6–13.

[12] In addition to the literature cited in n. 79 of chapter 3, see H. Gamble, *Textual History*, 36–129, and cf. Norman R. Petersen, "On the Ending(s) to Paul's Letter to Rome," in *The Future of Early Christianity* (Helmut Koester Festschrift; ed. Birger A. Pearson; Minneapolis: Fortress, 1991), 337–47. Petersen is right that there is a chiastic structure extending from Rom. 1.8 to 15.33. But Paul's unique epistolary situation and the names mentioned still make the double (or second) ending in Romans 16 probably integral to this letter.

[13] In addition to material cited in n. 80 of chapter 3, see Josephus, AJ 18.133, 135.

the rich freedman in Tiberius' household, who wielded significant authority in the reign of Claudius. He was forced to commit suicide by Nero (at Agrippina's instigation) in 54; his own slaves and freedmen remained in the powerful imperial household.[14] If these names in Rom. 16.10–11 correspond to those figures we know from history books, their household would most likely have been among the *potentes* within the Roman churches, given the political power and social status of the imperial household. Possible confirmation of this suggestion also comes from Phil. 4.22.

Roman citizenship

While not actually one of the specified orders (*ordines*) of Roman society, citizenship was a legally defined category best considered here. A significant difference among the Roman believers probably lay in the issue of Roman citizenship and the privileges it afforded. The Christians whom Nero crucified after the fire of 64 CE[15] were not citizens, for Roman law prohibited the crucifixion of citizens. Lampe argues that the testimony of Suetonius that such punishments were among Nero's proper acts of administration implies that those whom Nero crucified were not citizens.[16] While Nero did not show much regard for the law and Suetonius would not have been concerned with the niceties of citizenship, the argument is at least worth consideration. If there were resident foreigners (*peregrini*) in the churches, they would not have had the privileges of citizenship enjoyed by members who were citizens. The possibility that the "strong" included Roman citizens while at least some of the "weak" were *peregrini* is confirmed by an examination of the ethnicity of "strong" and "weak" groups under the "status" heading below.

Class

Social class as defined by Max Weber exists:

> when (1) a number of people have in common a specific causal component of their life chances, in so far as (2) this

---

[14] Bruce, *Paul*, 386–87. See also J. P. V. D. Balsdon, "Narcissus (2)," in *OCD*, 2nd ed., 722.

[15] Tacitus, *Ann.* 15.44.

[16] Lampe, *Die stadtrömischen Christen* 65–66, citing Suetonius, *Nero* 16.2; 19.3.

component is represented exclusively by economic interests in the possession of goods and opportunities for income, and (3) is represented under the conditions of the commodity or labor markets.[17]

I use this definition in the portraits of class to follow.

Wealth and poverty in Roman churches

If we seek to explain the social layers of the Roman churches in terms of social class, we need to marshal evidence for differences in property within the communities.[18] It is true that vegetarianism in antiquity has at times been taken as a sign of poverty.[19] But vegetarianism was never conclusive proof of poverty, and in first-century Rome there were strong precedents for vegetarianism even in the upper classes.[20] The asceticism of first-century Rome had not made the link with poverty that would later be the case in more distinctively Christian forms of asceticism.[21] Nor are those who are looked on as superstitious considered necessarily to be poorer in terms of property than the enlightened ones.[22] It is true that Paul does not explicitly ask the Roman Christians to contribute to his collection,[23] but this cannot be taken as evidence for their

[17] "Class, Status, Party," in *From Max Weber*, 181. For a survey of literature on the social class of early Christians, see Countryman, *The Rich Christian*, 1–18.

[18] To follow Weber, this is because the possession and the lack of property are "the basic categories of all class situations" ("Class, Status, Party," 182). On the general economic threat that Christianity posed to its surrounding society, see G. T. Oborn, "Economic Factors in the Persecutions of the Christians to A.D. 260," in *Environmental Factors in Christian History* (Shirley Jackson Case Festschrift; eds. J. T. McNeill, M. Spinka, and H. R. Willoughby; Chicago: University of Chicago Press, 1939), 131–48; esp. 133–36 on economic tensions caused in society by the Christian *familia*.

[19] Haußleiter, *Der Vegetarismus*, 4. Other texts that might be mentioned are: Prov. 15.17; Athenaeus, *Deip.* 4.161E–F; Juvenal, *Sat.* 3.229. See also Theißen, *Social Setting*, 128: "Members of the lower classes seldom ate meat in their everyday lives."

[20] Seneca was vegetarian for a year and then gave up the practice (*Ep.* 108.22), but in later life he is pictured as one again (Tacitus, *Ann.* 15.45) to avoid being poisoned. He also drank no wine (Seneca, *Ep.* 108.16). Another vegetarian, Musonius Rufus, at least moved in an upper class of Roman society in his associations with Rubellius Plautus, Barea Soranus, and Thrasea Paetus.

[21] Aside from the book of James, the evidence cited by Deems for the place of the Christian poor as evidence for practices of abstinence comes from after the composition of Romans ("The Sources of Christian Asceticism," 156–57).

[22] Though those who appeared to be superstitious in first-century Rome were not necessarily poor, I do argue in the text that follows that the "weak" were materially poorer than the "strong."

[23] On Paul's explanation about the collection in Rom. 15.25–32, see H. D. Betz, *2*

poverty.[24] Since they were not yet officially constituted as one of Paul's churches, Paul could not appeal to them for participation in the collection. Despite these considerations, which make descriptions of "strong" and "weak" in terms of social class difficult, five points may be observed that raise the following hypothesis: there was a class difference within the Roman community and the "weak" were perceived to be lower on the scale of social class than the "strong."

First, Paul's prohibitions of attitudes described with "judge" (κρίνω) for the "weak" and "despise" (ἐξουθενέω) for the "strong" (14.3, 10) seem to indicate that such attitudes existed in the community. While κρίνω could conceivably be characteristic of attitudes of either group (14.13), ἐξουθενέω fits best as an attitude exercised by those with material resources toward those without.[25]

Second, the hints of consumptive excess among the "strong" (13.13; 14.2, 17, 21) fit with the suggestion that the "strong" were viewed as wealthier than the "weak."[26] Such hints of consumption among "strong" in our text fit with what we know about how wealth was converted into social deference in Rome.[27] In the constitution of one burial club, for example, double portions at dinners are allotted to the president (*magister quinquennalis*) and one and a half portions to the secretary, messenger, and all former *magistri quinquennales*.[28]

Third, as Lampe has argued, Rom. 12.8, 13 indicate that there were different class levels in the church. He reads 12.16 as Paul's direction to those with material property to use it for those lower than themselves in social class. Lampe takes the four occurrences of

Corinthians 8 and 9: A Commentary on Two Administrative Letters of the Apostle Paul (Hermeneia; Philadelphia: Fortress, 1985), 141. Cf. M. A. Kruger, *"Tina Karpon*, 'Some Fruit' in Romans 1:13," *WTJ* 49 (1987) 167–73.

[24] On the position of Christians' social, economic, and vocational positions in relation to other inhabitants of the Empire, see Andreas Bigelmair, *Die Beteiligung der Christen am öffentlichen Leben in vorkonstantinischer Zeit: Ein Beitrag zur ältesten Kirchengeschichte* (VKHSM 8; Munich, 1902; reprint ed. Darmstadt: Scientia Verlag Aalen, 1970), 202–55; 293–330.

[25] See, e.g., 1 Cor. 16.11, where Paul's prohibition against looking down on Timothy immediately precedes a subtle command to provide materially for him. See also Juvenal, *Sat.* 3.152–53, who states that the worst thing about poverty is that it makes people prone to be ridiculed.

[26] For the common association between consumptive excess and luxury, see Sallust, *Cat.* 11.5–6.

[27] R. P. Saller, "Orders, Classes and Status," *CAH*, XI, forthcoming.

[28] *CIL* XIV 2.112.

"one another" (ἀλλήλων) in Romans 12 as evidence that the class difference effectively split the community.[29]

Fourth, there is evidence in the letter as a whole that Paul thinks that some in the church are relatively wealthy. Evidence I see for this is: (1) their faith is announced in the whole world (1.8); (2) "share" (μεταδίδωμι) and "show mercy" (ἐλεέω) are used in the list of spiritual gifts (12.8);[30] (3) μεστοί ἐστε ἀγαθωσύνης (15.14) may designate benefaction; (4) "to be sent on by you" (ὑφ' ὑμῶν προπεμφθῆναι) in 15.24 connotes material support;[31] (5) Paul states in 16.1–2 that the church may be a help to Phoebe, "patroness of many" (προστάτις πολλῶν).[32]

Fifth, since property continued to be a criterion of status in Roman society,[33] the upper hand that the "strong" enjoyed in status would likely have been related to perceptions of relative wealth within the community.

The foreign taint in the social caricature of the "weak" cannot be taken as conclusive evidence that they did not possess their own means of production.[34] Nor do Lampe's arguments for the servile background of some in the Roman community[35] necessarily make us conclude that the "weak" were of a preponderantly servile class.[36]

---

[29] Lampe, *Die stadtrömischen Christen*, 64. One may also note that the nine uses of this pronoun in Rom. 12.1–15.14 are a dense distribution for Paul. This may confirm Lampe's thesis that the section beginning at 12.1 is directed to a divided community.

[30] Neither term is used in the discussion of χαρίσματα in 1 Corinthians. "Helps" (ἀντίλημψεις) in 1 Cor. 12.28 and feeding the poor in 1 Cor. 13.3 may include material generosity, but the recognition of benevolence as a spiritual gift is stronger in Romans. Cf. 1 Cor. 1.26.

[31] See Bauer–Aland, s.v. "προπέμπω."

[32] On προστάτις here as equivalent to *patrona*, see Lampe, *Die stadtrömischen Christen*, 135.

[33] On the relevance of wealth for determining status, see Garnsey and Saller, *The Roman Empire*, 121–22. See also A. Stein, *Der römische Ritterstand* (Munich: C. H. Beck, 1927), 438–41. Weber ("Class, Status, Party," 190) allows for the influence that "class situation" can have in determining status.

[34] See the following discussion in this chapter on ethnicity of "strong" and "weak."

[35] *Die stadtrömischen Christen*, 136: οἱ ἐκ τῶν Ἀριστοβούλου (16.10) and οἱ ἐκ τῶν Ναρκίσσου (16.11) must designate either freedmen or slaves. On 153 he concludes that at least thirteen of the twenty-four names of Roman Christians listed in Romans 16 had servile origins. He rightly attempts no inference about the class composition of the community as a whole based on Romans 16. One may also note that if freedmen were among his thirteen servile names, some may have been relatively wealthy. Given the wealth and status of some freedmen in Rome, thirteen servile names provide no evidence for poverty or wealth in the community.

[36] One must remember that servile origins do not always indicate either poverty or a lack of social power in imperial Rome. See P. R. C. Weaver, "Social Mobility in

The "weak" as collegium

Jaquette suggests that Paul brings up the life and death topos in 14.7–9 and presents these as ἀδιάφορα in order to show that the divisive issues of food and day observance are ἀδιάφορα.[37] But given the description of judgment after death (14.10–12), I am not convinced that life and death are ἀδιάφορα here. Death is a pervasive theologoumenon in this letter;[38] I think that this is due to what Paul knows about the Roman communities of believers.

Why does Paul write about death when dealing with a controversy over food and the observance of days? He does so first because the "weak" appeared to be superstitious. Superstitious people in the first century were thought to be obsessively focused on keeping the body pure, and so could be concerned about food consumption. They were also known as very fearful of death.[39] When we encounter Paul's words of comfort related to death in Rom. 14.7–9, immediately following on a description of scrupulous behavior, the conclusion is inescapable that Paul is allaying some superstitious people's concerns about death. Indeed, Rom. 14.7–9 reads as though it were funereal liturgy, designed to comfort the bereaved. One might wonder if Paul knew that one or more of the Roman communities functioned, as did many *collegia*, as a burial club,[40] though of course it is clear that an officially Christian *collegium* would not have gained legal status in first-century Rome.[41] This suggestion fits with other evidence regarding the behavior of Christian communities who pooled their resources for the manumission of slaves in a way analogous to *collegia*.[42] It may

the Early Roman Empire: The Evidence of the Imperial Freedmen and Slaves," *Past & Present* 34 (1967) 3–20.

[37] Jaquette, *Discerning*, 130.

[38] Note the twenty uses of θάνατος between 5.12 and 8.39, as well as the underrated theme of lordship over the dead (1.4; 4.17, 24; 6.4, 9; 7.4; 8.11, 34; 10.7, 9; 14.9; 16.20?).

[39] Martin, *Corinthian Body*, 114, 156.

[40] The suggestion that early churches functioned in this way is not new. See E. Hatch, *The Organization of the Early Christian Churches* (1880 Bampton Lectures; London: Longmans, Green, and Co., 1909), 26–55; A. Yarbro Collins, "Vilification and Self-Definition in the Book of Revelation," in *Christians among Jews and Gentiles* (Krister Stendahl Festschrift; eds. G. W. E. Nickelsburg and G. W. MacRae; Philadelphia: Fortress, 1986), 317; R. S. Ascough, "Translocal Relationships among Voluntary Associations and Early Christianity," *JECS* 5 (1997) 223–41.

[41] Lampe, *Die stadtrömischen Christen*, 314.

[42] Harrill, *Manumission*, 178–82.

also explain why Paul describes Phoebe's ministry by stating that she has been patroness of many people, including himself.[43] Perhaps Paul is indicating to his audience that her entrée into the believing communities of Rome could include her assumption of the role of patroness/benefactress of a church. Just as a *collegium tenuiorum* would look for sponsors, so these early churches in Rome which perhaps functioned as *collegia* would need patrons or patronesses, "strong" people who could support the "weak."[44]

Class indicators for "strong" and "weak"

This look at the groups mentioned in Rom. 14.1–15.13 through the category of class allows us to conclude with the following suggestions about the place of these groups in the Roman class hierarchy. The difference between "strong" and "weak" included a difference in property. The "strong," who probably included some independent freedmen, were wealthier than the "weak." The term "independent freedmen" designates freedmen who were free of the practical ties by which masters continued to exercise authority over their freed slaves. This independence enabled these freedmen to accumulate wealth on their own, through various commercial ventures.[45]

The servile background of some of the members of the community is certain, but it cannot be used to infer that the "weak" were slaves. They may have been dependent freedmen. In general, I think it accurate to say that the "weak" included those from the more servile levels of the class hierarchy, excluding, of course, those from the imperial household. The "weak" were poorer than the "strong" and included more *peregrini* than the "strong" group.

We see that the text of Romans offers us evidence, in light of the social history of Rome, that the "strong" and "weak" groups fit with the tendency in imperial society to make distinctions on the basis of property and status. The presence of independent freedmen among the "strong," and poorer people – including *peregrini* – among the "weak," seems entirely consistent both with the letter of Romans and our knowledge of first-century Rome.

[43] Rom. 16.1–2.
[44] Rom. 15.1.
[45] With "independent freedman" I follow D'Arms's definition in *Commerce and Social Standing in Ancient Rome*, 148. See also Garnsey, "Independent Freedmen," 359–71.

Status

Ethnicity

In the discussion to follow, I use "ethnicity" with its sociological nuance of "national origin or distinctive cultural patterns," and not simply the physical characteristics that constitute "race."[46]

There is no evidence that the "strong" and "weak" groups of Rome had developed into distinct castes.[47] At the same time, the possibility that the segregation of "strong" and "weak" status groups occurred partially along ethnic lines deserves consideration, since ethnic identity plays such a significant role in the status that Juvenal, a writer in Rome a little later in the same century, assigns to people.[48] Unlike status groups that have reached the extreme of castes, "ethnic coexistences condition a mutual repulsion and disdain but allow each ethnic community to consider its own honor as the highest one."[49] Three arguments combine to support an hypothesis that ethnicity was a factor in the identity of "strong" and "weak" groups in the Roman church.

First, the scorn that the "strong" displayed toward the "weak" within the community (14.3, 10) fits with Roman attitudes toward foreigners.[50] When this consideration is combined with a recognition that "strength" was valued by the Romans and that foreign influence could be associated with "weakness,"[51] it seems possible that the attitude of "strong" toward "weak" in the church was simply part of the attitude that Romans had toward foreigners in society as a whole. We know that Rome in the fifties was a place of ethnic diversity. Within this diversity there was a definite ethnocentrism on the part of Roman citizens assimilated into the culture

---

[46] R. T. Schaefer, *Racial and Ethnic Groups* (3rd ed.; Glenview, Ill.: Scott, Foresman and Co., 1988), 26–27.

[47] See Weber, "Class, Status, Party," 188–89. Caste-related contamination is not evident in the scenario depicted in Rom. 14.1–15.13.

[48] Tony Reekmans, "Juvenal's Views on Social Change," 123. Although Reekmans frames it as a question of race, a reading of Juvenal indicates that it is actually an ethnic, rather than racial, criterion that he employs.

[49] Weber, "Class, Status, Party," 189.

[50] For a helpful survey of such attitudes, see A. N. Sherwin-White, *Racial Prejudice in Imperial Rome* (J. H. Gray Lectures, 1966; Cambridge: Cambridge University Press, 1967), 62–101.

[51] Horace, *Sat.* 1.9.71–72: "sum paulo infirmior, unus multorum." The same "strong" versus "weak" paradigm may be at work where Cicero, *Flac.* 67, portrays Flaccus' resistance to the diaspora temple collection as an instance of strength before barbarian superstition.

of Rome.[52] They resented the influx of foreigners and scorned their ethnic characteristics.[53] And it was a two-way street; *peregrini* looked down on the Romans and their culture.[54]

The merits of Roman culture were asserted from the Republic through the early Empire by the inclusion of the Romans within the category of Greeks in the general designation "Greeks and barbarians," though the ambiguous place the Romans occupied in terms of relative civilization is seen in the threefold distinction which also gained currency, "Greeks, Romans and barbarians."[55] The mixed character of Rome's urban population for our time period[56] is likely to have applied to the churches in Rome as well. The indications of a Jewish presence very early within Roman Christianity are clear,[57] but there is no reason to limit the foreign

[52] It is unlikely, especially in light of Rom. 11.17–24 and 15.9–12, that Paul, though calling himself "strong" (15.1), would endorse this ethnocentric aspect of their mindset.

[53] Greeks experienced slurs (Cicero, *Fam.* 16.4.2; *Tusc.* 2.65; *de Orat.* 1.102–105; 2.18; *Flac.* 9–10; 19 [but on Cicero's attitude toward Greeks, cf. *Q. fr.* 1.1.28]; Pliny, *HN* 15.5; Tacitus, *Ann.* 6.18). Despised also were Africans (Livy, 30.12.18; Sallust, *Jug.* 91.7). Cicero calls Africans, Gauls, and Spaniards "barbarians" (*Q. fr.* 1.1.27), though this term was not always meant with contempt; those races were defined as barbarian in the early Empire. The Jews, of course, were not exempt from such slurs by the Romans (Cicero, *Flac.* 66–69). See A. Momigliano, *Alien Wisdom: The Limits of Hellenization* (Cambridge: Cambridge University Press, 1975), 121–22, on Apollonius Molon as "a pioneer" in the genre of works against the Jews. Cf. J. G. Gager, *The Origins of Anti-Semitism: Attitudes toward Judaism in Pagan and Christian Antiquity* (New York/Oxford: Oxford University Press, 1983), 39–88, for examples of both positive and negative estimations of the Jews in the Roman sources.

[54] For a treatment of Jewish attitudes toward Rome, see N. R. M. de Lange, "Jewish Attitudes to the Roman Empire," in *Imperialism in the Ancient World* (eds. P. D. A. Garnsey and C. R. Whittaker; Cambridge: Cambridge University Press, 1978), 255–81.

[55] The development of Roman self-perception from barbarian to civilized is traced by Jüthner, *Hellenen und Barbaren*, 61–62.

[56] M. Rostovtzeff, *The Social and Economic History of the Roman Empire* (2nd ed.; Oxford: Oxford University Press, 1957), 100. Tenney Frank's conclusion, in "Race Mixture in the Roman Empire," *AHR* 21 (1916) 690, 693, that 90 percent of Roman-born urban plebeians were of foreign parentage, is surely skewed. See Taylor, "Freedmen and Freeborn," 129–32, for reasons why freedmen (with a majority who had foreign names) predominate in the epitaphs of the lower population in Rome, while no evidence remains for the freeborn. Though we might not accept M. P. Nilsson's thesis that racial mixture led to the downfall of Rome, his article "The Race Problem of the Roman Empire" (*Hereditas* 2 [1921] 370–90) certainly indicates the degree to which racial, and hence ethnic, mixture occurred in the Empire. A similar thesis, with charts and mathematical formulae, is advanced by Vittorio Macchioro, "Die anthropologischen Grundlagen des römischen Verfalls zur Kaiserzeit," *Politische-anthropologische Revue* 5 (1907) 557–81.

[57] Primary evidence includes the Jew/Greek distinctions in Rom. 1.16; 2.10; 3.9, 29. ("Ελλησίν τε καὶ βαρβάροις in 1.14 is not a Greek/Roman distinction. The

presence within the Roman church to Jewish Christians. If the ethnic mixture in first-century Roman society spawned ethnocentric abuse toward the non-Roman element, it is possible that the scorn we read of between "strong" and "weak" in the Roman churches was also partially motivated by such ethnocentrism.

A second argument is that Paul supports his command to the "strong" and "weak" (15.7 – προσλαμβάνεσθε ἀλλήλους) with a series of scripture proofs in 15.9–12 that envision the nations' future posture of praise toward God. Each of the four proofs mentions ἔθνη. Since these proofs are Paul's concluding argumentative tactic for "strong" and "weak," it seems likely that the difference between them was somehow related to ethnic diversity. Paul selected these scripture proofs to show both "strong" and "weak" that they must take their place among many nations who are drawn by God's mercy into his people.[58]

Third, from an anthropological perspective, differences in eating habits are often caused by ethnic differences. Diet is the factor that apparently divided the church in Rome. Once the link between diet and ethnicity is seen,[59] the possibility that the division between "strong" and "weak" was ethnically related is supported. This association between diet and ethnicity can be made because Romans for the most part were meat-eaters by the time of the early

Romans would be considered in the former designation, since this is an identification roughly analogous to "civilized and uncivilized" rather than "ethnic Greeks and non-Greeks.") Other evidence is 15.12, and if one accepts Romans 16, the repeated συγγενής may also indicate that the Jew/Gentile difference was quite marked. The book of Hebrews in its Jewish focus and possible Roman provenance might count as evidence of the Jewish element in the Roman church. See arguments also in Lampe, *Die stadtrömischen Christen*, 56, for a Jewish presence (although he opts for a Gentile majority, 53–55) in the Roman church; La Piana, "La primitiva communità cristiana di Roma," 215, takes the Roman church to have been predominantly Jewish Christian.

[58] See Hays, *Echoes*, 70–71, and "Christ Prays the Psalms," 134–36, for the rationale behind Paul's selection of these texts, and their relationship to the rest of Romans. Cf. also Dieter Zeller, *Juden und Heiden in der Mission des Paulus: Studien zum Römerbrief* (Stuttgart: Katholisches Bibelwerk, 1973), 218–23; 269–84; J. Ross Wagner, "The Christ, Servant of Jew and Gentile: A Fresh Approach to Romans 15:8–9," *JBL* 116 (1997) 473–85.

[59] See, e.g., F. P. Armitage, *Diet and Race: Anthropological Essays* (London: Longmans, Green, and Co., 1922). The three sections of his book, "Diet and Physique," "Diet and Colour," and "Diet and Cranial Form," all present his thesis that racial differences may be traced to dietary patterns. See also Ferro-Luzzi, "Food Avoidances," 97, on the difference between meat consumption in India and in other countries.

Empire. After acknowledging restrictions on consumption of meat, Mireille Corbier states,

> On the other hand, the use of meat seems to have been relatively banal and widespread, at least in the city, even if certain social categories (slaves, the rural population, the poor) did not have access to it or even were forbidden it as being above their social station.[60]

On the other hand, abstinence from meat could be linked to foreign influence in imperial Rome.[61] The social difference between "strong" and "weak" might therefore have arisen partially from an ethnic difference between them.

This possibility is illustrated by relations between peoples throughout history, in which ethnic slurs are made on the basis of diet.[62] Such slurs may be forcefully given and felt deeply when received, for a given culture's diet may be rooted in deeper, archetypical attitudes toward food and human existence unique to that culture.[63] To suggest that the groups who disrespected each other on the ostensible basis of eating habits were ethnically different is therefore consistent both with ways of defining ethnicity and with instances of ethnic relations among known cultures.

The ethnic difference between "strong" and "weak" suggested here is that the "strong" represented a pro-Roman background while the "weak" were of foreign extraction, or at least influenced by non-Roman habits. The question immediately arises, "What ethnic group would most likely be called 'weak'?"

The Hebrew Bible records "weakness" terminology applied to

[60] Corbier, "Ambiguous Status," 224. We note that the text of Rom. 14.1–15.13 does not state that the "strong" were consuming meat on a daily basis. We cannot make definite comparisons on the amounts or frequencies with which meat was eaten in Rome. But the "strong" habits of Rom. 14.1–15.13 still fit best with the meat consumption allowed in imperial Rome.

[61] See Seneca, *Ep.* 108.22. He returned to meat-eating lest his philosophically motivated vegetarianism be misconstrued for adherence to a foreign cult.

[62] Cf., e.g., the French doctor Edgar Bérillon's "discoveries" (published in 1915 and 1917) that Germans are prone to polychesia and have a large intestine much longer than other races' (J. Barzun, *Race: A Study in Modern Superstition* [New York: Harcourt, Brace and Co., 1937], 239–40; cf. also 294–95 for Barzun's own explanation of the relationship between diet and race).

[63] Cf. Ferro-Luzzi's suggestion for exceptionally long periods of meat abstinence in India ("Food Avoidances," 99): "These cases could be remnants of a more primitive belief which holds animal food to be spiritually dangerous for everyone, but above all, for women."

Jews.[64] Horace's *sum paulo infirmior*[65] in the mouth of one influenced by Jews is an example from Roman society. Roman Christianity also uses such language, for in *1 Clem.* 10.2 we find a
statement with "weakness" terminology applied to Abraham's
background.

> οὗτος δι᾽ ὑπακοῆς ἐξῆλθεν ... ὅπως γῆν ὀλίγην καὶ
> συγγένειαν ἀσθενῆ καὶ οἶκον μικρὸν καταλιπὼν κληρο-
> νομήσῃ τὰς ἐπαγγελίας τοῦ θεοῦ.

> He obediently went forth ... leaving a small country, a
> weak people, and an insignificant house in order that he
> might inherit the promises of God.

Though it is unlikely that the "weak" can be described as exclusively Jewish in composition, some Jewish influence was certainly
present among this group, to judge from Paul's use of κοινόν and
the Jewish background to Roman Christianity.[66] Paul probably
uses κοινόν in the Jewish sense of "impure" and uses a world
paradigm divided between ethnic Israel and the nations in 15.8–10,
12.[67]

Issues of ethnicity figure throughout the letter, and in matters of
salvation history seem oriented around a Jew/Gentile dichotomy.[68]
But these references do not prove that ethnic division within the
Roman church was Jew/Gentile in nature. As Jüthner observes, the
coming of Christianity changed the twofold (Greeks and barbarians) or threefold (Greeks, Romans, and barbarians) description of
humanity to a different one (Greeks, Jews, and Christians).[69] Paul's
repeated comparison of Jew and Greek is therefore meant to
encompass everyone outside of the scope of his gospel. Nor do his
comparisons run solely along a Jew/Gentile axis: Rom. 1.14,
Ἕλλησίν τε καὶ βαρβάροις, σοφοῖς τε καὶ ἀνοήτοις, is a vestige
of the formerly used civilized versus uncivilized division for

---

[64] See Amos 7.2, 5 (*qaton*); Hos. 4.3 (*'amal*); Neh. 3.34 (4.2 in ET – *'amelal* is
clearly an ethnic slur).

[65] Horace, *Sat.* 1.9.71.

[66] On κοινόν, see discussion toward end of chapter 6; on Jewish background for
Roman Christianity, see pp. 136–37, 201 above.

[67] But one must realize that these citations in themselves do not prove that the
"strong" versus "weak" tensions were essentially Gentile versus Jew in nature. Any
scripture proof related to ethnic unity must use the language of the nations and
Israel.

[68] E.g., Rom. 1.16; 2.9–10; 3.9; 9.24; 10.12.

[69] Jüthner, *Hellenen und Barbaren*, 91–92.

humanity.[70] And just as the letter is not exclusively oriented around a Jew versus Gentile dichotomy,[71] so he does not present the "strong" and "weak" issue as one that pivoted exclusively on Jew versus Gentile tensions. It therefore seems consistent with the evidence from Romans, as well as the first-century Roman church[72] and society, to posit that the difference in status in the "strong" and "weak" groups was related to the difference generally perceived between Roman and foreign elements of the city. Though not the only possible way of construing "strong" and "weak," this hypothesis fits with the use of terms for "strength" within Roman ethnocentrism. It also fits with the evidence that the Romans perceived the religions of the Jews and Egyptians to include vegetarianism.[73] The bulk of Rome's slaves and freedmen were orientals from Syria and Asia Minor.[74] If the "weak" were of more servile origins than the "strong," it is likely that there was a significant number from the East among the "weak." But I must qualify this generalization.

I have allowed for a Jewish presence among the "weak," but have refused to identify the "weak" as predominantly of one ethnic group. We therefore cannot generalize about the class level of the "weak" as a whole, but something may be said about the class level of Jews in ancient Rome. It has generally been assumed that under the early Empire they were poor.[75] This hypothesis has been questioned by Kraabel because of some gold glasses and finely

---

[70] This is the only place in Paul where he includes the uncivilized in his mission field (they are not listed in 1 Cor. 9.19–23), a statement motivated both by the composition of the Roman church and his intended trip to Spain.

[71] See J. M. Scott, *Paul and the Nations* (WUNT 1.84; Tübingen: J. C. B. Mohr [Paul Siebeck], 1995), 141–47.

[72] The idea of the nations found in 15.8–12 may reflect ethnic pluralism in the community itself. See such an emphasis in *1 Clement*, with its uses of κόσμος (5.7; 7.4; 19.2; 59.2), ἔθνη (55.1; 59.3*bis*, 4), πᾶσα σάρξ or πάντες ἄνθρωποι (59.3; 62.2; 64.1), and the examples drawn from foreign peoples (Nineveh – 7.7; Arabia/Egypt – 25.1, 3–5).

[73] Cf. Seneca, *Ep.* 108.22; Tacitus, *Ann.* 2.85.

[74] Frank, "Race Mixture," 700–701. While Taylor agrees that most freedmen were of "eastern origin" ("Freedmen and Freeborn," 115), she also shows how Latin *cognomina* replaced Greek in families of such freedmen (126–27) and how the freedmen assimilated to Roman values (129, 132).

[75] See Juvenal, *Sat.* 3.12–16, 296; 6.542–47; Martial, *Sat.* 12.57.13. Leon, *Jews*, 235–36, mentions the poor quality of the inscriptions (although most of these are third century CE at the earliest) and the traditional identification of locale for the Jewish settlement in Rome as sufficient evidence to posit a poor community of Jews in Rome.

carved inscriptions in the Jewish sector.[76] Kraabel and Leon are not in complete disagreement; Leon himself admits that there is evidence of wealth among some Jews in ancient Rome.[77] Discussions of the property holdings of Jews in Rome also need to take into account collections of the temple tax in the diaspora, still occurring when Paul wrote Romans. Thus not all those of foreign descent and servile background were necessarily considered "weak" at the grass-roots level of Roman society. Though the poor of foreign descent would be likely candidates for the "weak" label in Rome,[78] some of the foreign freedmen were quite wealthy. Foreign descent did not necessarily mean that one was poor. Still, it is likely that there was a foreign influence among the "weak." Thus, those foreign residents in Rome included some who were poor, though to be foreign was not a sufficient condition for being poor. Foreign extraction was linked not only to poverty; it was also linked to language usage.

If the "weak" did have a foreign element among them, there was probably a difference in language usage that contributed to their rift with the "strong." H. J. Leon considers the use of a foreign language in Rome as a sign of lack of assimilation to Roman culture, and concludes on the basis of inscriptions that "It is quite apparent that the Jews of Rome were a Greek-speaking group." He goes on to describe Roman Jews further: "Latin appears to have been the language of the more Romanized element."[79] Similarly, Carolyn Osiek has suggested that the "strong" were more literate and particularly more skilled in Latin than the "weak."[80]

With regard to ethnicity, then, it is likely that the "strong" contained a more purely Roman composition; the "weak" were ethnically diverse, containing some eastern influence. The ethnic

[76] A. T. Kraabel, "The Roman Diaspora: Six Questionable Assumptions," *JJS* 33 (1982) 453.

[77] Leon, *Jews*, 235–36.

[78] Juvenal, *Sat.* 3.14, describes the scarce furniture (as a sign of poverty) among Jews who have settled near the arch of Porta Capena; in 3.296 a stereotypical poor man is asked where he prays, as if poverty were a sufficient condition to demarcate one as a syngagogue member.

[79] "The Jews of Rome in the First Centuries of Christianity," in *The Teacher's Yoke* (Henry Trantham Festschrift; eds. E. J. Vardaman and J. L. Garrett, Jr.; Waco: Baylor University Press, 1964), 156.

[80] Carolyn Osiek, "The Oral World of the First Christians at Rome," paper read at the August, 1993 SNTS Meeting, 9–12. For the importance of Greek in the Empire of the second century, see G. W. Bowersock, *Greek Sophists in the Roman Empire* (Oxford: Clarendon, 1969), 15–16, 28–29.

difference between the groups is suggested on the basis of Roman attitudes toward foreigners resident in imperial Rome, Paul's use of scripture proofs related to "the nations" (τὰ ἔθνη), the place of diet in ethnicity and ethnic relations, class stereotypes that were linked to those of foreign extraction, and the differences in Latin usage among the foreign population.

Neighborhood presence

If we can assume that Christian churches in first-century Rome existed as neighborhood communities,[81] a status indicator on the neighborhood level may be relevant. We know that from the time of Augustus, the city's regions were divided into neighborhoods, with an official elected by each neighborhood as its neighborhood leader (*magister vici*).[82] Since this office was determined by local election, this official certainly held status at least within a given neighborhood. Thus Martial writes of two men in a quest for status: "consule Torquato vici fuit ille magister, non minor in tanto visus honore sibi" ("When Torquatus was consul the other was a vestryman, in such a dignity deeming himself no lesser man").[83] It is likely that the *magistri vici* of some of the neighborhoods may have been among the "strong" in the Roman churches. Such officials, if present in churches, would certainly have held higher status and wielded the privileges it brought. Also, to regard some people as "superstitious," as the "strong" probably did the "weak," inevitably lowered the status of those so regarded.[84]

The recognition of privileges according to status in the neighborhood (*vicus*) or association (*collegium*)[85] shows us that at any level, the Romans were ready to perceive and enforce a social hierarchy.

---

[81] See Lampe, *Die stadtrömischen Christen*, 10–35, for a detailed consideration of where in Rome the Christian communities were located. He identifies Trastevere as the place of the first Christian community in Rome (30–35). See also R. Jewett, "Tenement Churches and Communal Meals in the Early Church: The Implications of a Form-Critical Analysis of 2 Thessalonians 3:10," *BR* 38 (1993) 23–43.

[82] Suetonius, *Aug.* 30.1 describes how the city was divided up and leaders from among the people chosen for each neighborhood. See also Livy 34.7.2. Relevant secondary literature includes A. W. Van Buren, "*Vicus* (2)," *PW*, ser. 2, 8.A.2, cols. 2093–94; Lampe, *Die stadtrömischen Christen*, 445–46, who calculates the ratio between *magistri vici* and the inhabitants of Rome.

[83] Martial, *Epig.* 10.79.7–8 (trans. W. C. A. Ker; LCL; rev. ed.; London: William Heinemann, 1968).

[84] Martin, *Corinthian Body*, 156–57.

[85] See discussion above in this chapter on the meal portions of *collegia* leaders.

To read of "strong" and "weak" groups within a religious community of Rome, then, fits with this tendency.

Concluding portraits of "strong" and "weak"

As I have argued in chapter 3, it is very likely that the terms for "strong" and "weak" seen in Rom. 14.1–15.13 were in use among the believers in Rome for identifiable groups within their circles. This conclusion follows from the common usage these terms enjoyed in first-century Roman society, and avoids the difficulty of explaining why Paul would call some people "weak" within churches he was trying to win to his side (Rom. 1.8–15; 15.14–16).

The "strong"

The "strong" were a group of believers in one or more Roman churches who had more status, as defined by first-century Roman society, than the "weak." They had contact with the equestrian and senatorial orders through their members who were part of the imperial household. Most of the "strong" were Roman citizens, and identified positively with Roman culture. They spoke Latin. They had more money than the "weak." Some of them were independent freedmen who had acquired wealth through their own hard work. The "strong" group may have included some neighborhood leaders, responsible for maintaining order at the local level.

The "weak"

The "weak" were a group of believers with low status in the Roman churches. Some of them were convinced that Jewish dietary laws must be observed. Abstinence from meat was their way of making sure that they ate no meat from animals that had been improperly slaughtered. Though it was inevitable that food offered to idols was a concern to them, the dietary concerns of the "weak" certainly also included concerns about the type of meat being eaten and whether the blood had been properly drained from it.[86] But we cannot say that this was the only motivation behind the "weak" consumption habits. There were other reasons to abstain from meat in first-century Rome, which some could follow "for the

---

[86] Acts 15.20, 29; Gen. 9.4; Lev. 17.10–14; Dan. 1.8–16; 4 Macc. 5.2.

Lord" (14.6c). Some of the "weak" may have been vegetarian because of a distinct belief in animals' metaphysical equality with humans, or because they thought that a vegetarian diet would help them communicate with God in a way otherwise impossible, or because they thought that as the antediluvian, primitive diet, it was appropriate for those awaiting the redemption of their bodies (8.23).

In light of day observance within Roman society and Judaism, it is also likely that the difference over day observance (14.5–6) was an actual difference in the Roman churches. The "weak" were probably observing the Sabbath and perhaps other fast days. Some of the "weak" may also have been observing Sunday.

Relations between "strong" and "weak"

The "strong" considered the "weak" to be superstitious. We have seen that it was around the time when this letter was written that Christianity was called a superstition in Rome. With their abstinence from certain foods and observance of days, the "weak" were prime candidates for the charge of being superstitious. This behavior is called superstition in other texts of antiquity, and it was probably viewed as such by the "strong" and others outside of the Roman churches. The scorn that Paul prohibits among the "strong" (14.3a, 10b) probably represents a typical Roman reaction to behavior viewed as superstitious.

This label that the "strong" placed on the "weak" and the scorn that came with it effectively separated the "strong" and "weak" Christians. By the time Paul's letter arrived, "strong" and "weak" were in separate congregations. That is why Paul tells them to "accept" or "welcome" each other (14.1; 15.7), and hopes that they can learn to worship together (15.6, 9–12).

Paul's resolution of this controversy is profoundly theological. Indeed, theological "theory" is as much at work here as any practical concern to reconcile two estranged groups.[87] He recognizes all foods as clean, but calls on those free to eat anything to respect the sensibilities of those who do not share their freedom.

---

[87] See N. T. Wright, *The Climax of the Covenant* (Minneapolis: Fortress, 1992), 259: "Paul is thus driven to ask and answer (what we call) 'situational' and 'theological' questions at the same time, in the same breath, with the same words. I suggest ... that he would not have understood the difference between those two categories."

Maintenance of one's own clear conscience before God is prior to any general rule about diet or the observance of days. Paul's awareness of Roman society's "take" on the Jesus movement as superstition is evident from his tendency to define his gospel as above popular religion and above religious activity pursued in an *ex opere operato* manner (Rom. 1.18–21; 2.14–29; 12.1–2). Despite his awareness of this stigma in Rome, he asks the "strong" to allow the "weak" to continue in their practices, though they would appear superstitious to those outside of the churches. Paul uses the Roman social force of obligation to show how "strong" and "weak" ought to live in acceptance of one another. In particular, he tells the "strong" that they are obligated to swim against the current of Roman status relations and follow the "weak" diet (14.21; 15.1–2), so as not to offend the "weak." Paul is convinced that the rapprochement of "strong" and "weak" will be one specific instance of the ingathering of the nations under the reign of Jesus, Jewish Messiah for the world.

So far, in light of what we know of first-century Roman society and Christianity, the portraits seem plausible. But are they coherent with the rest of Romans? In the next, final chapter, I examine how this reading of Rom. 14.1–15.13 affects one's reading of the letter as a whole.[88]

---

[88] In this paragraph I am indebted to Wedderburn for his criteria of determining the plausibility of any reconstruction of what was going on in a church addressed by Paul: inherent plausibility; compatibility with other evidence about this and other early churches; coherence with Paul's text (*Reasons*, 64).

12

THE "STRONG" AND "WEAK" AND THE TOPOS OF ROMANS

τίς ἐνεπίστευσεν κυρίῳ καὶ κατῃσχύνθη;   Sirach 2.10

Who trusted in the Lord and was made ashamed?

This monograph has investigated Rom. 14.1–15.13 in light of its context in first-century Rome, as well as in relation to the context of the letter. The thesis of this book is that Rom. 14.1–15.13 fits both these contexts very well. The previous chapters have been written to show this. In this chapter I wish to offer some points of significance from the investigation of Rom. 14.1–15.13 for our understanding of early Christianity in Rome and for our reading of Romans.

First-century Roman context

Paul's letter fits first-century Rome

One prong of this book's thesis – that everything in Rom. 14.1–15.13, including Paul's description of the food controversy and his advice for its resolution, fits with what we know of first-century Rome – means that we should be more ready to look for connections between other parts of Romans and the actual state of affairs in Rome. If it is true that the Roman churches' faith was announced throughout the world (1.8), then the letter must deal with issues "on the front burner" in Rome.

For example, the articles of faith Paul mentions in his opening lines – different from what we read elsewhere in Paul – are probably not what he would put on his own pre-ordination statement of faith. They rather represent ways the Romans expressed their faith (1.3–4). The question of the Jew's advantage was certainly a question that would likely arise within Paul's audience (3.1).

Indeed, even the treatment of this and other questions as examples of Greek diatribe needs to be nuanced in light of the Jewish element within Paul's audience, and the underrated Jewish background and use of diatribe. Similarly, the question about remaining in sin in order to magnify grace probably reflected an actual caricature of Paul's teachings by some of his Roman audience (6.1). When Paul mentions the "kind of teaching to which you were entrusted" (6.17), it most likely means that he knew some of the features of Roman Christianity. When he says that he is writing to people who know law (7.1), it is most likely because there were people who were knowledgeable about and loyal to Torah and because first-century Roman society, like twentieth-century American society, was infested with lawyers. Paul instructs the Romans to pay their taxes most likely because taxes were a real problem in Rome (13.6–7).[1]

Since Paul's description and counsel regarding "strong" and "weak" is in line with what would be expected in first-century Rome and also coheres with the rest of Romans, this book casts a ballot for viewing the letter's contents as thoroughly occasional. Romans is situation-specific, written in a focused way to a specific church at a distinct moment in its development. Rom. 2; 6–8; 12.1–15.13 all seem to be addressed to the Romans' occasion, in which judgment was going on within the communities, communities divided over the place of Torah in the believer's life, the level of morality to follow in the believer's ethics, the obligation to obey government, and the questions of food consumption and the observance of days. Some of Paul's occasion has shaped chapters 6–8, for Paul is concerned to quiet the rumors that he has jettisoned Torah and so countenanced all kinds of shameful immorality.[2] But the references to the Romans' own situation in these chapters still prompt me to look mostly to their situation for these chapters' contents.[3] Rom. 15.17–32 arises out of Paul's occasion: he is concerned that he is viewed as one who has turned his back on his Jewish heritage and worried that he and his collection will not be accepted in Jerusalem, the center of Paul's universe.[4] Both occasions coalesce in Paul's desire to gain some "fruit" among the

---

[1] See the sources mentioned in n. 51 of chapter 2.
[2] Rom. 6.14–15; 7.1, 7, 12, 14; 8.2–4.
[3] Rom. 6.12, 17, 21; 7.1; 8.12–13.
[4] Scott, *Paul and the Nations*, 136–40.

Roman believers on his way to Spain (1.11–13; 15.24).[5] Both occasions also coalesce in Romans 9–11, where Paul needs to make clear that he has not abandoned his Jewish heritage (9.1–5) and also seeks to extinguish some Gentile boasting (11.13–24).

Though similar, Jews and Jesus-believers were distinct

All of our reconstructions of what was going on in the Roman community are hindered by a heritage two millennia long of distinct boundaries between Jew and Christian. But Romans was written before Nero's persecution, which singled out Christians and no doubt led to a distinct break between synagogue and church in Rome. Before Nero's persecution, the designations "Jew" and "Christian" could not always be made for sure. When Claudius expelled the Jews from Rome in 49 CE, no doubt some left. But others probably stayed on, joining Roman house churches that did not have the characteristics of Jewish synagogues.[6]

Paul's description of the "weak" shows us that there were people somehow associated with the churches of Rome who still retained the appearances of Jewish piety. In our historical reconstruction of the Roman churches, we cannot draw the line between Jew and Christian as rigidly as has been done in the past. Given the tenuous distinction between Jew and Christian, Paul's message in Romans 14–15 is clearly an attempt to keep what we now call Gentile Christianity ("strong") on good terms with and affirming of those Jewish believers (some of the "weak") who were associated with the Roman house churches. Paul's respect for the "weak" and his concern for Jews (9.1–3; 11.24) in this letter seem to indicate a Jewish-friendly position.

But given this point, there is evidence both in Rom. 14.1–15.13 and in the letter as a whole that Paul has an edge toward Torah that Tomson and Nanos ignore. Barclay might be overstating the case to call Paul's theology "a Trojan horse which threatens the integrity of those who sought to live according to the law,"[7] but

---

[5] Cf. Kruger, "*Tina Karpon*, 'Some Fruit' in Romans 1:13." His thesis is damaged by the timing of Paul's Rome visit; it is to come after his Jerusalem appearance (15.25, 28).

[6] I am indebted to Carolyn Osiek for this suggestion, made in November, 1992. She offered this possibility by analogy with the documented results of what happened when the Jews were expelled from Spain.

[7] See Barclay, " 'Do We Undermine the Law?,' " 308, and see discussion at end of chapter 10 above.

still Paul doth protest too much in this letter for us to place him as unequivocally Torah-friendly.[8] Something is going on in Paul's own occasion which stirs his anxiety about his homecoming in Jerusalem (15.30–32), and the best candidate for the cause of this anxiety is Paul's gospel of a righteousness apart from Torah (3.21; 9.31; 10.4). This gospel has clearly been construed as shamefully libertarian (6.1, 14–15), and Paul seeks to dissipate this notoriety throughout the letter.

There was no monolithic "Roman Christianity"

Closely related to the preceding point is a conclusion that we cannot speak of "Roman Christianity" or "the Roman church" in the mid first century. There was too much variety within the churches of Rome to warrant such a simple label.

In the first place, the audience of Paul's letter was more Jewish than reconstructions of a Gentile audience would have us believe.[9] Now that studies of Romans 7 and 12 show us the Jewish categories behind Paul's argumentation,[10] there is clear evidence that there must have been a segment of the audience who were Jewish and could follow Paul's allusions. This Jewish segment fits with my suggestion that the "weak" included a significant Jewish presence.

Second, Rome of the mid-fifties was so ethnically diverse that it is impossible to posit a monolithic expression of what we now call Christianity. With a population ever changing because of immigration and trade,[11] it stands to reason that there would be controversies among the house churches and within given churches. No wonder that Paul emphasizes the universality of his gospel in this letter.

---

[8] Rom. 3.31; 7.7, 12, 14.

[9] Here I must disagree with Neil Elliott, *The Rhetoric of Romans* (Sheffield: Sheffield Academic Press, 1990), 56–59, 67, 292, who understands Romans to be addressed to a predominantly Gentile audience.

[10] On Romans 7 see Dunn, *Romans*, 399–403; Wright, *The Climax of the Covenant*, 226–30. On Rom. 12.9–21 see Walter T. Wilson, *Love without Pretense: Romans 12.9–21 and Hellenistic-Jewish Wisdom Literature* (WUNT 2.46; Tübingen: J. C. B. Mohr [Paul Siebeck], 1991).

[11] See George La Piana, "Foreign Groups in Rome during the First Centuries of the Empire," *HTR* 20 (1927) 188–224.

The context of the Romans letter

Romans 14–15 in the context of the whole letter

In this monograph I have argued that Paul's attacks on judging in Romans 2 anticipate his commands to desist from judging in 14.3–4, 10, 13a. Karris has noted that Rom. 6.10–11 and 7.4 prepare the ground for the lordship statement of 14.9.[12] Paul also prepares the way for his treatment of the "strong" and "weak" controversy by mentioning the love command.[13] We have also seen with Tomson that the obligation Paul enjoins upon the "strong" is prepared for at least beginning with 13.8.[14] Also, at a fundamental level for the whole letter, the "strong" and "weak" section, including Paul's command not to bring blasphemy on the communities' "good," is anticipated by a series of statements designed to show his readers that his gospel and those who follow it are above shame, and therefore that the Romans should follow it. Paul's gospel itself is without shame (1.16; 3.8; 6.21). Those who follow it will not be ashamed (5.5; 9.33; 10.11). The believers in Rome should not live shamefully (12.17b; 13.1–14). Paul's gospel accounts for a ministry that is not shameful (15.17–21) and he asks his Roman readers to pray for him lest he be shamed in Jerusalem (15.30–32). It is this series of imbricate statements of being without shame, occurring in every major section of Romans, that leads me to look for a primary topos more focused than simply "the gospel" or "Paul's gospel."

Romans 14–15 as a key to the topos of Romans

Now that I have examined Rom. 14.1–15.13, it is appropriate to step back and ask how my study of this part of the letter affects how one reads the whole letter. After all, this is the only Pauline letter in which the practical teaching ("special exhortation") is situated at the conclusion of the letter's body, after what is regarded as more general parenesis.[15] It follows that this material in

[12] Karris, "Occasion," 76, following W. Thüsing, *Gott und Christus in der paulinischen Soteriologie*, Vol. I: *Per Christum in Deum* (3rd ed.; NTAbh 1; Münster: Aschendorff, 1986), 33 n. 88.

[13] Rom. 12.9–10; 13.8–10; 14.15.

[14] Tomson, *Paul and the Jewish Law*, 238, and p. 187 above.

[15] This point is rightly emphasized by Käsemann at the beginning of his discussion of Rom. 14.1–15.13, *Romans*, 364.

14.1–15.13 would likely have strong connections back to the rest of the letter, and would serve as an indication of the topos of the letter. Also, the chiastic relationship between Rom. 1.8–15 and 15.14–33 that has already been correctly observed[16] is incomplete until we also see that Rom. 1.16–17 is in chiastic relationship with 15.8–13. Both passages refer to faith, the divine power, and the inclusion of Jew and Gentile among God's people. Just as physicians find out what is happening in the heart by inserting their tubes through the femoral artery, so we can examine the primary topos of Romans by entering at a location usually considered far from the letter's heart.

The quest for the purposes behind this letter should allow us better to identify the primary topos, something like what we might call a "theme," or "main point" of the letter.[17] As other recent students of Romans have suggested, Paul seems to have more than one purpose in mind as he writes this letter.[18] Yet even those who find a number of purposes behind the composition of this letter tend to look for a unifying idea for the letter as a whole. Thus Dunn seems to introduce the theme of Romans as "the eschatological fulfillment of God in Christ for Gentile as well as Jew."[19] Cranfield and Moo treat the theme of Romans as if it is Paul's explanation of *the* gospel.[20] They differ from Käsemann, who emphasizes rather that divine righteousness is Paul's explanation of *his* gospel.[21] Now that we have examined Rom. 14.1–15.13 in detail, it is worth considering what this passage on "strong" and "weak" indicates about the primary topos of Romans. It seems to indicate that Paul's primary topos in Romans is not the righteousness of God. It is rather that Paul and his gospel are not shameful, nor does it bring shame on those who identify with it, but rather allows them to boast in God.

At the outset we must concede that Romans need not have only one primary topos. All of us compose written or oral communications that have more than one topos, and we must permit Paul that

[16] Petersen, "Ending(s) to Paul's Letter," 345.

[17] I prefer to use the term "topos" rather than "theme," since the former is closer to Paul's background. The difference between "primary topos" and "theme" is that the former is the topos that every other topos in the letter supports, while the latter implies that everything in the letter actually expresses the idea identified as "theme."

[18] Cranfield, *Romans*, 815; Dunn, *Romans*, lv; Wedderburn, *Reasons*, 5–6.

[19] Dunn, *Romans*, lxi.

[20] Cranfield, *Romans*, 823; Moo, *Romans*, 29–30.

[21] Käsemann, *Romans*, 24–25.

possibility as well. Still, those who read Romans are struck by its coherence, by its intratextual connections that seem to make it a fabric with one design. Also, it is best to start with a text-oriented look for a topos of the letter, since this is safer than speculation about the purposes of the letter, which are not fully recoverable to us, and cannot be evaluated with the controls available when we focus on the text. A look at the connections between Rom. 14.1–15.13 and the rest of the letter will help us evaluate others' suggestions of the topos of Romans and suggest a plausible alternative.

Romans 14–15 as part of Paul's self-introduction

William Countryman has suggested that Paul's main point in writing Romans was to solve the controversy over food, the task he handles in 14.1–15.13, after writing chapters 1–13 in such a way that both groups will listen to him.[22] Paul Minear takes a similar position. When he writes about the conflict between the various parties he envisions in the Roman churches, he concludes:

> I believe, then, that there is more than adequate evidence within the chapters themselves to indicate the importance of the issue to Paul and his correspondents. Evidence becomes really overwhelming when we see that Paul viewed the situation in chs. 14 and 15 as the target of the whole epistle.[23]

Countryman does help us understand the value Paul saw in the resolution of the "strong" and "weak" controversy for the success of this letter. Paul's gospel was distinctive in early Christianity for allowing Gentiles to remain Gentiles. He did not want a controversy caused in part by Jewish dietary laws to continue unabated in Rome, a key church in his mission area. Such a controversy generated interference for his message to Jew and Gentile. Since Jews and Gentiles were in the Roman churches, the controversy here had the potential to reverberate throughout the Mediterranean world. Paul needed this controversy resolved for the success of his mission anywhere in the Roman world. The Roman churches' favorable reception of the letter and welcome to Paul would

---

[22] Countryman, "The Rhetoric of Purity."
[23] Minear, *Obedience*, 33.

inevitably include following Paul's advice on "strong" and "weak."[24]

Countryman helps us to see, then, how this treatment of "strong" and "weak" in Rom. 14.1–15.13 fits with one of Paul's purposes in the letter – self-introduction and preparation of the Roman churches to support him. The purpose of this letter as a public relations release, designed to win the Romans over to Paul's side, would fail as long as such a division continued in the church. Paul's inclusion of his diagnosis and counsel on the "strong" and "weak" situation represents a gutsy move that risked the first readers' rejection of the letter, if they thought he had misdiagnosed their situation. But this diagnosis and counsel were necessary, if he was truly to succeed in recruiting the Roman churches to his support team.

Though Countryman and Minear are right to take seriously this latter part of Romans in their quest for understanding the letter as a whole, I am not persuaded that the whole letter is written to solve this difference. There is too much space devoted to issues that do not seem directly to impinge on the resolution of the "strong" and "weak" division. Paul seems intent on correcting misunderstandings of his gospel, simply for the sake of his own reputation (3.8, 31; 6.1–2, 15). He takes great pains to show his approval of his Jewish heritage, as we shall see in the next suggestion of a topos for Romans. These clarifications can all be forced to fit Countryman and Minear's position that the letter is written to resolve the "strong" and "weak" division. But the space Paul spends in the explanation of his gospel makes it unlikely that the issue of 14.1–15.13 is "the target" of the letter. There is not enough evidence in the letter to show that it is Paul's main point. It seems rather that Paul needed to address the "strong" and "weak" controversy on the way to an effective presentation of another topos that can take into account more of the letter.

Equality of Jew and Gentile

Second, the letter emphasizes the equality of Jew and Gentile before God and in God's covenant community on earth. In this sense, Romans has been viewed as a tract on ethnic equality to

---

[24] Countryman, "The Rhetoric of Purity," 9.

churches in a city that scorned foreigners.[25] We see this as early as
1.16, where Paul writes that his message contains divine power to
bring salvation to all who believe, apparently without distinction as
to their ethnicity.[26] While many students of Romans are ready to
see this issue of ethnic equality as one of several purposes behind
the letter, Kaylor takes it as the letter's topos. He writes:

> To be sure the concepts of sin, righteousness, faith, and
> grace are present in the letter, but underlying the whole,
> and dominant in Paul's thinking at the time of its writing,
> is the concern to affirm the unity of Gentile and Jew in the
> one new covenant people.[27]

We understand Paul's inclusion of Jew and Gentile in a fuller
sense when we note how this topos leads up to his treatment of
"strong" and "weak." While I have already noted Paul's emphasis
on "Jew and Greek" earlier in this chapter, it is also worth noting
the way in which Paul uses "all" or comparable expressions to
advance this purpose of promoting ethnic equality.[28] Indeed, it is
worth observing that major sections of Romans end with these
inclusive pronouncements of God's mercy to all (11.32, 36;
15.8–12).

I have already argued that the lines of the "strong" and "weak"
division were partially drawn along ethnic difference, so some
might use the "strong" and "weak" section of Romans to argue for
this topos. But what this book shows is how affirming Paul is of the
church members who continued in some habits included within
many forms of first-century Judaism, i.e., observance of *kashrut*
laws and observance of the Sabbath. In Romans 14–15 we see Paul
as more respectful of Jewish boundary markers than others have
noted in describing Paul's position on the Jews in Romans.[29] After
observing this in the "strong" and "weak" section, we start to

[25] On establishing Jew/Gentile equality as a purpose of this letter, see W. S.
Campbell, *Paul's Gospel in an Intercultural Context* (SIHC 69; Frankfurt-on-Main:
Peter Lang, 1991), 21–22; Cranfield, *Romans*, 822–23; Dunn, *Romans*, lvi–lviii;
Wedderburn, *Reasons*, 32–37.

[26] Other representative texts with the "no distinction" voice are 2.1–2; 3.9–18,
29–30; 10.12; 11.25–27.

[27] R. D. Kaylor, *Paul's Covenant Community: Jew and Gentile in Romans*
(Atlanta: John Knox, 1988), 19.

[28] Rom. 1.7, 14, 16; 4.16; 9.5; 11.32; 15.8–9.

[29] Here I agree with Campbell, who argues that it is mistaken to view Paul as
consistently against Jews in his Romans letter (*Paul's Gospel*, 138–41). Cf. Watson,
Paul, Judaism and the Gentiles, 97–98.

notice that instead of simply arguing for ethnic equality, Paul spends more space and expends more passion in this letter in arguing that his gospel is not anti-Jewish, but rather in continuity with Judaism. The "to the Jew first" refrain of this letter shows this, as do Paul's protestations that his gospel is really Torah-affirming (3.31; 7.12, 14; 13.8–10). Paul can find the essence of his gospel and its eschatological vision in Torah (10.6–10; 15.10). He is adamant about his Jewish identity (11.1),[30] and his identification with his people is clear (9.1–3; 11.11, 26–36; 15.8; 16.7, 11, 21).

Thus, a more careful look at Romans, beginning at 14.1–15.13, seems to eliminate the idea of ethnic equality, or even the new people of God, as the topos of Romans. Such an idea is eclipsed by Paul's repeated presentations of himself and his gospel as thoroughly Jewish.[31] If we are allowed to start with Rom. 14.1–15.13 on our quest toward a topos of Romans, the evidence would not clearly indicate ethnic equality. This section concludes with the mention of Christ's identity with "the circumcision" in order to confirm the promises of Israel's past (15.8). The eschatological vision is that Jew and Gentile praise God together, but their focus is on "the root of Jesse" (15.12, quoting LXX Isa. 11.10). In other words, the Gentiles are pictured as joining Israel, but the picture of ethnic equality or a new people of God is not clearly in view. The Jew first and then Gentile order seems to be at work even at Rom. 15.8–9.

The righteousness of God

Romans is concerned with the righteousness of God, and the righteousness of those who identify with Jesus in accordance with Paul's gospel. With this motif in mind, the letter appears as the earliest sustained Christian theodicy. In this letter Paul attempts to prove that God is just, or righteous, dependably keeping his promises to Israel while opening the covenant community to Gentiles.[32] In 1.17 Paul states that in his message the righteousness of God is revealed, and he will go on to explicate this righteousness

---

[30] See also his uses of συγγενής (9.3; 16.7, 11, 21).

[31] Nanos sees this agenda of Paul's everywhere in Romans (*Mystery, passim*). At least he helps us see the Jewishness of Paul and his letter, though one wonders why Paul would be worried about the Jews (15.30–32) if Nanos's portrait of Paul is entirely accurate.

[32] This purpose is treated by others as Paul's attempt to set forth his gospel. See Cranfield, *Romans*, 817–20; Dunn, *Romans*, lvi; Wedderburn, *Reasons*, 108–39.

throughout the book.[33] Besides showing God's righteousness, Paul also seems intent on showing that those who follow his gospel are righteous. His skirmishes against the charge of antinomianism[34] do not respond merely to an hypothetical objection he is considering. They represent Paul's defense of his position, learned in the thrust and parry of real attacks on his gospel.

One who considers the righteousness of God to be the topos of this letter can make Romans 14–15 fit this topos. Righteousness is a part of the essence of the kingdom of God, not eating or drinking (14.17). Paul contends that condemning fellow Christians who eat or drink in different ways ignores God's capacity to establish such believers as righteous (14.4). God's own righteousness will be vindicated at each person's appearance before the divine judgment seat, so it is unrighteous presumption to try to judge fellow Christians over consumption or day observance (14.10–12). God's righteousness is seen in Christ, who became a servant of the circumcision[35] on behalf of the faithfulness of God, which in Romans is the same as God's righteousness.[36] Christ's servanthood shows God's faithfulness, since it confirms the promises made to the Jewish ancestors (15.8). This work of Christ, who leads Jew and Gentile into the throng of the elect who praise God, obligates all in the church to live in peace with others in the community.

Also, my study of Paul's response to Roman "strong" and "weak" could be taken to highlight the connection between God's righteousness in Christ and the obligations of the "strong" to support the "weak" (14.21; 15.2–3) and the "weak" to desist from judging the "strong" (14.4, 10–13a). These obligations come in the series of obligations Paul presents in chapters 12–15, which all arise out of the benefits of Christ (Romans 5–8), included within the οἰκτιρμοὶ τοῦ θεοῦ of 12.1. It is because Christ has brought the righteousness of God to believers, with its benefits of freedom from sin, death, and the law, that believers are now obligated to present

[33] Representative passages on God's righteousness are 3.21–31; 5.17–21; 8.1–11; 9.14–33; 10.1–13.

[34] Rom. 3.5–8, 31; 6.1–4; 7.7–16.

[35] Paul uses "circumcision" here to emphasize the Jewishness of Jesus. Since "circumcision" was something the Jews took pride in and Gentiles mocked, its use here drives the point home that Christ came as a Jew, however distasteful and inappropriate that might seem to some of the more Gentile-oriented readers. It is certainly possible that the Jewish members of the "weak" group were called "circumcision," as Marcus, "Circumcision," 79, suggests.

[36] S. K. Williams, "The 'Righteousness of God' in Romans," *JBL* 99 (1980) 263.

their bodies back to God. Obligation as a social force was pervasive throughout Roman society, and Paul's use of it here must be seen as an attempt to use a social ethic common in his readers' world to make the implications of his gospel understood by them. Of course, though obligation bound Roman society together, Paul defines the obligation of the "strong" in a way they would not expect – they are to align their eating habits with the "weak" and support the "weak" (14.21; 15.1–2) – rather than force the "weak" to defer to their social status, as would be the norm in Roman society.

Paul's treatment of righteousness also shows us that righteous living means that one will respect the conscience of another. Adherence to rules is not what makes a person righteous, but loving one's fellow Christian and preserving the unity of the community (14.15–18).[37]

But the problem with this view, that the letter's primary topos is the righteousness of God, and that this is supported by 14.1–15.13, is that we should not think of the righteousness of God as the topos if we began looking for a topos at 14.1. It is true that Paul mentions righteousness first in his definition of the kingdom of God (14.17), but it is still stretching the category to say that chapters 12–16 are best placed under the topos of God's righteousness.[38] Though he is sensitive to the occasion of Romans,[39] Stuhlmacher's orientation around righteousness still falls into Melanchthon's perspective of Romans as *compendium*. This is also seen in the extensive use of other Pauline letters at the end of his essay to support his conclusion.[40] Even Schlatter briefly attempts to place Romans within Paul's life at the beginning of his commentary, but of course shows little concern for this occasion when explaining the text.[41]

Were we to start with Rom. 14.1–15.13 as indicative of the letter's topos while paying attention to the occasion of the letter, I think we should see that Paul is concerned to show how well his gospel brings honorable praxis within the community. We have

[37] See Minear, *Obedience*, 34, who describes how the "strong" might harm the faith of the "weak" and then comments, "To the apostle nothing could be more disastrous than such treasonable examples of Christian liberty."

[38] Cf. P. Stuhlmacher, "The Theme of Romans," in Donfried, *The Romans Debate*, 341.

[39] Ibid., 333–34 and also Friedrich, Pöhlmann, and Stuhlmacher, "Zur historischen Situation," 131–66.

[40] Stuhlmacher, "The Theme of Romans," in Donfried, *The Romans Debate*, 342–45.

[41] See A. Schlatter, *Gottes Gerechtigkeit* (Stuttgart: Calwer, 1952), 9.

seen that an understanding of the "weak" in light of the shame
some Romans saw in ascetic behaviors in consumption, as well as
the Roman scorn of superstition, leads us to view the "strong" and
"weak" discussion as centering around the question, "What is a
shame-free way of living before God and humanity?" This brings
us to my suggestion for the topos of Romans, based on the practical
teaching to "strong" and "weak" with which Paul concludes the
letter's body.

Paul, his gospel, and those who follow it are not shameful[42]

In Rom. 14.1–15.13, Paul is concerned to demonstrate that the
essence of faith as he understands it[43] leaves room for both the
"strong" and the "weak" to function. He must clarify Christ's
work as inclusive of both groups (14.4, 9; 15.8–9), and his understanding of divine judgment as a significant equalizer among
"strong" and "weak" (14.10–12). Paul here delimits the boundaries
of proper eating within a religious context, supporting his contention with a definition of the kingdom of God (14.14–17). His
benedictions provide his own defining portraits of what life ought
to be like in believing communities (15.5–6, 13). When we note the
clarifications of communal life (14.1–5, 13–23; 15.1–7) and instruction to live so as not to bring shame on the community (14.16), this
section points us to what Paul is doing in his whole letter, i.e.,
calling his readers to live in accordance with his gospel, which is
above shame and will enable them to live above shame.

The proposition of the letter contains a gospel definition in
support of Paul's statement that he is not ashamed of it (1.16–17).
Evidence that this letter in fact includes a tendency to define Paul's
gospel may be found in the occurrences of εὐαγγέλιον and
εὐαγγελίζομαι, especially at the beginning and ending of the
letter.[44] Though most of these references do not identify the
gospel as distinctly Pauline, we note that the bracketing uses of

---

[42] I am indebted to Steven E. Enderlein for helping me see this as the primary
topos and for the analogy of building blocks of topoi that I use in Figure 2. See his
dissertation "The Gospel is Not Shameful: The Argumentative Structure of Romans
in the Light of Classical Rhetoric" (Ph.D. dissertation; Marquette, 1998).

[43] I am using "faith" here both in the sense of *fides quae creditur* (the things that
are believed) and *fides qua creditur* (how one believes).

[44] εὐαγγέλιον occurs at 1.9, 16; 2.16; 10.16; 11.28; 15.16, 19; (16.25). εὐαγγελίζομαι comes at 1.15; 10.15 (LXX Isa. 52.7); 15.20.

εὐαγγελίζομαι in 1.15 and 15.20 are with reference to Paul. The noun εὐαγγέλιον is tied to Paul in 1.1, 9; 2.16; 15.16, 19. It does not seem accidental that the early addition at 16.25 repeats τὸ εὐαγγέλιόν μου from 2.16. The scribe correctly understood that this letter is really about *Paul's* gospel. It is not the same as what the Romans had received (6.17); indeed, one may observe that Paul does not use εὐαγγέλιον to describe the teaching they had received. If the Roman churches have no apostolic foundation, Paul in this letter seems ready to make his gospel clear,[45] in order that the Roman audience may follow it.

While Paul does show a tendency to define his gospel in this letter, including various liturgical elements,[46] it must be noted that the defining tendencies are all for a focused purpose. The letter is not a *compendium*-like definition of his own gospel or of religion; it is rather a presentation of his gospel to show its effectiveness in describing God's saving power (1.16), including its ability to guide people into moral goodness (3.5–8; 6.1–23; 14.16), its distinctiveness from (9.30–10.4) and continuity with Judaism (9.4–5; 11.25–32), and its consistency with Paul's scriptures (1.2; 3.21; 9.6; 15.8–12). Paul also presents himself and his ministry so that his Roman audience will understand and respect him for what he has done, and support him in the future (1.13; 15.17–29). The defining activity that occurs in this text is therefore not to define anything for its own sake. All the definitional nodes serve the focus, repeated throughout the letter, that Paul, his gospel, and those who follow it are not shameful. An advertisement for a certain kind of car can never be taken as a definition of an automobile.

One could argue for the positive formulation, "Paul's gospel is glorious," as a topos, based on the pairing of the understatement οὐ γὰρ ἐπαισχύνομαι in 1.16 with the sentence beginning ἔχω οὖν καύχησιν in 15.17.[47] But aside from 5.2 and 11.13, I do not see enough evidence that Paul is trying to show that his gospel is glorious in the letter as a whole. There is more going on in the letter than this agenda. Paul seems rather to be concerned with his gospel's consistency with God's ἀλήθεια and this gospel's capacity

---

[45] See G. Friedrich, "εὐαγγέλιον," *TDNT* II (1964), 729, where he writes of Paul's use of the term in an absolute sense, one that is the same as the other apostles' proclamation (734).

[46] Betz, "Christianity as Religion," 319–20, mentions the λατρεύω/λατρεία occurrences; ibid., 321 n. 26, lists the liturgical elements found in the letter.

[47] Conversation with Steven E. Enderlein in February, 1997.

to account for both Israel and the nations.[48] The primary topos expressed negatively fits these concerns and matches a topos Paul knows from his scriptures.[49]

Paul's gospel is also above shame because it contains the truth of the righteousness of God, but there is more to the letter than this. Paul and his gospel are without shame because they are in continuity with Judaism (9–11; 15.8–12) and teach the essence of Torah (3.27–31; 13.8–10) and the purpose of Torah (10.4). Paul identifies his own role as a minister of the gospel in terms reminiscent of Judaism (1.9; 15.16). The primary topos of the letter, then, is that Paul, his gospel, and those who follow his gospel are not shameful. The other topoi that can be identified, including "the righteousness of God," support this topos, but none of them can explain every part of this letter as well as the primary topos identified here. Figure 2 shows how the primary topos I have suggested is supported by other topoi of Romans, and how these topoi include the idea of being without shame, a prevalent idea in Paul's scriptures.[50]

Romans: its topos, occasional nature, and canonical prominence

Once one accepts the primary topos that Paul, his gospel, and those who follow it are without shame, the purpose of this letter emerges as deliberative.[51] This fits with how the classical rhetoricians defined deliberative rhetoric as that form of discourse that shows that a given course of action would avoid shame and keep or lead to honor.[52] Paul wants his readers not just to assent to the truths of his gospel; he wants them to follow it and expects changes in their behavior (2.1–4; 6.1–23; 13.1–14; 14.1–15.13;

---

[48] Paul's gospel is consistent with God's ἀλήθεια (1.18, 25; 2.2, 8, 20; 3.7; 15.8); Paul's gospel accounts for both Israel (2.17–29; 9–11) and the nations (2.12–16; 11.11–25; 15.8–12). On Israel, see also K. Stendahl, *Final Account: Paul's Letter to the Romans* (Minneapolis: Fortress, 1995), 1–7.

[49] Note the twice-quoted Isa. 28.16 in Rom. 9.33 and 10.11.

[50] Hays has already identified the LXX passages Pss. 24.2; 43.10; Isa. 28.16; 50.7–8 in his explication of Paul's "I am not ashamed" statement in Rom. 1.16 (*Echoes*, 38–39).

[51] For definitions, see Stowers, *Letter Writing*, 51.

[52] *Rhet. Her.* 3.2.3–3.3.8; Aristotle, *Rh.* 1.9.35–36; Quintilian, *Inst.* 3.8.1, 89 are the texts cited by D. A. deSilva as he makes this point about Sirach in "The Wisdom of Ben Sira: Honor, Shame, and the Maintenance of the Values of a Minority Culture," *CBQ* 58 (1996) 434–35.

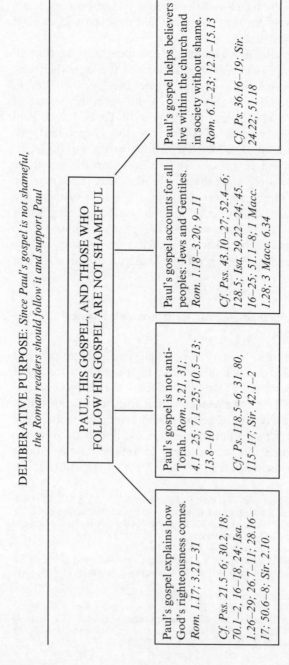

DELIBERATIVE PURPOSE: *Since Paul's gospel is not shameful,
the Roman readers should follow it and support Paul*

PAUL, HIS GOSPEL, AND THOSE WHO
FOLLOW HIS GOSPEL ARE NOT SHAMEFUL

Paul's gospel explains how
God's righteousness comes.
Rom. 1.17; 3.21–31

*Cf. Pss. 21.5–6; 30.2, 18;
70.1–2, 16–18, 24; Isa.
1.26–29; 26.7–11; 28.16–
17; 50.6–8; Sir. 2.10.*

Paul's gospel is not anti-
Torah. *Rom. 3.21, 31;
4.1–25; 7.1–25; 10.5–13;
13.8–10*

*Cf. Ps. 118.5–6, 31, 80,
115–17; Sir. 42.1–2*

Paul's gospel accounts for all
peoples: Jews and Gentiles.
Rom. 1.18–3.20; 9–11

*Cf. Pss. 43.10–27; 52.4–6;
128.5; Isa. 29.22–24; 45.
16–25; 51.1–8; 1 Macc.
1.28; 3 Macc. 6.34*

Paul's gospel helps believers
live within the church and
in society without shame.
Rom. 6.1–23; 12.1–15.13

*Cf. Ps. 36.16–19; Sir.
24.22; 51.18*

All references to Paul's
scriptures are from the LXX

Figure 2 The topoi in Romans

15.22–32). In that sense the letter is protrepsis; it is a call to follow a certain way of life.[53] When we see how Rom. 14.1–15.13 fits the context of first-century Rome and how it fits the context of the rest of the letter, the whole letter comes to be seen as thoroughly occasional. Its occasional nature confirms a view of this letter as deliberative in purpose. The occasion, a situation in Rome in which those who are following Jesus appear shameful to society outside of the churches, and in which one group is shaming another inside of the churches, prompts a call to a change of life for Paul's audience; the occasion does not simply result in a *compendium* of theological truths. The Romans' occasion is the predominant occasion behind this letter, though Paul resonates deeply with it, since he and his gospel are in danger of being shamed as he approaches Jerusalem (3.8; 15.17, 32). If we read the letter simply as a *compendium* about righteousness, we shall miss the letter's call for its readers to follow a new way of life, a life above shame in this world and the next.

While it is thoroughly occasional, we value this letter as part of our scriptural canon. And while we must first read the letter as not-scripture in order to understand its occasion,[54] our understanding of its occasional nature will then help us appreciate and benefit from its place within our canon.

As a letter written at a specific point in Paul's ministry and at a specific juncture in the Roman believers' lives, this letter cannot be taken as the completely definitive expression of our faith. As it would be a mistake to publish the transcripts of NASA's directions to the Mir space station crew as the reference guide to that space station, so Romans should not be read as the manual for our faith. Romans is rather an expression of Paul's gospel, probably fairly complete and characteristic, in which his driving topos is that it is not shameful.

The occasional nature of this letter opens our vista onto other expressions of the faith within our canon. The letter is placed first within the Pauline corpus. We can follow this decision by affirming that Romans is the most complete and characteristic expression of Paul's gospel that we have. But the Paul who wants us to appreciate the depths of divine mystery (11.33–36) would not want us to canonize this letter as the single or final expression of our

[53] Stowers, *Letter Writing*, 92; Aune, "Romans as a *Logos Protreptikos*," in Donfried, *The Romans Debate*, 278–96.
[54] Hays, *Echoes*, 5. See pp. 63, 197 above.

faith.[55] The Pauline corpus contains various expressions of the gospel, given on different occasions by one of its early masters. In that sense the corpus is like a published record of a series of chess games by a master such as Bobby Fischer. The first game in the publication would be considered characteristic of good chess; it would not be the one in which Fischer sacrificed his queen and went on to win. But still it is just one expression of the game; Fischer or any other chess master would not consider it to be the *compendium* of the game of chess. So within the Pauline corpus, we should be alert to differences within his letters, and not let the prominence of Romans obscure other expressions Paul makes of his gospel.[56] We can read Romans as scripture, treasuring and valuing principles that extend from its occasion into ours alongside other principles from other Pauline letters.

An understanding of the letter's thoroughly occasional nature will also free us up to read it alongside of other expressions of the gospel in the wider NT canon. Yes, Romans comes first within the Pauline corpus. But first within our canon is Matthew, a book with a different expression of the gospel. There is no reason to be found within the letter's occasion, the NT canon, or early church history[57] why Romans should be given more prominence than Matthew in our expressions of faith. Romans is an expression of Paul's gospel to show that it is not shameful, found among other expressions of the gospel, written by Paul and others.[58]

The primary topos in this letter, supported by the section on "strong" and "weak," allows us to account well for Romans historically, since it represents Paul's deliberative motive in the letter. Paul writes to change how his Roman readers live. The

[55] Brevard S. Childs argues that the process of canonization included editing of the Pauline correspondence "in a conscious effort to render these occasional writings into a normative collection for universal application within the community of faith," *The New Testament as Canon: An Introduction* (Philadelphia: Fortress, 1984), 23. But as Childs admits (ibid., 23, 251–52), the historical particularity in Romans has been retained, so I stand by my approach that seeks first to read the letter in light of its occasion. The letter's status as canonical does not exempt us from this first step.

[56] For example, with J. A. Fitzmyer, we should appreciate that in Galatians and Romans Paul gives different accounts for how the coming of Torah results in humanity's sinful condition, *Paul and his Theology: A Brief Sketch* (Englewood Cliffs, N.J.: Prentice-Hall, 1989), 78.

[57] K. Stendahl, *Paul among Jews and Gentiles and Other Essays* (Philadelphia: Fortress, 1976), 83: "It has always been a puzzling fact that Paul meant so relatively little for the thinking of the Church during the first 350 years of its history."

[58] See also J. D. G. Dunn, *The Living Word* (Philadelphia: Fortress, 1987), 141–74, on "levels of canonical authority."

problem with viewing the letter's primary topos as "the righteousness of God" or any of the other supporting topoi is that such a
view obscures for us the historical conditions of the letter's contents
(for example, 13.1–7) and the way in which this letter as protrepsis
calls for change. In that sense, our understanding of the thoroughly
occasional nature of this letter allows Romans to register at a
deeper level for us as scripture.

BIBLIOGRAPHY

Primary literature

The Apostolic Fathers: Greek Texts and English Translations of their Writings. Ed./trans. J. B. Lightfoot and J. R. Harmer, 2nd ed., ed. M. W. Holmes, Grand Rapids, Baker, 1992.

Apuleius. *Metamorphoses*, trans. J. A. Hanson, LCL, Cambridge, Mass., Harvard University Press, 1989.

Athenaeus. *The Deipnosophists*, trans. C. B. Gulick, LCL, London, William Heinemann, 1929.

Celsus, Aulus Cornelius. *On Medicine*, trans. W. G. Spencer, LCL, London, William Heinemann, 1935.

Cicero. *De natura deorum*, ed. A. S. Pease, 2 vols., Cambridge, Mass., Harvard University Press, 1955–58.

De officiis, trans. Walter Miller, LCL, London, William Heinemann, 1913.

De oratore, De fato, Paradoxa Stoicorum, De partitione oratoria, trans. E. W. Sutton and H. Rackham, LCL, London, William Heinemann, 1942.

Philippics, trans. Walter C. A. Ker, LCL, London, William Heinemann, 1926.

Cicero: Selected Letters, trans. D. R. Shackleton Bailey, London/New York, Penguin, 1986.

The Digest of Justinian, eds. Theodor Mommsen and Paul Krueger, trans./ed. Alan Watson, Philadelphia, University of Pennsylvania Press, 1985.

Dio Cassius. *Dio's Roman History*, trans. E. Cary, LCL, London, William Heinemann, 1925.

Diogenes Laertius. *Lives of Eminent Philosophers*, trans. R. D. Hicks, LCL, London, William Heinemann, 1925.

Gellius, Aulus. *The Attic Nights of Aulus Gellius*, Vols. I, III, trans. John C. Rolfe, LCL, London, William Heinemann, 1946, 1952.

Hesiod: The Homeric Hymns and Homerica, trans. H. G. Evelyn-White, LCL, London, William Heinemann, 1936.

Horace: Satires, trans. H. Rushton Fairclough, rev. ed., LCL, London, William Heinemann, 1929.

Josephus, Flavius. *Vita*, trans. H. St. John Thackeray, LCL, London, William Heinemann, 1926.

Juvenal and Persius, trans. G. G. Ramsay, LCL, London, William Heinemann, 1940.

Livy, Vol. VI, trans. Frank Gardner Moore, LCL, London, William Heinemann, 1940.

Musonius Rufus. "Musonius Rufus: 'The Roman Socrates,'" trans. Cora E. Lutz, *YCS* 10 (1947) 3–147.

Reliquiae, ed. O. Hense, Leipzig, B. G. Teubner, 1905.

Orphicorum Fragmenta, 2nd ed., ed. Otto Kern, Berlin, Weidmann, 1963.

Philo. *De vita contemplativa*, Vol. IX, trans. F. H. Colson, LCL, London, William Heinemann, 1941.

  Philonis Alexandrini De Animalibus: The Armenian Text with an Introduction, Translation, and Commentary, ed. Abraham Terian, SHJ 1, Chico, Scholars, 1981.

Pliny: Letters, trans. W. Melmoth, rev. W. M. L. Hutchinson, LCL, London, William Heinemann, 1915.

Pliny: Natural History, Vol. V, trans. H. Rackham, LCL, London, William Heinemann, 1950.

Plutarch. "De esu carnium orationes," *Moralia*, Vol. XII, trans. H. Cherniss and W. C. Helmbold, LCL, London, William Heinemann, 1968.

  "De Superstitione," *Moralia*, Vol. II, trans. F. C. Babitt, LCL, London, William Heinemann, 1928.

Porphyry. *On Abstinence from Animal Food*, trans. Thomas Taylor, ed. Esme Wynne-Tyson, n.p., Centaur, 1965.

Porphyry. *Opuscula selecta*, ed. Augustus Nauck, Leipzig, B. G. Teubner, 1886.

Seneca: Ad Lucilium epistulae morales, Vol. III, trans. R. M. Gummere, LCL, London, William Heinemann, 1925.

Seneca: On Benefits (De Beneficiis), trans. J. W. Basore, LCL, London, William Heinemann, 1935.

Sextus Pythagoreus. *The Sentences of Sextus: A Contribution to the Early Christian History of Ethics*, ed. Henry Chadwick, Cambridge, Cambridge University Press, 1959.

Suetonius: Lives of the Caesars, trans. J. C. Rolfe, LCL, 2 vols., London, William Heinemann, 1913–14.

Synesius. *Epistolographi Graeci*, ed. Rudolf Hercher, Paris, A. F. Didot, 1873, 638–739.

Tacitus. *The Annals*, trans. John Jackson, LCL, London, William Heinemann, 1937.

  The Histories, trans. C. H. Moore, LCL, 2 vols., London, William Heinemann, 1925–31.

Theophrastus. *The Characters of Theophrastus*, trans. J. M. Edmonds, LCL, London, William Heinemann, 1953.

Secondary literature

Commentaries on Romans

Barrett, C. K. *A Commentary on the Epistle to the Romans*, HNTC, New York, Harper & Brothers, 1957.

Chrysostom, John. *Opera omnia*. Vol. IX: *Homiliae XXXII in Epistolam ad*

Romanos, ed. J.-P. Migne, *PG* 60.395–682, Paris, Petit-Montrouge, 1853.

Cranfield, C. E. B. *A Critical and Exegetical Commentary on the Epistle to the Romans*, ICC, 2 vols., Edinburgh, T. & T. Clark, 1975–79.

Damascene, John. *Opera omnia*. Vol. II, ed. J.-P. Migne, *PG* 95.441–570, Turnhout, Brepols, n.d.

Dodd, C. H. *The Epistle of Paul to the Romans*, MNTC, New York, Harper & Brothers, 1932.

Dunn, J. D. G. *Romans 1–8*, WBC 38A, Dallas, Word, 1988.
Romans 9–16, WBC 38B, Dallas, Word, 1988.

Fitzmyer, J. A. *Romans*, AB 33, New York, Doubleday, 1993.

Godet, F. *St. Paul's Epistle to the Romans*, trans. A. Cusin and T. W. Chambers, New York, Funk & Wagnalls, 1883.

Huby, J. *Saint Paul: Epître aux Romains: traduction et commentaire*, rev. S. Lyonnet, Paris, Beauchesne, 1957.

Käsemann, Ernst. *Commentary on Romans*, trans. and ed. Geoffrey W. Bromiley, Grand Rapids, Eerdmans, 1980.

Kühl, Ernst. *Der Brief des Paulus an die Römer*, Leipzig, Quelle & Meyer, 1913.

Lagrange, M.-J. *Saint Paul: Epître aux Romains*, 4th ed., Ebib, Paris, Gabalda, 1931.

Leenhardt, Franz J. *The Epistle to the Romans: A Commentary*, trans. Harold Knight, London, Lutterworth, 1961.

Lietzmann, Hans. *Einführung in die Textgeschichte der Paulusbriefe: An die Römer*, 4th ed., HNT 8, Tübingen, J. C. B. Mohr (Paul Siebeck), 1971.

Lyonnet, S. *Les Epîtres de Saint Paul aux Galates, aux Romains*, 2nd ed., Paris, Cerf, 1959.

Melanchthon, Philipp. *Annotationes in epistulam Pauli ad Romanos et ad Corinthios, Opera*, vol. XV, ed. C. G. Bretschneider, Halis Saxonum, C. A. Schwetschke and Son, 1848; reprint ed., New York, Johnson Reprint, 1963.

Michel, Otto. *Der Brief an die Römer*, 4th ed., KEK 4, Göttingen, Vandenhoeck & Ruprecht, 1966.

Moo, Douglas J. *The Epistle to the Romans*, NICNT, Grand Rapids: Eerdmans, 1996.

Origen. *Opera omnia*. Vol. IV: *Commentariorum in epistolam beati Pauli ad Romanos*, ed. J.-P. Migne, *PG* 14.837–1292, Turnhout, Brepols, n.d.

Sanday, William, and Headlam, A. C. *A Critical and Exegetical Commentary on the Epistle to the Romans*, ICC 45, 13th ed., Edinburgh, T. & T. Clark, 1911.

Schlatter, Adolf. *Gottes Gerechtigkeit: Ein Kommentar zum Römerbrief*, 2nd ed., Stuttgart, Calwer, 1952.

Schlier, Heinrich. *Der Römerbrief*, HTKNT 6, Freiburg/Basle/Vienna, Herder, 1977.

Schmithals, Walter. *Der Römerbrief: Ein Kommentar*, Gütersloh, Gerd Mohn, 1988.

Sedulii Scotti collectaneum in apostolum 1. In Epistolam ad Romanos, eds. Hermann Josef Frede and Herbert Stanjek, VLGLB 31, Freiburg, Herder, 1996.

Stuhlmacher, Peter. *Der Brief an die Römer*, NTD 6, Göttingen, Vandenhoeck & Ruprecht, 1989.

Theodoret. *Opera omnia*. Vol. III: *Interpretatio Epistolae ad Romanos*, ed. J.-P. Migne, *PG* 82.43–226, Paris, Petit-Montrouge, 1859.

Wilckens, Ulrich. *Der Brief an die Römer*, EKKNT 6, Vols. I–III, Neukirchen-Vluyn, Neukirchener, 1978–82.

Ziesler, John. *Paul's Letter to the Romans*, TPINTC, Philadelphia, Trinity Press International, 1989.

Other works

Adams, J. N. "Conventions of Naming in Cicero," *CQ* 28 (1978) 145–66.

Aland, Kurt. "Der Schluß und die ursprüngliche Gestalt des Römerbriefes," in *Neutestamentliche Entwürfe*, Munich, Kaiser, 1979, 284–301.

Alföldy, Géza. *The Social History of Rome*, trans. D. Braund and F. Pollock, Totowa, N.J., Barnes & Noble, 1985.

Andrews, Scott B. "Too Weak Not to Lead: The Form and Function of 2 Cor. 11.23b-33," *NTS* 41 (1995) 263–76.

Arbesmann, P. R. *Das Fasten bei den Griechen und Römern*, RVV 21.1, Giessen, A. Töpelmann, 1929.

Armitage, F. P. *Diet and Race: Anthropological Essays*, London, Longmans, Green, and Co., 1922.

Attridge, Harold W. *The Epistle to the Hebrews: A Commentary*, Hermeneia, Philadelphia, Fortress, 1989.

Augustine. *Opera omnia*, Vol. X: *Contra Julianum*, ed. J.-P. Migne, *PL* 44, Paris, Petit-Montrouge, 1865.

Aune, David E. "De esu carnium orationes I and II (Moralia 993A–999B)," *PTWECL*, ed. H. D. Betz, SCHNT 3, Leiden, Brill, 1975, 301–16.

  Review of F. W. Danker, *Benefactor: Epigraphic Study of a Graeco-Roman and New Testament Semantic Field*, *Interp.* 38 (1984) 421–25.

Ausbüttel, Frank M. *Untersuchungen zu den Vereinen im Westen des römischen Reiches*, FAS 11, Kallmünz, Michael Laßleben, 1982.

Bacon, Francis. "Of Unity in Religion," in *Essays*, ed. R. F. Jones, New York, Odyssey, 1937, 8–13.

Bader, Günter. *Symbolik des Todes Jesu*, HUT 25, Tübingen, J. C. B. Mohr (Paul Siebeck), 1988.

Badian, E. *Foreign Clientelae (264–70 B.C.)*, Oxford, Clarendon, 1958.
"*Salutatio*," OCD, 948.

Barclay, John M. G. "'Do We Undermine the Law?' A Study of Romans 14.1–15.6," in *Paul and the Mosaic Law*, ed. J. D. G. Dunn, Tübingen, J. C. B. Mohr (Paul Siebeck), 1996, 287–308.

Barrett, C. K. *The First Epistle to the Corinthians*, HNTC, New York, Harper & Row, 1968.
  Freedom and Obligation: A Study of the Epistle to the Galatians, Philadelphia, Westminster, 1985.

Barzun, Jacques. *Race: A Study in Modern Superstition*, New York, Harcourt, Brace and Co., 1937.

Bassler, Jouette M. *Divine Impartiality: Paul and a Theological Axiom*, SBLDS 59, Chico, Scholars, 1982.

Beard, Mary, and Crawford, Michael. *Rome in the Late Republic*, London, Duckworth, 1985.

Beckwith, Roger T. "The Vegetarianism of the Therapeutae, and the Motives for Vegetarianism in Early Jewish and Christian Circles," *RevQ* 13 (1988) 407–10.

Berger, Peter L. *The Sacred Canopy: Elements of a Sociological Theory of Religion*, Garden City, N.Y., Doubleday & Co., 1967.

Berger, Peter L., and Luckmann, Thomas. *The Social Construction of Reality: A Treatise in the Sociology of Knowledge*, Garden City, N.Y., Doubleday & Co., 1966.

Bernays, Jakob. *Theophrastos' Schrift über Frömmigkeit: Ein Beitrag zur Religionsgeschichte mit kritischen und erklärenden Bemerkungen zu Porphyrios' Schrift über Enthaltsamkeit*, Berlin, W. Hertz, 1866.

Betz, Hans Dieter. *Der Apostel Paulus und die sokratische Tradition: Eine exegetische Untersuchung zu seiner "Apologie" 2 Korinther 10–13*, BHT 45, Tübingen, J. C. B. Mohr (Paul Siebeck), 1972.

"Christianity as Religion: Paul's Attempt at Definition in Romans," *JR* 71 (1991) 315–44.

2 Corinthians 8 and 9: A Commentary on Two Administrative Letters of the Apostle Paul, Hermeneia, Philadelphia, Fortress, 1985.

Galatians: A Commentary on Paul's Letter to the Churches in Galatia, Hermeneia, Philadelphia, Fortress, 1979.

Lukian von Samosata und das Neue Testament: Religionsgeschichtliche und paränetische Parallelen: Ein Beitrag zum Corpus Hellenisticum Novi Testamenti, TU 76, Berlin, Akademie, 1961.

Nachfolge und Nachahmung Jesu Christi im Neuen Testament, BHT 37, Tübingen, J. C. B. Mohr (Paul Siebeck), 1967.

Paul's Concept of Freedom in the Context of Hellenistic Discussions about Possibilities of Human Freedom, Protocol for the Center of Hermeneutical Studies 26, Berkeley, Center for Hermeneutical Studies, 1977.

"Das Problem der Grundlagen der paulinischen Ethik (Röm 12,1–2)," *ZTK* 85 (1988) 199–218.

Bigelmair, Andreas. *Die Beteiligung der Christen am öffentlichen Leben in vorkonstantinischer Zeit: Ein Beitrag zur ältesten Kirchengeschichte*, VKHSM 8, Munich, Lentner, 1902, reprint ed., Darmstadt, Scientia Verlag Aalen, 1970.

Black, David Alan. *Paul, Apostle of Weakness: Astheneia and its Cognates in the Pauline Literature*, AUS 7.3, New York/Berne, Peter Lang, 1984.

Blasi, Anthony J. *Early Christianity as a Social Movement*, TSR 5, New York/Berne, Peter Lang, 1988.

Bleich, J. David. "Survey of Recent Halakhic Periodical Literature: Vegetarianism and Judaism," *Tradition* 23 (1987) 32–90.

Boak, A. E. R. "*Officium*," PW XXXIV.2045–56.

Boas, George. *The Happy Beast in French Thought of the Seventeenth Century*, Baltimore, Johns Hopkins, 1933, reprint ed., New York, Octagon, 1966.

Bolkestein, Hendrik. *Theophrastos Charakter der Deisidaimonia als religionsgeschichtliche Urkunde*, RVV 21, Giessen, A. Töpelmann, 1929.
Wohltätigkeit und Armenpflege im vorchristlichen Altertum, Utrecht, Oosthoek, 1939, reprint ed., Groningen, Bouma, 1967.

Bousset, Wilhelm. *Kyrios Christos*, trans. John E. Steely, Nashville, Abingdon, 1970.

Bowersock, G. W. *Greek Sophists in the Roman Empire*, Oxford, Clarendon, 1969.

Bradley, David G. "The Origins of the Hortatory Materials in the Letters of Paul," Ph.D. dissertation, Yale, 1947.
"The *Topos* as a Form in the Pauline Paraenesis," *JBL* 72 (1953) 238–46.

Braun, Herbert. *An die Hebräer*, HNT 14, Tübingen, J. C. B. Mohr (Paul Siebeck), 1984.
"Glaube im NT," *RGG* II.1590–97.
Spätjüdisch-häretischer und frühchristlicher Radikalismus, BHT 24, 2 vols., Tübingen, J. C. B. Mohr (Paul Siebeck), 1957.

Bruce, F. F. *Apostle of the Heart Set Free*, Grand Rapids, Eerdmans, 1977.

Brunt, John Carlton. "Paul's Attitude toward and Treatment of Problems Involving Dietary Practice: A Case Study in Pauline Ethics," Ph.D. dissertation, Emory, 1978.

Brunt, P. A. "Cicero's *Officium* in the Civil War," *JRS* 76 (1986) 12–32.
"Free Labour and Public Works at Rome," *JRS* 70 (1980) 81–100.

Bultmann, Rudolf. *History of the Synoptic Tradition*, rev. ed., trans. John Marsh, New York, Harper & Row, 1963.
Theology of the New Testament, 2 vols., trans. Kendrick Grobel, New York, Charles Scribner's Sons, 1951, 1955.

Burkert, Walter. *Homo Necans: The Anthropology of Ancient Greek Sacrificial Ritual and Myth*, trans. Peter Bing, Berkeley, University of California Press, 1983.
Lore and Science in Ancient Pythagoreanism, trans. E. L. Minar, Jr., Cambridge, Mass., Harvard University Press, 1972.
Structure and History in Greek Mythology and Ritual, SCL 47, Berkeley, University of California Press, 1979.

Burrows, Millar. "Old Testament Ethics and the Ethics of Jesus," in *Essays in Old Testament Ethics*, J. Philip Hyatt Festschrift, eds. James L. Crenshaw and John T. Willis, New York, Ktav, 1974, 225–43.

Burton, Ernest De Witt. *A Critical and Exegetical Commentary on the Epistle to the Galatians*, ICC, Edinburgh, T. & T. Clark, 1921.

Butler, Christopher. "The Object of Faith according to St. Paul's Epistles," in *Studiorum Paulinorum Congressus Internationalis Catholicus 1961*, Rome, Pontifical Biblical Institute, 1963, I.15–30.

Calderone, Salvatore. "*Superstitio*," *ANRW* I.2 (1972) 377–96.

Campbell, W. S. *Paul's Gospel in an Intercultural Context*, SIHC 69, Frankfurt-on-Main, Peter Lang, 1991.

Capelle, Wilhelm. "Altgriechische Askese," in *Neue Jahrbücher für das klassische Altertum, Geschichte und deutsche Literatur*, Vol. XXV, ed. J. Ilberg, Leipzig/Berlin, B. G. Teubner, 1910, 681–708.

Casson, Lionel. *Travel in the Ancient World*, Toronto, Hakkert, 1974.

Charon, Joel M. *Symbolic Interactionism: An Introduction, an Interpretation, an Integration*, Englewood Cliffs, N.J., Prentice-Hall, 1979.

Childs, Brevard S. *The New Testament as Canon: An Introduction*, Philadelphia, Fortress, 1984.

Chow, John K. *Patronage and Power: A Study of Social Networks in Corinth*, JSNT Sup 75, Sheffield, JSOT, 1992.

Collins, Adela Yarbro. "Vilification and Self-Definition in the Book of Revelation," in *Christians among Jews and Gentiles*, Krister Stendahl Festschrift, eds. G. W. E. Nickelsburg and G. W. MacRae, Philadelphia, Fortress, 1986, 308–20.

Conzelmann, Hans. *1 Corinthians: A Commentary on the First Epistle to the Corinthians*, Hermeneia, trans. J. W. Leitch, Philadelphia, Fortress, 1975.

An Outline of the Theology of the New Testament, 2nd ed., trans. John Bowden, New York, Harper & Row, 1969.

Corbier, Mireille. "The Ambiguous Status of Meat in Ancient Rome," trans. R. P. Saller, *Food and Foodways* 3 (1989) 223–64.

Countryman, L. William. "The Rhetoric of Purity in Romans," unpublished paper, received in November, 1992.

The Rich Christian in the Church of the Early Empire: Contradictions and Accommodations, TSR 7, New York/Toronto, Edwin Mellen, 1980.

Cramer, Frederick H. *Astrology in Roman Law and Politics*, MAPS 37, Philadelphia, American Philosophical Society, 1954.

Cranfield, C. E. B. "ΜΕΤΡΟΝ ΠΙΣΤΕΩΣ in Romans XII. 3," *NTS* 8 (1962) 345–51.

Cumont, Franz. *After Life in Roman Paganism*, New Haven, Yale University Press, 1922; reprint ed., New York, Dover, 1959.

Dahrendorf, Ralf. *Homo sociologicus*, 4th ed., Cologne/Opladen, Westdeutscher, 1964.

Danker, Frederick W. *Benefactor: Epigraphic Study of a Graeco-Roman and New Testament Semantic Field*, St. Louis, Clayton, 1982.

D'Arms, John H. *Commerce and Social Standing in Ancient Rome*, Cambridge, Mass.: Harvard University Press, 1981.

"Control, Companionship, and *Clientela*: Some Social Functions of the Roman Communal Meal," *Echos du monde classique* 28 (1984) 327–48.

"The Roman *Convivium* and the Idea of Equality," in *Sympotica: A Symposium on the Symposion*, ed. Oswyn Murray, Oxford, Clarendon, 1990, 308–20.

Dederen, Raoul. "On Esteeming One Day Better Than Another," *AUSS* 9 (1971) 16–35.

Deems, Mervin Monroe. "The Sources of Christian Asceticism," in *Environmental Factors in Christian History*, Shirley Jackson Case Festschrift, eds. J. T. McNeill, M. Spinka, and H. R. Willoughby, Chicago, University of Chicago Press, 1939, 149–66.

Deidun, T. J. *New Covenant Morality in Paul*, AnBib 39, Rome, Pontifical Biblical Institute, 1981.

de Lange, N. R. M. "Jewish Attitudes to the Roman Empire," in *Imperialism in the Ancient World*, eds. Peter D. A. Garnsey and C. R. Whittaker, Cambridge, Cambridge University Press, 1978, 255–81.

deSilva, David A. "The Wisdom of Ben Sira: Honor, Shame, and the Maintenance of the Values of a Minority Culture," *CBQ* 58 (1996) 433–55.

Dibelius, Martin. *Die Formgeschichte des Evangeliums*, 3rd ed., Tübingen, J. C. B. Mohr (Paul Siebeck), 1959.

Die Geisterwelt im Glauben des Paulus, Göttingen, Vandenhoeck & Ruprecht, 1909.

Dickerman, Sherwood Owen. *De argumentis quibusdam apud Xenophontem, Platonem, Aristotelem obviis e structura hominis et animalium petitis*, Halle, Wischan & Burkhardt, 1909.

Dihle, Albrecht. "Gerechtigkeit," *RAC* X.270–87.

Dodds, E. R. *Pagan and Christian in an Age of Anxiety: Some Aspects of Religious Experience from Marcus Aurelius to Constantine*, Wiles Lectures, 1962–63, Cambridge, Cambridge University Press, 1965.

Donfried, Karl Paul. "False Presuppositions in the Study of Romans," in *The Romans Debate*, ed. K. P. Donfried, rev. ed., Peabody, Mass., Hendrickson, 1991, 102–25.

"The Kingdom of God in Paul," in *The Kingdom of God in 20th-Century Interpretation*, ed. W. Willis, Peabody, Mass., Hendrickson, 1987, 175–90.

ed. *The Romans Debate*, rev. ed., Peabody, Mass., Hendrickson, 1991.

Douglas, Mary. "Deciphering a Meal," in *Myth, Symbol, and Culture*, ed. Clifford Geertz, New York, W. W. Norton & Co., 1971, 61–81.

Purity and Danger: An Analysis of Concepts of Pollution and Taboo, New York, Frederick A. Praeger, 1966.

Droge, Arthur J. *Homer or Moses? Early Christian Interpretations of the History of Culture*, HUT 26, Tübingen, J. C. B. Mohr (Paul Siebeck), 1989.

Dumézil, Georges. *Archaic Roman Religion*, trans. Philip Krapp, 2 vols., Chicago, University of Chicago Press, 1970.

Dunn, J. D. G. *The Living Word*, Philadelphia, Fortress, 1987.

Duthoy, Robert. "La Fonction sociale de l'augustalité," *Epigraphica* 36 (1974) 134–54.

Dyck, A. R. "The Plan of Panaetius' ΠΕΡΙ ΤΟΥ ΚΑΘΗΚΟΝΤΟΣ," *AJPh* 100 (1979) 408–16.

Edwards, M. J. "Satire and Verisimilitude: Christianity in Lucian's *Peregrinus*," Historia 38 (1989) 89–98.

Ehrhardt, Arnold A. T. *Politische Metaphysik von Solon bis Augustin*, Vol. II: *Die christliche Revolution*, Tübingen, J. C. B. Mohr (Paul Siebeck), 1959.

Eisenstadt, S. N., and Roniger, L. *Patrons, Clients and Friends: Interpersonal Relations and the Structure of Trust in Society*, Cambridge, Cambridge University Press, 1984.

Eisler, Robert. *Orpheus – the Fisher: Comparative Studies in Orphic and Early Christian Cult Symbolism*, London, J. M. Watkins, 1921.

Elliott, N. *Liberating Paul: The Justice of God and the Politics of the Apostle*, BLib, Maryknoll, N.Y., Orbis, 1994.

The Rhetoric of Romans, Sheffield, Sheffield Academic Press, 1990.

Ellis, E. Earle. *Paul's Use of the Old Testament*, Edinburgh/London, Oliver and Boyd, 1957; reprint ed., Grand Rapids, Baker, 1981.

Enderlein, Steven E. "The Gospel is Not Shameful: The Argumentative Structure of Romans in the Light of Classical Rhetoric," Ph.D. dissertation, Marquette, 1998.

Feldman, Louis H. "The Orthodoxy of the Jews in Hellenistic Egypt," *JSS* 22 (1960) 215–37.

Fernandez, James W. "Persuasions and Performances: Of the Beast in Every Body ... and the Metaphors of Everyman," in *Myth, Symbol, and Culture*, ed. Clifford Geertz, New York, W. W. Norton & Co., 1971, 39–60.

Ferro-Luzzi, G. E. "Food Avoidances at Puberty and Menstruation in Tamilnad: An Anthropological Study," in *Food, Ecology and Culture: Readings in the Anthropology of Dietary Practices*, ed. J. R. K. Robson, New York, Gordon and Breach, 1980, 93–100.

Fitzmyer, J. A. *Paul and his Theology: A Brief Sketch*, 2nd ed., Englewood Cliffs, N.J., Prentice-Hall, 1989.

Foust, Dean. "Why Greenspan Should Keep Mum about the Market," *Business Week* (December 23, 1996) 35.

Fowler, W. Ward. *The Roman Festivals of the Period of the Republic: An Introduction to the Study of the Religion of the Romans*, London, Macmillan, 1908.

Fraenkel, Eduard. *Horace*, 1957; reprint ed., Oxford, Oxford University Press, 1970.

Frame, J. E. *A Critical and Exegetical Commentary on the Epistles of St. Paul to the Thessalonians*, ICC, Edinburgh, T. & T. Clark, 1912.

Frank, Tenney. "Race Mixture in the Roman Empire," *AHR* 21 (1916) 689–708.

Frazer, J. G. *Psyche's Task: A Discourse concerning the Influence of Superstition on the Growth of Institutions*, 2nd ed., London: Dawsons, 1968.

Friedrich, J., Pöhlmann, W., and Stuhlmacher, P. "Zur historischen Situation und Intention von Röm 13,1–7," *ZTK* 73 (1976) 131–66.

Furnish, Victor P. *The Love Command in the New Testament*, Nashville, Abingdon, 1972.

Gager, John G. *The Origins of Anti-Semitism: Attitudes toward Judaism in Pagan and Christian Antiquity*, New York/Oxford, Oxford University Press, 1983.

Gamble, Harry, Jr. *The Textual History of the Letter to the Romans*, SD 42, Grand Rapids, Eerdmans, 1977.

Gardella, Peter. *Innocent Ecstasy: How Christianity Gave America an Ethic of Sexual Pleasure*, New York/Oxford, Oxford University Press, 1985.

Garnsey, Peter D. A. "Independent Freedmen and the Economy of Roman Italy under the Principate," *Klio* 63 (1981) 359–71.

Garnsey, Peter D. A., and Saller, Richard P. *The Roman Empire: Economy, Society and Culture*, Berkeley, University of California Press, 1987.

Gärtner, Hans Armin. *Cicero und Panaitios: Beobachtungen zu Ciceros De officiis*, Heidelberg, Carl Winter, 1974.

Glad, Clarence E. *Paul and Philodemus: Adaptability in Epicurean and Early Christian Psychagogy*, NovT Sup 81, Leiden, Brill, 1995.

Godet, F. L. *Commentary on First Corinthians*, Edinburgh, T. & T. Clark, 1899; reprint ed., Grand Rapids, Kregel, 1977.

Godlovitch, Roslind. "Animals and Morals," in *Animals, Men and Morals: An Inquiry into the Maltreatment of Non-Humans*, eds. Stanley and Roslind Godlovitch and John Harris, New York, Taplinger, 1972, 156–72.

Goldenberg, Robert. "The Jewish Sabbath in the Roman World up to the Time of Constantine the Great," *ANRW* II.19.1 (1979) 414–47.

Goldman, David P. "The Fed Giveth, the Fed Taketh Away," *Forbes* (December 30, 1996) 172.

Gooch, Peter D. *Dangerous Food: 1 Corinthians 8–10 in its Context*, SCJ 5, Waterloo, Ontario, Wilfrid Laurier University Press, 1993.

Goode, Erich. *Sociology*, 2nd ed., Englewood Cliffs, N.J., Prentice-Hall, 1988.

Goodenough, E. R. *The Politics of Philo Judaeus*, New Haven, Yale University Press, 1938.

Goody, Jack. *Cooking, Cuisine and Class: A Study in Comparative Sociology*, Cambridge, Cambridge University Press, 1982.

Grodzynski, Denise. "*Superstitio*," *Revue des études anciennes* 76 (1974) 36–60.

Grundmann, Walter. *Das Evangelium nach Matthäus*, THKNT 1, Berlin, Evangelische Verlagsanstalt, 1968.

Gutbrod, Walter. *Die paulinische Anthropologie*, BWANT 4.15, Stuttgart, W. Kohlhammer, 1934.

Guthrie, W. K. C. *Orpheus and Greek Religion: A Study of the Orphic Movement*, New York, W. W. Norton & Co., 1966.

Haacker, Klaus. "Der Römerbrief als Friedensmemorandum," *NTS* 36 (1990) 25–41.

Hargrove, Barbara. *The Sociology of Religion: Classical and Contemporary Approaches*, 2nd ed., Arlington Heights, Ill., Harlan Davidson, 1989.

Harmening, Dieter. *Superstitio: Überlieferungs- und theorie-geschichtliche Untersuchungen zur kirchlich-theologischen Aberglaubensliteratur des Mittelalters*, Berlin, Erich Schmidt, 1979.

Harnack, Adolf von. *Brod und Wasser, die eucharistischen Elemente bei Justin*, TU 7/2, Leipzig, J. C. Hinrichs, 1891.

Harrill, J. Albert. *The Manumission of Slaves in Early Christianity*, HUT 32, Tübingen, J. C. B. Mohr (Paul Siebeck), 1995.

Haufe, Günter. "Reich Gottes bei Paulus und in der Jesustradition," *NTS* 31 (1985) 467–72.

Haußleiter, Johannes. *Der Vegetarismus in der Antike*, RVV 24, Berlin, A. Töpelmann, 1935.

Hays, Richard B. "Christ Prays the Psalms: Paul's Use of an Early Christian Exegetical Convention," in *The Future of Christology: Essays in Honor of Leander E. Keck*, eds. A. J. Malherbe and W. A. Meeks, Minneapolis, Fortress, 1993, 122–36.

Echoes of Scripture in the Letters of Paul, New Haven, Yale University Press, 1989.

Heil, Christoph. *Die Ablehnung der Speisegebote durch Paulus*, BBB 96, Weinheim/Berlin, Beltz Athenäum, 1994.

Heil, J. P. *Romans – Paul's Letter of Hope*, AnBib 112, Rome, Biblical Institute, 1987.

Heilmann, Willibald. *Ethische Reflexion und römische Lebenswirklichkeit in Ciceros Schrift De Officiis: Ein literatursoziologischer Versuch*, Wiesbaden, Franz Steiner, 1982.

Heinemann, I. *Poseidonios metaphysische Schriften*, Vol. I, Breslau, M. & H. Marcus, 1921.

Heinimann, Felix. *Nomos und Physis: Herkunft und Bedeutung einer Antithese im griechischen Denken des 5. Jahrhunderts*, SBAW 1, Basle, Friedrich Reinhardt, 1945.

Hellegouarc'h, J. *Le Vocabulaire latin des relations et des partis politiques sous la république*, Paris, Les Belles Lettres, 1963.

Hermann, Ingo. *Kyrios und Pneuma: Studien zur Christologie der paulinischen Hauptbriefe*, SANT 2, Munich, Kösel, 1961.

Herzfeld, Michael. "'As in Your Own House': Hospitality, Ethnography, and the Stereotype of Mediterranean Society," in *Honor and Shame and the Unity of the Mediterranean*, ed. David D. Gilmore, AAA 22, Washington, D.C., AAA, 1987, 75–89.

Hirzel, Rudolf. *Untersuchungen zu Ciceros philosophischen Schriften: De Natura Deorum*, Leipzig, S. Hirzel, 1877.

Hodgson, Robert, Jr. "Superstition," *ABD*, Vol. VI (1992), 239–41.

Hofius, Otfried. *Der Christushymnus Philipper 2,6–11: Untersuchungen zu Gestalt und Aussage eines urchristlichen Psalms*, WUNT 1.17, Tübingen, J. C. B. Mohr (Paul Siebeck), 1976.

Hooker, Morna. *A Preface to Paul*, New York, Oxford University Press, 1980.

Hopkins, Keith. *Death and Renewal*, SSRH 2, Cambridge, Cambridge University Press, 1983.

Ibscher, Gred. *Der Begriff des Sittlichen in der Pflichtenlehre des Panaitios: Ein Beitrag zur Erkenntnis der mittleren Stoa*, Munich, R. Oldenbourg, 1934.

Isaacs, Marie B. "Hebrews 13.9–16 Revisited," *NTS* 43 (1997) 268–84.

Janssen, L. F. "Die Bedeutungsentwicklung von *superstitio/superstes*," *Mnemosyne* 28 (1975) 135–88.

Jaquette, James L. *Discerning What Counts: The Function of the Adiaphora Topos in Paul's Letters*, SBLDS 146, Atlanta, Scholars, 1995.

Jeremias, Joachim. *The Eucharistic Words of Jesus*, trans. Norman Perrin, Philadelphia, Fortress, 1977.

Jewett, Robert. *Christian Tolerance: Paul's Message to the Modern Church*, Philadelphia, Westminster, 1982.

Paul's Anthropological Terms: A Study of their Use in Conflict Settings, AGJU 10, Leiden, Brill, 1971.

"Tenement Churches and Communal Meals in the Early Church: The Implications of a Form-Critical Analysis of 2 Thessalonians 3:10," *BR* 38 (1993) 23–43.

Johnston, George. "'Kingdom of God' Sayings in Paul's Letters," in *From Jesus to Paul*, F. W. Beare Festschrift, eds. Peter Richardson and John C. Hurd, Waterloo, Ontario, Wilfrid Laurier University Press, 1984, 143–56.

Judge, E. A. "Cultural Conformity and Innovation in Paul: Some Clues from Contemporary Documents," *TynBul* 35 (1984) 3–24.

The Social Pattern of Christian Groups in the First Century: Some Prolegomena to the Study of New Testament Ideas of Social Obligation, London, Tyndale, 1960.

Juster, Jean. *Les Juifs dans l'empire romain: leur condition juridique, économique et sociale*, 2 vols., Paris, Paul Geuthner, 1914; reprint ed., New York, Burt Franklin, 1965.

Jüthner, Julius. *Hellenen und Barbaren: Aus der Geschichte des Nationalbewußtseins*, EA, n.s. 8, Leipzig, Dieterich, 1923.

Kamlah, Erhard. *Die Form der katalogischen Paränese im Neuen Testament*, WUNT 7, Tübingen, J. C. B. Mohr (Paul Siebeck), 1964.

Karris, Robert J. "The Occasion of Romans: A Response to Professor Donfried," *The Romans Debate*, ed. K. P. Donfried, rev. ed., Peabody, Mass., Hendrickson, 1991, 125–27.

"Romans 14:1–15:13 and the Occasion of Romans," in *The Romans Debate*, ed. K. P. Donfried, rev. ed., Peabody, Mass., Hendrickson, 1991, 65–84.

Käsemann, Ernst. "'The Righteousness of God' in Paul," in *New Testament Questions of Today*, trans. W. J. Montague, Philadelphia, Fortress, 1969, 168–82.

Kaylor, R. David. *Paul's Covenant Community: Jew and Gentile in Romans*, Atlanta, John Knox, 1988.

Kircher, Karl. *Die sakrale Bedeutung des Weines im Altertum*, RVV 9.2, Gießen, Alfred Töpelmann, 1910.

Kirk, G. S. *Myth: Its Meaning and Functions in Ancient and Other Cultures*, SCL 40, Cambridge, Cambridge University Press, 1971.

Koets, P. J. Δεισιδαιμονία: *A Contribution to the Knowledge of the Religious Terminology in Greek*, Purmerend, J. Muusses, 1929.

Kraabel, A. T. "The Roman Diaspora: Six Questionable Assumptions," *JJS* 33 (1982) 445–64.

Krafft, Peter. *"Gratus animus,"* RAC XII.732–52.

Kruger, M. A. *"Tina Karpon*, 'Some Fruit' in Romans 1:13," *WTJ* 49 (1987) 167–73.

Kümmel, W. G. *Introduction to the New Testament*, 17th ed., trans. H. C. Kee, Nashville, Abingdon, 1973.

Lambrecht, Jan. "Strength in Weakness," *NTS* 43 (1997) 285–90.

Lampe, Peter. *Die stadtrömischen Christen in den ersten beiden Jahrhunderten: Untersuchungen zur Sozialgeschichte*, 2nd ed., WUNT 2.18, Tübingen, J. C. B. Mohr (Paul Siebeck), 1989.

La Piana, George. "Foreign Groups in Rome during the First Centuries of the Empire," *HTR* 20 (1927) 183–403.

"La primitiva communità cristiana di Roma e l'epistola ai Romani," *Ricerche religiose* 1 (1925) 209–26; 305–26.

Leach, Edmund. "Genesis as Myth," in *Genesis as Myth and Other Essays*, London, Jonathan Cape, 1969, 7–23.

Leeuw, Gerardus van der. *Religion in Essence and Manifestation*, Vol. II, trans. J. E. Turner, 1963, reprint ed., Gloucester, Mass., Peter Smith, 1967.

LeJay, Paul. "Le Sabbat juif et les poètes latins," *RHLR* 8 (1903) 305–35.

Leon, H. J. *The Jews of Ancient Rome*, Philadelphia, Jewish Publication Society of America, 1960.

"The Jews of Rome in the First Centuries of Christianity," in *The Teacher's Yoke*, Henry Trantham Festschrift, eds. E. J. Vardaman and J. L. Garrett, Jr., Waco, Baylor University Press, 1964, 154–63.

Levenson, Jon D. *Sinai and Zion: An Entry into the Jewish Bible*, San Francisco, Harper & Row, 1985.

Lincoln, A. T. "Abraham Goes to Rome: Paul's Treatment of Abraham in Romans 4," in *Worship, Theology and Ministry in the Early Church: Essays in Honor of Ralph P. Martin*, eds. M. J. Wilkins and T. Paige, JSNT Sup 87, Sheffield, Sheffield Academic Press, 1992, 163–79.

Lohse, Bernhard. *Askese und Mönchtum in der Antike und in der alten Kirche*, Religion und Kultur der alten Mittelmeerwelt in Parallelforschungen 1, Munich/Vienna, R. Oldenbourg, 1969.

Lorenzi, Lorenzo de, ed. *Freedom and Love: The Guide for Christian Life (1 Co 8–10; Rm 14–15)*, BMS 6, Rome, St. Paul's Abbey, 1981.

Lovejoy, Arthur O., and Boas, George. *Primitivism and Related Ideas in Antiquity*, Baltimore, Johns Hopkins, 1935; reprint ed., New York, Octagon, 1965.

Lucius, P. E. *Die Therapeuten und ihre Stellung in der Geschichte der Askese*, Strasburg, C. F. Schmidt, 1879.

Lüdemann, Hermann. *Die Anthropologie des Apostels Paulus und ihre Stellung innerhalb seiner Heilslehre nach den vier Hauptbriefen*, Kiel, Universitäts-Buchhandlung, 1872.

Lührmann, Dieter. "*Superstitio* – die Beurteilung des frühen Christentums durch die Römer," *TZ* 42 (1986) 193–213.

Luterbacher, Franz. *Der Prodigienglaube und Prodigienstil der Römer*, 2nd ed., Burgdorf, Langlois & Cie., 1904; reprint ed., Darmstadt, Wissenschaftliche Buchgesellschaft, 1967.

Macchioro, Vittorio. "Die anthropologischen Grundlagen des römischen Verfalls zur Kaiserzeit," *Politische-anthropologische Revue* 5 (1907) 557–81.

Macionis, John J. *Sociology*, Englewood Cliffs, N.J., Prentice-Hall, 1987.

Marcus, Joel. "The Circumcision and the Uncircumcision in Rome," *NTS* 35 (1989) 67–81.

Martin, Dale B. *The Corinthian Body*, New Haven/London, Yale University Press, 1995.

Mauss, Marcel. *The Gift*, trans. Ian Cunnison, Glencoe, Ill., Free Press, 1954.

Méautis, Georges. *Recherches sur le pythagorisme*, Université de Neuchâtel, Recueil de travaux publiés par la Faculté des lettres sous les auspices de la Société académique 9, Neuchâtel, Paul Attinger, 1922.

Meeks, Wayne A. *The First Urban Christians: The Social World of the Apostle Paul*, New Haven/London, Yale University Press, 1983.

"Judgment and the Brother: Romans 14:1–15:13," in *Tradition and Interpretation in the New Testament: Essays in Honor of E. Earle Ellis*, eds. G. F. Hawthorne and O. Betz, Grand Rapids/Tübingen, Eerdmans/J. C. B. Mohr (Paul Siebeck), 1987, 290–300.

Mette, Hans Joachim. " '*Genus tenue*' und '*mensa tenuis*' bei Horaz," *MH* 18 (1961) 136–39.

Metzger, Bruce M. *A Textual Commentary on the Greek New Testament*, rev. ed., London/New York, United Bible Societies, 1975.

Minear, Paul S. *The Obedience of Faith: The Purposes of Paul in the Epistle to the Romans*, SBT 2.19, Naperville, Ill., Alec R. Allenson, 1971.

Moellering, H. Armin. *Plutarch on Superstition: Plutarch's "De Superstitione," its Place in the Changing Meaning of Deisidaimonia and in the Context of his Theological Writings*, rev. ed., Boston, Mass., Christopher, 1963.

Moir, Ian A. "Orthography and Theology: The Omicron–Omega Interchange in Romans 5:1 and Elsewhere," in *New Testament Textual Criticism: Its Significance for Exegesis*, Bruce M. Metzger Festschrift, eds. Eldon Jay Epp and Gordon Fee, Oxford, Clarendon, 1981, 179–83.

Moiser, Jeremy. "Rethinking Romans 12–15," *NTS* 36 (1990) 571–82.

Momigliano, Arnaldo. *Alien Wisdom: The Limits of Hellenization*, Cambridge, Cambridge University Press, 1975.

Mommsen, Theodor. *Die römische Chronologie bis auf Caesar*, 2nd ed., Berlin, Weidmann, 1859.

Mott, Stephen C. "The Power of Giving and Receiving: Reciprocity in Hellenistic Benevolence," in *Current Issues in Biblical Interpretation*, M. C. Tenney Festschrift, Grand Rapids, Eerdmans, 1975, 60–72.

Moule, C. F. D. "Obligation in the Ethic of Paul," in *Christian History and Interpretation*, John Knox Festschrift, eds. W. R. Farmer, C. F. D. Moule, and R. R. Niebuhr, Cambridge, Cambridge University Press, 1967, 389–406.

Murphy-O'Connor, Jerome. *Paul: A Critical Life*, Oxford, Clarendon, 1996.

Nababan, A. E. S. "Bekenntnis und Mission in Römer 14 und 15: Eine exegetische Untersuchung," D.Theol. dissertation, Heidelberg, 1962.

Nagel, Peter. *Die Motivierung der Askese in der alten Kirche und der Ursprung des Mönchtums*, TU 95, Berlin, Akademie, 1966.

Nanos, Mark D. *The Mystery of Romans: The Jewish Context of Paul's Letter*, Minneapolis, Fortress, 1996.

Nebe, Gottfried. *"Hoffnung" bei Paulus: Elpis und ihre Synonyme im Zusammenhang der Eschatologie*, SUNT 16, Göttingen, Vandenhoeck & Ruprecht, 1983.

Nebel, G. "Der Begriff des ΚΑΘΗΚΟΝ in der alten Stoa," *Hermes* 70 (1935) 439–60.

Neufeld, Vernon H. *The Earliest Christian Confessions*, NTTS 5, Leiden, Brill, 1963.

Nilsson, Martin P. *Die Entstehung und sakrale Bedeutung des griechischen Kalenders*, Lund, Gleerup/Leipzig, O. Harrassowitz, 1918.

Geschichte der griechischen Religion, 2 vols., 2nd ed., HKAW 5.2.1–2, Munich, C. H. Beck, 1955, 1961.

A History of Greek Religion, trans. F. J. Fielden, 2nd ed., Oxford, Clarendon, 1949; reprint ed., Westport, Conn., Greenwood, 1980.

"The Race Problem of the Roman Empire," *Hereditas* 2 (1921) 370–90.

Nola, Alfonso M. di. "Superstizione," *EDR*, 1973.

Nutton, V. "The Beneficial Ideology," in *Imperialism in the Ancient World*, eds. Peter D. A. Garnsey and C. R. Whittaker, Cambridge, Cambridge University Press, 1978, 209–21.

Oborn, George Thomas. "Economic Factors in the Persecutions of the Christians to A.D. 260," in *Environmental Factors in Christian History*, Shirley Jackson Case Festschrift, eds. J. T. McNeill, M. Spinka, and H. R. Willoughby, Chicago, University of Chicago Press, 1939, 131–48.

O'Brien, Peter T. "Thanksgiving within the Structure of Pauline Theology," in *Pauline Studies*, F. F. Bruce Festschrift, eds. D. A. Hagner and M. J. Harris, Grand Rapids, Eerdmans, 1980, 50–66.

Ollrog, Wolf-Henning. "Die Abfassungsverhältnisse von Röm 16," in *Kirche*, Günther Bornkamm Festschrift, eds. Dieter Lührmann and Georg Strecker, Tübingen, J. C. B. Mohr (Paul Siebeck), 1980, 221–44.

Osiek, Carolyn. *Rich and Poor in the "Shepherd of Hermas": An Exegetical-Social Investigation*, CBQMS 15, Washington, D.C., CBA, 1983.

Otto, Walter. "*Religio* und *superstitio*," *Archiv für Religionswissenschaft* 12 (1909) 533–54.

Parker, Robert. *MIASMA: Pollution and Purification in Early Greek Religion*, Oxford, Clarendon, 1985.

Paschen, Wilfried. *Rein und Unrein: Untersuchung zur biblischen Wortgeschichte*, SANT 24, Munich, Kösel, 1970.

Penna, Romano. "Les Juifs à Rome au temps de l'apôtre Paul," *NTS* 28 (1982) 321–47.

Peristiany, J. G., ed. *Honour and Shame: The Values of Mediterranean Society*, Chicago, University of Chicago Press, 1966.

Peterman, G. W. *Paul's Gift from Philippi: Conventions of Gift Exchange and Christian Giving*, SNTSMS 92, Cambridge, Cambridge University Press, 1997.

Petersen, Norman R. "On the Ending(s) to Paul's Letter to Rome," in *The Future of Early Christianity*, Helmut Koester Festschrift, ed. B. A. Pearson, Minneapolis, Fortress, 1991, 337–47.

Peterson, Erik. "᾿ΕΡΓΟΝ in der Bedeutung 'Bau' bei Paulus," *Biblica* 22 (1941) 439–41.

Philip, J. A. *Pythagoras and Early Pythagoreanism*, Toronto, University of Toronto Press, 1966.

Pohlenz, Max. *Antikes Führertum: Cicero De Officiis und das Lebensideal des Panaitios*, Leipzig, Teubner, 1934.

Radin, Max. "*Obligatio*," PW 34.1717–26.

Rauer, Max. *Die "Schwachen" in Korinth und Rom nach den Paulusbriefen*, BibS(F) 21.2–3, Freiburg im Breisgau, Herder, 1923.

Reasoner, Mark. "The Theology of Romans 12:1–15:13," in *Pauline Theology*, Vol. III: *Romans*, eds. David M. Hay and E. Elizabeth Johnson, Minneapolis, Fortress, 1995, 287–99.

Reekmans, Tony. "Juvenal's Views on Social Change," *AS* 2 (1971) 117–61.

Reinhardt, Karl. *Poseidonios*, Munich, C. H. Beck, 1921.

Ridderbos, H. *Paul: An Outline of his Theology*, trans. J. R. de Witt, Grand Rapids, Eerdmans, 1975.

Rieß. "Aberglaube," PW Sup 1.29–93.

Riggenbach, E. "Die Starken und Schwachen in der römischen Gemeinde," *TSK* 66 (1893) 649–78.

Rist, J. M. *Stoic Philosophy*, Cambridge, Cambridge University Press, 1969.

Roberts, Colin H. *Manuscript, Society and Belief in Early Christian Egypt*, Schweich Lectures, 1977, London, Oxford University Press, 1979.

Robson, John R. K., ed. *Food, Ecology and Culture: Readings in the Anthropology of Dietary Practices*, New York, Gordon and Breach, 1980.

Rohde, E. *Psyche: The Cult of Souls and Belief in Immortality among the Greeks*, trans. W. B. Hillis, London, Routledge & Kegan Paul, 1935.

Rostovtzeff, M. *The Social and Economic History of the Roman Empire*, 2nd ed., Oxford, Oxford University Press, 1957.

Rudd, Niall. *Themes in Roman Satire*, London/Norman, Okla.: University of Oklahoma Press, 1986.

Saller, Richard. "Patronage and Friendship in Early Imperial Rome: Drawing the Distinction," in *Patronage in Ancient Society*, ed. Andrew Wallace-Hadrill, London/New York, Routledge, 1989, 49–62.

Personal Patronage under the Early Empire, Cambridge, Cambridge University Press, 1982.

Sampley, J. Paul. "The Weak and the Strong: Paul's Careful and Crafty Rhetorical Strategy in Romans 14:1–15:13," in *The Social World of the First Christians: Essays in Honor of Wayne A. Meeks*, eds. L. M. White and O. L. Yarbrough, Minneapolis, Fortress, 1995, 40–52.

Sänger, Dieter. "Die Δυνατοί in 1 Kor 1:26," *ZNW* 76 (1985) 285–91.

Schaefer, Richard T. *Racial and Ethnic Groups*, 3rd ed., Glenview, Ill., Scott, Foresman and Co., 1988.

Schmekel, A. *Der Philosophie der mittleren Stoa in ihrem geschichtlichen Zusammenhange*, Berlin, Weidmann, 1892.

Schmithals, Walter. *Der Römerbrief als historisches Problem*, SNT 9, Gütersloh, Gerd Mohn, 1975.

Schneider, Nélio. "Die 'Schwachen' in der christlichen Gemeinde Roms: Eine historisch-exegetische Untersuchung zu Röm 14,1–15,13," D.Theol. dissertation, Kirchliche Hochschule Wuppertal, 1989.

Schott, Theodor. *Der Römerbrief: seinem Endzweck und Gedankengang*, Erlangen, Andreas Deichert, 1858.

Schottroff, Luise. *Der Glaubende und die feindliche Welt: Beobachtungen zum gnostischen Dualismus und seiner Bedeutung für Paulus und das Johannesevangelium*, WMANT 37, Neukirchen-Vluyn, Neukirchener, 1970.

Schrage, Wolfgang. *Die konkreten Einzelgebote in der paulinischen Paränese: Ein Beitrag zur neutestamentlichen Ethik*, Gütersloh, Gerd Mohn, 1961.

Schubert, Paul. *Form and Function of the Pauline Thanksgivings*, BZNW 20, Berlin, A. Töpelmann, 1939.

Schürer, Emil. *The History of the Jewish People in the Age of Jesus Christ (175 B.C.–A.D. 135)*, eds. Matthew Black, Fergus Millar, and Geza Vermes, rev. ed., 2 vols., Edinburgh, T. & T. Clark, 1973, 1979.

Scott, James M. *Paul and the Nations*, WUNT 1.84, Tübingen, J. C. B. Mohr (Paul Siebeck), 1995.

Scullard, H. H. *Festivals and Ceremonies of the Roman Republic*, Ithaca, Cornell University Press, 1981.

Segal, Alan F. *The Other Judaisms of Late Antiquity*, BJS 127, Atlanta, Scholars, 1987.

Shaw, Brent D. "'Eaters of Flesh, Drinkers of Milk': The Ancient Mediterranean Ideology of the Pastoral Nomad," *AS* 13/14 (1982/83) 5–31.

Sherwin-White, A. N. *The Letters of Pliny: A Historical and Social Commentary*, Oxford, Clarendon, 1966.

   Racial Prejudice in Imperial Rome, J. H. Gray Lectures, 1966, Cambridge, Cambridge University Press, 1967.

Shklar, Judith N. "Subversive Genealogies," in *Myth, Symbol, and Culture*, ed. Clifford Geertz, New York, Norton, 1971, 129–54.

Siker, Jeffrey S. *Disinheriting the Jews: Abraham in Early Christian Controversy*, Louisville, Westminster/John Knox, 1991.

Smith, Dennis E. "Social Obligation in the Context of Communal Meals: A Study of the Christian Meal in 1 Corinthians in Comparison with Graeco-Roman Communal Meals," Th.D. dissertation, Harvard, 1980.

Smith, J. Z. "Fences and Neighbors: Some Contours of Early Judaism," in *Imagining Religion*, Chicago, University of Chicago Press, 1982, 1–18.

   Map Is Not Territory, Leiden, Brill, 1979.

Smith, Morton. "Paul's Arguments as Evidence of the Christianity from which he Diverged," in *Christians among Jews and Gentiles*, Krister Stendahl Festschrift, eds. George W. E. Nickelsburg and George W. MacRae, Philadelphia, Fortress, 1986, 254–60.

   "Superstitio," *SBL 1981 Seminar Papers* 20, ed. K. H. Richards, Chico, Scholars, 1981, 349–55.

Sollenberger, Michael G. "Identification of Titles of Botanical Works of Theophrastus," in *Theophrastean Studies: On Natural Science, Physics and Metaphysics, Ethics, Religion, and Rhetoric*, Rutgers University Studies in Classical Humanities 3, eds. W. W. Fortenbaugh and R. W. Sharples, New Brunswick/Oxford, Transaction, 1988, 14–24.

Stählin, Gustav. *Skandalon: Untersuchungen zur Geschichte eines biblischen Begriffs*, BFCT 2.24, Gütersloh, C. Bertelsmann, 1930.

Stanley, D. M. *Christ's Resurrection in Pauline Soteriology*, AnBib 13, Rome, Pontifical Biblical Institute, 1961.

Stein, Arthur. *Der römische Ritterstand*, Munich, C. H. Beck, 1927.

Steinmetz, Peter. *Theophrastus, Charaktere*, Vol. II: *Kommentar und Übersetzung*, Das Wort der Antike 7, Munich, Max Hueber, 1962.

Stendahl, Krister. *Final Account: Paul's Letter to the Romans*, Minneapolis, Fortress, 1995.

   Paul among Jews and Gentiles and Other Essays, Philadelphia, Fortress, 1976.

Stengel, Paul. *Die griechischen Kultusaltertümer*, 3rd ed., HKAW 5.3, Munich, C. H. Beck, 1920; reprint ed., New York, Arno, 1975.

Stowers, Stanley K. *The Diatribe and Paul's Letter to the Romans*, SBLDS 57, Chico, Scholars, 1981.

Letter Writing in Greco-Roman Antiquity, LEC, Philadelphia, Westminster, 1986.

A Rereading of Romans: Justice, Jews, and Gentiles, New Haven/London, Yale University Press, 1994.

Strack, Hermann I. *Das Blut im Glauben und Aberglauben der Menschheit: Mit besonderer Berücksichtigung der "Volksmedizin" und des "jüdischen Blutritus,"* rev. ed., Schriften des Institutum Judaicum in Berlin 14, Munich, C. H. Beck, 1900.

Strathmann, Hermann. *Geschichte der frühchristlichen Askese bis zur Entstehung des Mönchtums im religionsgeschichtlichen Zusammenhange*, Leipzig, A. Deichert, 1914.

Stuhlmacher, Peter. *Gerechtigkeit Gottes bei Paulus*, FRLANT 87, Göttingen, Vandenhoeck & Ruprecht, 1965.

Das paulinische Evangelium, Vol. I: *Vorgeschichte*, FRLANT 95, Göttingen, Vandenhoeck & Ruprecht, 1968.

Stuiber, Alfred. "Geschenk," *RAC* X.685–703.

Syme, Ronald. "Astrology in the Historia Augusta," in *Historia Augusta Papers*, Oxford, Clarendon, 1983, 80–97.

Taylor, Lily Ross. "Freedmen and Freeborn in the Epitaphs of Imperial Rome," *AJPh* 82 (1961) 113–32.

Party Politics in the Age of Caesar, SCL 22, 1949, reprint ed., Berkeley, University of California Press, 1961.

Theißen, Gerd. *The Social Setting of Pauline Christianity: Essays on Corinth*, ed. and trans. John H. Schütz, Philadelphia, Fortress, 1982.

Untersuchungen zum Hebräerbrief, SNT 2, Gütersloh, Gerd Mohn, 1969.

Thesleff, Holger, ed. *The Pythagorean Texts of the Hellenistic Period*, Acta Academiae Aboensis, series A, 30, no. 1, Åbo, Akademi, 1965.

Thornton, T. C. G. "Jewish New Moon Festivals, Galatians 4:3–11 and Colossians 2:16," *JTS* 40 (1989) 97–100.

Tomson, Peter J. *Paul and the Jewish Law: Halakha in the Letters of the Apostle to the Gentiles*, CRINT 3.1, Assen/Maastricht, Van Gorcum, 1990.

Vellian, Jacob. "Lenten Fast of the East Syrians," *A Tribute to Arthur Vööbus: Studies in Early Christian Literature and its Environment, Primarily in the Syrian East*, ed. Robert H. Fischer, Chicago, Lutheran School of Theology at Chicago, 1977, 373–78.

Veyne, Paul. *Le Pain et le cirque: sociologie historique d'un pluralisme politique*, Paris, Seuil, 1976.

"Vie de Trimalcion," *Annales, E.S.C.* 16 (1961) 213–47.

Vielhauer, Philipp. *Geschichte der urchristlichen Literatur*, 2nd ed., Berlin/New York, Walter de Gruyter, 1978.

Vogt, Joseph. *Kulturwelt und Barbaren zum Menschheitsbild der spätantiken Gesellschaft*, Abhandlungen der geistes- und sozialwissenschaftlichen Klasse 1, Mainz, Akademie der Wissenschaften und der Literatur, 1967.

Vögtle, Anton. *Die Tugend- und Lasterkataloge im Neuen Testament*, NTAbh 16.4–5, Münster, Aschendorff, 1936.

Wächter, Theodor. *Reinheitsvorschriften im griechischen Kult*, RVV 9.1, Gießen, A. Töpelmann, 1910.

Wagner, J. Ross. "The Christ, Servant of Jew and Gentile: A Fresh Approach to Romans 15:8–9," *JBL* 116 (1997) 473–85.

Walters, J. C. *Ethnic Issues in Paul's Letter to the Romans: Changing Self-Definitions in Earliest Christianity*, Valley Forge, Pa., Trinity Press International, 1993.

Watson, Francis. *Paul, Judaism and the Gentiles*, SNTSMS 56, Cambridge, Cambridge University Press, 1986.

Weaver, P. R. C. "Social Mobility in the Early Roman Empire: The Evidence of the Imperial Freedmen and Slaves," *Past & Present* 34 (1967) 3–20.

Weber, Max. *From Max Weber: Essays in Sociology*, trans. and eds. H. H. Gerth and C. Wright Mills, New York, Oxford University Press, 1946.

Wedderburn, A. J. M. *Baptism and Resurrection: Studies in Pauline Theology against its Graeco-Roman Background*, Tübingen, J. C. B. Mohr (Paul Siebeck), 1987.

The Reasons for Romans, SNTW, Edinburgh, T. & T. Clark, 1988.

Weiss, Hans-Friedrich. "Zur Frage der historischen Voraussetzungen der Begegnung von Antike und Christentum," *Klio* 43–45 (1965) 307–28.

Wendland, Paul. *Die Therapeuten und die philonische Schrift vom beschaulichen Leben*, Leipzig, B. G. Teubner, 1896.

Wernle, Paul. *Der Christ und die Sünde bei Paulus*, Freiburg/Leipzig, J. C. B. Mohr (Paul Siebeck), 1897.

Westerholm, Stephen. *Preface to the Study of Paul*, Grand Rapids, Eerdmans, 1997.

Wibbing, Siegfried. *Die Tugend- und Lasterkataloge im Neuen Testament und ihre Traditionsgeschichte unter besonderer Berücksichtigung der Qumran-Texte*, BZNW 25, Berlin, Alfred Töpelmann, 1959.

Williams, Sam K. "The 'Righteousness of God' in Romans," *JBL* 99 (1980) 241–90.

Willis, Wendell Lee. *Idol Meat in Corinth: The Pauline Argument in 1 Corinthians 8 and 10*, SBLDS 68, Chico, Scholars, 1985.

Wilson, Walter. *Love without Pretence: Romans 12:9–21 and Hellenistic-Jewish Wisdom Literature*, WUNT 2.46, Tübingen, J. C. B. Mohr (Paul Siebeck), 1991.

Winter, Bruce W. "The Public Honouring of Christian Benefactors: Romans 13.3–4 and 1 Peter 2.14–15," *JSNT* 34 (1988) 87–103.

Wissowa, Georg. *Religion und Kultus der Römer*, HKAW 5, Munich, C. H. Beck, 1902.

Wright, N. T. *The Climax of the Covenant: Christ and the Law in Pauline Theology*, Minneapolis, Fortress, 1992.

Zahn, Theodor. *Geschichte des Sonntags vornehmlich in der alten Kirche*, Hanover, Carl Mener, 1878.

Zeller, Dieter. *Juden und Heiden in der Mission des Paulus: Studien zum Römerbrief*, Stuttgart, Katholisches Bibelwerk, 1973.

Zucker, Conrad. *Psychologie de la superstition*, trans. François Vaudou, Paris, Payot, 1972.

INDEX OF BIBLICAL REFERENCES

INDEX OF EARLY CHRISTIAN
LITERATURE

INDEX OF HELLENISTIC AND RABBINIC JEWISH SOURCES

INDEX OF GRECO-ROMAN SOURCES

INDEX OF AUTHORS

INDEX OF SUBJECTS